D1242661

eye-opening, *Digging Up Armageddon* reveals the reality-show level of human relationships on archaeological excavations at one of the world's most extraordinary sites, Megiddo, and just how little archaeology has changed in a hundred years. Essential reading for anyone who wants to know how archeological magic truly happens."
—SARAH PARCAK, author of *Archaeology from Space:*
How the Future Shapes Our Past

"*Digging Up Armageddon* is a riveting account of the search for Solomon's lost city in the years prior to World War II. Eric Cline, who himself excavated for many years at Megiddo, adds a human dimension to the archaeology by interweaving the fascinating personal stories behind these exciting discoveries."
—JODI MAGNESS, author of *Masada:*
From Jewish Revolt to Modern Myth

"Megiddo is the mother of all ancient mounds, the cradle of biblical archaeology, a place related to great historical figures such as Thutmose III, Solomon, and Josiah. The excavations at Megiddo were the largest and most romantic in the history of Near Eastern archaeology. Thanks to them, unparalleled monuments from biblical times—gates, palaces, temples, and water systems—were unearthed. But Megiddo has also become the focus of every problem in the archaeology of the region, from questions about the beginning of urbanism to the historicity of a united monarchy of David and Solomon. In this deeply researched, beautifully written, and engaging book, Eric Cline writes the history of the dig at Megiddo, and by doing so, he sheds light on the entire history of the Bronze and Iron Ages in the Levant, including that of ancient Israel."
—ISRAEL FINKELSTEIN, coauthor of *David and Solomon: In Search of the Bible's Sacred Kings and the Roots of the Western Tradition*

"Enjoyable, fascinating, and engaging. *Digging Up Armageddon* is an extremely well written and lively account of perhaps the most important excavations ever conducted in Israel. Cline has, once again, written an excellent book."
—AREN M. MAEIR, coeditor of *The Shephelah during the Iron Age:*
Recent Archaeological Studies

"Cline's successful detective work in figuring out the interpersonal relationships among these archaeologists, including the scandals and gossip that severely impacted their fieldwork, is extremely important."
—RACHEL S. HALLOTE, author of *Death, Burial, and Afterlife*
in the Biblical World: How the Israelites and Their Neighbors
Treated the Dead

DIGGING UP
ARMAGEDDON

DIGGING UP ARMAGEDDON

The Search for the Lost City of Solomon

ERIC H. CLINE

PRINCETON UNIVERSITY PRESS
PRINCETON AND OXFORD

Published by Princeton University Press
41 William Street, Princeton, New Jersey 08540
99 Banbury Road, Oxford OX2 6JX

press.princeton.edu

First Paperback Printing, 2022
Paperback ISBN 9780691233932

The Library of Congress has cataloged the cloth edition as follows:
Names: Cline, Eric H., author.
Title: Digging Up Armageddon : The Search For the Lost City of
Solomon / Eric H. Cline.
Description: Princeton, New Jersey : Princeton University Press, [2020] |
Includes bibliographical references and index.
Identifiers: LCCN 2019022505 (print) | LCCN 2019022506 (ebook) |
ISBN 9780691166322 (hardback) | ISBN 9780691200446 (ebook)
Subjects: LCSH: Megiddo Expedition (1925-1939) |
Excavations (Archaeology)—Israel—Megiddo (Extinct city) |
Megiddo (Extinct city)—Antiquities.
Classification: LCC DS110.M4 C58 2020 (print) | LCC DS110.M4 (ebook) |
DDC 933/.45—dc23
LC record available at https://lccn.loc.gov/2019022505
LC ebook record available at https://lccn.loc.gov/2019022506

British Library Cataloging-in-Publication Data is available

Editorial: Rob Tempio and Matt Rohal
Production Editorial: Lauren Lepow
Text Design: Carmina Alvarez
Cover Design: Karl Spurzem
Production: Erin Suydam
Publicity: Maria Whelan and Amy Stewart

Cover image: Excavating the water tunnel at Megiddo. Courtesy of the Oriental
Institute of the University of Chicago.

This book has been composed in Sabon Next LT Pro

Printed in the United States of America

As I write these lines, . . . behind me rises Har-Megiddo, "the Mount of Megiddo," or as known to the Western world in its Hellenized form, "Armageddon." Towering high above the plain, Armageddon was an imposing stronghold, . . . now deeply covered by the rubbish of thousands of years, green with billowing grain and bright with nodding anemones. Our first trenches have been thrust into the vast mound, . . . [and] already . . . [our] workmen have brought out an inscribed block bearing Egyptian hieroglyphs.[1]

—*James Henry Breasted, March 1926*

Contents

List of Illustrations   ix

Preface   *"Welcome to Armageddon"*   xiii

Prologue   "Have Found Solomon's Stables"   1

PART ONE
1920–1926

Chapter I   "Please Accept My Resignation"   5

Chapter II   "He Must Knock Off or You Will Bury Him"   23

Chapter III   "A Fairly Sharp Rap on the Knuckles"   34

Chapter IV   "We Have Already Three Distinct Levels"   47

PART TWO
1927–1934

Chapter V   "I Really Need a Bit of a Holiday"   59

Chapter VI   "They Can Be Nothing Else than Stables"   85

Chapter VII   "Admonitory but Merciful"   93

Chapter VIII   "The Tapping of the Pickmen"   125

Chapter IX   "The Most Sordid Document"   144

Chapter X   "Either a Battle or an Earthquake"   185

PART THREE
1935–1939

Chapter XI   "A Rude Awakening"   205

Chapter XII   "The Director Is Gone"   218

Chapter XIII   "You Asked for the Sensational"   241

Chapter XIV	"A Miserable Death Threat"	261
Chapter XV	"The Stratigraphical Skeleton"	274

PART FOUR
1940–2020

Chapter XVI	"Instructions Had Been Given to Protect This Property"	289
Epilogue	"Certain Digging Areas Remain Incompletely Excavated"	297
Cast of Characters: Chicago Expedition Staff and Spouses		301
Year-by-Year List of Chicago Expedition Staff plus Major Events		303
Acknowledgments		309
Notes		313
Bibliography		371
Index		387

Illustrations

MAPS

Map 1. Detail from the Survey of Western Palestine (Sheet VIII) by
      Conder and Kitchener   6
Map 2. Megiddo and surrounding area, drawn by Edward DeLoach   9

FIGURES

Fig. 1. Early view of Megiddo   xiv
Fig. 2. James Henry Breasted   xviii
Fig. 3. Cable from Guy to Breasted, 4 June 1928   2
Fig. 4. Clarence Fisher at work   13
Fig. 5. Megiddo team members with Egyptian workmen, fall 1926   20
Fig. 6. Chicago tents at Megiddo, first week of season in 1925   25
Fig. 7. Megiddo dig house   27
Fig. 8. (a) Breasted at Megiddo, with Sheshonq fragment against
      wall and DeLoach with a turkey; (b–c) Photograph
      and drawing of Sheshonq fragment   28
Fig. 9. Breasted visit to Megiddo, March 1926   35
Fig. 10. Sorting pottery in the Megiddo dig house   38
Fig. 11. Olof Lind, clad in local garb   44
Fig. 12. Lower end of a chute with railcar waiting to be filled   48
Fig. 13. (a) Clearing surface levels in Squares M13 and M14;
      (b) workers in late 1926   50
Fig. 14. Megiddo Stratum I   54
Fig. 15. P.L.O. Guy, undated photograph   60
Fig. 16. Megiddo excavation staff and spouses, 7 September 1928   74
Fig. 17. Memorial plaque for Rosamond Dale Owen
      Oliphant Templeton, in Maple Hill Cemetery,
      New Harmony, Indiana   82
Fig. 18. Megiddo excavations, during Guy's directorship ca. 1931–34   87

Fig. 19. Portion of northern stables found by Chicago team,
June 1928   88

Fig. 20. Model and detail of "Solomon's Stables" by Olof E.
Lind and Laurence Woolman   90

Fig. 21. "Great Royal Visit" by Rockefellers and Breasted,
March 1929   94

Fig. 22. Megiddo excavation staff and spouses, 22 May 1929   97

Fig. 23. Engberg excavating skeletons   117

Fig. 24. Balloon photography in Solomon's Stables   129

Fig. 25. The first aerial photo mosaic created at Megiddo   130

Fig. 26. Beginning of excavation of water system, with
surface soil removed   135

Fig. 27. Water tunnel   137

Fig. 28. Skeleton/burial of "guard" in the water system at Megiddo   138

Fig. 29. Mending pottery at Megiddo, during Guy's
directorship ca. 1931–34   155

Fig. 30. Pottery room at Megiddo, during Guy's
directorship ca. 1931–34   155

Fig. 31. Ramses VI bronze statue-base   186

Fig. 32. Plan of Stratum III   188

Fig. 33. Plan of Stratum IV   192

Fig. 34. Reconstruction of Stratum IV structures in Area
A from the northwest by Concannon   194

Fig. 35. Removal of bronze vessel hoard in Locus 1739
from Stratum VIA   195

Fig. 36. Crushed skeleton and pottery in Locus 1745 from
Stratum VIA   196

Fig. 37. Gordon Loud ca. 1930 in the courtyard of the
expedition house at Khorsabad   207

Fig. 38. Aerial view in 1937   219

Fig. 39. Canaanite bronze statuette, covered with gold foil   225

Fig. 40. Temple 2048 in Area BB   226

Fig. 41. (a) Northern Trench (Area AA); (b) Eastern Trench
(Area BB); (c) Southern Trench (Area CC)   230

Fig. 42. Stratum IV gate, viewed from the north after
clearing and before removal of right side   234

Fig. 43. Coded cable sent from Loud to Wilson on 11 May 1936   238

Fig. 44. Stratum VIII gold hoard under floor of Room 3100   246

Fig. 45. The Treasury (3073) viewed from the south 250
Fig. 46. Complete animal skeleton and ivories in the
          western half of the northern room of the Treasury,
          looking east 251
Fig. 47. Ivory pen case with cartouche of Ramses III 253
Fig. 48. City wall of Megiddo Stratum XVIII 267
Fig. 49. Stone Altar 4017 in Area BB 269
Fig. 50. Stratum XV plan showing round stone altar
          behind one of the megaron temples 282
Fig. 51. Megiddo car overturned and totaled in collision in Iraq 290

"Welcome to Armageddon"

Each day throughout the year, the tour buses begin arriving at Megiddo soon after 9:00 a.m., disgorging fifty tourists at a time. By the time the site closes at 5:00 p.m., several dozen buses will have deposited hundreds of visitors. "Welcome to Armageddon," the tour guides say, as they march their flocks up the steep incline and through the ancient city gate. Reciting their practiced patter as they go, they reach the first stopping point. The group members catch their breath and, frequently, burst into hymns or prayers, especially if they are on their way to Nazareth, located almost directly across the valley.

Our small group of archaeologists smile tolerantly, having been at the site since before dawn. Wielding pickaxes, trowels, and dustpans, filling buckets and wheelbarrows full of freshly excavated dirt, we play our game of guessing the nationality of each group from fifty yards away, as they come around the last corner of the incline before heading past our excavation area. From the nearby Northern Observation Platform, they gaze up the length of the Jezreel Valley on one side and down into the depths of the Chicago excavation trench on the other. Attached to the chain-link fence, which only rarely deters tourists from coming into the excavation area, is our sign that jokingly reads, "Please do not feed the archaeologists." We may not get their nationalities right, but that doesn't stop us from hoping that they might have some extra cookies.

Megiddo is mentioned a dozen times in the Hebrew Bible, and in a multitude of other ancient texts, but it is especially well-known as the setting in the New Testament for the penultimate battle between the forces of good and the forces of evil. We are told in Revelation 16:16 that the two opposing armies will assemble "at the place that in Hebrew is called Armageddon."[1]

FIG. I. Early view of Megiddo (courtesy of the Oberlin College archives)

In fact, the very word *Armageddon* comes from *Har Megiddo*—Hebrew for the "mound" or "mountain" (*har*) of Megiddo. By the Middle Ages, multiple nationalities, languages, and centuries had added an *n* and dropped the *h*, transforming *Har Megiddo* to *Harmageddon* and thence to *Armageddon*.[2]

There have actually been numerous Armageddons at the ancient site of Megiddo already, as one civilization, group, or political entity gave way to another over the millennia—one world ending and another beginning— from the Canaanites to the Israelites, and then the Neo-Assyrians, Neo-Babylonians, Persians, Greeks, and Romans, followed in turn by the Muslims, crusaders, Mongols, Mamlukes, Ottomans, and, most recently, World War I and the 1948 Israeli War of Independence.[3] However, it is the New Testament's Armageddon that is the most famous and which is responsible for attracting the tourists.

The ancient mound once stood more than one hundred feet (thirty-six meters) above the surrounding fields, at its highest point in the north. A visitor to the site in 1904 was surprised at just how high it was. Instead of the low mound that he expected to see, he found instead "a proper hill that dominates the plain." The Chicago archaeologists reduced its height by re- moving the topmost occupation layers, but even so it still towers over the

Jezreel Valley today, easily more than seventy feet high and readily visible from a great distance.[4]

Early photographs show the mound in its pristine state, as yet untouched by the excavators' shovels and picks and without all of the huge spoil heaps of excavated earth that now litter the area. Taken from the north, they show the mound rising majestically in the distance. From this side, two distinct levels can be discerned: a lower level with a perfectly horizontal terrace about halfway up the mound, upon which Gottlieb Schumacher, the first excavator, said he found the remains of a fortification wall protecting the city; and a slightly smaller upper level that sits directly on top of this lower level, like a second story on a house or the upper layer of a cake.[5]

Within the mound itself, we now know, are the remains of at least twenty ancient cities, built one on top of another over the course of nearly five thousand years, from about 5000 BCE to just before 300 BCE. The various excavators have given a Roman numeral to each one, I–XX, numbering them sequentially. Stratum I, at the very top, is the most recent, dating to the Persian period. Stratum XX, located just above the native bedrock, is the oldest settlement, dating to the Neolithic period. The strata in between date to the Copper, Bronze, and Iron Ages, including the time of the Canaanites and the Israelites (see table 1).

It isn't easy for us to get to the site by 5:00 a.m. every day. We need to, though, in order to get in an eight-hour workday before it gets too hot. The alarm clocks are set to go off very early at the kibbutz where we are staying; by the ungodly hour of 4:35 a.m., we are packed into several large buses and a small fleet of cars—though a fleet of small cars is perhaps a more apt description. There are nearly 120 of us, counting both the professional archaeologists and graduate students who make up the staff plus the volunteer team members who have come from all walks of life—doctors, lawyers, nurses, accountants, schoolteachers, students, and others—for a "once in a lifetime" experience.

The staff members, all of whom have been working with us at Megiddo for several seasons, are in the cars for the most part, though some are with the volunteers in the buses, reclining in air-conditioned comfort even at this early hour and desperately trying to grab a few last minutes of sleep. I am usually behind the wheel of a Mazda 3, or a *shalosh*, as we affectionately call it, a type of car that most Israelis also seem to drive, though I don't use the

TABLE I. Chronological Overview of the Ancient Near East in Relation to Megiddo Stratigraphy (after Ussishkin 2018: 15; all dates approximate)

Time Period	Megiddo Strata	Approximate Dates	Known For:
Neolithic and Chalcolithic	XX	5000–3400 BCE	Domestication of plants and animals; invention of pottery; use of copper
Early and Intermediate Bronze Age	XIX–XIV	3400–2000 BCE	Invention/use of bronze; writing; first cities
Middle Bronze Age	XIII–X	2000–1550 BCE	Canaanites; Hyksos
Late Bronze Age	IX–VII	1550–1130 BCE	Egyptian New Kingdom
Israelite (Iron Age)	VI–IV	1130–734 BCE	Early Israelites, United Monarchy, Divided Kingdoms
Neo-Assyrian	III–II	734–600 BCE	Neo-Assyrian Empire; destruction of Israel
Neo-Babylonian and Persian	I	600–330 BCE	Neo-Babylonian Empire; destruction of Jerusalem; Cyrus the Great
Hellenistic	—	330–30 BCE	Seleucids and Ptolemies; Maccabees
Roman/Byzantine	—	1st–6th centuries CE	First and Second Jewish Revolts; destruction of Jerusalem (again)

horn nearly as much as the rest of them do. It was originally dark blue when I first picked it up in Tel Aviv, but now it is a solid brown, thanks to the layer of dirt that coats every inch of the outside. I mentally remind myself to take it through a car wash before returning it to the rental company at the end of the dig season, but I'll probably forget to do so and have to throw myself on their mercy, as has happened several times in the past. Israel Finkelstein, codirector of the dig and probably the best-known archaeologist working in Israel today, is in the passenger seat, as he is most days. I concentrate on driving safely as we speed through the darkness.

We reach Megiddo some twenty-five minutes later and leave our cars in the parking lot next to the Visitor Welcome Center, which was converted from what remained of the original Chicago dig house, first built during the mid-1920s. It now features a restaurant, bathrooms, a few gift shops, and two rooms presenting a brief history of the excavations, complete with a model of the ancient site that has moving parts if you push the right buttons.

We begin walking up the ancient mound, lugging our digging tools, water jugs, and other supplies, clutched in both hands or carried on our backs. Our sleep-deprived brains barely register the fact that beneath our feet are layers of remains stretching back through human history.

Passing through the Late Bronze Age city gate, which dates back to before the time of the heretic Egyptian pharaoh Akhenaten in the fourteenth century BCE, we proceed along the tourist path and eventually reach the top of the mound. Dotted with palm trees, the surface is covered by a tangle of ancient ruins as far as the eye can see. Here the team members split into groups, each heading to their different excavation areas.

After quickly raising the poles that support the black shades covering each area to protect us from the sun, we have a few minutes to relax. Sipping cups of coffee and munching on breakfast bars, we watch the sun rise from behind Mount Tabor and burn the early morning mist off the floor of the Jezreel Valley. The dawn temperature is already seventy degrees Fahrenheit. The mosquitoes are biting, for the light wind is not enough to disperse them, but it is a temporary annoyance. They will soon disappear as the temperature rockets into the nineties and beyond over the course of the next few hours. By the time we leave in the early afternoon, the site feels like an oven. It's not hard to imagine that we are indeed working at Armageddon, even though it is only June. And we are lucky. The real heat will come in August. Nobody, not even archaeologists, is crazy enough to dig then.

Megiddo was my home away from home every other summer for twenty years, from 1994 to 2014. I dug at the site as a member of the Tel Aviv Expedition for almost as long as I have been married to my wife, Diane Harris Cline. She was the one who spotted the original flier advertising for volunteers and staff to take part in a new series of excavations at the site.

I was interested in participating for several reasons, including the fact that Megiddo has been at the center of biblical archaeology for more than a century, but also because of James Michener's book *The Source*, which I have read six times and which was influential in my choice of career. His book

FIG. 2. James Henry Breasted (courtesy of the Smithsonian Institution Archives)

was published to worldwide acclaim in 1965 and ranked number 1 on the *New York Times* best-seller list for almost a year. In it, Michener dramatically portrays the history of an archaeological site in Israel as well as the story of the archaeologists who were uncovering it. Although his site of "Makor" (Hebrew for "source," as in "a source of water") is fictitious, Michener visited Megiddo, among numerous other sites, during the year that he spent researching and writing the book while living at the Dan Carmel Hotel in Haifa in 1963. The parallels are obvious to those familiar with both Makor and Megiddo.[6]

Michener also quite clearly based his fictitious archaeologists upon real ones, including specifying that John Cullinane, the director of the dig at Makor, came from "the Biblical Museum in Chicago." This can only be a tip of the hat to James Henry Breasted, the preeminent Egyptologist and distinguished founder and director of the Oriental Institute at the University of Chicago, who favored three-piece suits, rimless glasses, and a debonair mustache. It was he who sent the team of actual archaeologists to Megiddo during the years from 1925 onward.

By the time I retired from active participation at the site, only Israel Finkelstein, the patriarchal Israeli archaeologist who has been codirector of the project since it began in 1992, and David Ussishkin, his longtime colleague, had worked there longer. Over the course of ten seasons in twenty years, I dug in most of the areas that we opened up, as I rose through the ranks from a volunteer to eventually join Finkelstein as codirector of the expedition.

Our daughter, Hannah, first came with us when she was eighteen months old, digging in the dirt with a trowel that seemed immense in her tiny hands, wearing a shirt cut down to size that read, "I Survived Armageddon." Our son, Joshua, was born five years after I joined the excavation team, and he was with me at Megiddo as I began to write the opening chapters of this book—by the time he turned eighteen, he had celebrated almost as many birthdays on excavations in Israel as he had at home in the United States.

I met many interesting people and made longtime friends during my summers at Megiddo. Above all, each excavation season, I was able to introduce anywhere from four to forty students from my university to the trials and tribulations of digging, along with countless other volunteers from elsewhere who were fulfilling a lifelong dream to participate in an excavation.

We were the fourth group of excavators to have dug at Megiddo over the course of the past century. The first was Gottlieb Schumacher, an American of German ancestry whose excavations from 1903 to 1905 were sponsored by the German Oriental Society and the German Society for the Exploration of Palestine. Twenty years later, in 1925, the Chicago excavators who are the focus of this book arrived at the site, determined to find Solomon's city. They stayed for fourteen excavation seasons, halting only because of World War II.

The famous Israeli archaeologist Yigael Yadin was responsible for the third expedition to investigate the ancient mound. He came with his graduate students for a few seasons in the 1960s and 1970s to test various hypotheses, including whether he could identify Solomon's building activities at the site.[7]

And then our Tel Aviv Expedition, under the continuous codirection of Israel Finkelstein and David Ussishkin, began with a trial season in 1992 and started in earnest in 1994.[8] Like the other archaeologists who had dug at Megiddo before us, we were hoping to uncover more secrets of its past, including more precisely dating the various levels and more accurately determining the historical sequence within the mound. We were also interested in answering specialized queries about what the inhabitants ate, wore, feared, and believed in each time period. The answers often remain debated and frustratingly elusive, although the advent of new scientific techniques is now shedding additional light and providing fresh data for Megiddo, frequently at a micro-archaeological level.[9] A final set of questions pertained to Finkelstein's controversial suggestion that much of what archaeologists thought were tenth-century BCE remains from the time of Solomon at various sites, including Megiddo, should in fact be redated to the ninth century BCE and the time of Omri and Ahab. This is known as the "Low Chronology" hypothesis and is still the focus of much discussion among archaeologists.[10]

Since Megiddo has been excavated on and off for more than a century at this point, virtually every building uncovered at the site has been the subject of multiple articles and scholarly debates as to its form, function, and especially date. This includes everything from the city gate in each level, to the water tunnel, the stables, the palaces, and even the private houses.[11]

As usual in archaeology, much of what the earlier excavators said about their discoveries at Megiddo now needs to be reconsidered in light of more recent discussions. Even the final publications of the Chicago team, especially the volumes usually called *Megiddo I* and *Megiddo II*, were the subject of debates virtually as soon as they were published in 1939 and 1948, respectively. Therefore, we placed some of our trenches in areas that we hoped would clarify the issues and provide some more definitive answers.

It is also frequently the case that archaeologists working at an ancient site like Megiddo, while trying to answer one question, will unexpectedly confront several more. However, that is in part why archaeology is so intriguing, and it simply motivates us to eagerly head back out into the field each season. It was the same in the 1920s and 1930s, for the Chicago archaeologists who spent a decade and a half trying to unlock its secrets.

It was the Chicago archaeologists who were responsible for having dug all the way down to bedrock. They were led by a succession of field directors: first Clarence Fisher, then P.L.O. Guy, and finally Gordon Loud, all sent to Megiddo by Breasted.

Breasted made it clear that he was particularly interested in discovering the remains of two cities out of the many that lay within the ancient mound.

One was Solomon's, which that ancient king had reportedly fortified during the tenth century BCE, according to the Hebrew Bible. The other had been captured by the Egyptian pharaoh Thutmose III nearly five hundred years earlier, in 1479 BCE, according to his own records.

However, the search for Solomon and for Thutmose III was not as straightforward as the Chicago archaeologists expected. The excavations rarely provided answers to their questions, and what they uncovered at the site was often unexpected. There were some years when they found next to nothing except tangled architecture and pottery sherds by the thousands, which were of interest only to themselves and other archaeologists. And there were other times when their discoveries made the front page of newspapers around the world, especially when they announced that they had found "Solomon's Stables" at the site.

Despite consisting largely of architects and geologists retrained as archaeologists and pottery specialists, and notwithstanding changes in personnel on an almost yearly basis, this team was among the best to excavate in the Middle East at the time. They retrieved the entire chronological history of Megiddo, from the Neolithic period to the Persian era, and noted the later Roman graves and adjacent remains as well. Along the way, they incorporated cutting-edge innovations and techniques, including balloon photography, vertical excavation, and the use of the Munsell color system for describing soil color. Their discoveries and innovations still resonate throughout biblical archaeology.

The scholarly publications by the Chicago excavators present their final thoughts on the results of their excavations. Their discoveries are justifiably famous, including stables, ivories, and an impressive water tunnel. The books and articles that they published are still used, and debated, by archaeologists working in the region today. However, these provide only a small window into the daily activities of the team members and the stories behind their discoveries.

Fortunately, they also left behind a treasure trove of other writings—more than three decades' worth of letters, cablegrams, cards, and notes exchanged by the participants, as well as the diaries that they kept. In working through these archival materials, currently housed at the Oriental Institute, the Rockefeller Archive Center, the Israel Antiquities Authority, and elsewhere, I realized that they provide us with a glimpse behind the scenes, a peek at the internal workings of the dig, playing out against the backdrop of the Great Depression in the United States as well as the growing troubles and tensions in British Mandate Palestine between the two world wars. We also get a glimpse of what the early years of biblical archaeology were like, including the backstory of *how* they actually did the archaeology, and the tools and techniques that they used at the time; in some ways, it is a far cry from what we do and use today, while in other ways it has not changed at all.

As a result, my research for this book took an unexpected and interesting turn. I had originally envisioned writing just about the archaeology of Megiddo, describing it layer by layer, building by building, from the beginning of its occupation to the end, without paying much attention to the archaeologists who had actually revealed the ancient remains. However, the wealth of detail contained in the letters, diaries, cables, and notes of the Chicago personnel revealed so much about their interactions, as well as the specific details of what went on during each of the excavation seasons, that I decided that they—and their efforts—should be the primary focus of the story (or should at least get equal billing).[12]

I should also note that I came to more fully appreciate the work of archivists—in particular their friendliness and patience, even with a naive researcher asking endless questions that usually had obvious answers. Furthermore, to my surprise, and delight, I found the archival research to be unexpectedly similar to doing an archaeological excavation, except that it involved digging through paper rather than dirt. Just as with a dig at an ancient site, where the presence (or absence) of a single item can sometimes make a tremendous difference, trying to resolve a specific issue at an archive often raised a whole host of other questions even while answering the original query. There was also the same thrill of finding something, especially the unexpected; the same dejection at coming up dry despite a promising beginning; and the same satisfaction that comes from putting together enough puzzle pieces to yield a plausible hypothesis for a past event.

Moreover, subsequent communications with descendants of the Chicago team members, as well as very basic genealogical research on Ancestry.com, resulted in the acquisition of additional material and information, ranging from letters and diaries to war records and details about their careers after Megiddo, which shed more light on individual team members such as Edward DeLoach, Daniel Higgins, Laurence Woolman, and even Gordon Loud and both Clarence and Stanley Fisher. I hope that I have been able to bring all of them to life in the pages of this book, for the material allowed me to better understand and discuss these team members as real people in the context of their times, with hopes, fears, dreams, problems, ambitions, and desires, rather than simply as names on the spines of books or in bland lists of participants, which is what they had been to me previously.

As a whole, their story includes intrigues, infighting, romance, and dogged perseverance, as well as the details underlying the drastic changes in staff and directors, before the digging came to an abrupt and unexpected end because of World War II. It frequently reads more like the script for a daytime soap opera, for the improbable cast of characters included an architect who became one of the best excavators of his day, but who couldn't manage a team of diggers, and a British Zionist who was married to the daughter of the man who reinvented Hebrew as a modern language, but who himself had neither a college degree nor any formal training in archaeology, and was fired for writing "one of the most scurrilous letters ever received" by the Oriental Institute. There was also a surveyor who sued for wrongful termination, but who may also have been spying for the Haganah while at the site; a young scholar arrested for smuggling antiquities on his way home, but who went on to a successful academic career nevertheless; and a high school dropout without a degree in archaeology and a geology student initially without an undergraduate degree, who together published more of the final excavation reports than anyone else—all micromanaged by Breasted from far-off Chicago and funded by one of the wealthiest men of the day, John D. Rockefeller, Jr.

That story, of their quest to uncover biblical Armageddon and to lay bare the city of Solomon, and of their intertwined personal and professional interactions during the search, can now be untangled and told. However, a brief word of explanation is necessary before we start. Beginning with the third chapter, the chapters in parts I and II have been written as a series of pairs. In each case, the first chapter in each pair (e.g., chapter 3) deals with the Megiddo personnel and their issues during a particular period, while the other chapter (e.g., chapter 4) discusses the actual archaeology that they conducted during the same period.

This was done in order to separate the personal from the professional during the seasons directed by Fisher and by Guy (it is not necessary for the seasons directed by Loud). However, the format is also meant specifically as an homage to the memory of James Michener, in gratitude and admiration, for his book was also written as a series of alternating chapters. I hope that readers will find my factual account of Megiddo and its Chicago excavators even half as interesting and entertaining as I found Michener's fictional story about Makor and its archaeologists.

DIGGING UP
ARMAGEDDON

"Have Found Solomon's Stables"

Everything changed in early June 1928, when James Henry Breasted, director of the Oriental Institute at the University of Chicago, received a Western Union cablegram. Sent by P.L.O. Guy, field director of the team of excavators that Breasted had sent to dig at Megiddo, the cable read: "FIRST KINGS NINE FIFTEEN TO NINETEEN AND TEN TWENTYSIX STOP STRATUM FOUR APPARENTLY CORRESPONDS STOP BELIEVE HAVE FOUND SOLOMON'S STABLES."

Considering that he had been waiting nearly three years for such a discovery, Breasted demonstrated remarkable restraint. He calmly cabled back a single word that same day: "CONGRATULATIONS."[1]

The rest of the world wasn't nearly as calm, cool, or collected. It's not every day that an archaeological team cites chapter and verse from the Hebrew Bible to describe their new finds, especially when those discoveries are tentatively identified as King Solomon's stables. In fact, Breasted was far more excited than he had let on. "I have now received full confirmation of the discovery of the stables of Solomon in our excavations at Armageddon," he told John D. Rockefeller, Jr., alerting him to the news before the official announcement was made public.[2]

The *New York Times* breathlessly reported on the discovery in early August, after receiving detailed information from Breasted. A longer article ran later that month, entitled "Digging Up the 'Glory' of King Solomon."[3] What more could a newspaper—or an excavation sponsored by Rockefeller—want? Armageddon and King Solomon in the same story was a scoop of the highest magnitude. It also made Breasted, and their financial backers in New York, especially happy, for it seemed that they had finally found the first remains from the city of Solomon for which they had been searching.[4]

The story also ran on page 1 of the *St. Louis Post-Dispatch*, with the headline "Excavators Find Stables of Solomon at Armageddon." In it, Breasted was quoted as saying: "Such a discovery will be of the greatest historical

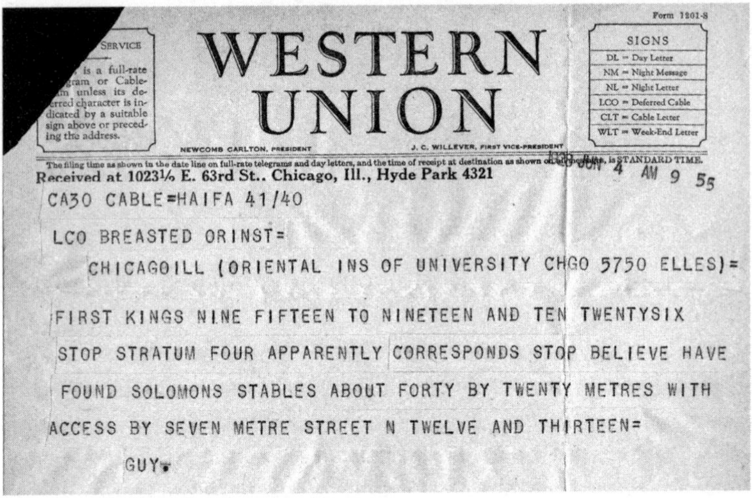

Form 1201-S

SERVICE

is a full-rate gram or Cable- m unless its de- rred character is in- dicated by a suitable sign above or preced- ing the address.

WESTERN UNION

NEWCOMB CARLTON, PRESIDENT J. C. WILLEVER, FIRST VICE-PRESIDENT

SIGNS
DL = Day Letter
NM = Night Message
NL = Night Letter
LCO = Deferred Cable
CLT = Cable Letter
WLT = Week-End Letter

The filing time as shown in the date line on full-rate telegrams and day letters, and the time of receipt at destination as shown on all messages, is STANDARD TIME.

Received at 1023½ E. 63rd St.. Chicago, Ill., Hyde Park 4321 JUN 4 AM 9 55

CA30 CABLE=HAIFA 41/40

LCO BREASTED ORINST=

CHICAGOILL (ORIENTAL INS OF UNIVERSITY CHGO 5750 ELLES)=

FIRST KINGS NINE FIFTEEN TO NINETEEN AND TEN TWENTYSIX STOP STRATUM FOUR APPARENTLY CORRESPONDS STOP BELIEVE HAVE FOUND SOLOMONS STABLES ABOUT FORTY BY TWENTY METRES WITH ACCESS BY SEVEN METRE STREET N TWELVE AND THIRTEEN=

GUY.

FIG. 3. Cable from Guy to Breasted, 4 June 1928 (courtesy of the Oriental Institute of the University of Chicago)

importance. Few people are aware that Solomon was not only an Oriental sovereign, but likewise a successful merchant. Not the least of his activities was his enterprise as a horse dealer."[5]

Breasted may have been thinking of horse-trading, but the two verses that Guy cited in his cable are the ones more usually quoted in tandem still today, in order to describe Megiddo as one of Solomon's "chariot cities":

> And this is the account of the forced labor which King Solomon levied to build the house of the LORD and his own house and the Millo and the wall of Jerusalem and Hazor and Megiddo and Gezer. (1 Kings 9:15)

> And Solomon gathered together chariots and horsemen; he had fourteen hundred chariots and twelve thousand horsemen, whom he stationed in the chariot cities and with the king in Jerusalem. (1 Kings 10:26)[6]

The discovery of these buildings launched Megiddo into the limelight of biblical archaeology, where it has remained ever since, even as suspicions emerged that Solomon may not have built them and that they might not even be stables.[7] This is the story of that site and of the Chicago archaeologists whom Breasted sent to search for Solomon's city.

PART ONE

1920–1926

CHAPTER I

"Please Accept My Resignation"

Chicago's excavations at Megiddo almost ended less than a week after they officially began. Just four days into the first excavation season, in early April 1926, Clarence S. Fisher, the newly appointed field director, sent a cable back to Chicago. In it, he stated bluntly: "HIGGINS' ATTITUDE MAKES FURTHER ASSOCIATION IMPOSSIBLE STOP DUAL DIRECTION ALWAYS DESTRUCTIVE OF BEST RESULTS STOP PLEASE ACCEPT MY RESIGNATION."[1]

It is perhaps fitting for a site that has seen so many major battles fought in its vicinity during the past four thousand years to also be the scene of a struggle for control of the excavations meant to unearth its secrets. However, Megiddo is not the first archaeological site at which such power struggles have taken place, nor will it be the last.

Breasted cabled back almost immediately, refusing to accept Fisher's resignation and assuring him that there was only one director: "DEEPLY REGRET TROUBLE," he wrote. "PLEASE UNDERSTAND YOU ARE SOLE DIRECTOR AT MEGIDDO STOP THERE IS NO DUAL DIRECTION AM CABLING HIGGINS STATING WORK IS UNDER YOUR SOLE INSTRUCTIONS."[2]

The tension had begun months earlier, when Clarence Fisher and Daniel Higgins both arrived at Megiddo in September 1925. However, the full story actually begins nearly a hundred years before that, in mid-April 1838, when Edward Robinson, an American minister, stood with his missionary colleague Eli Smith on top of a tall mound known in Arabic as Tell el-Mutesellim—"the Hill of the Governor."

Robinson and Smith were in the Jezreel Valley of what is now the modern state of Israel, intent on locating biblical sites in the Holy Land. Already they had pinpointed dozens to their satisfaction, based on similarities between modern village names and ancient places.

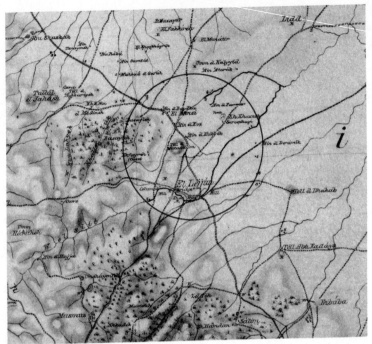

MAP 1. Detail from the Survey of Western Palestine (Sheet VIII) by Conder and Kitchener (PEF-M-WS-54.2; courtesy of the Palestine Exploration Fund)

Robinson, who was a professor at Union Theological Seminary, was certain that Megiddo lay somewhere in the vicinity of Tell el-Mutesellim. However, he didn't realize that he was actually standing on top of Megiddo at that very moment. In fact, he dismissed the mound as a possibility, stating, "The Tell would indeed present a splendid site for a city; but there is no trace, of any kind, to show that a city ever stood there."[3] Ultimately, Robinson decided that the nearby village of Lejjun covered both ancient Megiddo and Roman Legio.

Thirty-five years after Robinson and Smith, Lieutenants Claude R. Conder and Horatio H. Kitchener, who were surveying the western Galilee on behalf of the Palestine Exploration Fund (PEF), also stood on top of Tell el-Mutesellim. This time, though, they did notice traces of ancient remains. The upper parts of the mound were covered with thorns or cultivated, but under the vegetation lay "a city long since completely ruined." Everywhere they looked, there were foundations of buildings and broken pieces of pottery.[4]

Nevertheless, like Robinson and Smith, they still didn't identify Tell el-Mutesellim as Megiddo.[5] Their reluctance was based in part on the fact that, three years earlier, Conder had suggested that Megiddo might be located farther down the valley, at "the large ruined site of Mujedd'a at the foot of Gilboa,—a mound from which fine springs burst out."[6]

The debate over the location of biblical Megiddo continued for another two decades, until the Scottish theologian George Adam Smith convincingly showed that Megiddo and Tell el-Mutesellim were one and the same. He did so by using both direct and indirect evidence, including connecting biblical passages to geographical locations and documenting mentions within Egyptian inscriptions in his 1894 book *The Historical Geography of the Holy Land*, which was a landmark publication in all senses of the word.[7]

Breasted had been wanting to begin digging at Megiddo ever since June 1920, for the site had lain untouched following the conclusion of Schumacher's excavations fifteen years earlier. It was Lord Edmund Allenby, hero of the Allied forces in the Middle East during World War I and victor of the battle fought at Megiddo in 1918, who convinced Breasted that he should begin a new series of excavations at the ancient site. "Allenby of Armageddon," as he was frequently called, though his official title was "Viscount Allenby of Megiddo," had won the 1918 battle at the ancient site in part because of Breasted's multivolume publication, *Ancient Records of Egypt*, which appeared in 1906. In one of those volumes, Breasted translated into English the account of Pharaoh Thutmose III's battle at Megiddo. Breasted's translation allowed Allenby to successfully employ the same tactics thirty-four hundred years later.[8]

However, June 1920 was a tense time. There had been riots in Jerusalem a few months earlier, back in February and March, when the British announced their intention to implement the Balfour Declaration of November 1917 and create a national home for the Jewish people in Palestine. More riots, with nine people killed and nearly 250 injured, took place just a month before Breasted's attempted visit to Megiddo, when Easter Sunday and the Muslim celebration of Nebi Musa coincided.[9]

As it was, Breasted had to content himself with seeing Megiddo from a distance that June. In part, this was because it wasn't considered safe to cross the last few miles owing to bandits, but it was also because of a frustrating series of car problems and dysfunctional directions. "After having driven for hours along the hills on the north side of the plain of Megiddo, until we were far up toward Nazareth," Breasted wrote the next day, "we found that neither of our drivers knew the road. . . . For over two hours we drove over plowed fields and dry stubble land . . . staring helplessly at the walls of distant Megiddo which challenged us from across the plain."[10]

Although he had failed to make it to Megiddo, from Nazareth Breasted could see a mixture of sights and sites—geographical, historical, and religious. From here, the Jezreel Valley appeared like a triangle lying on its side. Its tip was out of view, off to the west by Haifa and the Mediterranean Sea, while its broad base lay approximately twenty-four miles (38 km) to the east, at the Jordan River.

The valley itself is quite narrow where Breasted stood, just eleven miles (18 km) across as the crow flies, which is why Napoleon reportedly once called it "the most perfect battleground on the face of the earth."[11] Perhaps fittingly, somewhere between Megiddo and Nazareth, in the heart of the valley, the "secret" Israeli air force base of Ramat David is now located. It is not shown on any maps of the region but, ironically, has its own Wikipedia page. It's certainly not a secret to any of the inhabitants in the valley, or the modern excavators at the ancient site, who are treated to daily sights of F-16 jets taking off and then landing again at ear-shattering volume.

To the west, just shy of the Mediterranean, Breasted could see Mount Carmel in the distance. Here, the Hebrew Bible says, Elijah once had a contest with the prophets of Baal (1 Kings 18:16–46); a Carmelite monastery now marks the reported spot.

To the east, he could see Mount Tabor. According to the biblical account, the Israelite troops of Deborah and Barak charged down its slopes, fighting against the forces of the Canaanite general Sisera, probably in the twelfth century BCE (Judges 4:1–24). The Transfiguration of Christ reportedly took place here more than a thousand years later; three separate churches now mark the spot at the summit of the mountain—the largest one was commissioned by Benito Mussolini.

Even farther east, and almost out of sight for Breasted, lay Mount Gilboa. Here, the Bible tells us, King Saul and three of his sons met their deaths at the hands of the Philistines in the eleventh century BCE (1 Samuel 31:1–12; 1 Chronicles 10:1–12). Nearby is the site of ancient Jezreel, where Jezebel was reportedly thrown out of a window and then trampled to death (2 Kings 9:10, 30–37).

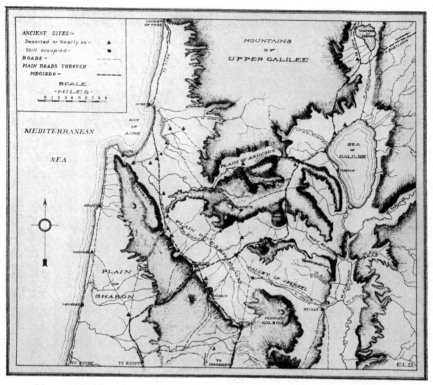

MAP 2. Megiddo and surrounding area, drawn by Edward DeLoach; published in Guy 1931: fig. 2 (courtesy of the Oriental Institute of the University of Chicago)

Much closer, also to the east and not more than a thousand yards away from the site of Megiddo, Breasted spied the junction where the Musmus Pass—also known as the Wadi Ara and the Nahal Iron—comes into the valley. It was through this pass that the armies of both the Egyptian pharaoh Thutmose III and the Allied commander General Edmund Allenby successfully marched in 1479 BCE and 1918 CE, respectively, en route to capturing Megiddo. In recording his victory on the walls of a temple in Luxor down in Egypt, Thutmose said that the capturing of Megiddo was "like the capturing of a thousand cities."[12]

Thutmose was not exaggerating, for Megiddo controlled the entrance to the Jezreel Valley from the west throughout antiquity. The Via Maris (literally the "Way of the Sea," as the later Romans called it) ran through the valley, serving as a main road for travelers and armies alike moving between Egypt in the south and Anatolia (modern Turkey) or Mesopotamia (modern Iraq) in the north. As both Breasted and Thutmose III well knew, if you controlled Megiddo, the rest of the region followed. Virtually every invader of the area fought a battle here in antiquity.

For Breasted, as it is for visitors today, the view across the length and breadth of the Jezreel Valley was breathtaking and the sense of history overwhelming. With just a bit of imagination, he could visualize the armies of Napoleon, the Mongols, Mamlukes, Egyptians, Canaanites, crusaders, Israelites, and others marching across the valley floor. All have fought here: biblical Deborah, Gideon, Saul, and Jonathan; Pharaohs Thutmose III and Sheshonq; Generals Kleber, Baibars, and Allenby; and unnamed soldiers in the hundreds and thousands. Many have died here. It is a sobering reminder of our place in the grand scheme of things.

At the time that he was trying to visit Megiddo, Breasted had just founded the Oriental Institute (OI) at the University of Chicago, courtesy of a large grant from John D. Rockefeller, Jr. He was now on the hunt for promising sites that the new institute might excavate, making "a daring reconnaissance trip through the Near East to survey the possibilities for research work . . . [c]rossing territory which was still virtually in a state of war."[13]

Breasted contacted John Garstang, who was the director of the brand-new British School of Archaeology in Jerusalem. More importantly, Garstang had also just been named director of the newly established Department of Antiquities in British Mandate Palestine. Breasted requested that a formal application be made on his behalf to the Archaeological Advisory Board, such that "the site of Megiddo be reserved for the period of one year to the University of Chicago with a view to excavation under the terms of the Law." By late November, he had been promised an excavation permit, valid for one year.[14]

Breasted's actions were part of a larger movement by American archaeologists at that time. Archaeology in the region was still in its infancy in those days, and archaeological expeditions up to that point had been rather haphazard. Even the headquarters of all the foreign schools of archaeology in Jerusalem were still relatively new, with the German Protestant Institute of Archaeology, the École biblique et archéologique française, and the British School of Archaeology, as well as the American School of Oriental Research, having been recently founded. In fact, even the field of archaeology as a discipline was still young at that time. Heinrich Schliemann's excavations at Troy, in which he was actively searching for proof of the Trojan War, had begun only fifty years earlier, in 1870, and Howard Carter was still two years away from finding the tomb of Tutankhamen, in 1922.[15]

The British archaeologist Sir William Matthew Flinders Petrie and the American Frederick Jones Bliss, digging at the site of Tell el-Hesi one after the other (1890 for Petrie, 1891–92 for Bliss), had been at the forefront of the field.[16] They were the first to realize that "tells" were man-made, consisting of multiple cities built one on top of another. They also borrowed from geology by introducing the concept of stratigraphy, which held that the lowest levels in the tells were usually earlier than the ones nearer the top. And they realized that because pottery types go in and out of style over time, they could be used to help date the various stratigraphic levels within a mound, as well as to indicate which levels at different sites were contemporary with each other.[17]

Their techniques were adapted and improved upon by other archaeologists. With some exceptions (notably the Irish archaeologist R.A.S. Macalister, who tended to ignore both stratigraphy and the precise location of the small finds that he came across while digging at the biblical site of Gezer during the periods 1902–5 and 1907–9), each archaeologist continued to improve upon the methods of the others.

Having been promised an excavation permit, Breasted approached Harry Judson, president of the University of Chicago, to discuss how he might finance the proposed excavation. Judson told him to put his thoughts into a letter that could be used in a pitch made to Rockefeller and other possible donors. Breasted promptly did so, ending his letter with a succinct financial assessment: "To make a complete clearance of the ancient city, its walls, its stronghold, citadel, palace, and houses, and to publish the results, would require a budget of Sixty Thousand Dollars ($60,000.00) each year for four years."[18]

Judson, in turn, immediately contacted Rockefeller, to ask whether he would be willing to fund this additional project. It would be a worthwhile endeavor, he suggested, for the results "may . . . cast a flood of light on the past of civilizations."[19]

Rockefeller was intrigued. Moreover, he liked Breasted. "I enjoyed knowing him and seeing him," Rockefeller once said. "He was a charming gentleman and a distinguished scholar, with the modesty of the truly great. My interest in archaeology was wholly the result of his influence."[20] However, since Rockefeller was not prepared to underwrite all four years of exploration, he offered to give $60,000 for the first year of excavation, on the condition that money for the additional three years came from elsewhere.[21] In early July 1921, the *New York Times* briefly announced the plan to excavate Megiddo, with the headline "To Excavate Armageddon; John D. Rockefeller Jr. Gives $60,000 to Dig Up the Site."[22] Unfortunately, Breasted was unable to raise the additional funds at the time, but he retained the option to dig at the site at some point in the future.

Three years later, in August 1924, probably stimulated by a letter that Clarence Fisher had sent to him a few weeks earlier, Breasted wrote to Rockefeller, asking whether the initial pledge was still on the table. He reiterated his interest in excavating "this remarkable stronghold of Armageddon," as he called it, noting that it "has become the proverbial symbol of the struggles of man, where Asia and Africa fought for supremacy for thousands of years." By mid-November, Rockefeller agreed to extend his pledge of $60,000 until July 1925, on the continuing condition that Breasted was able to procure the additional money needed from elsewhere.[23]

⚬

At this point, although it may seem that we are getting too far down in the weeds, it is necessary to continue our deep dive into the events leading up to the first season of excavation at Megiddo. The excursus will be worthwhile, for it is here that we meet the initial team members, some of whom will play a role at the site for years to come, as well as some of the other archaeologists with whom they would interact.

We therefore pick up the action again with the letter that Fisher sent to Breasted in mid-July 1924. In it, he asked whether Breasted planned to begin digging at Megiddo soon, and, if so, whether he could assist in any way.[24] Fisher was familiar with the site, having visited it in 1921 as part of a tour of the area arranged by William Foxwell Albright and the American School of Oriental Research in Jerusalem.[25]

Although originally trained as an architect at the University of Pennsylvania, from which he had graduated in 1897, Fisher identified himself as an archaeologist on all his passport applications and other official documents. A slim bookish man of about five feet eight, who also favored wire-rim glasses and sported a mustache, Fisher had quite a bit of experience by that

Fig. 4. Clarence Fisher at work (courtesy of the Oberlin College archives)

point. He had excavated at Nippur in Mesopotamia in 1900 and with George Reisner of Harvard University at Samaria in Ottoman Palestine in 1909–10. He had also directed excavations in Egypt for several seasons. At the time that he wrote to Breasted, he was back at the University of Pennsylvania, employed at the University Museum as a curator, and had been directing their excavations at Beth Shean (Beisan) in British Mandate Palestine for three seasons, from 1921 to 1923.[26]

Fisher was among the best practitioners of his time, having adapted and improved upon Reisner's methods, mainly by opening up large horizontal areas all at once while digging at Beth Shean, in order to see as much as possible of a single level before proceeding down into the next one. He would later teach many others over the years, including Albright in the early 1920s.

At the time, Albright was just getting his own start in the field of biblical studies and archaeology, having received his PhD from John Hopkins

University in 1916. He would later go on to become one of the most influential people in the field of biblical archaeology, as well as related disciplines, including serving as director of the American School of Oriental Research in Jerusalem, which is now named after him. He would also become Breasted's greatest rival in certain ways, and though there was mutual respect, there was no love lost between the two men.[27]

Fisher did not mention to Breasted what had prompted his inquiry in mid-July 1924, but he was not happy about the salary that he was receiving at the University Museum at the time, nor with his unsuccessful attempts to get permission from George B. Gordon, director of the museum, to hire an assistant.[28] He also probably foresaw that his time at the University of Pennsylvania was about to end, for he had been removed from the directorship of the Beth Shean excavations several months earlier. In fact, Fisher took matters into his own hands and fired off a letter of resignation in early December, although it took nearly a month for it to reach Dr. Charles C. Harrison, president of the museum's Board of Managers.[29]

Meanwhile, having heard from Rockefeller that his pledge would be extended, Breasted reached out to Fisher later that same month.[30] At the same time, he contacted Garstang again, asking that the permit for the excavation of Megiddo be extended until the end of 1925, which would give him enough time to raise the necessary funds.[31]

In early January, Garstang and the Archaeological Advisory Board agreed to extend the permit for Megiddo.[32] The official letter was sent on the exact same day that Philadelphia-area newspapers announced that Fisher and the University Museum had parted ways.[33]

The museum's official explanation was that Fisher had been let go because of ill health and his poor physical condition, but Fisher afterward insisted that he had resigned rather than been fired, because he had not been allowed to select his own assistant. In fact, he provided his letter of resignation to the Philadelphia newspapers, declaring, "If I leave the University Museum, I shall most certainly associate myself with the expedition of some other institution and continue my researches in the East." He subsequently did exactly that, at Megiddo.[34]

Eventually Gordon provided more of the backstory to Alan Rowe, who had taken over from Fisher as director at the Beth Shean excavations. According to Gordon, Fisher had been let go at Beth Shean because his "mental and physical health made it impossible for him to represent the Museum or to conduct the work of our Expeditions in the field." Fisher was ordered to return to Philadelphia, but there "his symptoms grew more aggravated [and] he . . . appeared to labour under the false idea that he was persecuted."[35] In the end, when Fisher offered his resignation from the museum, both Gordon and Harrison were undoubtedly relieved.

Fisher remained in contact with Breasted, writing again in February to indicate his continued interest—which was not surprising, since by that time he was out of a job.[36] Meanwhile, Gordon was sure that Breasted had no idea of the events that had transpired both at Beth Shean and in Philadelphia, writing to Rowe, "I understand that Professor Breasted is in charge of the University of Chicago Expedition at Megiddo. I should add to what I have said that Professor Breasted knows nothing at all about Mr. Fisher's conduct while connected with this Museum nor the circumstances under which he left its employ."[37] However, Breasted was probably quite aware of what had happened, for he was extremely well connected and often had news of events long before others did.[38]

Breasted next wrote to Raymond Fosdick, who was close to Rockefeller. At the time, Fosdick was a member of the board for all three Rockefeller philanthropic organizations that subsequently would be involved with the Megiddo excavations: the Rockefeller Foundation (RF), the General Education Board (GEB), and the International Education Board (IEB); he later became president of the first two boards.[39]

In his letter, Breasted reiterated much of what he had written in his original sales pitch back in March 1921, particularly about the importance of Megiddo/Armageddon.[40] He also told Fosdick that he had been unable to raise the additional funds beyond Mr. Rockefeller's pledge to fund one season of work at Megiddo because of an endowment campaign being run concurrently by the University of Chicago. Therefore, but also because expenses in the Near East had fallen slightly in the interim, Breasted now proposed an "entirely new Megiddo Project" for which he needed $15,000 for equipment (including tents, furniture, and Decauville railway cars and tracks for hauling away the dirt) plus funds for five years of work at $40,000 per year, for a total of $215,000.[41]

As an impetus to get Fosdick to persuade Rockefeller to pledge the entire amount, Breasted wrote that another factor relevant to the revised project was that "an admirable man is in sight to take charge of the Megiddo excavations." We might be forgiven for thinking that Breasted then extolled at length the virtues of Fisher, with his previous dig experiences in Egypt and at Samaria and Beth Shean, but that was not the case. Instead, Breasted wrote, "This man, whose name is Higgins, is firstly a trained geologist with wide field experience in many parts of the world. He has, for example, made a survey of the Peninsula of Sinai and knows all about its resources in oil and minerals. He can accept at any moment tempting commercial offers. But his heart is in archaeological field work. Such a man is a far better field director than the academic scientist. I am very anxious to save Higgins for such work."[42]

What had happened? It seems that—possibly because of the events relating to Fisher and the University of Pennsylvania Museum—Breasted had initially decided not to offer Fisher the directorship of the dig, but instead to put this geologist, Daniel F. Higgins, Jr., in charge. It is unclear why Higgins's heart lay "in archaeological field work," as Breasted put it, because he had no specific archaeological experience whatsoever. Nevertheless, in all other respects, Higgins's credentials certainly seemed impeccable—he had been trained at the University of Illinois, Northwestern University, and the University of Wisconsin, and was currently teaching geology at the University of Chicago. He had worked in Korea and China, and then for the US Geological Survey, fought in World War I with the British Expeditionary Force, and conducted explorations and surveys in both the Sinai and Egypt. He had also been married for fifteen years by that point; as newlyweds, he and his wife, Ethel, had served as Methodist missionaries and taught in Korea for two years, from 1910 to 1912. They had two young daughters: Mary, who had been born while they were in Korea and was now fourteen years old, and Eleanor, who was born while they were in China and was now nine years old. As might be expected, they were all quite willing to move to the Middle East.[43]

However, Fosdick very nearly torpedoed the entire proposal. Although he dutifully forwarded it to Rockefeller, he began by noting, "At first sight this new proposition seems to propose an arrangement of doubtful wisdom, inasmuch as it puts the entire burden [of funding the work] upon you." Nevertheless, he also pointed out that "in Dr. Breasted we have a uniquely trained man . . . certainly there is no one better in the world at the present time. The question is whether we ought to avail ourselves of the services of Dr. Breasted while he is still living and in his prime."[44]

Rockefeller felt that the answer was yes. After an additional conversation with Fosdick, Rockefeller authorized him to go all in and pledge the entire amount of $215,000 that Breasted had requested, which is the equivalent of nearly $3,000,000 today.[45]

The welcome news reached Breasted just hours before he departed for England on the SS *Homeric*. This was a splendid and luxurious passenger ship that began life as the German superliner *Columbus* in 1913. It was acquired by Great Britain in 1919 as part of the Treaty of Versailles, sold in 1920, and then finally completed and put into service by the White Star Line in 1922.[46]

As the ship pulled away from the North American coastline, Breasted cabled Daniel D. Luckenbill, whom Breasted affectionately addressed as "D.D." in all of his communications. Luckenbill was a distinguished professor of Assyriology and one of Breasted's closest colleagues at the Oriental Institute, with whom he had been discussing the various possibilities concerning Megiddo.[47] Swearing him to secrecy, Breasted followed up a few days later with a letter, also sent from on board the ship.

He asked Luckenbill whether, rather than Higgins, Fisher were still available. However, he also asked whether Luckenbill had any other suggestions for a field director, since Breasted wasn't completely sold on Fisher in that capacity.

It is not entirely clear why Breasted had decided not to ask Higgins to head the project after all, as he had proposed to Fosdick back in May. His decision may be related to the fact that Breasted was initially unsure about hiring Higgins at all but had been persuaded by Luckenbill, who swore that Higgins was the best photographer he had ever met, in addition to being a geologist and a surveyor.[48] More likely, it had to do with the fact that Breasted had realized Higgins needed additional archaeological training before he could be put in charge of the entire operation. Therefore, he decided that Higgins would be second in command, under Fisher's direction, and Fisher would train Higgins in how to run an excavation.

Although he had concluded that there was no one else available on such short notice, Breasted confided to Luckenbill, "poor Fisher is almost neurotic. It is very likely that after having started our expedition and gotten it into good running order for a few months, he will go off the deep end as he has done now with several successive groups of men." He continued: "I don't mean that I am taking Fisher with the deliberate intention of splitting with him. He is a very valuable man, and if his health will permit him to go on with us, I am and would be strongly in favor of keeping him; but there is every likelihood that things will go as I have suggested above."[49]

As it turned out, Breasted was prescient, for that was exactly what happened. But all of that lay in the future, and so, with no other suggestions forthcoming, Breasted cabled Fisher as soon as he reached London. "CAN YOU ACCEPT FIELD DIRECTORSHIP MEGIDDO EXCAVATIONS?" he asked.

Fisher accepted the offer almost immediately, but only after Luckenbill went to Philadelphia to talk it over with him in person. "FISHER ACCEPTS," Luckenbill cabled Breasted tersely. He then followed up with a longer cable and an even longer letter, for Fisher had suggested that they should begin immediately, by surveying the mound from September through March and then excavating from April through October. Both Breasted and Luckenbill liked the plan.[50]

Luckenbill and Fisher also discussed the arrangement to have Fisher train Higgins, which Fisher found appealing. Luckenbill reported that Fisher would take Higgins "in hand at once and train [him] for the work. He seems to think that one season would do that job. So do I. Thereafter, we would still have Fisher's advice and help, but things would fall to Higgins and assistants."[51]

Breasted was pleased to hear that Fisher had accepted the position. He filled Fisher in on the financial details, noting that they had enough money for a five-year campaign: $55,000 for the first season, which included $15,000 for equipment and the construction of a dig house at the site and $40,000 for the actual season, plus $40,000 for each season thereafter. Since that came to $215,000—exactly the amount that Breasted had requested in his modified plan and which Rockefeller had just donated—Fisher's salary of $5,000 per year plus traveling expenses would come from somewhere else in Breasted's annual budget for the Oriental Institute.[52]

At the same time, Breasted contacted Garstang once again, this time requesting that the official excavation permit finally be issued. He told Garstang that they had succeeded in procuring the funds and that Fisher would be directing the field operations.[53]

Overall, as Breasted saw it, they needed four people on staff: (1) a manager/administrator; (2) an archaeologist; (3) an epigrapher/philologist (to read the inscriptions he was expecting that they would find); and (4) a surveyor/draughtsman/plan-maker. He also suggested that they should take on a student to assist with the work.[54] Of course, on an excavation conducted today, we would have many more staff members; it is unfathomable to have only a single archaeologist present at a site during the digging season now, but that was common practice in those days.

As for the student whom he had envisioned taking part in the project, Breasted settled on a young man named Edward DeLoach as an assistant for Higgins, whom both Higgins and Luckenbill had recommended. DeLoach was twenty-four years old, the son of a good friend of Luckenbill's. He was originally from Georgia but as a student at the University of Chicago had taken surveying classes taught by Higgins. Fisher approved of this plan as well, since he had suggested to Luckenbill that they should take with them "a youngster or two and interest them in archaeology." At the time, DeLoach was working as a surveyor down in Post, Texas, but he responded promptly and positively to the invitation to participate at Megiddo that Higgins sent to him in July 1925. His only question, as he told his mother, was how much they were going to pay him.[55]

Breasted was pleased with all of this and told Fisher that he was confident Higgins would be "a very useful and good man," for Higgins not only understood how to make maps and plans but was also accustomed to managing men.[56] In fact, Fisher found Higgins to be neither useful nor good; nor did any of the other Megiddo team members have a more positive reaction. This was eventually made clear by separate correspondence between Breasted and others, including a former Yale student named John Payne Kellogg, who—unbeknownst to the others—became Breasted's informant from mid-May 1926 onward, surreptitiously reporting directly to him on everything from their emotions to the discoveries made by the team.

Breasted later told Garstang that Higgins had come highly recommended by the Department of Geology at the University of Chicago. However, as he concluded, "Regarding our complete disappointment in this direction I need not say more. The fact that our one year contract with Higgins has not been renewed is probably sufficient comment."[57]

By early July 1925, before all the trouble with Higgins came to pass, and exactly one year after he had first written to Breasted, Fisher began making plans to have equipment purchased and shipped to Megiddo. Higgins did the same, beginning in early August. This included equipment for surveying and photography, as well as for the light railway that would be used to haul away the excavated dirt. Fisher requested a car, specifically a Dodge or a Buick sedan, and proposed that a young Egyptian, with whom he had worked in Egypt, serve as overseer of the workmen. He also suggested that Higgins might sail over on the same steamer, so that they "could then get acquainted and talk over plans," though that didn't materialize.[58]

In the meantime, Garstang sent Breasted the official permit to dig at Megiddo, confirming that the work would be conducted under the field directorship of Fisher. Fisher himself made arrangements to sail by mid-August, so that he could begin work at Megiddo in early September.[59] This would allow the team to do a preliminary survey of Megiddo, begin building their dig house, and prepare everything for the first season, which would begin in April 1926 and last until October of that year, as Fisher had previously suggested.

FIG. 5. Megiddo team members with Egyptian workmen, fall 1926: Clarence Fisher, with hat on knees in center of photograph; Stanley Fisher is on his left and then Olof Lind; Ruby Woodley is on his right, wearing a hat, and then Edward DeLoach, with two-toned shoes, with Labib Sorial in a fez to his right (courtesy of the Oriental Institute of the University of Chicago)

Fisher planned to have a trained team in place by the spring. He proposed that their small group should be supplemented by the registrar from his excavations in Egypt, whom he had trained "in careful preparations of notes and plans." He also suggested that they bring from Egypt "a body of trained workmen, around whom we can build up a body of locals."[60]

These trained workmen from Egypt came from the village of Quft, where Petrie had begun this tradition in the 1890s. The descendants of the men whom he originally trained had created a quasi–caste system, in which certain families provided the overseers, while others provided the pickmen, the shovel men, and other necessary workers. According to stories told today at Megiddo, it is these men, eating Egyptian dates during their breakfast, lunch, and work breaks, who were responsible for the date palms now growing all over the top of the mound at the site, but this may be apocryphal. They formed the backbone of the excavation team for the Chicago archaeologists, working for them each season until the end of the excavations in 1939.

When Breasted finally received the official permit for the Megiddo excavations in early August, he forwarded it to Fisher. Two weeks later, the team members left the United States, but on two different ships. On one was Fisher and his twenty-six-year-old nephew (his brother's son) from St. Louis, who bore the same name but was known as "Stanley." The plan was to have him serve as their record keeper and accountant/financial officer, in addition to learning how to do archaeology. On the other was Higgins, who would be the surveyor and photographer, along with his wife and daughters, and DeLoach, who was appointed the expedition's cartographer as well as assistant to Higgins.[61] Fisher was the oldest, having just turned forty-nine, but Higgins was only about five years younger.[62]

The plan was to have these four men begin the preliminary surface survey of the site immediately. Four additional Americans would join them six months later, so that the excavation season could begin as planned in April 1926, with the Egyptian workmen having arrived in the meantime. The four additional men never materialized, however. Only one more team member joined them, the former Yalie named Kellogg, whom we have already met, and who was twenty-eight years old at the time.[63]

There were no women included among the initial staff; Fisher left behind his wife, Florie, and their seventeen-year-old son, Clarence Stanley, Jr., in the Philadelphia area. Although Higgins brought his wife, Ethel, and their two daughters, the three women chose to live in Beirut, near the American University, rather than at Megiddo; Ethel promptly began teaching first-year Latin to the American schoolchildren there.[64]

Apart from Fisher, none of the members of the expedition had any actual excavation experience, and only Fisher and Higgins had been outside the United States before. Though we can commend Breasted for having a reasonably multidisciplinary team, insofar as there was an architect, a surveyor, a cartographer, and an accountant among their members, it is truly surprising that there was nobody else experienced in doing actual archaeology. Even Fisher had been trained as an architect rather than as an archaeologist, though that wasn't all that unusual for the age.

That there were such people available with at least classroom knowledge, and some with actual excavation experience, is beyond question, though. Courses in archaeology, Egyptology, and the like, were already in place in England at Liverpool University by 1904 (established by Garstang) and the University of London (where Petrie had been appointed professor of Egyptology already in 1892). Established curricula were in place even earlier in continental Europe, including at the Humboldt University in Berlin, where Breasted himself had become the first American to receive a PhD in Egyptology, back in 1894. Even in the United States, archaeology courses were being offered at schools, including Bryn Mawr and Smith, as early as 1900.

Furthermore, Breasted could easily have filled his team with pioneering women archaeologists alone, such as Harriet Boyd Hawes, Edith Hall Dohan, and Hetty Goldman. All had directed their own excavations in Greece, Crete, and/or Turkey years before the Chicago team went to Megiddo. It is probably unfair to castigate Breasted in hindsight, given the general tenor of those times, but it is also interesting to speculate as to whether he would do things differently if he were staffing the excavation today.[65]

CHAPTER II

"He Must Knock Off or You Will Bury Him"

Fisher and his nephew Stanley sailed on 18 August 1925, having booked passage on the SS *Aquitania*, an attractive Cunard ocean liner often called "Ship Beautiful." Two weeks later they arrived in Alexandria. With stops in Cairo, Jerusalem, and Haifa to get supplies and arrange for the workmen, they eventually made it to Megiddo by mid-September.

Higgins and his family, plus DeLoach, arrived in Beirut about ten days afterward, having embarked on 29 August on the SS *Canada* from New York. After getting his family settled near the American University in Beirut, Higgins and DeLoach reached Megiddo before the end of the month. Fisher, Stanley, and seventeen Egyptian workmen and laborers were waiting.

Sunny skies and mild temperatures had greeted the team members in both Haifa and Beirut, but so did a cacophony of sounds, dust, and, in the case of Haifa, a town that was not yet even fifty years old. It had grown tremendously in the interim, but wandering the streets of Haifa was still a bit like being in the American Wild West back in the day.

Moreover, the road to Megiddo was unpaved. It took hours to get there—it was the type of place that one visited as a deliberate destination, rather than stopping by while en route to somewhere else. Even the tiny Arab village of Lejjun, located nearby, was more likely to be the actual destination than the ancient mound of Tell el-Mutesellim.

Sheep and goats wandered the area, looked after by the occasional herder. Clouds of gnats and mosquitoes hovered above the standing pools of water in the swampy marshland that made up the valley floor. It was bucolic, beautiful, and potentially deadly. The young Americans, and no doubt the older ones as well, were both excited and homesick—some were probably having second thoughts about their grand adventure. DeLoach's letters home, though, were filled more with descriptions of their new home away from home than with anything else.

In the meantime, the world's media had caught wind of the search that was about to begin. The *St. Louis Post-Dispatch* ran several stories about the expedition, perhaps in part because they were the hometown paper for Stanley Fisher. In mid-July, fully a month before the team had even left, the newspaper published an article with the headline "Armageddon to Be Unearthed by Archeologists." Subsequently, a longer feature article appeared in the pages of the Sunday Magazine supplement in mid-September, just as the team was arriving at the site.[1]

In the weeks that followed their arrival at Megiddo, the four intrepid team members began their initial work at the site. They started by surveying the mound, as planned, at the same time as they began the construction of a dig house in which they could live and work during the coming years.[2]

Soon a representative from the Department of Antiquities arrived, to help them negotiate with the local landowners.[3] Fisher had been told there were "some ninety separate owners holding varying amounts of shares," all living in the nearby village of Umm el-Fahm. In fact, because there were so many, it was not until nearly a month later that they were able to complete the negotiations with Hassan Saad, who claimed to be the largest of these landowners and so was serving as their representative. Fisher paid him in advance, signing a lease for the right to excavate on the eastern half of the mound. They promised to return the land as it had been, ready for cultivation, after three years.[4]

Finally, Fisher decided that it was time to begin trial excavations. Higgins immediately intervened, however, claiming that he had been told by those back in Chicago—that is, Breasted and Luckenbill—that they were only to survey and construct the house during these first weeks, and to begin excavating later. That was the first argument between the two men, but by no means the last.[5]

In fact, Fisher and Higgins disagreed on almost everything, including what time they should eat breakfast. Higgins wanted to get up at 5:30 a.m. and eat at 6:00 a.m. sharp, while Fisher wanted breakfast at 7:00 a.m. As a result, they ate separately, with the others joining along the way. Higgins also wanted to hold church services every Sunday morning—remember that

Fig. 6. Chicago tents at Megiddo, first week of season in 1925 (from the estate of C. Stanley Fisher, courtesy of Barbara A. Keller)

he and his wife had previously served as missionaries in Korea—to which Fisher grumbled quite specifically that they were there to do archaeology, not to run a religious mission.[6]

One would think that the living conditions for their team would necessarily have been quite primitive for the first few months, for they had to live in tents while the house was being built.[7] However, the six tents were all luxuriously furnished, complete with white bedsheets, finely woven grass carpets on the floors, and a small washstand for each of the Americans. The meals were better than those served at most hotels, young DeLoach told his mother, with five-course lunches and seven-course dinners each day, plus tea every afternoon at four p.m.[8]

At first, they pitched their tents near the Ain el-Kubbi spring, on the floor of the Jezreel Valley just to the north of the mound. One of the tents was used as a dining room, office, and sleeping quarters for the staff; another was for the Egyptian workmen; and the smallest was for the cook and the kitchen. They had chosen a picturesque spot; from their camp they could see Nazareth, Mount Gilboa, Mount Tabor, and, on a clear day, Mount Hermon off in the far distance. They could also see across the river Jordan, DeLoach told his mother, though that was a bit of an exaggeration.[9]

Unfortunately, they were constantly visited by the sheep and goats that they had noticed earlier. There were also too many mosquitoes. Soon thereafter, they decided to change locations and build their headquarters on the lower part of the mound itself. There they also put up another large tent, to be used as the office and dining room, so that the original first tent could be used just as a bedroom. Higgins also got his own tent, which served as his office as well as living quarters, since he was responsible for all the equipment that was to be used in the preliminary survey.[10]

However, the move did not alleviate the mosquito problem. By mid-December 1925, just three months after arriving at the site, Fisher came down with malaria. Within a month, everyone else on the team had contracted it as well. "Dr. Fisher was down with fever again when we left camp," DeLoach told Breasted. "He never goes more than two weeks without a spell and seldom that long. The spells usually last about three or four days, and always chills and fever about 102°F. . . . I have had two spells since I last wrote you, but I am following the quinine treatment given by the government as a result of a recent survey they made and it seems to be working well."[11]

Garstang said much the same a few days later, ending with a dire warning: "My dear Breasted. I have just returned from Megiddo after an adventurous ride. . . . Fisher is ill, & at the time of our call none of his staff was there. Higgins [is] in Beyrout, having had malignant malaria, & the other two in Haifa. All have had malaria: I cannot explain that. Fisher has had malignant malaria on & off with a spell in hospital for about 6 weeks. He is very run down & if he doesn't stop work he will collapse. . . . Now he must knock off or you will bury him."[12] In fact, Breasted himself later noted that when Lord Plumer, the British high commissioner, came to visit the site, "every member of the staff was in bed with malaria and there was no one to receive him."[13]

It wasn't until much later that Fisher could be persuaded to go to Jerusalem for convalescence. He spent two weeks there and eventually looked much better than he had upon arriving. However, he returned to Megiddo shortly thereafter and never fully recovered.[14]

In January, an anonymous note arrived in Chicago. Postmarked from Nazareth, it registered a complaint that Higgins was not yet back from Beirut, even though he had recovered from malaria. It also said that he had been doing geological work up in Lebanon rather than participating in the activities at Megiddo, including helping to oversee construction of the dig house.

Fig. 7. Megiddo dig house (after Fisher 1929: fig. 10; Courtesy of the Oriental Institute of the University of Chicago)

This was causing problems, according to the anonymous writer, not only because of Higgins's absence, but because he had left orders that they were not to touch any part of the house that had anything to do with his work, nor to put in any electrical wires at all, for some reason. The writer—who could only have been Fisher, Stanley, or DeLoach—noted that this meant the other rooms also could not be completed, because the wiring had to go in before the ceilings could be put into place.[15]

Soon thereafter Higgins returned to Megiddo and construction of the house resumed. By the latter part of January, it was nearly complete; the team was living in one part, while the rest was being finished. There were bedrooms for the team members, DeLoach said, as well as a kitchen, a dining area, and a common room. There were also areas for drawing architectural plans and for studying and storing the artifacts, and a large interior courtyard for washing and mending the pottery sherds as they brought down from the mound. DeLoach did note, though, that their fears about tents and high winds had been realized just a few weeks earlier: "Several weeks ago all of our tents were blown down in a very severe rain and wind

Fɪɢ. 8. (a) Breasted at Megiddo, with Sheshonq fragment against wall and DeLoach with a turkey; (b–c) Photograph and drawing of Sheshonq fragment (courtesy of the Oriental Institute of the University of Chicago)

storm. We were all in bed. We got soaked and many papers and books were damaged, and dishes broken. We have no more of that to fear now that we are in the house."[16]

Undoubtedly alarmed by what he had been hearing, Breasted made arrangements to visit the expedition during his upcoming trip to the Middle East. However, when he arrived at the site in early March, Fisher greeted him with good news. While the workmen were up on the tell gathering stones to use for the foundations of the new dig house, as Fisher had written in an earlier memo that they would be doing, they had found a broken piece of stone upon which were carved Egyptian hieroglyphics, including what looked like a pharaonic name in a cartouche.

(b)

(c)

The Chicago workmen found the fragment in a dump of dirt and stones that had been left during Gottlieb Schumacher's excavations twenty years earlier.[17] It was not surprising that Schumacher's team had missed it—although it was nine and a half inches (24 cm) tall and quite thick, the hieroglyphs were very worn and nearly unreadable at first, so that it looked like just another stone among many.[18]

As mentioned, Schumacher had excavated at Megiddo from 1903 to 1905. He had hired as many as two hundred workmen at a time, who dug a huge trench from north to south across the entire mound, as well as several smaller secondary trenches. Later dubbed the "Great Trench," it wound up being more than 20 meters wide, expanding to 30 meters in at least one area, more than 250 meters long, and 12 meters deep in places.[19]

In employing this strategy, Schumacher was following that used by Heinrich Schliemann at the site of Troy just a few decades earlier. There were problems, of course, including workmen not noticing and then throwing out many smaller objects, such as this stone fragment, and Schumacher may have done as much damage at Megiddo as Schliemann did at Troy. However, like Schliemann, Schumacher did publish the stratigraphic results of his excavations promptly, in 1908, although it took another twenty years—and another scholar (Carl Watzinger)—to publish the artifacts, which he did in 1929, four years after Schumacher's death.[20]

Breasted immediately translated the royal cartouche as belonging to Pharaoh Sheshonq, the Libyan pharaoh who founded the Twenty-Second Dynasty of Egypt and ruled from about 945 to 920 BCE.[21] He also realized that the fragment was obviously part of a much larger inscription, possibly a stele standing close to ten feet tall originally, and that they might yet find additional pieces that belonged to it.[22] Breasted took this to be a most auspicious sign, an omen foretelling that levels dating to the Egyptian New Kingdom period did indeed lie within the mound, waiting to be revealed.

All of the later reports published by the Chicago team implied that they had discovered the Sheshonq fragment just before Breasted's visit in March 1926. However, Higgins noted in private that it had actually been found four months earlier. As he wrote to Luckenbill, "Breasted did not seem too pleased that it had been resting here since last November without his hearing about it!"[23]

Nevertheless, as mentioned, Breasted felt that this was a good sign, especially coming before the excavation had even officially begun. He subsequently penned a quick note to Fisher from his hotel in Haifa, asking him to keep news of the discovery quiet until a cable could be sent to Mr. Rockefeller. Only then would they alert the press.[24] Such a concern is noteworthy in reflecting the financial needs of an excavation beholden to its sponsor even back then, just as is frequently the case today.

Four days later, having moved on to Cairo in the meantime, Breasted wrote to Luckenbill, noting rather gleefully that Schumacher's team had missed the fragment.[25] Alerting Garstang in Jerusalem as well, he said that Fisher would be sending a report about the fragment, and asked him to "keep the matter confidential for a short time." He claimed that he hadn't yet sent the news to Rockefeller, "whose interest in Biblical history is such that he will at once appreciate the value of this find, and a first account of it to him will, I have no doubt, stimulate his interest in such researches in Palestine."[26]

In actuality, Breasted had already written to Rockefeller about the discovery. "This is a first greeting from the great mound covering the fortress of Armageddon," he began. "Our great task of clearing the huge mound is just beginning." He went on to tell the tale of how one of the Egyptian workmen had noticed the hieroglyphs on the stone fragment, which they then set aside until his arrival, and how reading it had transported him back to "a Sunday school in a little church on the far-off prairies of Illinois."[27]

However, news always spreads fast in the archaeological world, even back then, especially when a momentous discovery has been made. Garstang had already heard about the discovery of the fragment and told Breasted that, in the future, Fisher should keep him informed about "anything he wishes to keep quiet, so that I may know how to reply when 'rumours' reach me."[28]

The Department of Antiquities also realized the significance of the discovery. They took possession of the fragment when the finds from the season were divided between them and the expedition, as was supposed to be done just before the dig shut down each year, and transported it to Jerusalem, where it is now in the Rockefeller Archaeological Museum (formerly the Palestine Archaeological Museum) in East Jerusalem.[29]

Why they wanted it, and its significance, can be stated fairly simply. According to a very lengthy inscription that Pharaoh Sheshonq ordered to be carved onto a wall in a temple in Egypt, he had attacked and captured

Megiddo, among many other cities in the area. We know that this took place a few years before the end of his reign, about 930 BCE. Thus the fragment overlooked by Schumacher's workmen at Megiddo may corroborate Sheshonq's boast that he had captured the city. In addition, to a number of scholars and members of the public it was even more important because of its biblical implications, for many today equate Sheshonq with Pharaoh Shishak, who the Bible says attacked Jerusalem and other cities soon after the death of King Solomon—that is, also approximately 930 BCE.[30]

Breasted eventually wrote at length about the stone fragment, using almost the same words that he had written to Rockefeller:

> On my first arrival at the mound after work had begun in the spring of 1926, Dr. Fisher informed me that a fragment inscribed with Egyptian hieroglyphs had been brought down from the top of the mound as a building block during the construction of the house. It was with considerable satisfaction on the first sunny day after the rains had diminished that I was able to make out the name of Shishak or Sheshonk I, in hieroglyphs very dimly glimmering from a badly weather-worn and almost illegible inscribed stone surface. As a lad in a country Sunday school, I had so often read the familiar words of the Old Testament historian in I Kings 14:25–26, that they came back to me very vividly as this record of the ancient conqueror's name, found in the midst of ruins of one of his captured cities, slowly became legible.[31]

Eventually word got out to the wider world. In late June 1926, the *St. Louis Post-Dispatch* ran a feature story about the find on page 2 of its Sunday Magazine supplement, complete with pictures of the fragment and of Megiddo, as well as Sheshonq's inscription on the wall in Luxor down in Egypt, and a fine photo of Breasted himself looking very elegant and sophisticated. Although the article itself is full of erroneous information, the best part is a quote from Breasted, in which he states: "It was by mere chance that we came upon this stone. Already it had been thrown into the dump heap by a former expedition which I do not care to name."[32]

Breasted also tried to explain how they were digging and ventured to describe the makeup of the ancient mound in terms that the newspaper's readers might understand. "Certainly, a priceless find was thrown away when the Shishak stone was discarded. That goes to show how careful the excavator must be in throwing aside this or that as worthless," he said. "We are trying to avoid such pitfalls by removing the soil from the mound a thin layer at a time and sifting every square inch of it. You may or may not know that the Mound of Megiddo, or Armageddon, is made up of layers something like a huge layer cake. Each layer represents the ruins of a city or an age. . . . Nobody knows how many cities have flourished and died on the site of Megiddo. That is one of the many things this Armageddon expedition of the Oriental Institute hopes to determine. As yet our work is only in its beginning."[33]

Momentous as the discovery of the Sheshonq fragment was, it would have been even more meaningful had the Chicago team found the inscribed piece of stone still in situ, or if Schumacher's workmen had noticed it, whether built into a later wall or in its original context. As both Fisher and then Guy noted in their subsequent reports on their excavations at Megiddo, it might then have been possible to tell which city at Megiddo dated to the time of Sheshonq. By extrapolation, we would then also know which city at Megiddo was the one that Solomon built.

However, since Schumacher's workmen had simply thrown the inscribed fragment into a spoil heap of dirt and other stones by the side of one of their trenches, there was no record of the level or stratum in which it was actually found. Therefore, in his 1929 preliminary report, Fisher was able to say only, "The fragment of the Shishak stela . . . came from one of the old surface dump heaps near the eastern edge [of the mound]." Guy mentions it again in the 1931 second preliminary report, but he was able to add only the following: "From somewhere in a minor trench of Schumacher's (No. 409 in Square M14 on our plan . . .) which penetrates barely below Stratum IV came the stela fragment of Shishak which was found by Fisher's foreman in the rubbish heap beside it."[34]

In his 2004 book on Megiddo, Tim Harrison noted that this findspot was most likely close to what is now the Northern Observation Platform at the site.[35] In 2014, the Tel Aviv team conducted excavations in this area, but no further fragments of the original inscription were found. Despite Breasted's optimistic statement to Luckenbill—"It is not impossible, indeed probable, that the remnant containing a narrative of his [Sheshonq's] Palestinian campaign may still be lying in the mound awaiting our excavations"—no other piece from this monument has ever been found.[36]

CHAPTER III

"A Fairly Sharp Rap on the Knuckles"

Preparations for Chicago's first season of actual excavation at Megiddo began in the early months of 1926, well before Breasted's visit. The team needed to procure visas for their Egyptian workmen, so that the men could travel to British Mandate Palestine. They also wanted to make certain that they didn't have to pay customs duties on any of the equipment that they had shipped over, from their automobile to tents, photographic material, steel filing cabinets, and pieces of the light railway that they planned to build (and which they referred to in correspondence simply as "the Decauville," after the French manufacturing company that made it). And, perhaps more important than anything else, at least in terms of their health, they hoped to work with the government to get the swamps filled in, in order to eradicate the mosquitoes and thus the malaria infecting all of them.[1]

During his visit in March, Breasted thought that everything was going well—so much so that he cheerily remarked to Luckenbill afterward, "Everything is going splendidly at Megiddo." All of the team members had recovered from their bouts with malaria, according to Breasted; the house was almost finished and was very comfortable; and the digging was to begin soon.

A photo taken during his visit confirms much of this—gathered in front of the house are the team members, including DeLoach, Higgins, Breasted and his son Charles, and Fisher, as well as a number of workmen, with Stanley perched on the sill of an upstairs window. The house looks stout and well built, with shutters open on every window. Next to the men is parked the team's "International" truck, in very good shape, with open sides covered by a grille and with shades that could be rolled down as protection from the dust and sun.

Breasted's later description of the dig house differed slightly from DeLoach's earlier one. In the Oriental Institute handbook issued in

Fig. 9. Breasted visit to Megiddo, March 1926; left to right: Edward DeLoach, Daniel Higgins, James Henry Breasted, Charles Breasted, Clarence Fisher, with Stanley Fisher perched on the sill of an upstairs window (from the estate of C. Stanley Fisher, courtesy of Barbara A. Keller)

August 1928, he said that it was "built of heavy stone masonry," with a double roof. There was actually more than one building, as can be seen in photographs from that time. The largest one contained the living and working quarters, including the drafting rooms and the darkroom for photography. The other buildings contained workshops, the kitchen and provision storage rooms, an area for storing the antiquities, and a three-car garage.[2]

Breasted specifically said that Fisher and Higgins were being "perfectly courteous to each other."[3] In fact, it was all an act—the two men were being cordial to each other strictly for his benefit, but he became aware of that only long after the fact.[4]

The workmen arrived by mid-April and the first season of excavation finally began a few days later. The plan was to work in two main areas: the lower part of the eastern slope, where everything would be investigated and then cleared away so that the material removed from the top of the mound could be dumped in this area; and on the top of the mound, where an area on the eastern side, near Schumacher's Great Trench, would be investigated and the various layers removed after each had been investigated in turn—first Stratum I, then Stratum II, III, and so on.[5]

Less than a week into the dig season, however, the power struggle between Fisher and Higgins finally erupted into the open.[6] Instead of having it out with Higgins on the spot, Fisher fled to Jerusalem.[7] From there he sent the cable to Chicago, resigning his position as field director and citing irreconcilable differences with Higgins. As we have seen, Breasted refused to accept the resignation and confirmed instead that Fisher was the sole director at Megiddo.[8] Breasted also cabled Higgins at the same time, "giving him a fairly sharp rap on the knuckles," as he later told Luckenbill. The terse message read simply, "WORK AT MEGIDDO MUST BE DONE UNDER FISHER'S SOLE INSTRUCTIONS LOYAL COOPERATION WITH HIM INDISPENSABLE."[9]

Eventually the details began to emerge as to what had happened, courtesy of letters written by DeLoach and by Kellogg, who joined the team in May. Kellogg had been studying with Luckenbill at the Oriental Institute, after graduating from Yale in 1921. However, he wished to gain experience in the field as well as learn the ancient languages and history in the classroom, so he contracted with Breasted to join the Megiddo expedition after the university's winter quarter had ended.

A good-looking young man, standing five feet eleven, with blue eyes and brown hair, Kellogg was twenty-eight years old at the time, hailing from Watertown, New York. He quickly became the "inside man" at Megiddo, reporting back to both Breasted and Luckenbill about the goings-on between Higgins, Fisher, and the others. He kept firm to his plan to excavate only for the portion of the season that remained that year and to return to Chicago for courses in the fall. And so we eventually find him on a ship's manifest returning to New York in October 1926, never to return to Megiddo again.[10] However, at the moment, all of that still lay a few chaotic months ahead.

According to Kellogg, it was hard to say who was more to blame. While Higgins was extremely tactless and had antagonized everybody since his arrival, Fisher had his own faults, including some that probably made him unfit to serve as director.[11]

"Dr. Fisher certainly is a good technician," Kellogg noted, "but absolutely without a practical hair in his head and with no ideas at all of organization, and because of temperament unable to assume a dictatory attitude." His assessment of the situation was blunt and straightforward: "Fisher has too much reticence and Higgins too much of the opposite. He (Higgins) has a good deal of ability and great breadth of interest which however should be kept a good deal of the time within narrower limits. Fisher isn't the man to see that this is done."[12]

Those back home in Chicago clearly agreed with Kellogg's appraisal, for Luckenbill later told Breasted, "Of Fisher's lack of executive ability I have been aware for twenty-five years. . . . And it is true that Higgins has the American bluff that puts things over. Allah be with us and them!"[13]

However, in the meantime, Breasted's reply to Fisher had the desired effect on him. Reassured as to his status, Fisher cabled back, "EVERY EFFORT WILL BE MADE TO INSURE MEGIDDO SUCCESS."[14] Kellogg later reported that Breasted's cable had given Fisher sufficient courage to come back to the dig and resume his duties.

However, the cable to Higgins had the opposite effect. He was not happy in the least. In his opinion, Fisher was simply a spoiled child who shouldn't have bothered Breasted with their trivial differences, just as Higgins had refrained from troubling Breasted about them during his recent visit. Feeling that he was blameless in all of this, and that Fisher was the one who was actually at fault, Higgins sent back a snarky reply to Breasted.

Breasted's cable to him was "amazing" (and not in a good way), said Higgins. He then itemized five possible causes for Fisher's complaints about him; all were written in the third person. The first item on the list read: "Recalcitrant Higgins and DeLoach did cause to have removed a gigantic latrine ('the skyscraper'), erected by Fisher prominently by the main gate, to a less unseemly site." Another entry continued the theme, declaring: "Said Higgins did on numerous occasions willfully resent the promiscuous deposition of human excrement in immediate juxtaposition to our camp and excavations . . . and that at last he insisted on latrines for the workmen."[15] Breasted was not pleased; he did not appreciate receiving such a letter in response to his "knuckle-rapping" cable, even if several of Higgins's points did have obvious merit.

Meanwhile, by now it was mid-May and so, at the same time that all of this was going on, they began work on the East Slope of the mound. Fisher wanted to start in on the top of the site as well, but he was stymied by the fact that Higgins had not yet completed, or perhaps had not even begun, his survey of the area and had not created an initial plan. So they continued to dig only in the same area on the eastern slope where they had been working in the fall, in an effort to clear the area before using it as a dump for dirt and debris that would come from the excavations at the top of the tell.[16]

It was slow going, since they didn't have many workmen. Moreover, the whole area was honeycombed with tombs from different periods, a number of which had collapsed, crushing the pottery and other burial goods that were inside. It had also been used as a quarry sometime later, and Fisher surmised that those quarrymen of antiquity had frequently stopped to rob the tombs that they came across during their work. He was also keenly aware that Schumacher had excavated in the area previously and had already cleared out a number of the tombs.

As the weeks wore on, Higgins, who should have been occupied with surveying the top of the mound so that they could begin digging there, instead filled his days by photographing some of the pottery and other objects, as well as the details of the excavations. He was also frequently gone for a week or more at a time, visiting his family in Beirut and taking on external projects, which frustrated Fisher no end. DeLoach was kept busy doing the real drafting work, drawing and planning the tombs as they were excavated.

Fig. 10. Sorting pottery in the Megiddo dig house (courtesy of the American School of Oriental Research Archives, Nelson Glueck Photograph Collection)

One Egyptian workman, Ali, was in charge of washing the baskets full of pottery sherds that came in from the tombs and elsewhere, and then fitting the various pieces together. Three local boys helped him, but even so the courtyard of the house quickly filled up with baskets of pottery waiting to be sorted.

Fisher noted that as soon as the pottery had been drawn, "only those which are worthy of being kept for Museum purposes are placed in the storeroom with registry numbers." Complete pots were always saved, he said, as were decorated pieces, but the other undecorated pieces were simply discarded, by being reburied in one of the tombs.[17] Even so, with the amount of pottery that was coming in, and with no one else available to help him but his nephew Stanley upon occasion, Fisher was soon overwhelmed and rapidly fell behind in drawing and recording everything.

Fortunately, everything suddenly slowed down in early June. Only six of the Egyptian workmen were actually digging at the time and many of the local workers had returned to the fields to harvest their crops. The Chicago team had also used up all of their money and were playing for time until the next installment arrived on 1 July.[18] It is unclear how many men had been employed at the height of the season, though we know Fisher complained at one point that he had only 80 local workmen when he could have used 150.[19]

Two weeks later, in mid-June, a cable arrived from Breasted. Without preamble, it simply declared: "UNIVERSITY IS RELIEVING HIGGINS BY CABLE TODAY OF ALL FURTHER DUTY IMMEDIATELY YOU ARE AUTHORIZED [TO] PAY HIM RETURN TRAVELLING EXPENSES WHEN HE LEAVES."[20] Fisher's relief was palpable.

Breasted also sent a second cable that same day. This one went directly to Higgins. We do not have the original, but a handwritten draft in the Oriental Institute archives states bluntly: "University will not require your services after July thirty-first and you are hereby relieved of further duty as of this date. Your return travelling expenses will be paid by Doctor Fisher who is in no wise responsible for nor until today aware of this action. Please cable date leaving and balance salary to end July will be deposited immediately [to] your bank account."[21]

Higgins had been in Beirut for several weeks beforehand but happened to be at Megiddo on the day that both cables arrived. Rather than talking it over with Fisher, Higgins replied directly to Chicago instead, first offering to work for only $100 per month for the next year and then demanding to be paid for August and September. Subsequently, he departed for Beirut, returned briefly to get his belongings in mid-July, and then moved with his family back to the United States.[22]

It is quite clear from the extant letters exactly why Higgins was suddenly fired, for his snarky response to the earlier cable had antagonized Breasted, as mentioned. Breasted had responded immediately with a letter berating Higgins for his lack of loyalty and obedience, which Breasted valued above all else in his team members. He ended the letter by telling Higgins how disappointed he was in him. Then, on 16 June, the same day that he sent Higgins the cable telling him that he had been fired, Breasted sent him another long letter that itemized, point by point, exactly how Higgins had disappointed him and the reasons for which he was being fired.[23] Such a letter, it seems, was typical of Breasted, for he eventually sent a similarly detailed letter to Guy, when he fired him almost exactly six years later, in August 1934.

In the long letter to Higgins, Breasted wrote that additional facts had come to his attention since they had met at Megiddo back in March, including the fact that, while en route to Megiddo the previous August, and before having ever even been to the site, Higgins had hired an Armenian as an assistant surveyor, without first consulting Breasted. Apparently, the man was eventually dismissed, but only after he had cost the expedition hundreds of dollars and filed a lawsuit against both Fisher and Higgins. This lawsuit, which is nowhere else mentioned in the archives, seems to have been settled without Breasted's knowledge until after the fact. Breasted also noted that Higgins's total lack of the tact and graciousness that are necessary on a field excavation had "all but wrecked the Expedition." He concluded, "What you have failed to see is that it is just as important to maintain successful working relations with other members of an Expedition as it is to know how to do the work at all."[24] In that, Breasted was absolutely correct, for the same still holds true on archaeological excavations today.

However, there was one other episode that Breasted did not mention in his letter, but which likely also contributed to Higgins's firing. It is alluded to only in passing, in various places, beginning with an aside that Kellogg made to Breasted in mid-July. While discussing, after the fact, their good fortune in being rid of Higgins, for he wasn't the type of man whom they wanted associated with the work that they were doing at Megiddo, Kellogg also said that Higgins had created "quite a mess between Luckenbill and

Albright."[25] He didn't elaborate further on what had happened, but then again he probably didn't need to, for Breasted was undoubtedly all too well aware of what had transpired. It had taken place months earlier, soon after the men arrived at Megiddo.

Albright had come to visit the dig back in mid-October 1925 but, as later biographers of Albright have delicately put it, there was "a misunderstanding . . . and Albright was forbidden access to the mound." Outraged, Albright sent a letter to Luckenbill, telling him what had happened, but Luckenbill—thinking that Albright was traveling in Mesopotamia—didn't answer for nearly six months. When he did reply, in mid-April 1926, Luckenbill said that he had no idea why anyone at Megiddo would "exclude Albright from the site." Albright, in turn, wrote back two months later, saying that he had long since decided that it was all the result of a misunderstanding, and that he was certain that neither Luckenbill nor Breasted had meant for him to be denied permission to see the site.[26] Higgins also confirmed that, by then, the "Albright matter," as he called it, had gone quiet.[27] In the meantime, Fisher, who apparently was not there at the time, also tried to smooth things over, telling Albright that he was always welcome at the site, and that he would show Albright around himself.[28]

But who would have denied Albright, the director of the American School in Jerusalem, access to the site? We know that there were only four staff members present in October 1925—Clarence Fisher, Stanley Fisher, Edward DeLoach, and Daniel Higgins. Of those, both DeLoach and Stanley Fisher were young and very junior; they would never have done such a thing. It could only have been Fisher or Higgins who denied entry to Albright, but based on Kellogg's letter, it appears that it was Higgins. However, in his defense, Higgins may not have been acting entirely on his own, because back in June, even while they were still appointing the staff members, Luckenbill and Breasted had discussed the fact that "the Oriental Institute was not ready to have any supervision of its work by Dr. Albright." Luckenbill, in fact, said that he had made it clear to Fisher that "we could not be expected to do much cooperating with him [Albright]."[29]

So even if Higgins had denied entry to Albright, he might not have been completely out of line. Still, as Albright's biographers note, the incident "nearly shattered the expedition."[30] Thus the firing of Higgins, even so belatedly—eight months after the event—will have begun to set things right and to patch up what could have been a professional disaster pitting some of the best-known names in archaeology and Assyriology against each other just as the excavation was getting under way.

Fisher and the others undoubtedly held at least a mild celebration after Higgins was sacked in mid-June. However, another cable, sent by Breasted three days later, poured cold water on the festivities. This one read: "GREATLY INTERESTED IN RESULTS ON SLOPES. PLEASE CABLE WHO IS RESPONSIBLE FOR DELAYED SURVEY AND EXCAVATION OF TOP. PLEASE BE PERFECTLY FRANK. SHIELD NOBODY. BREASTED."[31]

Fisher's reply must have cost a pretty penny, for it is by far the lengthiest cablegram in the Megiddo archives at the Oriental Institute. In it, Fisher laid the blame squarely upon the just-fired Higgins:

DESPITE SUMMIT PLANS NOT BEING STARTED BEGAN EXCAVATING THERE APRIL EIGHTEENTH STOP HIGGINS DEMANDED WORK BE SUSPENDED UNTIL MAP FINISHED, CLAIMING HE REPRESENTED CHICAGO'S INTEREST I THEN CABLED MY RESIGNATION STOP HIGGINS PLACED MEN ON NEW SLOPE AREA WHERE INTERESTING MATERIAL WAS DISCOVERED I ASSUME FULL RESPONSIBILITY FOR FAILURE TO INSIST UPON OUR ORIGINAL SCHEME BEING FOLLOWED BUT ACCEPTED HIGGINS' STATEMENT OF HIS AUTHORITY WITHOUT QUESTION STOP ALWAYS WILL FOLLOW YOUR SUGGESTIONS. DELOACH NOW LOOKING AFTER SURVEY OF EXCAVATIONS.[32]

Fisher later elaborated further, in a sworn statement that he was required to make in late July. In it, he answered fifteen separate questions concerning Higgins and his work. Within his responses, he noted that Higgins had spent two weeks out of each month away from Megiddo, even during the excavation season: one week was spent in Beirut—though Fisher neglected to say that Higgins was visiting his family there—and the other was spent at Tell en-Nasbeh, where he was making a map of the excavations for Dr. William Badè, who was excavating the site.[33]

The most damning information was given in reply to the eighth question: "At what date did he [Higgins] begin the survey at the top of the Megiddo Mound?" Fisher responded by saying that "there was no map started of the hill until April 18th. . . . Then no more than five days work was done on this map until Mr. Higgins left the expedition [i.e., in mid-June]. All we have to show for this work are a few contour lines covering a small portion of the northeast summit." In subsequent answers, he noted that Higgins himself had estimated that the summit could have been plotted in three to four weeks of sustained effort, and agreed that the excavations on the top of the mound had been delayed by at least two months because of Mr. Higgins's failure to complete the promised survey.

Fisher concluded his answers by noting, "Mr. Higgins antagonized every member of the Expedition by constant criticism and cutting remarks, especially at meals," and that he had alienated the Egyptian workmen in a variety of ways, including letting them know that he suspected them all of being thieves. Just to make certain that there was nothing left to ask, he made the final point that "all the members would have left the Expedition at the end of this season, if not sooner, had Mr. Higgins not been set free."[34]

When these answers reached Breasted in mid-August, he instructed Luckenbill to refuse to see Higgins if he appeared in Chicago before Breasted himself returned to the area. And from that day on, nothing more was said about Higgins, apart from a brief mention that he had attempted in July to get two thousand more dollars from the expedition but had been satisfied when they agreed instead to pay the two additional months' salary (August and September) beyond his year's contract, the amount he had demanded before leaving Megiddo. Breasted noted ironically to Luckenbill that he also received "a pathetic letter from Mrs. Higgins for whom I feel very sorry. She regards her gifted husband as a prodigy."[35]

Higgins died just four years later, in 1930. At the time he was employed as a professor of geology at Lincoln Memorial University, in Tennessee. His obituary noted that he had been ill for several weeks before his death, and that "the doctors say that his death was really due to the long siege of sickness he had in Egypt ten years ago" (which would have been back in about 1920).[36]

Soon thereafter, new personnel joined the team, including Miss Ruby Woodley, who had previously been the secretary of the British School in Jerusalem. She had worked with Fisher when he was at Beth Shean, as well as earlier, at Thebes in Egypt. Now she came on board at Megiddo in August 1926, at the age of thirty-five, at first as a secretary and general housekeeper. She soon graduated to recorder/registrar, and a good deal of mischief, before departing exactly two years later, in August 1928.[37]

FIG. 11. Olof Lind, clad in local garb (courtesy of the Oberlin College archives)

Another new hire was a photographer named Mr. Olof Lind, who proved to be an excellent addition to the staff. Lind, whom the Chicago team consistently called Olaf rather than Olof, was a six-foot-tall Swede. Until 1925 or so, he had been a member of the American Colony in Jerusalem, a small Christian utopian community that had originally been established by American expatriates in the 1880s. Olof had been kicked out of the colony and later filed a lawsuit, though he did not win in the end.[38] He remained as the photographer of the expedition for a decade, until the end of the 1935–36 season, working for all three successive directors, from Fisher to Guy to Loud. Fisher was very pleased that he was able to hire both of them for less than he had been paying Higgins alone, "so that we get two active workers instead of one, at less cost."[39]

Perhaps most importantly for the health of the team, the British Mandate government had finally started to drain the swampy land in the vicinity of Megiddo, laying down terracotta pipes connected to the main drain.

Fisher noted, without irony or exaggeration, that the situation had played havoc with them during the season, and that "for the past month, there has not been a day when one or more of the staff have not been in bed. Several times I've had to eat alone."[40]

Strangely enough, given the reports from the other team members of his bouts of malaria, Fisher claimed to "have escaped remarkably well so far." According to him, though, "the others have been great sufferers, including Mr. Lind, our new photographer. Now even Miss Woodley, who had been looking after the others, is . . . seriously ill. Malaria seems to be the main thing, but all of the fellows seem to have some sort of stomach trouble in connection with it. As many as half of the Egyptian workmen were down one or two days. Then we have had fever and typhoid raging in the Jewish colony at Afula and in the villages from which we draw most of our work people." Regardless, he remained optimistic, stating that "all of these problems at the start make me feel that we are going to have a great deal of good fortune later on."[41]

Indeed, by early October, Fisher noted that the health of the staff was much improved, with only Miss Woodley still in the hospital at Haifa, and that the swamp was drying up quickly, so that they should be able to control the malaria in the future.[42] However, that would not happen soon enough for Fisher's nephew Stanley, who had been serving as the expedition's accountant as well as the chauffeur, in addition to drawing pottery as needed. In early December 1926, he suddenly returned to the United States and then submitted an official resignation on the last day of that month, owing "to ill health."[43] His departure and resignation took place so suddenly that it was not made known to those back in Chicago until late February 1927,[44] more than two months later.

The stage was now set for a remarkable change, although neither Fisher nor Breasted knew it at the time. Already at the end of September, Fisher had suggested that they should consider adding to their staff at Megiddo an archaeologist named Philip Langstaffe Ord Guy (generally referred to simply as P.L.O. Guy), who was chief inspector for the Department of Antiquities in British Mandate Palestine but was about to retire. "I wonder if you remember Mr. Guy, the Inspector of Antiquities who was stationed at Jerusalem and Haifa," Fisher wrote to Breasted. "He is leaving the Government service and would like I feel sure to get back into field work. I have not broached the matter to him, but if you would consider him a useful man, I might try and see if he would join us, and if so, upon what terms."[45]

Breasted replied that he didn't remember ever meeting Guy, but said that Fisher should ask whether Guy would be willing to take charge of the field activities at Megiddo, while Fisher remained in charge of the scientific and archaeological record. Following up shortly thereafter, Breasted asked whether Fisher had been able to get in contact with Guy and "gain some reaction from him about joining the Megiddo staff."[46]

However, in contacting Guy, Fisher was unknowingly signing away his own position. Negotiations between Breasted and Guy, for the latter to take over as field director, began as early as the end of December 1926.[47]

CHAPTER IV

"We Have Already Three Distinct Levels"

In the meantime, in terms of the archaeology that they were there to do, work at the dig continued after Higgins's departure. By mid-July, they had constructed a wooden chute to carry debris from the top of the mound to the bottom, in anticipation that work would finally begin in that area. Railroad cars on a track carried the dirt from the digging areas to the top of the chute, while additional cars on another spur of track then took the dirt from the bottom of the chute to the dumping areas.[1] It was an elaborate, and efficient, process.

One week later, digging finally began on the top of the mound, a full three months after it had originally been scheduled to start. At first, they mostly cleared away Schumacher's dumps and debris, but they did almost immediately find what Kellogg called "a complete [A]shtarte clay incense shrine," which was in pieces and would have to be put back together.[2] Ashtarte, also called Astarte (as subsequent Chicago letters spell it) and perhaps better known as Ishtar, was the ancient Semitic goddess of fertility, venerated throughout the ancient Near East for millennia.

Fisher, apparently giddy at being able to excavate without further hindrance, began laying out squares on the top of the mound. As he put it, he hoped to clear "the later, uninteresting levels out of the way, so that succeeding years could be devoted entirely to investigating the more important historical portions of the hill."[3]

They were working on the eastern part of the mound, reaching as far as Schumacher's Great Trench. Part of their assignment was to clean out and connect Schumacher's old trenches, so that they could create a new complete plan of the area. Along the way, their results showed that Schumacher had destroyed almost as much as he recovered: "Our new work on the east side shows that many strata must have been destroyed by him between the surface and his deep series of houses. In the first four meters we have

Fig. 12. Lower end of a chute with railcar waiting to be filled (after Fisher 1929: fig. 27; courtesy of the Oriental Institute of the University of Chicago)

already three distinct levels and four if we include the Arabic tower which he cleared and removed."[4]

We must keep in mind that archaeology was still a relatively new discipline, as has been mentioned, and that experiments in using various methods of excavation and recording were taking place at different sites across the area and the world. However, as also mentioned, Fisher was considered at the time to be one of the best archaeologists working in the Middle East. He implemented innovative approaches to excavation, including at Megiddo: "The whole area has been divided into 25-meter squares, the corners of which are marked on the ground with red topped pegs. The squares are designated with a letter and a number, running in regular sequence from North to South and East to West, thus P12, P13, Q12, Q13, etc."[5] This is the same system in use at Megiddo even today by the current excavation team, although the squares are now much smaller (5 m × 5 m).

Fisher later also elaborated upon their manner of utilizing the workmen, which almost exactly mirrored the system that Schumacher had used previously at the mound. There were three large "work gangs," with each overseen by an Egyptian foreman, and with a chief foreman (known as a *reis*) overseeing them all. Each group had three of the trained Egyptian workmen—the quftis—working with the local laborers. As Fisher put it, "a gang consists of pick-men, scrapers or basket-fillers, and a number of carriers."[6]

The Chicago team used local men and women, as well as boys and girls, as the basket carriers. These took the baskets full of soil, after a careful search had been made for artifacts, and carried them to the waiting railway carts. Each group had its own branch of the small railway system that the Chicago team had laid out, encircling the mound at the edge of the summit.[7]

However, this rather dry description doesn't really give a sense of the action, as it were, of the dust flying as the workmen cleared each ancient room of debris and artifacts, leaving only the walls standing. There were literally hordes of these local workmen, vastly outnumbering the members of the archaeological team, sometimes at a ratio of 100:1, all supervised by the trained Egyptian overseers. The archaeologists and architects came around only when something exciting had been found or needed to be drawn.

As the season progressed, days of excruciating boredom, with few finds to report, were interrupted by periods of intense activity. All staff members were expected to pull their weight, and if any slacked off or were perceived as not doing their fair share, tempers flared. Even on an excavation today, with between fifty and two hundred people working together for several weeks at a time, things can get volatile. Back then, with so few team members living and working together virtually year-round, it is no wonder

FIG. 13. (a) Clearing surface levels in Squares M13 and M14; (b) workers in late 1926 (courtesy of the Oriental Institute of the University of Chicago)

that there were internal conflicts and interpersonal problems more often than not.

Fisher also detailed the system used to record the architecture that they found, which was important since they were opening up huge areas at once, across a large horizontal area. When the tops of walls were revealed, the pickmen followed them down until they ascertained the room or area to which they belonged. They then gave each room or area a specific number, so that they could accurately refer to it and label it on a plan.

The room or area was then excavated down to the floor level, with each artifact given a unique identification number. When the floor was reached, any objects found in situ were left in position and a photograph was taken, after which one of the trained Egyptian foremen carefully excavated and removed each artifact.[8]

Furthermore, since the Chicago excavators planned to remove the strata one by one, in order to reach the lower levels, Fisher implemented a system that he had successfully used previously. After they had exposed an entire layer, with all of its buildings clearly visible, they would create a topographic plan and take photographs, documenting it completely and accurately, as he later explained: "Then begins the search for the next period. The gangs return to their original squares and first demolish the finished walls of the stratum, layer, or level just excavated. The work then proceeds." It was straightforward, he said. "Thus level after level is found, thoroughly examined, and recorded as though no other period were represented on the hill. Each becomes quite simple and clear in turn. . . . By this method one keeps in touch with the historical sequence and feels tremendous satisfaction in seeing the story of the hill develop."[9]

On the one hand, Fisher's system certainly worked to record all of Stratum I in the area they were excavating, followed by all of Stratum II lying beneath it, as well as a stratum that he called "Sub-II," and then his Stratum III. This allowed them to get much more than just a glimpse into the levels, as would have happened if they had worked in smaller squares dug vertically rather than horizontally. It has allowed us to fairly definitively date these levels, even though Fisher's numbering system was later changed. His "Sub-II" is now our Stratum III and dates to the Neo-Assyrian period, while Strata II and I date to the Neo-Babylonian and then the Persian periods; his Stratum III will be further discussed below (see table 2).

TABLE 2. Levels and Assignation to Approximate Dates/Periods for Topmost Strata at Megiddo, with Renumbering by the Various Chicago Excavators

Initial Strata Designation (Fisher 1929)	Strata Designation Revised by Guy (1931)	Strata Designation Revised by Lamon and Shipton (1939)	Strata Designation Revised by Loud (1948)
I	I	I	I
II	II	II	II
Sub-II	Sub-II	III	III
III	III IV	IVB (only in Area CC); IV across rest of site	IVB IVA
—	—	V (newly detected level)	Subdivided into VB and VA in Area DD; V across rest of site
—	V	VI	VIB VIA

However, completely removing the remains from an entire stratum so that the next one could be revealed, as Fisher did, means that no future archaeologist can come back later to check the results and conclusions. And that is why we almost never do such total removal at a site today, especially since stratigraphic levels in a mound rarely come as neatly as those in a layer cake. There are almost always pits, trenches, remodeling, renovations, and other aspects of human behavior and construction that can render both the initial excavation and the subsequent reconstruction of habitation of each level difficult.

Even more problematic is when the original excavator does not keep good field notes, or any at all, as is sometimes the case. Indeed, after Guy took over from Fisher, he complained to Breasted that there were almost no notes from the previous season: "I find practically no fieldnotes dealing with the strata already laid bare," he said. "I do not know whether Fisher has any notes with him but if he has not, there is only his memory to be relied on for a lot of evidence, and unless he can produce something the publication will not be full."[10]

When Fisher finally began digging at the extreme southeastern edge of the site, he found that the two upper levels were missing entirely, so he was able to start right in on what he called Stratum Sub-II and then Stratum III. Among the interesting small finds that Fisher and his team discovered in this area were a "seal of stone which has a scene of Gilgamesh slaying a stag" and, strangely, a "Spanish dollar of Philip II dated 1588," which was heavily coated with a gray patina and was found just under the surface. They also recovered some fifty scarabs; a number of additional coins, including some of late date that were surface finds; "many bronze arrow heads and implements"; and the largest flint collection that Fisher had ever seen.[11]

In addition, they came across a city wall along the side of the mound, which Fisher said was built during Stratum III and continued in use in Sub-II. He was optimistic that they would find it running around the entire circuit of the mound. The city wall was given the number 325 on the plans, by which it is still known today, though the strata were later relabeled Stratum IV and Stratum III, respectively (see table 2).[12]

Working right through August, they stripped the entire area between Schumacher's trench and the eastern edge of the hill down to the Persian level by mid-September. Fisher was confident of their dating, for all of the pottery in this level dated to about 400 BCE; moreover, they had found two silver coins of Tyre, dating to 400–332 BCE (at which point Alexander the Great had conquered Tyre).[13] By early October, the light railway and chute were in operation, and they began removing the walls of Stratum II. Fisher predicted that before they closed down in November, "the whole eastern part of the Astarte temple should be laid bare."

Because of the excavations of both Schumacher and the Chicago excavators, there are no remains of Strata I and II left at Megiddo today. Fisher was not impressed with what they found in these top two levels anyway, though the photographs left to us show that the remains of both strata were actually fairly extensive. Overall, he said, the remains in these top two levels were "irregular and rooms of two successive periods are often built on nearly the same level, side-by-side. All are of the poorest rubble, and represent the period when Megiddo was in its decay."[14] He also later noted that Stratum I lay so near the modern surface that most of the remains had been plowed

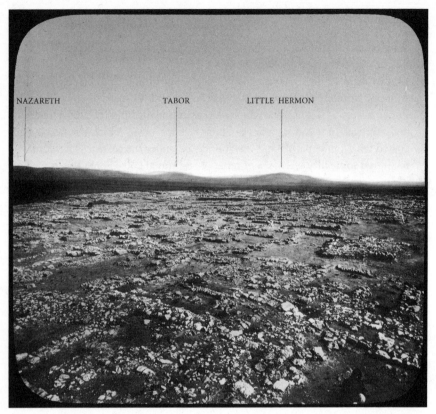

NAZARETH   TABOR   LITTLE HERMON

FIG. 14. Megiddo Stratum I (courtesy of the Oriental Institute of the University of Chicago)

up and the stones reused in field walls by the local villagers, leaving little for the excavators to find.[15]

Fisher was correct in saying that the remains in the top two levels were not very impressive, consisting primarily of small domestic buildings constructed haphazardly, but there is one larger building that he found, which has been identified as a fortress. It still remains a matter of debate as to who first built this fortress—some have argued for Egyptians, some for Judeans, and others for Persians. Lamon and Shipton, in their *Megiddo I* volume, suggested that the destruction of this fortress, and portions of the Stratum II town, was caused by the forces of Pharaoh Necho II at the time that he killed Josiah, king of Judah, at Megiddo in 609 BCE, though there is no real evidence for this.[16]

One thing is clear: during this time, in both Strata II and I, Megiddo was little more than an unwalled town protected only by this fortress. Its sole importance was that it was located along the route known as the Via Maris.[17]

At the time of Josiah's challenge, Necho was simply marching his army through the area. He was en route to a larger confrontation at Carchemish that was to determine the fate of the entire ancient Near East. Had Josiah allowed Necho and his forces to proceed unmolested, as the Egyptian pharaoh had requested, he would have lived to see another day. His religious reforms might have continued, as would his dreams of creating another kingdom like that of David and Solomon, but all came to an end in 609 BCE.

Moreover, the Neo-Babylonians and their crown prince Nebuchadnezzar won at Carchemish, defeating both the Egyptians and the Neo-Assyrians. The balance of power shifted immediately, as the Neo-Babylonians established the next empire ruling over the area, including destroying Jerusalem in 586 BCE and taking the king, his family, and high-ranking officials to far-off Mesopotamia. Their rule did not last even a century, though, and soon, when Cyrus the Great captured Babylon in 539 BCE, the Persians became the next great empire to rule over the entire Near East. Cyrus allowed the exiled Judahites to return home from Babylon, where they had spent nearly five decades by that point, and the cities in the region, from Megiddo to Jerusalem and beyond, became Persian vassals, having long since lost their independence.

The end of this final phase at Megiddo—that is, the end of Stratum I— seems to date to about 350 BCE, give or take a few decades, according to both Fisher and Guy.[18] The ancient site lay abandoned, but it is not clear why. At least one scholar has suggested that the city ended in a blaze of glory and destruction by Alexander the Great and his Macedonian army in about 331 BCE,[19] but there is no evidence for such a cinematic finale. It seems more likely that Alexander's men marched past an unoccupied mound, if indeed they ever swung far enough inland en route from Tyre to Egypt to even catch a glimpse of the ancient site. Later inhabitants lived elsewhere in the valley, of course, both near the ancient mound and farther away, but Megiddo's day had ended.

By the time the Romans established a camp for the Sixth Legion near the foot of the mound in the early centuries of the first millennium CE, the ancient site of Megiddo had slipped into obscurity: uninhabited, used primarily as a cemetery by the Roman legionnaires, and no longer the object of fierce battles for control of the region. These were now fought elsewhere in the Jezreel Valley for the next fifteen hundred years or more, from the coming of Islam in the seventh century CE through the crusaders and Saladin, the Mongols and the Mamelukes, and the Ottomans.[20] It was only with World War I and then the 1948 Israeli War of Independence that Megiddo came alive again with the sound of men, horses, and the clamor of battle. But the mound itself was never again the location of a living, breathing site after the Persian period, more than twenty-three hundred years ago.

PART TWO

1927–1934

CHAPTER V

"I Really Need a Bit of a Holiday"

In his initial overture to Guy in late December 1926, Breasted said simply, "The task at Megiddo is a large one and I have the feeling that Fisher needs additional help in carrying his responsibility."[1] It is no wonder that Breasted was eager to bring Guy on board, for naming the retiring chief inspector (and acting director) for the Department of Antiquities in British Mandate Palestine as the field director at Megiddo would certainly be seen by many to be a coup.

Guy was a thin, rather wiry, man. He usually parted his hair in the middle and almost always wore spectacles. He also frequently wore a military-style shirt when he wasn't wearing a jacket and tie, for he had risen to the rank of captain and then lieutenant colonel during the course of his life, having served in both the British and French armies during World War I.[2]

Born in Scotland in 1885, Guy was forty-two years old at the time that he took over from Fisher at Megiddo. He had attended Oxford University from 1903 to 1906, where he studied classics (Greek and Latin). He then enrolled at Glasgow University from 1906 to 1909, where he studied law. However, he did not receive a degree from either school. His career in field archaeology didn't begin until after World War I, when he was invited by Sir Leonard Woolley to become the photographer at Carchemish in 1919–20, taking the place of T. E. Lawrence (better known as "Lawrence of Arabia"). He also dug with Woolley at the site of Amarna in Egypt in 1921–22.[3]

Although he had no formal training in archaeology, and no field experience beyond the seasons spent at Carchemish and Amarna, Guy was subsequently appointed chief inspector for the Department of Antiquities in British Mandate Palestine in 1922. He split his time between Haifa and

Fig. 15. P.L.O. Guy, undated photograph (courtesy of Michael Stanner and Jack Green)

Jerusalem for the next five years, being responsible primarily for sites in the northern part of the region.[4]

During this time, he also met Yemima Ben-Yehuda, whom he fondly referred to as "Jimmie" in his letters. They married in 1925, after the death of her father, Eliezer Ben-Yehuda, an extremely well-known scholar responsible for the revival of Hebrew as a spoken modern language. She already had a daughter, Ruth, from a previous marriage; Guy embraced the entire package and treated Ruth as if she were his own daughter. With this union, which brought him into the upper echelons of the Yishuv (the Jewish community), Guy became firmly entrenched in Zionist circles, even though he himself was not Jewish.[5]

The end for Fisher seems to have come suddenly, with almost no warning. A letter that he sent to the director of antiquities in late March listed the members of the expedition for the coming season, of whom he mentioned only four staff—himself, DeLoach, Lind, and Woodley, since both Stanley and Higgins were now gone—as well as twenty-two Egyptian workmen, most of them from Quft.[6] The letters and cables subsequently exchanged right up through 12 April 1927 between Breasted, Fisher, and assorted others also contain absolutely no indication that Guy would replace Fisher as quickly as he did.[7]

However, one week later, on 19 April, after arriving at Megiddo again a few days earlier and meeting with both of them in person, Breasted sent a letter to Fisher. The next day he sent one to Guy. Breasted explained to Fisher that he would now have a "new advisory directorship of our Oriental Institute work in Palestine" and would thereafter be "Advisory Director" rather than "Field Director" at Megiddo. In the letter to Guy, Breasted stated that he intended to appoint him field director, replacing Fisher, for a term that would begin in just two weeks, on 1 May.[8]

Although such potential changes had obviously been in the works for some time, it seems likely that what Breasted found when he arrived at Megiddo precipitated the sudden change. "When I reached Megiddo I found Fisher in a very serious condition," Breasted later wrote. "He was then in the hospital at Haifa having lain unconscious for four hours at our expedition house at Megiddo before he was taken to the hospital."[9]

The official reason given for Fisher's resignation and reassignment was his health. "With the advance of the Spring of 1927, the health of the expedition, including that of Dr. Fisher himself, was in a very precarious state," Breasted noted in his foreword to Fisher's preliminary report, which was published in 1929. "He [Fisher] was therefore appointed as advisory director."[10] In his own subsequent preliminary report, published in 1931, Guy similarly stated that "when it had become impossible for Fisher to continue the work that he had begun some eighteen months before, and he had gone to recuperate at Ramallah, Professor Breasted invited me to take charge of the excavations."[11]

Fisher's problems also extended beyond recurring bouts of malaria. Obviously, he had been under a great deal of stress during the 1925–26 season, both in dealing with Higgins and in terms of running the expedition as a whole. This seems to have been more than Fisher had anticipated or could handle. In fact, Breasted said as much to James A. Montgomery, the president of the American Schools of Oriental Research (the entire organization, not simply the archaeological outpost in Jerusalem): "As you know he [Fisher] has always been afflicted with nervous trouble and this has been aggravated by long years of loneliness and exile from America complicated by successive attacks of malaria since his work in Babylonia. . . . [T]here is no question but that his nervousness has so developed that he suffers from delusions, super-sensitiveness and complexes. He has insisted to me that people were trying to get him out of his post, etc, etc. . . . Responsible as I was for the future conduct of an elaborate expedition at Megiddo, I could not of course leave him in sole charge of the work."[12]

Word that Fisher had been replaced spread quickly throughout the archaeological community in British Mandate Palestine and Egypt. Writing to the University Museum in Philadelphia from Cairo in late April 1927, Alan Rowe, the archaeologist who had previously taken over from Fisher at Beth Shean, said: "I have just heard privately . . . that Dr. Fisher's health has given way, and that he has had to give up his work with the Chicago Expedition at Megiddo. His place will be taken by Mr. P.L.O. Guy, at present acting Director of the Department of Antiquities, Jerusalem."[13]

It is probably not a coincidence that Fisher had been removed from his directorship of the excavations at Beth Shean in 1923 and from the directorship of the excavations at Megiddo in 1927 for essentially the same physical and mental reasons. In fact, he seems to have had problems while in the field even from the very beginning of his career, for when Fisher was a young architect on his first excavation in 1900, at Nippur in Mesopotamia, he reportedly had "suicidal homosexual yearnings," as one scholar put it.[14] He threatened to kill himself several times in despair over unrequited feelings for his tent mate on the dig, a young British archaeologist named Valentine Geere, whom he had nursed back to health when he fell ill while they were en route to the excavation. As another scholar described it, "the atmosphere at the [Nippur] dig house began to resemble an Edward Albee play."[15]

However, Fisher's feelings might not have been as completely unrequited as they may have seemed to him during those days at Nippur. Geere subsequently published a book entitled *By Nile and Euphrates: A Record of Discovery and Adventure*, in which the dedication read, "To Clarence S. Fisher as a token of friendship, and of gratitude for the care with which through nine weeks of typhoid fever he nursed The Author."[16]

After being appointed field director at Megiddo, Guy directed the expedition for the next seven seasons. During this period, there was a constant stream of personnel problems. Some of these he had inherited from Fisher, but others seem to have been caused by Guy's unspoken resentment of the more educated scholars whom Breasted simply assigned to his staff and sent from the United States to join the team.[17]

For example, Breasted now suggested to Guy that a man named John A. Wilson should be assigned to work as a surveyor with DeLoach.[18] Wilson would, much later, succeed Breasted as director of the Oriental Institute, but at the time he was a very junior twenty-eight-year-old draftsman and surveyor on Chicago's Epigraphical Project in Luxor, Egypt. He was also part of a short-lived experiment in which the staff members of the two expeditions (Megiddo and Luxor) each worked at the other project during their respective "off seasons." He and his wife, Mary, had arrived at Megiddo with Breasted during the latter's fateful visit in April, following which the change in field directors took place.

For some reason, Guy did not list Wilson among the staff members, or even mention him as a participant, when he published his 1931 preliminary report. However, Wilson is listed in the archival records and in the final publication of these seasons (i.e., the *Megiddo I* volume) as having participated in the excavations at Megiddo from April through June 1927, so we know that he was present. Moreover, DeLoach himself soon told Breasted that both Mr. and Mrs. Wilson "have been a great help to us." Mr. Wilson was helping with the registration and surveying, while Mrs. Wilson was helping with the library and generally around the house, as DeLoach put it.[19]

However, Guy did get along well with the people whom he himself hired. Probably the best example was Guy's aide-de-camp Ralph B. Parker. Somewhere between twenty-five and thirty years old at the time that he was hired at Megiddo, Parker was a military man who went by "Harry" for reasons now unknown. He had served in the Army Cyclist Corps and the Sixteenth Welsh Regiment during World War I. On a 1926 ship manifest, while journeying from Australia to England, he listed his profession as "police man" and his place of residence as "Palestine," for he was serving as an officer in the "British Gendarmerie" at the time. Winston Churchill had created the unit back in 1922, to serve as a paramilitary force in British Mandate Palestine.[20]

Guy hired Parker in June 1927, after getting a recommendation from General MacNeill, Parker's commanding officer, when the unit was being disbanded. Guy gave Parker the responsibility of maintaining order in the dig house and other general duties. Though he had taken part in a small excavation at a crusader castle before coming to Megiddo, Parker was never again active in the field, and Guy himself said that Parker would never be an archaeologist.[21] Nonetheless, he ended up serving at Megiddo longer than any other staff member—not only right through the final season in 1939, but even thereafter, for he stayed on to oversee and take care of the dig house and the site through World War II, the 1948 War of Independence, and beyond, until 1954 when he finally retired to Cyprus (and then to London by 1957).[22]

Parker's hire was not without some bumps, however. For example, DeLoach complained to Breasted in late May, before Parker's arrival, that Parker "has had no university training along such lines," and that it seemed a waste of money to put him on staff.[23] A month later, after Parker had arrived toward the end of June, DeLoach changed his tune somewhat, noting that Parker was "a very jovial sort of a chap." But, he also added, "I don't believe I ever saw a person who hated the Jews more, much to our (including the Guy's [sic]) surprise."[24]

In early June, even before Parker arrived, DeLoach reported to Breasted that there were already tensions at the dig. "The Jewish question is getting to be a problem with us," he wrote, "and we can't say much about it without running the danger of offending Mrs. Guy. We have Jewish carpenters, last week we had a Russian Jewess with us studying pottery, and Mr. Guy is getting a Jewish assistant for me. The men are dissatisfied with it as much or more than we are. Reis Hamid came in to me last night and said that the men were working for me, and not for Mr. Guy, for he is "half Jewish himself now.""[25]

The ongoing situation in British Mandate Palestine was clearly reflected at the dig. It had been only ten years since the Balfour Declaration of November 1917. During that decade, tensions ran high between Arabs and Jews in the region, including riots in 1920 and 1921, as mentioned. Although the situation was only going to get worse during the remaining years that the Chicago excavators were at Megiddo, at this point they had no way of knowing any of that, for the August 1929 Arab riots were still two years off, the general strike of 1933 and the Arab Revolt of 1936–39 were even further away, and World War II was only a glimmer on the horizon.

Within a few days of taking over and beginning to dig in early May, Guy found himself faced by a number of problems. Some were ongoing and some beyond his control, but in others he seems to have played a large role. One problem, which should have been anticipated since the swamps had not yet been fully drained, was malaria, which continued to plague the staff.[26]

In his autobiography, published in 1972, Wilson recalled the situation as follows:

> At the end of the 1927 season at Luxor, I had gone to Megiddo in Palestine, to spend a few weeks learning about excavation. When Mary and I had arrived, we found that there was not a Western man left at the mound. Malaria had ravaged the staff. Fortunately, the work had been well organized, and the mound was marked with a grid of squares for precise location. For two weeks I kept the workmen digging away at the same level. I supervised the moving of earth and listened solemnly to the report of the foreman, of which I understood only about half. At the end of a day, I labeled the baskets of finds by square and level and took them into the house for the woman registrar to catalogue. By the time the staff had been reorganized, the new director [Guy] was too busy learning his mound to bother about teaching me. So I ran a dig briefly without knowing the principles and detailed techniques of excavations.[27]

Wilson also noted elsewhere that it took them fully four hours to drive the fifteen miles from Haifa to Megiddo because of the state of the roads at that time. Once they were at the site, he and his wife dosed themselves with quinine until their ears rang, as he put it, in order to avoid coming down with malaria themselves. When in their room at the dig house, they also suffered from the intense heat, which reached 117 degrees Fahrenheit at one point, because of the corrugated iron roof on the building. "I never did learn field archaeology," he later said, "except by the experience of being pitched into it head first."[28]

Another immediate setback impacted Breasted's offer to increase the number of workmen, for some of the Egyptian foremen demanded higher wages at the first opportunity. Instead of agreeing to their request, Guy simply let them go, with Breasted's evident approval.[29]

Then J. G. O'Neill arrived at the dig. He was on a traveling fellowship from the University of Dublin in Ireland, where he was a student of R.A.S. Macalister—the same Macalister who had excavated at Gezer twenty years earlier. However, he left in indignation less than a month into the season, after having been chastised by Guy for a variety of unstated missteps. In retaliation, O'Neill sent a letter to Guy from Jerusalem during the first days of June that contained statements no student or subordinate should ever send to the field director of an excavation, including one that read, "I knew that you were a mere substitute during Dr. Fisher's unfortunate absence."[30] This, of course, was far from the truth, since Guy had just been appointed permanent field director in Fisher's place.

It was only much later, in August, that Guy finally brought the subject up with Breasted, noting simply that "O'Neill turned out to be a most objectionable person, who irritated everybody." He followed this up with more details in late September, after which Breasted expressed regret that Guy had been forced to deal with such unpleasantness and that "the O'Neill experiment turned out so unsuccessfully."[31] It was the second such failed experiment in as many years: first Higgins and now O'Neill. It would not be the last.

At the same time that all of this was going on, William F. Badè reported to Breasted that there were unsubstantiated rumors about "goings-on" at Megiddo. Badè was a professor at the Pacific School of Religion in Berkeley, California. He is perhaps better known to the general public as the literary executor and biographer of the naturalist John Muir, and as a former president of the Sierra Club and editor of the *Sierra Club Bulletin*.[32] Badè was also an archaeologist, however, and at the time he was directing the excavations at Tell en-Nasbeh, an Iron Age site near Jerusalem, which may have been biblical Mizpah. A year earlier, Higgins had been working for him on the side, without receiving prior permission from Breasted, so Badè had had inside information about Megiddo at the time, and still had his ear to the ground in terms of gossip and "goings-on" in the general archaeological community.[33]

He told Breasted that he was a "disinterested source," noting, "What has happened or is now happening at Megiddo is, of course, not my affair. But I naturally have a friendly interest in the success of the Expedition." However, it was clearly more than just a "friendly interest," and Badè may not have been as disinterested as he claimed, because he seems to have taken a certain amount of glee in reporting the rumors to Breasted.[34]

According to Badè, one archaeologist told him that "the best interests of the Megiddo Expedition have unwittingly been sacrificed to the intrigues of a middle-aged stenographer, infatuated with a young man who is himself ill and apparently completely under her influence."[35] While the stenographer was quite obviously none other than Miss Woodley, it is less clear who the specific young man was, though it was most likely DeLoach or, less likely, O'Neill.

In fact, it may well have been O'Neill who was the archaeologist quoted by Badè and who was the source for these rumors. To be fair, though, these could just have easily been told to Badè by Fisher himself, because Fisher had already cabled Breasted near the end of May, about the time that O'Neill was let go. He claimed that the doctors in Beirut had now given him a clean bill of health and reported: "CONDITIONS AT MEGIDDO VERY UNSATISFACTORY WOULD SUGGEST MY TAKING CHARGE TO SAVE SITUATION." To this, Breasted simply cabled back the same day, "REGRET SUGGESTION IMPOSSIBLE."[36]

Badè further informed Breasted that the archaeological material on the tell at Megiddo was not being competently excavated, because Guy was there only part of the time. Furthermore, the stenographer—that is, Miss Woodley—was busy getting rid of everyone whom she disliked on the dig by reporting "alleged incivilities" to either Guy or DeLoach. He concluded by saying, "Meanwhile the field observations and the archaeological records of the mound are getting disrupted at a most critical and important stage of the dig," and asserted that "Dr. Fisher stands ready to save the situation as much as he can."[37]

In addition, a few weeks later, Breasted received in the mail an anonymous handwritten letter signed only "An Observer." It read in part: "You should be advised that a scandal is brewing at Megiddo and that the scientific part of the work is so badly done that the excavations should be closed under the rules of the Department of Antiquities. Mr. Guy is ill and has not been at the mound for two weeks or more. Meanwhile the messing-up continues. You should also inquire into the respectability of one of the persons whom you have left in charge."[38] It is unclear who sent this anonymous letter, though it was most likely O'Neill, Badè, or Fisher.

This is hardly the sort of situation that a new field director wishes to face, especially if it is the previous field director who may have played a part in the machinations. To his credit, Breasted backed Guy fully. In mid-June, he wrote to say that he understood Guy had been "confronted with such an exodus of the native staff but this is simply a continuation of the situation which was obviously impending before I left the place. I am sure that you will be able to consolidate the organization and build it up again."[39] In a separate and confidential letter, he also advised Guy of the rumors that had reached his ears via Badè and the anonymous source, and suggested that they would be put to rest if Mrs. Guy could begin living in the Megiddo house as soon as possible.[40]

Breasted also sent a polite response to Badè, in which he noted that many of the problems had been caused by "the unexpected delay in the release of Mr. Guy from his duties in Jerusalem."[41] This was, in fact, a very real problem because the British authorities were having difficulty finding someone to replace Guy as director of antiquities in British Mandate Palestine and had therefore kept him on in the position of acting director long after his originally scheduled resignation date. This, in turn, meant that Guy could be at Megiddo only on a part-time basis, until the situation was finally resolved in late August.

Guy himself said that each week he spent three days in Jerusalem and three days at Megiddo, with a day taken up traveling between the two. As he put it, in a rather understated manner several years later, the four months that followed his arrival at Megiddo on 30 April 1927 "were somewhat strenuous."[42]

In the meantime, DeLoach and Breasted had also been discussing "the inability of the London government to find the right man as Director for the Palestine Department of Antiquities," which Breasted described as being "a great misfortune for us."[43] Since DeLoach had been doing a good job overseeing operations on the top of the mound during this period, Breasted promoted him to the position of assistant field director in late June. Not only was this a recognition of the good work that he was doing; it was also done, as Breasted told Guy, so that the work at Megiddo would not be seen by outsiders as being "in the casual control of a member of the expedition without defined powers."[44]

Eventually, in mid-July, Guy attempted to counter the rumors, informing Breasted that Mrs. Guy had accompanied him every time he went to Megiddo. Moreover, she would now be there with him continuously, which should help put the rumors completely to rest. He also added that they had both been absent for much of June, because of sandfly fever, a fact that

DeLoach separately confirmed, and that he believed the rumors and reports were being spread by Fisher, "whose behavior even towards myself is odd."[45]

DeLoach also chimed in at about the same time, confirming that things were now more peaceful at the dig. Mrs. Guy was there full-time, working on translating one of Breasted's books into Hebrew and trying to learn Egyptian hieroglyphics. She and Mr. Guy had their own living room, DeLoach said, and the dig house was nearly complete, with only the large roof still remaining to be installed. Miss Woodley had also planted flowers and lawn seed in front of the entrances, which eased the stress among the personnel.[46]

On 11 July, a large earthquake hit Jericho, Nablus, and other nearby communities, causing severe damage and the loss of many lives. However, it was barely felt at Megiddo. DeLoach immediately sent a cable to Breasted the next day, informing him that everyone on the team was okay; the only damage they had suffered was to two dozen pots that fell off a shelf in the storeroom. Others, including Lind, later said the same.[47]

However, the attempted sabotage, or perhaps it was more like unintended consequences, continued, for Guy received a cable from Breasted in early August that read, "SURPRISED HEAR FROM SEVERAL SOURCES MEGIDDO WORK STOPPED PLEASE CABLE REASONS AND DATE OF RESUMPTION." To this, Guy could only reply, probably quite bewildered, "CANNOT UNDERSTAND WORK HAS CONTINUED AND IS CONTINUING WITHOUT INTERRUPTION."[48]

The matter was quickly resolved, with Breasted attributing it to erroneous reports brought back by "passing travelers," but one wonders who the real sources were, which he never mentioned. It may have been as simple as a complaint in a letter sent by DeLoach to Breasted in mid-July, which began, "Mr. Guy has stopped all of the work on the Tell before I left [for a medical appointment in Beirut] . . . which was extremely disappointing to me." DeLoach did not specify why the work was temporarily stopped, but went on to say that it was discouraging to him personally, for some reason, and also not what Breasted would have wanted.[49]

Furthermore, DeLoach also said that Parker was causing problems at the dig, including cursing at the workmen and even kicking a little boy to the ground. As DeLoach put it, "Such a thing as this might be all right in the famous Irish [sic: Welsh] regiment, of which he was a member, but I think that is very unbecoming to an expedition such as ours." On a different matter altogether, DeLoach also noted that he was training the Russian chauffeur, Serge Tchoub (who had taken the position after Stanley Fisher returned home to the United States), to help him do the mapping and measuring for the survey and plans. "He is very bright and seems willing to learn," said DeLoach, adding also, "This way we save a salary."[50]

During the first week of August, Parker's treatment of the workmen and locals worsened. In particular, there was an incident one evening when Parker "kicked one of the locals on the shin just below the knee, causing a bad injury," according to DeLoach. Miss Woodley bandaged the wound up immediately and the man was able to hobble around using a stick, but the workmen, including those who came from the two villages nearest to the expedition, went on strike in protest. DeLoach and Lind were eventually able to get Parker to apologize to some extent, and they then cajoled everyone into going back to work, but, as DeLoach put it, "the locals are very much upset."[51]

DeLoach, who had by now become Breasted's inside source on the dig (like Kellogg the year before), tended to send more details of the sordid underbelly of the excavation than he did news of the exciting discoveries. He did this deliberately, saying, "I am including a great many details which may not amount to very much in themselves, but I have found, during the last two years, most of the big things that affect the destiny of an expedition grow up from the small ones, and that if these small ones can be settled in time, a great deal of time and trouble may be saved later. I do not like to be always complaining and finding fault, but I think that you want to know all these things if they are really going on."[52]

DeLoach was correct on both counts, for such minor incidents can grow to be big problems even on excavations today, and Breasted surely needed an ear to the ground, especially on a dig that had already seen more than its share of personal squabbles and personnel problems. However, if his letters of mid-July and early August were what caused Breasted to send the cable to Guy, asking why reports of the dig shutting down early had reached his ears, then DeLoach himself may have unintentionally contributed to some of the ongoing problems.

Eventually, in late August, Ernest Richmond was appointed director of antiquities, a position that he held for the next decade, through 1937. Guy could finally begin working at Megiddo full-time, although the dig lasted only another month that year before they closed up at the end of September.[53]

Just after the season ended, Badè apologized to Guy and, de facto, to Breasted. He retracted the rumors he had conveyed and the statements he had made earlier, saying to Guy, "You have had a very difficult task to administer the Department of Antiquities and the affairs of the Megiddo Expedition at the same time, and I have only admiration for the ability with which you have done it."[54]

Charles Breasted, executive director of the Oriental Institute and elder son of James Henry Breasted, who would be an integral part of the Megiddo story from then on, noted that, even back in Chicago, they realized "this has been an exceptionally trying time in Palestine."[55] It was probably with a tremendous feeling of relief, therefore, that Guy sent DeLoach, Lind, and Woodley off on holiday first and then on to Luxor in Egypt, where they were to work on Chicago's dig there for the winter. He and his wife, Yemima, then left for Europe, to take a vacation that they both desperately needed. As he put it, "I really need a bit of a holiday."[56]

However, just as soon as they got back from their vacation, Breasted began to ramp up the pressure once more. In early January 1928, he told Guy, "This coming season, beginning next April, is one of vital importance for the future of our work . . . and I am looking to you to put through a vigorous and aggressive season's work." Breasted had specific interests in mind, of course, for he also wanted Guy to get down into the levels of the mound that would yield the Egyptian and Solomonic monuments for which he had been waiting with ever-growing impatience and frustration.[57]

The season ultimately proved to be successful in terms of personnel as well, but in an unexpected way. Since Higgins had been let go at the end of the 1926 season, DeLoach had served as their surveyor during the 1927 season, as well as acting as temporary assistant field director for part of that time, as mentioned. However, in early 1928, DeLoach was ordered by his doctors to remain in Chicago for health reasons, since he continued to suffer from malaria.[58]

It was clear that the team needed to hire an experienced surveyor for the season, which was scheduled to begin in early May and last through the end of July. It was a good thing that they did, for DeLoach was not cleared by the doctors to return to Megiddo until September.

At first, they tried to hire a surveyor named Ivan Terentieff, who was working on a University of Michigan expedition at Karanis (Kôm Aushim) in Egypt, but it turned out that he would not be available until early June. In the interim, therefore, Guy hired a young Ukrainian-born architect named Emmanuel Wilensky, who was passionate about archaeology. He was twenty-five years old and had already been working on a Harvard University excavation at the site of Nuzi in Iraq.[59] Wilensky arrived at Megiddo in late April, just before the season began.

Although he was sick for much of the time, because of some bad fish that he had eaten, Wilensky performed his job quietly and professionally. He worked with the team until early June, at which point Terentieff arrived and took over for the rest of the season and beyond (until the end of September).[60] As a result, Wilensky was a known quantity; he would return to the expedition a few years later, in 1932 and 1933, as we shall see.

Other new members also joined the team in 1928, including Charles Little, who had previously worked at Beth Shean as a draftsman, and whose family ran a hotel up in Lebanon. Like Wilensky, Little was frequently ill during the season, but in Little's case the malady was heart trouble that was thought to have been caused by his excessive smoking—up to forty cigarettes and ten pipes a day, according to one eyewitness. He arrived at Megiddo by mid-April and barely made it through the season, resigning and leaving on the last day of July. Guy was not impressed by him, remarking, "I have not observed that he takes much interest in his work, which, I am inclined to think, he regards as a task to be got through, and not something to be done <u>con amore</u>." He added that he eventually found out that Rowe had fired Little, which is why he had left Beth Shean; it is a wonder that he was ever even hired at Megiddo.[61]

But it was two other young men who arrived that year, one before the season and one after, who would prove to be essential to the expedition and its publications, although nobody could have predicted that at the time. One was Geoffrey M. Shipton, the seventeen-year-old nephew of Harry Parker, Guy's aide-de-camp. Shipton, who went by "Geoff," was a high school dropout from Wales. He initially joined the project in mid-January 1928, before the season began, in large part to keep Parker company and to give Shipton himself something to do. A visitor to Megiddo described him a few years later as "a boy in his teens . . . without any college education and of course lacking all scientific background."[62]

Shipton had no training in archaeology whatsoever and was originally hired for only three months as a draftsman with a salary of $75. He ended up being one of the longest-serving members of the expedition, from 1928 right up through the final field season in 1939. He learned everything on-site at Megiddo, having been repeatedly denied admission to study at Chicago, despite the best efforts of the others on the team.[63] He finally left the expedition as it came to an end, when he got a job offer that he couldn't refuse and went to work for a company called Spinney's, which based him in Haifa and Cyprus.[64]

The other fortuitous hire that year was Robert Scott Lamon, a six-foot-tall, twenty-two-year-old geology student and member of Beta Theta Pi fraternity from the University of Chicago, who had decided to take a break from his undergraduate studies. He was "on the slim side, good looking, and comes of excellent family," as Charles Breasted noted in a letter of introduction sent to Guy in late August 1928. However, he had also never before been outside the United States and had never participated in an archaeological excavation.[65]

Lamon was sent over in September 1928, in time for the fall season, to serve double duty—as a surveyor in place of Terentieff and as a draftsman in place of Little, both of whom had just left at that point. Lamon ended up serving the expedition almost as long as Shipton, including temporarily serving as the field director after Guy was fired in 1934. His last season in the field was in 1935–36, after which he returned to Chicago to work on the publications. He later became a petroleum geologist working for Standard Oil, Northern Natural Gas, and other companies in Calgary, Canada, and Bogota, Colombia, before retiring to Arizona, where he passed away in 1975.[66]

Between the two of them, Lamon and Shipton eventually wrote or co-authored five of the publications associated with the results of the project, which is the same number as the three field directors (Fisher, Guy, and Loud) combined. Perhaps surprisingly, especially given their initial lack of archaeological training, Lamon and Shipton's publications included two books on the pottery found at the site, a book on the water tunnel system, a guide-book, and—most importantly—the *Megiddo I* volume.[67] The fact that such young, junior, and initially untrained and inexperienced members of the staff ended up being entrusted with and responsible for the final publication of the ten field seasons directed by Fisher and Guy—that is, all of the

Fɪɢ. 16. Megiddo excavation staff and spouses, 7 September 1928; front row, sitting (left to right): William Staples, Yemima Guy, P.L.O. Guy (with dog), Margaret Staples, Ivan Terentieff; back row, standing (left to right): Harry Parker, Edward DeLoach, Olof Lind, Robert Lamon, Geoffrey Shipton (courtesy of the Oriental Institute of the University of Chicago)

Chicago seasons except for those directed by Loud from 1935 to 1939—is interesting, if not downright shocking.

They were not the only newcomers that season either, for on the same boat as Lamon, and beginning work on the same day in late September, came William E. Staples, who had been hired by Breasted and sent over to serve as epigrapher and recorder for the expedition. Described by Charles Breasted as "a man of great ability, likable personality, and great industry," Staples was Canadian, a graduate of Victoria College and the University of Toronto. He had recently married, in 1926, and his wife, Margaret Ruth (who was known simply as "Ruth" to her friends), came with him to Megiddo, beginning a trend of married couples living in the dig house.[68]

Guy eventually suggested to Breasted that a permanent team should be based at Megiddo all year round, if they were to properly deal with all of the material that was coming out of the ground. Thus, rather than having the team members present just during the digging season and only a skeleton crew left during the other months of the year, he wanted team members to be available for a full twelve months, with as little change in personnel as possible, so that the registration, drawing, photography, and planning could be kept up to date at all times.[69]

He made this plea because of the experiment that had been put in place the previous year, when—as mentioned above—some of the Megiddo staff members had been sent to the Chicago dig at Luxor in Egypt after the season at Megiddo had ended. The experiment had not been successful and so Breasted agreed entirely with Guy's logic, though he pointed out that they should also give the team members a reasonable vacation period each year.[70]

By this time, Guy also had very firm ideas about the personnel, and about their personalities. He very much liked Olof Lind, whom he described as a first-class photographer who did his work just as Guy would have done, recalling his days as Woolley's photographer at Carchemish early in his career. He also noted that Lind was loyal and pleasant, and got along well with the others.[71]

In contrast, he described Miss Woodley, who was by then the registrar, as rather odd and quite devious. Not only did she have too much to look after, according to Guy, but she was very protective of her role on the dig, to the extent that she made things difficult for others by not allowing them to help out even when they offered to undertake chores that remained undone. Even more disgraceful, in his eyes, was that "she cannot draw at all, and does not even check properly. . . . When a mistake is found, she will never admit that it is her fault."[72]

Guy also itemized some of the problems that Miss Woodley was causing among the other staff members, including possibly making advances on DeLoach, Shipton, and Little, one after the other. "Now Miss Woodley has dropped Shipton and rather nags at him," he wrote. "She has, however, taken up Little and coddles him as she used to want to coddle DeLoach."[73] Those three were the only single and available men at the dig during the spring of 1928. Miss Woodley would have been thirty-seven years old at the time, while Shipton was twenty years her junior, still being only seventeen or eighteen. DeLoach would have been about twenty-seven, just ten years younger than Miss Woodley, while it is unclear how old Little was. It is perhaps also appropriate to recall that, exactly one year earlier, Badè had specifically warned Breasted about "the intrigues of a middle-aged stenographer, infatuated with a young man who is himself ill and apparently completely under her influence"—that young man was most likely DeLoach, as mentioned just a few pages ago.[74]

Guy ended his comments by saying that Miss Woodley "has a character which makes her an extremely dangerous member of my staff." He refused to go into further specifics, but rather mysteriously remarked only that there were "many little things, difficult to take hold of, which . . . combine to make a story of intrigue, hintings and devious dealing which causes me to tell you that I do not want Miss Woodley to remain at Megiddo any longer than can be helped."[75]

In the end, it is perhaps not surprising that Miss Woodley was let go after the season was over, in August 1928, almost exactly two years since Fisher first hired her. Reaction had been quick, for her severance came just two months after Guy complained to Breasted about her.[76]

She landed on her feet soon enough, although this outcome entailed a move westward to Greece. She began working in 1932, at first part-time, as the secretary of the British School of Archaeology in Athens, just as she had previously been the secretary of the British School in Jerusalem before being hired at Megiddo. She was eventually hired full-time and served in that position for more than a decade, from 1936 to 1946, after which she retired to Leeds.[77]

Meanwhile Guy was still also having problems with Fisher, who was living not too far away, in Ramallah. The two men had a strained relationship, with each complaining to Breasted about the other.[78] In late June, for example, Guy told Breasted: "I feel that Fisher has behaved very discourteously . . . apart from discourtesy when we have met, he has completely ignored letters of mine to which no-one could take exception. . . . Also, he seems to lose no opportunity of speaking ill of us here." He concluded: "So far as I can hear and see, Fisher has shown himself to be a trouble-maker wherever he has gone: with Hilprecht, with Reisner, at Beisan [Beth Shean], and certainly with us. He is not clean, and I earnestly hope that you will sever his connexion with Megiddo."[79]

He further besmirched Fisher by referring to an unspecified incident that they had apparently managed to keep quiet. "If it were made public," Guy claimed, it "would . . . have the most serious results for Fisher himself." He reassured Breasted, however, that "though people have mentioned the thing to me, I have spoken of it to nobody except Pere Vincent [from the École Biblique in Jerusalem]. . . . He told me that he was thinking of recommending Fisher as head of the Baghdad School; would I tell him, frankly and freely, what I thought of the idea? I thought of what had happened here, and what might so easily happen there if Fisher were put in charge of young men, and I could do no other than advise against it, giving the reasons why I did so."[80]

What had happened at Megiddo? Unfortunately, we simply don't know. Guy never did elaborate upon what had happened and why he was concerned about the problems that might ensue if Fisher were placed in charge of young men. There is nothing else in the archives at the Oriental Institute about this supposed episode. However, given what we know about Fisher's previous unrequited love for his tent mate at Nippur, as well as about a young boy named Nasir el-Hussein whom he brought home to America from that dig (but who returned to his own home shortly thereafter),[81] plus an adopted son from Ramallah named David (or, rather, Daoud), and a school for young boys in Jerusalem with which he was associated, it is probably safe to say that the unspecified incident did not involve a tryst with Miss Woodley. Regardless of what Fisher may or may not have done, this pattern of using innuendo and gossip against colleagues and fellow team members, even if founded in truth, would not serve Guy well in the coming years, and it eventually got him fired in 1934.

There is one additional strange mention in a very long and detailed letter that Guy sent to Breasted in late June. He wrote rather enigmatically about an attack that had been made on Parker and Shipton, remarking only that an investigation into it had closed satisfactorily, with the perpetrators being let off with a warning after apologizing for what they had done.[82] As with the unspecified incident with Fisher that Guy had mentioned, there is no other discussion anywhere else in the archives of this episode involving Parker and Shipton. Thus it is unclear what might have happened or why, though perhaps the matter can be traced back to the previous year, in July and August 1927, when DeLoach detailed Parker's abusive treatment of the local workmen and the abortive strike that resulted when he physically attacked one of them.[83] Perhaps further information will turn up in the future, but for now all that can be said is that relations between the Megiddo staff and the nearby villagers apparently were not always courteous and friendly during these years.

⚛

In fact, regarding such relations with the locals, something else that Guy accidentally discovered at about the same time is of supreme importance. Realizing that the three-year lease on the land at Megiddo that Fisher had originally negotiated back in 1925 was going to expire in October, Guy wrote to Breasted during the summer, listing four potential courses of action regarding future work at the mound, three of which required renewing the lease. The fourth involved purchasing, rather than renting, a specific area of the mound.[84]

He had already made inquiries at the Department of Antiquities about what could be done, and had been told that, if they were willing to pay for it, the land could be expropriated and would become government property, which they could then excavate at their leisure. Guy thought this might be something worth investigating. As it turned out, it was.[85]

Less than two weeks later, matters played straight into Guy's hands. When he mentioned to the other staff members that the lease that Fisher had previously signed with the local landowners was due to expire soon, Miss Woodley, who was friends with a British expatriate living in Haifa named Miss Frances E. Newton, passed along the surprising information that Megiddo did not legally belong to the people to whom they had been paying rent for the past three years. She also said that Miss Newton had told Fisher the same thing back when he had signed the original lease in 1925, but that he hadn't paid attention.[86]

Fisher should have listened to her, for it turned out that almost 20 percent of the mound—thirteen acres—was actually owned by an American named Mrs. Rosamond Dale Owen Oliphant Templeton. She was the granddaughter of Robert Owen, who had founded a well-known but ultimately failed utopian community at New Harmony in Indiana. She was also the second wife and widow of Laurence Oliphant, a popular Scottish novelist and travel writer who had lived next door to Gottlieb Schumacher in Haifa from 1882 to 1888.[87]

Laurence met and married Rosamond a little more than two years after his first wife died suddenly. However, just six months after their wedding, he passed away in turn, succumbing to lung cancer in late December 1888. Rosamond then spent the next few decades sorting out his affairs, including dealing with land that he had purchased in Ottoman Palestine. She also married a disciple of Oliphant's named James Templeton, only to have him commit suicide within two years by jumping overboard while sailing back from Beirut to Haifa. The only thing she retained from that marriage was her new name, Mrs. Templeton, by which she was known for the rest of her life.[88]

As a result of her marriage to Laurence Oliphant, Mrs. Templeton inherited more than just Tell el-Mutesellim. According to the New York Times, her overall holdings in the Jezreel Valley were extensive.[89] In fact, when Schumacher began his excavations at the site in 1903, several newspaper articles appeared in British newspapers that same year, describing her as the "owner of a portion of the plain of Armageddon." The Edinburgh Evening News even ran the story with the headline "English Lady Owns Armageddon." One British newspaper reporter asked, "How much of Armageddon do you own, Mrs. Templeton?" to which she replied, "About 1200 acres, and it is the central and best part."[90] However, two different tales, which she told at different times, emerged as to how she had acquired the land in the first place.

According to the earlier version, Laurence Oliphant became the owner of the property in the Jezreel Valley somewhat by accident in 1884 or 1885.[91] In a detailed letter that he published about Armageddon in the New York Sun, dated 11 September 1884, Oliphant said that the villagers who owned the land on and around Lejjun and Tell el-Mutesellim were in a tremendous amount of debt and had begged him for loans, which he said he was unable to provide. It is possible, though, that he did eventually take out mortgages on this land in return for loaning them money after all, and when the owners defaulted on their payments, the land became his.[92]

In fact, when Mrs. Templeton was interviewed by the reporter in London in 1903, she told him that Laurence had acquired the land in the Jezreel Valley and Haifa back in the 1880s. However, as she said, "Mr. Oliphant bought the land, but Europeans were not allowed at that time to have land in their names, so he held it in the name of an Arab."[93]

She said further that she had tried to secure it in her own name but was unsuccessful for fifteen years. At last, she prevailed; it was at that point that she told the reporter that she owned twelve hundred acres of Armageddon, complete with documentation and a valid title to back up her claim.[94]

However, in her book My Perilous Life in Palestine, which she published in 1929, the story did not end in 1903 but continued for nearly three more decades.[95] In that book, she also told an entirely different tale of her acquisition of Armageddon. There she wrote that, sometime during the 1890s, the Turkish government had put Armageddon up for auction to the highest bidder. She said that she was guided by her inner voice, to which she had listened her whole life, to purchase the famous site. Moreover, as she noted, the local landowners were the ones who had told the government to sell the land, and she had been asked by the government to buy it, so she wouldn't be robbing anyone if she bought the thousand acres of land that were being offered to her.[96]

She repeated the same story in a letter that she sent to the commissioner of lands in British Mandate Palestine, a copy of which she eventually sent to Guy. In it, she said, "I bought the land put up at auction by the Turkish Government at the earnest request of the fellaheen in order to assist them, as they badly needed the money being much in debt."[97]

In her own book, published in 1948, Miss Newton confirmed this version of the story, writing that "more than half a century ago the widow of Lawrence [*sic*] Oliphant bought a share in the 'Armageddon' land when the Turks put it up to auction to recover taxes due from the peasants. Her name appears in the Turkish Land Registry books as part-owner."[98]

After doing some research, Guy concluded that it did seem very likely that the people to whom they had been paying rent since 1925 had no right to the money—at least not without Mrs. Templeton's consent. He also said that he couldn't understand why a search of the Land Registry had not been done when they had signed the original lease, especially since Miss Newton had told Fisher about Mrs. Templeton at the time. It seemed obvious to Guy that Fisher, and the small committee that had been formed at the time, had simply ignored what Miss Newton had said.

Guy outlined to Breasted why the new situation might be turned to their advantage, for they would be able to overturn their current lease, including the part about handing over the dig house, and could negotiate new terms with the proper owner, that is, Mrs. Templeton. He also suggested that Breasted should meet with Mrs. Templeton, because she might be willing to sell everything to them at a good price.

A visit was indeed made to Mrs. Templeton, but it was Guy who went to meet her, rather than Breasted. In early September, Guy related to Breasted what had transpired. "I duly visited Mrs. Templeton at 201 Brighton Road, Worthing. She is 82, but her faculties are still acute. She is . . . keenly interested in some kind of Christianity which she herself describes as 'unorthodox', and which aims at closer brotherhood among mankind, and higher uplift."[99]

She was eager to sell the land to them, Guy said, but first she had to definitively establish her title to it. He also reported that she was very interested in their work at Megiddo and wouldn't put any obstacles in their way, in terms of selling the land to them. He ended by saying: "I am glad I called upon her: it lets us know how things lie. She is a pleasant old lady, and we got on famously together . . . although she only eats two meals a day, breakfast and supper, she had prepared various little cakes and things for my delectation."[100]

He subsequently sent a cable to Breasted in late September, in which he wrote that the British Mandate government was prepared to expropriate the land, as long as the Oriental Institute was willing to pay for it: "GOVERNMENT WROTE YOU TWENTYFIFTH PREPARED TO EXPROPRIATE AT OUR EXPENSE TITLE TO VEST IN THEM STOP I BELIEVE THIS BEST COURSE IRRESPECTIVE OF PRESENT OWNERSHIP STOP PROBABLE COST UNDER 3750 DOLLARS. PLEASE CABLE DECISION."[101]

Breasted's return cable said simply, "THIS AUTHORIZES AGREEMENT WITH GOVERNMENT FOR EXPROPRIATION AND PURCHASE ON TERMS CABLED ME." He also asked Guy to let him know when the government had proceeded with the expropriation of the land, so that they could pay the bill.[102]

Finally, at the beginning of November, Guy was able to tell Breasted that the expropriation of the land was going forward, but very slowly. The area had been officially surveyed, all boxes on the various forms had been duly checked, and notice was about to be served to the local owners. He ended on the hopeful note that he expected to gain entry to the whole area in about a week.[103]

As it transpired, however, the process of expropriation was not well received by the local landowners or the villagers who were farming the land, which might have been expected. Nevertheless, it had been made quite clear to them that the expropriation would take place, regardless of their feelings. The final word was given to Hassan Saad, the representative of the local landowners, on 12 November.

The next morning, when Guy and the other team members climbed to the top of the tell to begin work, they found that "malicious damage" had been done to their equipment during the night. One of the railway cars for transporting the dirt had been pushed down an embankment; the field telephone was knocked over and broken; a water jar was smashed; a box was taken from one of the tents and thrown into Schumacher's Great Trench; and "an unpleasant and unsanitary souvenir [was] left in a prominent place." They reported the damage to the local police, who began an investigation, though Guy was pretty certain that Hassan was behind it.[104] Undoubtedly, he was correct, given the timing and the circumstances.

Meanwhile, even though Mrs. Templeton's formal claim to the land still had to be heard by the Anglo-Turkish Mixed Arbitral Tribunal, and then by the Land Court in Jerusalem—all of which would proceed at a snail's pace until 1931[105]—she was happy to go ahead and sell her part of Tell el-Mutesellim to Breasted and the Oriental Institute, as part of a larger deal in which the local government compensated the rest of the landowners. In early December 1930, therefore, it was announced with great fanfare in the *New York Times* that the Oriental Institute of the University of Chicago had purchased Armageddon from Mrs. Templeton. The headline declared: "Armageddon Battlefield Bought for $3,500 from an American Widow for Exploration." Although $3,500 may not sound like a lot, it was the equivalent of just over $48,000 today.[106]

FIG. 17. Memorial plaque for Rosamond Dale Owen Oliphant Templeton, in Maple Hill Cemetery, New Harmony, Indiana (courtesy of Dan Elliott)

Note, however, that this did not necessarily end the matter of expropriation, for letters now in the archives of both the Oriental Institute in Chicago and the Israel Antiquities Authority in Jerusalem, as well as in the Israel State Archives, show that the dialogue continued right through the 1930s and into the 1940s, until the 1948 War of Independence ended the discussion, when the land simply became part of the new state of Israel.[107]

After Mrs. Templeton's death in 1937, her adopted son Carlos oversaw her burial in the cemetery at Llanwrtyd Church in Newtown, Wales, near her Welsh grandfather. He also arranged for the installation of a memorial plaque in the Maple Hill Cemetery at New Harmony, Indiana, where her father and other family members were buried. On the plaque, Carlos saw to it that her connection to Armageddon would never be forgotten, for the inscription reads:

> This Tablet in Loving Memory of
> Rosamond Dale Owen Oliphant Templeton
> Author, Philosopher, Traveler, Ardent Christian.
> Daughter of
> Robert Dale Owen.
> Member of Minerva Society.
> Charter member of New Harmony Woman's Library Club.
> Formerly Owner of Armageddon.
> Born—New Harmony—December 13, 1846
> Died—Worthing, England—June 19, 1937
> Erected by her Devoted Adopted Son,
> Carlos Ronzevalle.
> Peace! Peace![108]

Apart from the events surrounding the expropriation of the land, life at the Megiddo compound was otherwise pretty harmonious from September through December 1928. Edward DeLoach had finally recovered from his bouts of malaria, and whatever else had been ailing him, so he had been cleared by the doctors in Chicago to return to the site, which he did by the end of September.[109] As mentioned, Dr. and Mrs. Staples and Robert Lamon had also arrived together at about the same time as DeLoach, in late September, so that by early December they were all "a pretty happy family," with no "signs of mutiny," at least according to Guy's account.[110]

Since the days were getting shorter, Guy changed the working hours, giving them all time off after lunch, so that they could go on long walks or occasional shooting expeditions, before working again until dinner. He also forbade them to work after dinner, encouraging them instead to read, and even envisioned starting a "study-circle" where they could informally discuss their own finds late into the evening, presumably over a glass of wine or whiskey.[111]

Guy also made a list of things for them to do during these winter months, before the digging season began again in April. These included making working plans of all the excavation areas; completing the recording of all the pottery and other artifacts from the season that had just concluded; and checking over everything from the 1927 and 1928 seasons. He also envisioned writing two small publications, although he did not manage to complete either one at that time, despite his best intentions.

Chief among the items on his list was a plan to clear away the surface soil in the new areas that he wished to excavate—that is, in the region on the top of the tell that was about to be made available for digging because of the land expropriation. The team had already laid out the boundaries and set the pegs for the new squares by early November, but, as he complained to Breasted a month later, heavy rains put an end to those plans because the top half meter of soil was now completely waterlogged. Instead, he simply sent the Egyptian workmen home to their families until the early spring, rather than continuing the futile efforts.[112]

CHAPTER VI

"They Can Be Nothing Else than Stables"

The discovery of "Solomon's Stables" came near the beginning of Guy's second season, but we need to start earlier than that in order to appreciate what it meant for the expedition. When he had first taken over from Fisher the previous year, in early May 1927, Guy had high hopes that they would find something dramatic.[1] So did Breasted. They initially spoke about acting on a proposal that had been made by Fisher, in which they would confine their excavations "to the six northernmost squares on top of the mound and . . . go down as deeply as possible." Instead, Guy first continued the practice of opening up as much area as possible, having received permission to hire as many as three hundred workers, as long as he could use them efficiently.[2] That would have been a lot of workmen—a force larger than that at most contemporaneous digs—but there were almost never that many available at one time, as it turned out.

Even though, as discussed, his initial 1927 season turned out to be shorter than Guy would have liked, and despite the fact that it was beset by malaria, staffing problems, innuendo, and gossip, as well as the fact that he himself was present only part-time right through the end of August, the Chicago team actually accomplished quite a lot during that first year under his leadership. While they had no major discoveries to report, that year's work set the stage for the momentous 1928 season. We know this in part from a twelve-page letter that Guy wrote to Breasted in mid-August, detailing their accomplishments to that date, although only part of it deals with the actual digging; the rest is taken up with budgetary and personnel matters.[3]

This seems to have been the only time that Guy actually sent such a detailed report during the 1927 season. The closest he got at any other time that year was a brief note back at the beginning of the season, from the end of May, in which he simply said: "All goes well meanwhile: clearing of dump area is finished & we have about 100 men clearing exposed levels at the top of the chute. 2 caves on dump area yielded much pottery. Nothing much coming out of the upper dig as yet, of course."[4]

Much of the season was taken up with laying down two parallel lines of railway tracks on the mound and setting in place more chutes for getting rid of the dirt and stones that they were removing. There were at least four chutes in use by that point; one of these was a sturdy iron chute that they had ordered from Egypt and which was put in place alongside the old wooden chute that they had been using. This also meant moving one of Fisher's dumps on the side of the mound and enlarging the space on the eastern slope at the bottom of the tell for dumping. During this process they uncovered more graves and shaft tombs, including some from the Iron Age and others that Guy thought might date to the Middle Bronze Age. One contained a beautiful cylinder seal, perhaps made of lapis lazuli. In all, they found a total of forty-one more tombs during the 1927 season, ranging in date from the Early Bronze Age to the Early Iron Age, in addition to the sixty tombs that had already been excavated by Fisher.[5]

They also uncovered more of the city wall from the Iron Age levels. This is City Wall 325, previously mentioned, which seems to have been built and encircled the entire mound during what is now called Stratum IV, lasting into Stratum III (Guy's III and Sub-II). Guy thought that the wall had been built about 700 BCE. He was close; we now know that it was still in use in 700 BCE, though it had originally been built earlier than that.[6]

On the top of the mound, since the area that they had begun to clear "revealed no buildings of outstanding interest," Guy decided to dig slightly to the north, where Fisher had already found a number of buildings. In this area, they were following the policy of total excavation, and then total removal, of the various strata, one by one. As Guy noted, for instance, "When the work of clearing on the E[ast] slope was finished, we transferred work to the summit, and moved the level II Temple (?). . . . We shall shortly, I hope, have the big level III Temple (?) out of the way, and then I hope for something of interest."[7] He was unsure at that time about the identifications of these buildings, but clearly both needed to be moved, or removed, so that the team could get down to the more "interesting" levels, as he put it.

By mid-August, they had already reached in some places what Guy called Strata IV and even V (later renamed V and VI by Lamon and Shipton, in the final publication), "owing to the remains of IV being scanty and broken up" in the area where they were digging. They were also running into

Fig. 18. Megiddo excavations, during Guy's directorship ca. 1931–34 (courtesy of the Oberlin College archives)

stratigraphic problems. As Guy noted, "The levels all over the area of which I am writing are very mixed and run into one another in a manner which demands the closest archaeological supervision while they are being dug, and this seems likely to be the case everywhere on the tell itself."[8] All of that changed, however, in 1928.

After the Egyptian workmen arrived in late April 1928, they began work at the northern end of the tell, in order to clarify some points and questions left over from the previous season.[9] The initial discovery of "Solomon's Stables" came a few weeks later, just a month into the season. It was at the time of transition between the two surveyors, for Terentieff arrived on 3 June, while Wilensky left two days later, on 5 June. Guy sent the cable announcing the discovery of the stables to Breasted on the day in between (see the prologue, above). However, the first parts of the stables had apparently come to light sometime earlier, as Guy later told Breasted.[10]

Guy sent the complete details, in a very long letter full of news, at the end of June, several weeks after a division of their finds to that point had been made with the Department of Antiquities.[11] This was the type of letter that he was supposed to send once a month but instead ended up sending only once, or sometimes twice, a season . . . and sometimes not at all.

FIG. 19. Portion of northern stables found by Chicago team, June 1928 (courtesy of the Oberlin College archives)

After describing their continuing clearance of City Wall 325, including the fact that there were rooms built up against its inner face, Guy finally got to the important matter of the stables. He wrote: "Our big find, of course, is the great complex of buildings which covers practically the whole of Squares N12 and N13. They can be nothing else than stables, and very good stables too, with room for somewhere about 150 horses. The 'standing stones' have no religious significance whatever: they are nothing more or less than hitching-posts, and lots of them have still got the rope holes unbroken." He thought that there were 12 passages within the stables, with room for 12 horses within each passage, for a total of 144 horses (rather than 150).[12]

In large part because of these discoveries, Guy asked the draftsmen to begin drawing their plans at a scale of 1:200, rather than the previous 1:100. This resulted in smaller renderings of the buildings and other remains, but they were able to get much more of the site, and the squares that they were excavating, onto a single working plan. This, in turn, permitted them to easily see how everything was connected, even remains that were some distance apart, as Guy reported to Breasted.[13]

Guy also noted problems with Fisher's previous methods of recording and registration, complaining that they were pretty theoretical and hard to actually use. He said that others elsewhere, such as at Beth Shean where Fisher had previously worked, had difficulties with them as well, so he had modified them accordingly.[14] All of these changes made it easy to better record the discoveries that they were now making.

In early July, Guy elaborated on his previous remarks to Breasted, stating that the stables appeared to be "composed of several units divided from each other by common party-walls. Each unit consists of three passages— the central passage a real passage, the two flanking passages rows of stalls in which the heads of the animals faced inwards so that they could be fed and watered easily from the central passage."[15] By the time the *New York Times* articles about the stables appeared in August,[16] the number of hypothesized horses that could fit into the stables had been reduced to 120, but the rest of the details remained essentially the same.

Each stable was a tripartite arrangement, consisting of a plastered central aisle with a cobblestone aisle to either side. In each of the side aisles, the stalls were arranged in rows with a manger in front of each horse, separated by massive stone hitching posts. Each of the stable buildings that they eventually uncovered had the same plan, usually consisting of at least five such "stable units." Guy was completely correct about the food for the horses brought in via the plastered central passage, although it now seems that they were probably taken outside for watering.[17]

Guy also said that they had found grain in one of the stables, which he was submitting to the Department of Agriculture for identification. However, if it was ever done, the results of the analysis seem never to have been reported anywhere.[18]

Similar structures had been found at other sites, such as Tell el-Hesi and elsewhere, where they had also been dated to the time of Solomon, but nobody had previously been able to identify them. The proper identification of these buildings has, in fact, been the source of continuous debate for most of the last century. While most archaeologists now agree that these are in fact stables, others see them as storehouses or barracks, or as fulfilling some other unidentified purpose. Guy was certain from the outset that they were used as stables, at least initially, when they were built during Stratum IV.

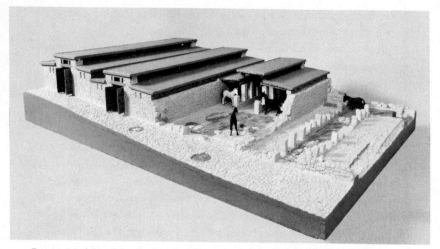

Fig. 20. Model and detail of "Solomon's Stables" by Olof E. Lind and Laurence Woolman (courtesy of the Oriental Institute of the University of Chicago)

However, as he told Breasted, "the stables were re-used in [Stratum] III partly as stables (we have the late mangers in places) and partly, I believe, as dwellings."[19]

As it happens, the most recent expedition to the site, by Tel Aviv University, has uncovered yet more such structures, in the same northern area where the Chicago excavators first found theirs. Their findings have settled the debate in favor of Guy's identification of them as originally built and used as stables.[20]

However, there is one other problem—the date of the stables. Guy was sure that they were built during the time of Solomon, as indicated by his initial cable in early June, but he confessed that there were also some stratigraphic difficulties. While he told Breasted that "our Stratum IV, in which our stables occur, is to be pushed back beyond the time of Omri and Samaria to the time of Solomon," he also noted that "III follows closely on IV, and there is practically no difference between the pottery of the two. . . . All the Megiddo strata are, so far as I have dug them, mixed up with one another in a way I have seldom seen elsewhere, and III and IV are peculiarly difficult to disentangle in many places."[21]

Guy did not realize that the two levels were much later in date than he thought they were. It is now generally accepted that the stables were first built during the second half of Stratum IV, in the period now called IVA. Many archaeologists have dated this phase to the ninth century BCE and the time of Ahab and Omri. It also fits quite well because of a mention on the Monolith Inscription, erected over in Mesopotamia by the Neo-Assyrian king Shalmaneser III, which says that Ahab brought two thousand chariots to the Battle of Qarqar, which was fought in Syria in 853 BCE. However, following the additional excavations by the current Tel Aviv Expedition, a number of scholars would now go even lower and argue that the initial construction of the stables dates to the first half of the eighth century, during the reign of Jeroboam II.[22] Either way, it is now clear that this city of the stables, our Stratum IVA, was not built by Solomon.

Not knowing any of this at the time, Guy continued to believe that he had uncovered Solomon's Stables. He spelled out his reasoning to Breasted, writing: "Horses and chariots were of great importance to Solomon: it would be natural, taking into consideration the importance of Megiddo, the traditional connection of the Plain with chariots, the convenience of its situation for dealings with Kings of the Hittites and of Syria, that Solomon should make a Chariot City of it."[23] Of course, horses and chariots were of great importance to the kings who came after Solomon as well, so the same arguments could apply to them, but that went unsaid.

Overall, in large part because of the discovery of the stables, the 1928 season proved to be much more successful than the previous one. As a result, Guy stated rather melodramatically, "Our current discovery of a city of the tenth century B.C.—well planned and built as a homogeneous whole—leads me to recommend to you that the whole of our plan of campaign should be changed."[24]

To his mind, Stratum IV had been "conceived and built by one authority": Solomon. Therefore, as he put it, they now had the opportunity—or, rather, almost a duty—of excavating the entirety of what he thought was one of Solomon's largest cities. He noted that previous excavators at sites elsewhere had dug right through strata and cities dating to the time of Solomon almost without a second thought, but that at Megiddo they were lucky to have realized what they had come across before excavating farther.[25]

Guy therefore asked Breasted for permission to uncover the entire town, thereby continuing their practice of what we would call today "horizontal archaeology," in which the entire stratum is revealed before any of it is re-moved. It was for this reason that they needed to acquire the entire mound of Megiddo, he said, and not just the portion that they had been renting and excavating up to that time. And it was for that reason Breasted readily agreed to purchase the land from Mrs. Templeton.[26]

Guy sent the workmen home because of the rains in November 1928,[27] but up until that time they worked in fifteen new squares on the top of the mound, removing the surface strata. Guy noted that "there is very little of Stratum I remaining . . . the first buildings we find belong chiefly to II." He was pleased about this, he said, "because of the relative unimpor-tance of [Stratum] I." Such an attitude would not be tolerated in archaeol-ogy today, where every stratum is seen as important in terms of the history of an ancient site. They also weren't finding many ancient remains or arti-facts in the upper level, which delighted Guy, since it meant that they could dig quickly. He did realize that he shouldn't be admitting to such feelings, however, noting parenthetically, "(is this wicked, [coming] from an archaeologist?)."[28]

Guy also said, probably trying to get on Breasted's good side, that he had cleared a bit off the South Slope of the tell, by Square T9. Here he had found City Wall 325, and just below it some pottery from the earliest part of the Iron Age, dating just after 1200 BCE, he thought. Just eighteen inches (half a meter) farther down, they uncovered some Late Cypriot pottery, so he thought that it wouldn't be long before they reached the period of Ramses and then the Amarna period. The "Thothmes" stratum, as he put it, would not be far below this. "There is thus," he concluded, "no great depth of de-bris to be excavated . . . and I know that you will be glad of this."[29] Unfor-tunately, Guy could not have been more wrong; it would take another seven years of digging, and a different field director, before they got down to the Egyptian levels that Breasted had long anticipated.

CHAPTER VII

"Admonitory but Merciful"

At the beginning of 1929, the new year dawned calmly and peacefully for the excavators at Megiddo, with no hint of the clashes that would occur between Jews and Arabs in Jerusalem, Haifa, Hebron, and Safed later that summer, nor of the stock market crash that would rock the United States on Black Tuesday, 29 October.[1] Instead, it was the sad condition of the single road that served Megiddo which weighed heavily on Guy and the team that January. Guy mused gloomily that they would "undoubtedly be cut off from time to time during the winter," and indeed they were.[2]

By mid-January, the track was impassable because of the heavy rains. In order to get supplies from Afula, they had to ride horses rather than drive.[3] Although the excavators—and Breasted, to his credit—had been complaining to the authorities for quite some time, the situation became even more dire when the prospect arose of a visit by the Rockefellers sometime in the spring.[4] The excavation team immediately began preparing for the "Great Royal Visit," as Charles Breasted called it.

Charles arrived a week ahead of the rest of the party, on 1 March, in order to spend time productively with the team and catch up on their activities and needs.[5] Then, on the morning of 8 March, several cars pulled up to the dig house. Out of them emerged various Rockefellers and James Henry Breasted, suitably dressed for an excursion.[6] The government had come to the rescue just in time, "rushing [the] road through to a state which made the route at least passable," so that the visitors were able to reach the site. However, they had still spent nearly two hours bumping and lurching over the "unrolled macadam road," as Breasted described it.[7]

The Rockefeller interest in Megiddo had been long-standing of course; recall that John D. Rockefeller, Jr., had first promised Breasted funding to excavate at the site nearly a decade earlier and had then come through so that work could begin in 1925. Now, just a few months previously, in

FIG. 21. "Great Royal Visit," 8 March 1929; left to right: P.L.O. Guy (above), A. Murray Dyer, David Rockefeller, Geoffrey Shipton, Mary "Tod" Clark, Edward DeLoach, Robert Lamon, Abby Rockefeller, John D. Rockefeller, Jr., James Henry Breasted, Harry Parker, unidentified man wearing a fez (courtesy of the Oriental Institute of the University of Chicago)

December 1928, the Rockefeller Foundation and the General Education Board, two of the philanthropic entities associated with the Rockefellers, had approved a large grant for the construction of a building for the Oriental Institute on the University of Chicago campus, as well as for a ten-year period of research and publication, which included work at Megiddo as well as at numerous other sites in Egypt and the Near East.[8]

The group had spent the previous night at the Royal Hotel in Nazareth, so they were able to arrive at Megiddo by 11:00 a.m. After showing them around the various facilities, Guy and the other team members took their visitors up on the ancient tell. They gathered together for a photograph, clustered tightly between upright stones in one of the stables. Guy stood head and shoulders above the others, on the left. He, Shipton, DeLoach, Lamon, and Parker were all in jacket and tie, each wearing a fedora, though DeLoach also sported a cane and wore his usual bow tie in contrast to all of the others, who wore more somber neckties.

The Rockefellers and Breasted were interspersed among them, including young David Rockefeller and his tutor, Murray Dyer, who stood on the left with a fashionable cap and a cane. In between Shipton and DeLoach was Mary "Tod" Clark (the future Mrs. Nelson Rockefeller), wearing a fur-lined coat and a chic hat. Abby Rockefeller, also with a stylish hat and coat, stood between Lamon and her husband, John D. Rockefeller, Jr. The famous man himself, dressed in an overcoat, warmly grasped the crook of Breasted's right arm, with a slight smile on his face, while Breasted, quite somber, can be seen clad in his traveling "plus fours" along with the de rigueur (for the day) tweed jacket and tie; both men also have canes, needless to say.

On a side note, and purely as a matter of coincidence, it was on that very same day—8 March 1929—that Rockefeller won a major proxy fight back home and forced out Col. Robert Stewart as chairman of the board for the Standard Oil Company of Indiana, the company that had been cofounded by Rockefeller's father. (Much later, in the 1980s, it was renamed Amoco and then merged with British Petroleum in the 1990s.) His eldest son, John D. Rockefeller III, then a senior at Princeton, noted in his own diary entry, "Another famous day. The annual meeting of the Board of Directors of the Standard Oil Co. of Indiana met . . . to elect the Board of Directors. Father had over 50% of the stock in his control by proxy and hence was able to get Stewart out as Chairman of the Board. . . . Father will be terribly pleased as [it] has meant a lot to him."[9]

After descending from the mound and eating an elaborately prepared lunch, the various Rockefellers and Breasted climbed back into their cars, heading for Tiberias and the Sea of Galilee, and on to Beirut, Baalbeck, Damascus, and then a return to Cairo. In the meantime, Charles Breasted headed in the other direction from Megiddo, bound for Haifa and then Cairo, where he eventually reunited with the rest of the party before they all departed for New York a week later.[10]

In all, it was a whirlwind trip, of which the visit to Megiddo was but a very small part. Although Rockefeller had been very good about writing detailed letters back home throughout the earlier part of the trip, especially from Egypt, he stopped doing so at the end of February, since their group would arrive back home before the letters did. As a result, it is hard to know what he thought of Megiddo, for he made only a very brief entry in his daily diary, under the heading "Fri. Mch. 8"—"Left 9 [a.m.] drove to the Oriental Institute of Chicago house at Megiddo. Mr. Guy in charge. Mr. Noble [*sic*] the Eng. road engineer and wife also there. Saw excavation of Solomon's stables. Left after lunch over same new road to highway near Haifa then back through Nazareth and on ¾ hour to Tiberias on Sea of Galilee."[11] That was it; no other comments, notes, or reaction from the man who had been funding the entire enterprise.

He did, however, take the time later that day in Tiberias, after checking in to the Elisabetha Haven of Rest Health Resort, to write a note of thanks to Peter Nobel, the district engineer for the Public Works Department in Haifa, who had been responsible for finishing the road to Megiddo in time for their visit. He also wrote a similar letter to Sir John Chancellor, the high commissioner of British Mandate Palestine, calling the work that Nobel and his staff had done on the new road "little short of miraculous."[12] Breasted, also grateful for the show of hospitality to himself and their major benefactor, sat down right away as well and wrote a nice letter of appreciation to Guy and his wife, Yemima.[13]

Several days later, Abby sent a telegram to their son Nelson, the future New York governor and vice president of the United States, who was an undergraduate living in Hitchcock Hall at Dartmouth College at the time. She wrote simply: "HOLY LAND MORE BEAUTIFUL THAN DREAMED TRIP DELIGHTFUL STARTING HOME TOMORROW." To this, written in pencil below her message, Nelson scrawled "any signs of second coming?"[14] (We should note that it is not clear whether he actually sent that as a reply.)

After the entourage departed from Megiddo, the team members at the dig all breathed more easily. The visit had gone well. One of the immediate fringe benefits for all concerned was that they had been granted permission to construct a tennis court, which Breasted and the Rockefellers had all agreed was much needed.[15] Breasted himself also benefited unexpectedly some months later, when Rockefeller promised him $100,000 for his personal use, as thanks for leading them on the tour of Egypt and the Near East, and as a sign of his "admiration for what you have and are doing [and] my genuine affection for you."[16]

Lamon also benefited from the visit, for he had taken the opportunity to discuss with Charles Breasted how he might finish his undergraduate degree from Chicago. He had put his schooling on hold when he joined the team, and so a plan was now made for him to return to Chicago after the 1929 season, spend some time in residence, and then complete the rest of his remaining credits by correspondence. Cables and letters were exchanged in April, and it was tentatively arranged that Lamon would return to Chicago in mid-June and that a temporary replacement for him would be found,

FIG. 22. Megiddo excavation staff and spouses, 22 May 1929; front row, sitting (left to right): Florence and Edward DeLoach (with small dog), Yemima and P.L.O. Guy, Margaret and William Staples; back row, standing (left to right): Harry Parker, Charles Kent, Reis Hamid, Robert Lamon, Olof Lind, Geoffrey Shipton (courtesy of the Oriental Institute of the University of Chicago)

in the person of a young man named Robert W. Hamilton from Oxford, who would be with them for a few weeks until they all left for vacation in July.[17]

Hamilton did come to excavate with them from 24 June to 10 July, but his presence went completely unremarked in the letters and other correspondence from that two-week period. Little did they know that, just two years later, he would be appointed chief inspector of antiquities in British Mandate Palestine and would interact continuously with the Megiddo team in that capacity for seven years, from 1931 to 1938. The relationship continued even beyond, in fact, since he then was appointed director of antiquities, a position that he held until 1948 and the end of the British Mandate. Even later, he would become keeper (curator) of the Department of Antiquities at the Ashmolean Museum in Oxford.[18]

There was yet another young man, Charles Kent, who arrived at Megiddo soon after the "Royal Visit" and stayed through June 1929. We see him in a photograph of the team members taken on 22 May, but otherwise his time at the dig, like Hamilton's just after him, went undocumented. He does not seem to be directly related to the well-known biblical scholar Charles Foster Kent, who would have been more than sixty years old at the time, though their names are quite similar.

In April, before the dig season started, Fisher's long-awaited preliminary excavation report finally appeared. Covering the period from the beginning of work in 1925 through the end of the 1926 season and entitled *The Excavation of Armageddon*, it was the first publication from the excavation team to appear in print. Discussion about it had begun a year earlier, in February 1928, when Breasted first laid out for Fisher exactly what should be in it and what it should look like, right down to the size of the paper and the typeface that would be used.[19] Guy sent around copies when they became available in late April 1929, including three to the director of antiquities in Jerusalem.[20] No doubt this gave him motivation to produce his own report, as he told the director, but, as we shall see, that would take two more years, for it did not appear until 1931.

April also brought some very unexpected news from DeLoach: he was engaged to be married to Miss Florence Adele Burnham (Flo, or Sis, as her family called her). She was a young woman from Winnetka, Illinois, who stood five feet five, with brown hair and a winning smile. They had first met through a mutual friend before he left for Megiddo in 1925, but had begun dating only in 1928, while he was home in Chicago recuperating from malaria. She and her entire family—mother, father, and several siblings—had begun traveling the world (for a second time) shortly thereafter, visiting such exotic lands as China, Japan, Korea, Siam (as they called it), India, and Egypt. She and DeLoach had been corresponding throughout the trip, including a postcard that she sent from Cairo in late March.[21]

The family met up with DeLoach (and possibly Bob Lamon) in Jerusalem at the beginning of April and spent the day touring around. According to a book later published by Flo's mother, Anita Willets-Burnham (who was an artist, author, and teacher at the Art Institute in Chicago), DeLoach then invited Flo and her older sister Carol-Lou to be his guests at the dig house at Megiddo for a week. Unfortunately, it seems that DeLoach hadn't asked for permission ahead of time, and so this interruption of the daily routine was not at all appreciated.[22] At some point while they were all there, De-Loach proposed to Flo; upon returning to Jerusalem, they broke the news to her parents that they were engaged. They set the date for three weeks thence, which was the soonest that the local (and international) laws allowed.[23]

As soon as he learned of the engagement, Guy tried to talk the young man out of it but was unsuccessful. The marriage was to take place soon after the beginning of the dig season, which would create all sorts of problems for the dig team if DeLoach then promptly left on a honeymoon. In despair, Guy asked Breasted whether he could authorize a fortnight's vacation for the couple, only to be told that the matter would be left to his discretion.[24]

The wedding was held at high noon on 29 April 1929, in St. George's Cathedral in Jerusalem. She was just nineteen years old; he was twenty-seven. In attendance were Lamon, Staples, and Shipton, with Olof Lind serving as the best man, but Mr. and Mrs. Guy were nowhere to be seen. A photograph taken that day, on the steps of the cathedral, shows the entire Burnham family plus the newlyweds, Lind, and the others from Megiddo. The new couple then left on a quick honeymoon, sailing the Nile, but returned in time to show the rest of the family around Megiddo before bidding them goodbye. Her parents and siblings traveled on to Damascus and beyond, but Flo stayed at Megiddo with her new husband. As her mother later wrote, "It was difficult saying goodbye to Sis; one hates to leave a daughter, when it may be forever, even though she is left in the Holy Land."[25]

It must have been a rather difficult and shocking change for Flo as well. Up to that point, she had been happily gallivanting around the world with her family. Even though she had been eager to get married, she was now stuck in the boondocks at Megiddo with a group of people she didn't even know. Despite all that, she appears to be reasonably happy in a photograph taken of the Megiddo excavation staff and spouses in late May 1929, about three weeks after their wedding and probably very soon after they returned from their honeymoon.

While the two of them were undoubtedly very much in love, their sudden marriage wasn't met with complete enthusiasm by the senior administration, either back in Chicago or at Megiddo. For one thing, the unexpected marriage upended the careful positioning of the living arrangements in the dig house, because the new couple had to be moved into a larger bedroom and there was now another mouth to feed at every meal.[26]

Charles Breasted wrote to Guy before the wedding, expressing doubt and concern about DeLoach's judgment in light of the apparently sudden rush to marriage to someone they erroneously thought he had just met. However, he did also state that DeLoach "is entitled to all the happiness he can get from life and from his job in particular, so long as any move he makes does not interfere with his job but rather serves to contribute to his efficiency."[27]

But what is especially interesting is what we do *not* find after the wedding. There are no more letters or cables exchanged directly between DeLoach and either Charles or James Henry Breasted. The last communication had been a cheery cable full of best wishes to DeLoach in late August 1928, when he was returning to Megiddo after his long convalescence at home,[28] but there is now a deafening silence. There are no immediate cables of congratulations to the newlyweds; no discussions of how the room and board costs associated with Flo's now staying permanently at the dig house would be covered and by whom; no mention at all of the nuptials until a thoughtful letter sent by Breasted's wife, Frances, on behalf of them both, but not until more than two months after the event, in mid-July. Instead, Guy and Charles Breasted exchanged letters and cables with snide and belittling remarks about the couple, both individually and together. It is clear that DeLoach's move, which appeared both impromptu and impetuous to them, since they did not know the full backstory of the romance that had begun back in Chicago, did not sit well with these grandees.[29]

Bear in mind that absolutely nothing negative had ever been said about DeLoach in the years before his sudden marriage; that he had even been appointed assistant field director for a brief period in 1927; and that they were sympathetic when he had to go home to Chicago in 1928 in order to recover from malaria. Now, however, the administration viciously turned on him as well as his new bride, with character assassinations of both. Although Guy did defend him as "a really competent surveyor, and a careful one," and said that "the plans he produces are accurate and good to look upon," he also said that, in his opinion, it appeared that DeLoach had made a grievous error and "blotted his copy-book pretty effectively" because of the marriage.[30]

Charles Breasted was even more brutal in his reply to Guy, damning DeLoach with faint praise and casting aspersions on his character. His statements and accusations are, quite frankly, very surprising, especially since there had not been anything untoward said about DeLoach during the entire four years of his association with the expedition to that point. In fact, back in 1927, when temporarily promoting him, James Henry Breasted had said, "I have great confidence in the character and ability of this young man."[31]

Charles Breasted also maligned Flo, despite the fact that he had never met her, including a strange claim that her presence was creating problems in the group. However, there is no indication that anything he said about her was true, and he could not possibly have known whether Flo's presence was causing problems, because he was in Chicago and she was at Megiddo. In fact, we know from other letters and diaries, such as those of Janet Woolman, who arrived at Megiddo in September and was in daily contact with Flo for the next six months, that Flo actually fit in quite well with the group and with the other spouses who were present that season.[32]

Charles was, however, gracious enough to say that DeLoach "has displayed qualities of loyalty and faithfulness in the face of real hardship and the most discouraging circumstances" and that, as noted, he was entitled to his happiness.[33] Since the marriage subsequently lasted for nearly forty years, until DeLoach's death in Dallas at age sixty-seven, one year after his retirement from a long and successful career at the Atlantic Refining Company as a geologist/geophysicist, and produced three children and numerous grandchildren, it is clear that he and Flo made the right choice for themselves, regardless of what others may have thought.[34]

Nevertheless, given the above, and with the advantage of twenty-twenty hindsight, it comes as no surprise that the marriage marked the beginning of the end of DeLoach's association with Megiddo. By August 1929, he had apparently requested to be transferred to another expedition, though that did not come to fruition. He also wrote to his father saying that he no longer wished to pursue a career in archaeology and was thinking of resigning from the expedition. And indeed, he and Flo left for America within the year, in March 1930, as we shall soon see.[35]

In mid-July, the team temporarily stopped work at the site. Everyone took a timely vacation, in order to avoid the heat of the summer. When they began again in October, new members had joined their team, namely, another pair of newlyweds, Laurence Woolman and his wife, Janet, who had been sent by Breasted.

Laurence Woolman was a twenty-five-year-old architect with both an undergraduate degree and a master's degree from the University of Pennsylvania. At six feet one, he barely fit into the bed provided for them at Megiddo, according to Janet.[36] (This was also a problem for both Lind and Lamon, who were of similar height.) He also had no archaeological training, and neither he nor Janet had ever been out of the United States before.

Much of the Megiddo correspondence in the Oriental Institute archives that dates from May 1929 deals with Woolman's selection as a new member of the team. In part, this was because of a new policy being instituted by the Oriental Institute. Breasted had traveled around the United States, auditioning architects for potential positions on the Oriental Institute excavations in Egypt, Iraq, and Turkey, in addition to Megiddo. Woolman had been selected for Megiddo, although Guy, of course, was not keen on the idea by any means.[37]

After initial strong protests that he didn't need an additional draftsman, since Lamon intended to come back in September after finishing his coursework at Chicago, Guy reluctantly gave in.[38] He probably would have put up much more of a fight had he realized that Woolman, who was single at the time that he was offered and accepted the position, was scheduled to get married just a week before leaving the United States for British Mandate Palestine in late August,[39] and that this would mean hosting yet another set of newlyweds in the Megiddo dig house.

Guy actually didn't have much choice in the matter, as usual, but at least this time Charles Breasted took the time to tepidly apologize: "I hope you will not feel that the new man . . . is being inflicted upon you against your wishes" (which of course he was). He continued, "In sending him to you, the Director is not only giving you an exceptionally able man who will unquestionably be of the greatest assistance to you, but he is hoping to afford an archeological training to men of sound architectural preparation." He also explained further that this was a new policy on the part of the institute, and that two other young architects were being sent to join the team working at Luxor in Egypt, another was being sent to the team in Iraq, and yet another to the team in Turkey. And, as he concluded, returning to Woolman specifically, "His drafting ability is only incidental, but even at this he excels any one at present on your staff."[40]

Knowing Guy as we do, this was hardly the way to endear the new man to him, but perhaps by this time he was getting a bit more used to such orders—and new staff members—sent by the Breasteds. He replied in late

May with a cable stating that Woolman should plan to arrive by mid-September at the latest; it was not until July that he was informed there would be two Woolmans rather than one.[41]

The Woolmans set sail for British Mandate Palestine on 24 August, just as news was reaching the United States of a riot that had broken out in Jerusalem and rapidly spread to Haifa, Hebron, Safed, and elsewhere. Cables exchanged between the Breasteds in Chicago, Guy in London, and those back at Megiddo (Parker, Shipton, and Lind) confirmed that all was well at the site, and that the British police forces were checking in on them from time to time.[42]

The riots, which lasted from 23 to 29 August, began in Jerusalem over a question of access to the Wailing (Western) Wall by the Temple Mount, but quickly spread throughout the country. More than 130 Jews and nearly as many Arabs were killed, with close to 500 additional people injured during the week of rioting. A British inquiry set up in the aftermath, known as the Shaw Commission, concluded that the situation had been exacerbated by Arab fears of the ever-increasing number of Jewish immigrants into the country and what this might portend for the future.[43] In the meantime, Parker, who had been kept busy fetching supplies from Haifa on and off during the entire period, enlisted in the Military Police and began carrying a gun at all times.[44]

By the time the Woolmans arrived in Haifa on 17 September, the riots were long over, but the wounds and scars were still fresh. Parker picked the couple up at the train station when they arrived. The drive to the dig house at Megiddo took hours over the potholed road that once again needed work. Throughout, Parker held forth on the "troubles" that had just boiled over, blaming everything on the Jews and pitying the Arabs, who were blameless, he said. The monologue continued at the dining table, where Shipton joined them for supper. "The Jew is to blame," Woolman wrote the next day, in a letter to his parents. "They have antagonized the Arabs. All told, about 300 were killed and the newspaper stories you read of the poor persecuted Jew were all Jewish propaganda. All this business was premeditated and planned by them. . . . Mr. Parker told us the whole story last evening and it is a big mess to handle."[45]

It is, frankly, astonishing to read these words, written by someone who hadn't been in the country for even twenty-four hours and who hadn't yet met any of the locals—Jews or Arabs—except for those employed at the dig house. Woolman's subsequent letters home over the next few days, and even some thereafter, contained additional diatribes against the local Jews, whom he called "a lousy race" and the "scum of the earth" on more than one occasion. He also frequently protested the general treatment of the Arabs.[46] However, Woolman's son David, writing his own memoir of his parents, attributes these perspectives to the initial influence of Parker, and he is most likely correct.[47]

Anti-Semitism had always been present at Megiddo to some degree, as mentioned above, including DeLoach's letter of two years earlier, in June 1927, in which he described the workmen's perception of Guy being "half Jewish," but now it seems to have festered and grown more poisonous. While it is difficult to point fingers nearly a century later, the increasing anti-Semitism at the site appears to have been specifically fomented and encouraged by Parker. He seems to have been pretty fervent as well as vocal in his opinions, but he was hardly alone in the country, for many of the British Mandate government administrators seem to have felt much the same way.

In any event, just two days after the Woolmans had settled in, both the Stapleses and the DeLoaches arrived from Trieste, having spent their summers in Europe. Lind had arrived during the day in between, so the dig house was now almost full.

The Woolmans were both rather amused at the daily dining schedule. They reported that breakfast was at 8:30 a.m., followed by tea at 11:00 a.m., then lunch at 12:30 p.m., with more tea at 4:30 p.m., and then finally dinner at 8:00 pm. Woolman eventually decided that the amount of tea they were required to drink was "a nuisance, really," but that it would be an insult if they did not drink it. He also complained that the day was broken up so much by the meals and tea that they worked only five and a half hours each day, which he considered to be a joke. By early October, he had reached the conclusion that these were the most peculiar hours that he had ever worked, and that it was not surprising that nothing ever got done.[48]

P.L.O. and Yemima Guy had been scheduled to return to Megiddo from London on 12 September, but his mother died unexpectedly as they were heading for the ship.[49] As a result, they did not arrive until 3 October, well after all of the others. Coincidentally, they joined up with Lamon in Trieste, when he was returning from his stay in Chicago for his coursework, and sailed together with him back to British Mandate Palestine.

It is clear, from the letters sent back home by Woolman, that during those weeks before the Guys arrived, there was very little for him to do, and very little work done by anyone, apart from more surface cleaning on the tell.[50] It is also clear that a viper's nest of anti-Semitism was now omnipresent in the house, pulling apart the supposed "congenial" members of the team. By this time, there had been more than two weeks of unabashed criticism and condemnation of the local Jews by Parker and others during the Guys' prolonged absence, and the damage to the conviviality of the team lasted for the remainder of that season, and probably beyond.[51]

Of course, as Woolman also noted, "Mrs. Guy is a Jewess and all this anti-Jewish talk about the house will stop when they arrive."[52] On that point, he was quite correct, for within three days of the Guys' return, Woolman said: "All anti-Jewish conversation about the house has ceased now that the Guy's [sic] have returned. It is quite funny too as everyone is so careful of what they say. It is rather awkward at times."[53] That may have been somewhat of an understatement.

However, it is also interesting to see how the bloom came off the rose, for it was not long before Woolman became less enamored of Parker. By early November, he was describing Parker as "a cantankerous individual who is continually putting his fingers in the pie and making himself disagreeable. . . . He is absolutely impossible to work harmoniously with and has an intelligence which is limited to pounds and piasters."[54]

As soon as the Guys finally arrived at Megiddo, they ordered that preparations be made for the remodeling of the dig house, because of the increased number of team members now present. When the partition between the dining room and library was taken down, in order to make more room at the dinner table, they found a note tucked in between the boards, which read, "By golly, Mister, you'll tear down this house." Suspicion naturally fell upon the long-departed Higgins, but it was never clear who had left it.[55]

Within a week, Guy was able to report to Breasted that they had begun to dig again up on the mound, as well as continuing to clear the top of the mound in their new area. He also put both Lind and Woolman to work constructing a 1:50 model of the stables that they had found, which would ultimately be sent to Chicago after it was completed. We should note that he had previously suggested to Charles Breasted that they should send a portion of one of the actual stables to Chicago, to be displayed at the World's Fair scheduled for 1933, but that never came to fruition.[56]

Guy also sent the bad news that malaria had struck the local laborers with a vengeance, as well as some of the Egyptian workmen, because of heavy rains earlier in the year.[57] However, there was no mention at all of unrest among the team members or anti-Semitic comments at the dining table, because those had all immediately ceased with the return of the Guys, as Woolman had noted.

Woolman also reported intermittently throughout the fall regarding work on the model of the stables. He described it as "mostly imagination," but said that they would use the results of the excavation to help in making it, since they could discern the actual plan, stalls, mangers, and hitching posts still in situ on the mound. It was difficult work, he said; they were attempting to construct it using potter's clay with a plaster of paris base on a wooden frame. He was also pessimistic, saying that the final result would probably not be very imposing, but that it would be valuable insofar as it would satisfy "to a certain extent the curiosity of those who wonder what kind of a building he [Solomon] kept the horses in."

On the other hand, Woolman had a marvelous time discussing the proposed model with Leonard Woolley, who visited them on 22–23 October, while on his way to his own excavations at Ur in Iraq. Woolley was still digging in the cemetery where he had some years earlier discovered the famous "Death Pits of Ur" with their treasures (now split between the British Museum and the University Museum at the University of Pennsylvania), and the Megiddo team members were undoubtedly enthralled by his stories.[58]

"Black Tuesday," 29 October, came and went at the dig, with no hint that anything traumatic had happened anywhere in the world. However, the crash of the stock market that day in the United States marked the beginning of the Great Depression, which would have a dramatic impact on the excavation in the coming years. Of more immediate impact, quite honestly, was Janet Woolman's twenty-second birthday on 11 November, which everyone helped her to celebrate. We have to remember just how young some of these Megiddo people were at the time. Janet wasn't the youngest, though; that honor went to Flo DeLoach, who was two years younger. Today that is the age of our typical college volunteer at Megiddo, rather than the staff members and their wives.

Woolman also noted at the time just how bad the road to Haifa was once again. The dirt that had been layered over the stone foundation of the road had by now been "pulverized to dust," as he put it, and so they were literally driving on rock. It was also maintained by prison laborers, who had neither inclination nor incentive to work quickly. This affected the archaeologists on a weekly basis, of course, since they frequently went to Haifa on the weekends, but it also affected any visitors that they might have. By December, the road was again virtually impassable, despite the work done on it before the Great Royal Visit back in March.[59]

In the meantime, Charles Breasted came through on a flying visit from 17 to 20 November, stopping by Megiddo and Jerusalem while en route from Beirut to Cairo.[60] Woolman was pleased by the visit, because it represented an opportunity to talk with the "Chicago people" about the specifics of the expansion to be made to the dig house. He had begun working on the plans back in early October, and by later that month the stones for the foundation were being cut, but other than that, he hadn't been able to make much headway.

Because of the visit, major changes were made to the plans, which kept Woolman busy for a few more weeks. As he described it, "Charles Breasted's visit was like a tornado descending upon us and as a consequence there is much to be done around here in the way of improvements. A tennis court will be made, a new water system will be installed, and the electric voltage is to be increased so that the ladies can have a sewing machine and use their electrical equipment."[61]

It was a good thing that Woolman was working on the renovations to the dig house, because Guy had been absolutely correct during his correspondence with Charles Breasted the previous May. They really did not need Woolman at Megiddo, especially since Lamon had returned at almost the same time as the Woolmans had arrived. Remember that Woolman had been foisted upon them from Chicago, albeit with the best of intentions—to give him architectural training in the field—but in actuality there was very little for him to do at Megiddo. There was not much for the others to do either, Woolman said; at one point, in mid-October, he reported that they had enough excavation staff to oversee three hundred laborers but that there were only one hundred available, so the digging was going very slowly.[62]

There was even less to do for Janet Woolman, who must have been bored out of her mind, along with the other young newlywed, Flo DeLoach. They helped each other learn French, knitted sweaters, and whiled away endless days, going from breakfast to tea to lunch to tea to supper . . . and then learning how to play bridge in the evenings.[63] She also kept busy by writing dozens of letters, as did Woolman, and by maintaining a diary.

The entries in Janet Woolman's diary and the letters that they both sent home paint a picture of daily life at the dig and provide a window into what it was like at Megiddo for them. According to her, Mrs. Staples was kind and amiable, but Dr. Staples craved arguments. Guy was an "Oxford" type, affected, but courteous, while Yemima Guy was small, blond, and comely, but "pleasing in manner"—together they are "right interesting types."[64]

Woolman tells a similar story when writing home to his parents. His first impression of the Stapleses and DeLoaches, upon their arrival from Trieste, is that they seemed to be "very congenial, both men and women," and that he thought they would get along harmoniously, as he put it. He described Lind as talkative, a good-natured sort, with a good sense of humor.[65]

They continued to get along with the Stapleses and DeLoaches, eventually playing bridge with the Stapleses after dinner on many evenings throughout the fall,[66] but Woolman grew less and less enamored of both Mr. and Mrs. Guy as the weeks went by. In one letter home, he describes Guy as being "conceited and set in his ways." In another, he wrote: "The Guys are peculiar people. Guy is rather effeminate, extremely conceited and self-centered. He treats us all like school children and as a result there is a great deal of dissension in the camp. Nobody gets credit for what they do." He also grew impatient, writing at one point: "It is disgusting sometimes the way things are managed here, a complete lack of organization. But I am not the Field director and hence will let the business ride and make the most of it."[67]

Janet Woolman also provides us with another description of the dig house. It was built, she said, of brownish stone, with lots of windows, green shutters, and a red tile roof. There was a garden with geraniums and palms, "so it is right colorful." Inside, she noted, the floors were simple rough planks and the walls just "plaster and boarding." However, it was comfortably furnished and had all sorts of conveniences (including showers and bathtubs). There was also a big lounge in which they gathered during off-hours and downtime. She said that their own room faced the tell and also looked over the garden; we know that the rooms on the other side of the house had a marvelous view across the Jezreel Valley. Woolman added the fact that the flower garden went all around the house; he knew that there were geraniums and roses, but wasn't certain about the identification of the other plants and flowers.[68]

There were also, she said, six servants—three men and three women—all of them locals. He said there were actually more—two waiters, two kitchen boys, a cook, four cleaning ladies, and a general caretaker, all either Arab or Russian. He noted that the Arabs did the kitchen work, "cooking and serving, carrying water, shining shoes," while the Russian women did the housework, "making beds, cleaning rooms, laundry work." The waiters, he said, "wear white robes, a red band around their stomach, and a fez, like Shriners."[69]

The Woolmans' letters also shed light on their weekend excursions to Haifa, where they eventually joined the Palestine Railway Club, at the urging of Harry Parker. It gave them a place to go when they were in Haifa for the day, with tennis courts, pool tables, magazines, and dances. Originally, he thought that it cost only $1 per year to join, though it turned out to actually be $5.20.[70]

Back at the dig house, they received the *London Times* and the *Egyptian Gazette*, Woolman said, and were looking forward to receiving the *Christian Science Monitor* when his parents arranged for it (note that this was in addition to the expedition's subscriptions to *Scientific American*, *Century*, and *Atlantic Monthly*, which were paid for back in Chicago).[71] As for exercise, they played deck tennis, on a court just one-third the size of a tennis court; apparently they were all familiar with this game since it had originated as a sport on the ships that they took to and from the United States. It gave them a good workout, according to Woolman, but they were happy to hear that Charles Breasted had confirmed that the full-sized tennis court should be built.[72]

They also began taking walks during the afternoons and on the weekends, in the vicinity of Megiddo. One day in late September, they went to visit the ruins left by the Roman legions when they were stationed in the area. Woolman noted that it was only a thirty-minute walk, and that there were remains of Roman tombs and what he described as an amphitheater. He later elaborated, saying that the amphitheater had disintegrated "into practically nothing," but that there were still stones present and that the hollow in the side of the hill was "so symmetrical that you can tell what it was."[73] The scenery was gorgeous, he added. Although they could never see the actual sunset, since it was behind a hill, "the reflections on distant hills and the sky and clouds is indescribable, like a dream, such soft and warm color, purples, greens, browns and reds all softened to a grayish tone like an artist's conception of the ideal."[74]

And, once it started raining every day, the valley looked like a large lake early in the morning, since the mist was always very thick and settled low on the ground. It is, Woolman said, "a gorgeous sight."[75] With the coming of the rain, the hills and fields began to bloom. He waxed poetic about it: "The country is gorgeous now. The colors of the landscapes are indescribable. The fields are becoming greener and greener. We can see storms coming miles away across the plain and they cause many fantastic effects together with the clouds such that you can't imagine. If an artist should paint such a picture you would not believe it."[76]

However, as he noted, their walks also took them through the local villages. He was less than impressed with these, writing: "You should see the dirty places these natives live in, some in tents (Bedouins), wandering Arabs, some in mud clay houses, no roofs and lousy dirty and so poor and ill kept. You wonder that here 3000 years ago our civilization received its beginning and it is said that they lived far better in King Solomon's time than they do now."[77] He also observed that "in the country away from the towns there has been no progression since biblical times. The people are very primitive . . . [and] remain uneducated, backward. . . . At present, they are like animals, slightly advanced like people of the Bronze Age 7000 years ago."[78]

One day, in mid-December, the Woolmans went for a walk with the Stapleses around the tell and through the village of Lejjun, to the outlet of the Wadi Ara pass, though which both Thutmose III and General Allenby with their armies had passed, though thirty-four hundred years apart. Woolman was horrified by what he saw in Lejjun, writing home: "That is where our laborers on the tell come from. It is a purely Arab village and the houses are ramshackles [*sic*] and falling to pieces. Such hovels these people live in. Dead dogs were lying in the streets, blood stains where a cow had been slaughtered, and for sanitary facilities they don't even resort to the 'Specialist.' The rain washes away their houses bit by bit and when it stops they get out with their mud plaster and patch up the damage."[79]

The digging season ended for the year on 28 November, no more than a week or so after Charles Breasted's visit. The Egyptian workmen were allowed to return home on 1 December. As Guy proudly noted, the team had put in 185 days of work that year, as compared to 143 the previous year, when he had just taken over and they had a shortened season.[80]

With the season over, they all left for their vacations in late December. The Woolmans went to Egypt, along with the DeLoaches, who were heading for Luxor. The Stapleses went to Beirut. The Guys went to Port Said. The others scattered. They weren't gone very long, however, for by 30 December, the Woolmans were back at Megiddo. Though Woolman told his parents, "We hated to come back," they were glad to sit down and relax with the bundles of letters as well as the newspapers and magazines that had arrived in their absence.[81]

However, even the brief vacation that everyone had taken over the Christmas holidays didn't help much, for by this point the congeniality that Guy professed to see in his team had dissipated. Actually, the team members themselves all got along; it was Guy with whom they were no longer enchanted.

Woolman minced no words in writing home on the first day of the new year. "Guy is a dawdler and does not care to hurry," he told his parents. "You have him well sized up when you asked if he guarded well his own interests. He is very careful, afraid of making a mistake."[82] He elaborated a few weeks later, writing in mid-February:[83]

> He [Guy] is a stubborn Englishman and seems to be getting away with murder but it is not for us to judge but to do our work and cooperate for the interests of the Oriental Institute. It is for them to learn the truth about this man. There is much to be said but it would accomplish nothing. I am hoping to get my work finished up so we can be sent to Luxor next year. There is some pushing to be done tho in the next three months and that <u>spirit</u> is entirely lacking in this expedition. When you drink tea 3 times a day you can understand why little is accomplished.

He hadn't changed his mind by early March, writing, "Guy is timid, so afraid of making a false step and too willing to take a slow pace."[84]

More than anything else, it was the situation of the DeLoaches that consumed Charles Breasted, Guy, and others, including the Woolmans, during the early months of 1930. In late January, Guy sent a cable to Charles that read: "THE LADY REJOINS HER FAMILY SHORTLY STOP DOES THIS AFFECT DECISION STOP UNDER CIRCUMSTANCES AM PREPARED TO BE ADMONITORY BUT MERCIFUL." To any telegraph operator transmitting the message, or anyone other than the two correspondents, it might as well have been in code, but obviously they both knew what it meant. Charles replied on the same day, as part of a longer cable: "WE HAVE BEEN ADMONITORY BUT MERCIFUL SINCE FIRST EMPLOYING HIM MY DEFINITE REACTION UNCHANGED SINCE OUR DISCUSSION BUT PREFER LEAVE FINAL DECISION YOUR HANDS."[85]

Now, almost ninety years later and with additional information from others present at the time, we are able to figure out a portion of the story, but even so, not everything is yet clear. We know, for instance, that "the lady" can only have been Flo DeLoach and the "him" whom they were employing can only have been Ed DeLoach, for there is no other couple that matches this description. We have seen already that these two were figuratively in the doghouse with the Megiddo administration by this point, because of their sudden marriage, which had taken everyone by surprise.

We can also figure out the meaning of "The lady rejoins her family shortly," but it remains a mystery how Guy would have known that already in late January, for it was not until the first week in March that Woolman wrote home with the news that the DeLoaches would be leaving in a few days. According to him, Flo had found out she was pregnant and therefore they had decided to return home, in part so that the baby would be born in America, and in part because there was no room in the dig house for a new mother and baby; they would have had to live separately from the others. As he put it, "No one here knows of it except us. Janet has been Mrs. DeLoaches' confidant more or less and we knew of it from the beginning, which was discovered when she was examined by a doctor while in Beirut."[86]

But, as Woolman also noted, there was a question in his mind about whether DeLoach had actually been quietly fired by Guy. As Woolman put it initially, "Whether he [DeLoach] received the skids here or not we don't know but it was evident that conditions around here were none too pleasant for them." He later added, "The truth of his leaving is not exactly known, but I am of the impression that he was not in good standing with the Oriental Institute more or less, because of personal reasons." His final statement on the matter indicates that he was certain by then that DeLoach had been let go; he claimed not to understand why, but was certain that "DeLoach was not given a square deal."[87]

The DeLoaches broke the news of their impending departure to the rest of the team just five days before leaving. It was a momentous declaration, for it meant that the last remaining member of the original team from 1925 was leaving the project.

On 10 March, they boarded the RMS *Mauretania*, known as the "Grand Old Lady of the Atlantic,"[88] when it stopped for the day in the harbor of Haifa, and then headed for home. The Woolmans came to see them off, even going so far as to accompany them on board; Janet said later: "We surely wanted to stay on that boat—only 20 dollars to N.Y. second class, too. Well, we may be next, who knows."[89]

Olof Lind was also crestfallen that they had left. They would not lose touch with him, however, for eventually he came to live with them and served as the caretaker for Ed's father, first in Texas and then in Georgia.[90]

Both Guy and Charles Breasted were undoubtedly pleased at this sudden turn of events. Almost a week after the DeLoaches' departure, Guy sent a cable to Charles, saying that they had left and that he was optimistic this would speed up the surveying, though he didn't say why or how.[91] However, when the DeLoaches arrived in Chicago, James Henry Breasted was supposedly caught completely by surprise, for he "knew nothing of their departure from Megiddo," according to Woolman, who concluded, "It looks like a queer business all the way then."[92]

It may be that everything had been orchestrated by Guy and Charles Breasted, but it also could be that James Henry Breasted was not as unaware as he professed, for we can see a pattern here of targeted firings over the years. First it was Higgins, who was targeted and then fired by Breasted in 1925/26. Then it was Fisher, who was targeted and then fired by Breasted in early 1927. Now it was DeLoach who was targeted beginning right after his marriage in April 1929 and quite possibly fired just before leaving in March 1930. We will run across this again in future seasons, until eventually Guy himself was targeted and then fired in 1934, hoist with his own petard.

The digging season finally began in late March, two weeks after the DeLoaches' sudden departure.[93] By that time, Woolman was able to report that he expected to be done with the model of the stables within the month.[94]

Regarding the new additions to the house, he had earlier said in letters sent home in late February that his plans called for a total of twelve new rooms, including five bedrooms, two baths, a new dining room, and a new layout for the kitchen.[95] Now, a month later, he was able to confirm this, stating: "The new addition has two baths, one for Mr. and Mrs. Guy, a private one, and one for the others. There are four other bedrooms in the addition and a library. Guys have two rooms and a bath. And there is also plenty of closet space. The floors are to be of tile upon concrete and the ceiling as high as possible so as to make it cool in summer. They are about 17 feet high."[96]

What is perhaps most surprising, however, is a single sentence that Woolman included in his letter home: "We do not expect Dr. Breasted this year but I hope he does get out here soon as I have never met him."[97] Charles Breasted came through instead, once again on a flying visit, staying for less than twenty-four hours on 11 April. He gave his final stamp of approval to all of the proposed renovations, though a subsequent cable that he sent from Chicago in mid-May made it clear that the expenses were beginning to mount up and could not go any higher. In fact, he specifically said in the cable, and in a follow-up letter, that he needed to stress the necessity of employing "exceptionally strict" economic measures during the next few seasons. Clearly the Great Depression was already beginning to have some impact on the Oriental Institute and its endeavors, both at home and overseas. Ironically, he was at pains to say, "Please note in this connection that we shall regard a new tennis court as a necessity and not a luxury."[98]

Overall, the letters and cables exchanged during this year (1930) are far more concerned with personnel matters and the new addition to the house than they are with details of the actual excavations. For instance, throughout the season, Staples continuously pushed for various raises, travel arrangements, and even support for his application to be the new director of the American School of Oriental Research in Jerusalem, a position that was about to become vacant. To all of these, both Breasteds replied negatively, especially since Staples was Canadian, but reiterated that they would like him to continue at Megiddo for three or even four more years. In response, Staples said that he would be happy to serve in whatever capacity they needed him, but that he trusted it would be with an increase in his annual stipend at some point.[99] As it happened, the appointment to the American School did not come to pass, and Staples stayed for only one more season at Megiddo, leaving for good in July 1931.[100]

Guy also asked for a salary raise for himself, as well as a salary for his wife. The two Breasteds again pushed back immediately: it was absolutely out of the question to give Mrs. Guy a salary, Breasted said in mid-January, because of the precedent that it would set, not to mention the optics of a salary line for the director's wife in the annual budget. Instead, they would give Guy himself a small raise.[101]

In addition, Charles Breasted said at the end of May, they could offer Guy a five-year contract renewal at a total salary of $6,000 per year. Would he take it? Charles appealed specifically to Guy's sense of taking part in an expedition of tremendous scientific importance: "We are all engaged in this campaign because we are devoted to science. . . . There has gradually grown up among the members of the Oriental Institute a fine sense of fellowship in this great scientific Crusade to which we are devoting our lives, and I have been convinced from the beginning that you share in this feeling, not least because it is so broadly human and transcends the boundaries of nationality." However, the offer letter went astray, and Guy didn't receive it until early October, leaving Charles to wonder for several months whether his message had been heeded. They finally resolved the matter and Guy signed on for another five years.[102]

Also toward the end of May, the Oriental Institute sent out a bulletin with information for the next year, which stated that the Woolmans would be relocated to the Chicago dig in Luxor. Woolman expressed relief, writing home: "The profession called archaeology does not appeal to me in any way and I have been most fortunate here at Megiddo in not having to indulge in it to a great extent. The type of architecture they are unearthing here is totally barren of charm and impressiveness."[103]

In mid-June, a number of the Megiddo excavators went to Jerusalem, to attend a ceremony for the laying of the foundation stone for the new Palestine Archaeological Museum. Its construction was being underwritten by John D. Rockefeller, Jr., at the urging of Breasted. Guy sent Breasted a cable afterward, with the news that the ceremony had been successful.[104]

Breasted had provided remarks for the ceremony, which included several prescient phrases. He viewed the building as something more than what is usually denoted by "museum," for he suggested that it would also serve as the headquarters for the Department of Antiquities, house a library of archaeological books, and host lectures in a theater-like setting. All of these functions, along with the exhibition galleries, "will be the means whereby archaeological knowledge will be made accessible or will be distributed to the Public and to students."[105] Breasted's words have held true up to the present day, for the headquarters of the Israel Antiquities Authority (IAA) are still in the building, as are the galleries and other public spaces; they are only now—nearly ninety years later—being moved into new facilities in West Jerusalem.

Ten days later, the Woolmans left Megiddo, on 29 June, at the end of the first half of the season. They did not return to the region until they were en route to Luxor for the beginning of the season there in early October, but they did stop by Megiddo at that point.[106] They met the new members of the team, who had joined for the fall portion of the 1930 season. There were two, Dudley W. Phillips and Robert M. Engberg, plus their wives.

Although Phillips had been taking classes in Egyptian hieroglyphics and Oriental history while at the University of Chicago on a fellowship, he had previously been a student at University College in South Wales, Cardiff. There he had taken courses from the well-known British archaeologist Sir Cyril Fox, who was the keeper of archaeology at the National Museum of Wales. As an undergraduate and after his graduation in 1928, Phillips had done survey work with Fox, following a series of earthen banks and ditches across Mercia. These were known collectively as Offa's Dyke, a construction that dated to the seventh and eighth centuries CE. Fox described him as a "good companion," noting that his "fiddle always accompanied him on these expeditions, and his talk, interlarded with appropriate music (either invented or drawn from memory) will be remembered, I am sure, in many an inn parlour on the Welsh border till our generation passes away."[107]

Although the British connection and the fact that Phillips was big and strong were appealing to Guy, Charles Breasted warned him ahead of time that, although Phillips was "of sterling qualities and exceptional intelligence," he was also young. He was just twenty-four years old and had a tendency to be overly critical, particularly of Americans. Charles's precise words were that Phillips was "perhaps inclined to be a little blunt and tactless." He also noted that Phillips usually thought of himself first and the team second. And, just to make matters even less palatable to Guy, Charles warned him that Phillips was engaged to a Frenchwoman, and that they would probably get married beforehand and come to Megiddo together (as indeed they did).[108] As it turned out, Phillips and his wife were at Megiddo

Fig. 23. Engberg excavating skeletons (courtesy of the Oriental Institute of the University of Chicago)

for only just over three months, from early October 1930 until he was suddenly fired in mid-January 1931.[109]

However, the other new team member, Robert M. Engberg, and his wife, Irene, stayed for the next four years. Engberg had graduated from the University of Chicago in 1928 and then done postgraduate work there in both anthropology and American archaeology from 1928 to 1930. He was sent out by Breasted to replace DeLoach as the topographic assistant. He proved to be an essential member of the expedition before leaving in June 1934, in order to head back to Chicago for a fellowship at the Oriental Institute and to serve as a research assistant and instructor. He later finished up his PhD in 1937, with a dissertation written on the Hyksos.[110]

Engberg also published the very first volume to appear from the expedition, a study of the Chalcolithic and Early Bronze Age pottery from the site, which he coauthored with Shipton (1934). He also contributed a chapter to Herbert May's book on the cult remains at Megiddo (1935) and helped Guy to finally publish the Megiddo tombs (1938), as well as eventually writing two accessible overview articles that appeared after the excavation had ended

(1940, 1941). In short, although they lost DeLoach, by gaining Engberg as his replacement the expedition found someone who would be instrumental in helping to publish their results.

By early October, everyone was in place and the dig resumed. Breasted, Guy, and Staples were in communication throughout the fall, concerned with the manuscript that would become the second preliminary report, on the 1927–29 seasons of excavations, which included a chapter by Staples on an inscribed scaraboid that they had found. It would eventually see the light of day the following year, in 1931, but not without a certain amount of hair pulling and teeth gnashing, for Breasted did not like Guy's paragraphs on the geological background of human development and liked Staples's contribution even less.

Guy accepted the criticism in fairly good spirits and suggested that the entire section on geology should be cut, though they eventually reached a compromise regarding the material.[111] However, Staples's section took quite a bit more thought. Breasted and the editors completely reworked it back in Chicago since the scholars there totally disagreed with Staples's analysis. In fact, they had rewritten it so much that, as the editorial secretary told Staples, "the conclusion to which your article now leads is quite different from its former one."[112]

A final letter, which Guy sent on the last day of the year, contained only details about the newly completed quarters in the dig house. These allowed everyone much more room, including larger bedrooms for each of the married couples—the Stapleses, Phillips, and Guys—as well as for the bachelors, who had taken over the upstairs rooms of the original house. They had also been making new purchases, including wicker furniture and other tables and chairs, but were holding off on new curtains and carpets until Charles Breasted's imminent arrival, which was to take place early in the new year.[113]

Considering the dearth of discoveries that season, it is especially ironic that in late December, during the winter break, Guy was told to start using a codebook when sending cables to Chicago. He was specifically instructed to purchase something called *Bentley's Complete Phrase Code*, which had been published in 1923 and was currently in its eighth reprint. It was already in use by those in the Chicago office, by the OI archaeologists at Luxor in Egypt, and by Charles Breasted while he was traveling, or so Guy was informed. Rather apologetically, he was also told, "Since this code was devised for business communication, it lacks archaeological and scientific words and phrases, as well as many other terms peculiar to our field. At the end of the code book will be found a supplement of over 2000 blank symbols. A list of words and phrases is being compiled in Chicago for use in connection with the supplement. This office will be glad to receive suggestions for this private supplement. A copy of the list will be forwarded to you as soon as it is prepared."[114] In fact, although the codebook was used only sparingly rather than for every cable, the news of some of the momentous discoveries and events at the site that still lay in the future would indeed be sent in code.

As per usual during the "Guy years," much of 1931 was consumed with personnel matters, although that was also the year that they discovered the water tunnel, as we shall see. First and foremost, Phillips, who had arrived just the previous October, apparently lived up to all of the dire warnings that Charles Breasted had relayed to Guy before his arrival. We are not provided with details of what happened during the last months of 1930, for the letters are suspiciously silent until January, but we then are informed that Phillips was given a stern talking-to by Charles Breasted, and then fired on the spot, during the latter's quick visit to Megiddo on the eleventh of that month. Guy also had it out with him the next day, reiterating what had been said. As a result, Phillips and his wife abruptly departed a day or so later, sailing for Europe on 14 January.[115]

As Guy later explained, he had let Phillips know in no uncertain terms that he had not been given responsible work up on the tell because he wasn't fit to tackle it; when given a project, of dealing with a group of objects from a tomb, "he had shown a good deal of inaccuracy and a lack of application, and obviously considered it beneath his dignity to draw the pottery." He had also wanted to supervise the work of other people "without himself knowing how to do it." In the end, Guy said, he had warned Phillips that he was "in acute danger of becoming, permanently, an intellectual prig." To all that, Phillips had no response in the end except to ask whether Guy would be willing to shake hands, which they did.[116] We do have to remember that Phillips was still very young, and that Guy had been given fair warning that Phillips had a tendency to be blunt, tactless, and overly critical, but nobody had told him that Phillips was also both arrogant and unwilling to do the actual work that was necessary.

No sooner had they finished dealing with Phillips than an issue arose with Staples and his wife, Ruth, who by this point had told the rest of the team that she was pregnant. Guy had mentioned it, as inside information acquired from his wife, Yemima, in a confidential letter to Breasted in early November 1930,[117] but by mid-January it was no longer a secret. Mrs. Staples had been planning to return to Canada to give birth, probably sometime in May, and then return to Megiddo with the newborn, but she had now learned that babies were not welcome at the Chicago house down in Luxor, and was worried that the same would be true at Megiddo.[118]

She was quite right in her fears, for apparently there had been yet another "decision which had been arrived at," but concerning which the Stapleses had not yet been informed. Moreover, Guy straight-out lied to them, by his own admission, telling them that the news of her pregnancy had not yet even been discussed, so they shouldn't worry about it. In fact, Guy and Charles Breasted had been conferring about it for quite some time by this point, and had floated various options, including having the Stapleses stay in Haifa, with Mr. Staples commuting to the dig. Nevertheless, the Stapleses were reassured by Guy's bald-faced lie, and so Mrs. Staples left for Canada on 31 January on the SS *Britannic*. Perhaps to make up for his duplicity, Guy wrote to the captain of the ship, arranging for Mrs Staples to be waited on hand and foot for the duration of the voyage home.[119] Of course, in hindsight, and given what happened with the Stapleses, we can now say with certainty that the DeLoaches were quite right to have left when they did, the previous year, after similarly realizing that they were about to become parents.

However, everything was fairly happily resolved when Staples announced that he was taking a position as associate professor of Semitics and Old Testament at Victoria College, part of the University of Toronto, which was his alma mater. He would be leaving the dig in July, when their spring season ended. Perhaps to his surprise, both Breasteds as well as Guy were very supportive and congratulated him.[120] Actually, they were relieved, because they had been hoping that just such a situation would materialize. The only thing that marred an otherwise happy parting, since the Stapleses never learned that they would not have been welcomed back to the dig house with a newborn, was a fight over finances and reimbursements that continued throughout the summer until it was finally resolved, with hard feelings remaining on both sides.[121]

And with that, another multiyear partnership with a member of the Megiddo team came to an end, for Staples and his wife had been part of the expedition since September 1928. All ended well for him, for he taught at Victoria College for the next thirty years, from 1932 to 1962, enjoying a stellar career as professor of Ancient and Near Eastern Studies and a good reputation as a Bible scholar. Their daughter Elizabeth, conceived at Megiddo, also graduated from the college two decades later, like her father before her.[122]

In the meantime, in order to make up for the loss of Phillips, Guy sought, and gained, permission to hire a young English surveyor named Hucklesby, for June and July. Hucklesby came highly recommended by other archaeologists, including Fisher, who was now working at Jerash (in what is now Jordan). However, as it turned out, Guy did not like Hucklesby personally, though he did good work, so Hucklesby's contract was not renewed after the initial term ran out at the end of July.[123]

Guy subsequently told the Breasteds that he needed two new people, "a genuine surveyor, who does not want to do other things, but is content to continue for some years to survey," and "a young draftsman who is prepared to continue to be a draftsman." He wanted to select these two himself, Guy said, and would seek them out in London over the summer.[124] As for a recorder for the expedition, to replace the departing Staples, who had been serving in that role, Guy didn't want anyone new; he had already told Shipton that he could have the job. As Guy told Charles Breasted, Shipton "knows the ropes, takes kindly to the job, and can be trusted to carry it out neatly and well."[125] However, as usual, the Breasteds had other ideas, and so Herbert Gordon May eventually joined the Megiddo team in October as the new recorder, much to Guy's chagrin in both the short term and the long term.

It could be said, without exaggeration, that May's tenure at Megiddo started out on the wrong foot and ended on an even worse note three years later. It began when Breasted cabled Guy in early July, and told him that May and his wife, Helen, would be joining the team. He said that May was an excellent Old Testament and Hebrew scholar, and that Mrs. May was a graduate of the Boston Art Institute and not only could draw but had actually taught drawing.[126]

Rather than simply accepting the decision, Guy fired off a cable and then a letter, stating that he needed a draftsman, not another student of Hebrew and the Old Testament (for that description had fit Staples as well). Moreover, the fact that Mrs. May could draw was irrelevant, Guy said, because all of the wives who had been at Megiddo to that point "have in the past kept out of the drafting and recording rooms." As he wrote, "I fancy this is an arrangement common to all the expeditions, and I find it a sound one."[127]

All of this back-and-forth caused a great deal of confusion for poor May and his wife, who were still back in the States, trying to arrange for passports and turning down other job opportunities that had come their way. One of May's sponsors, a professor at the University of Chicago named J.M.P. Smith, wrote to Breasted, appalled that Guy would prefer Shipton; it was he who referred to Shipton as a teenage boy who hadn't been to college.

Of course, although those statements about Shipton were true, Smith did not account for the fact that Shipton had by that point been at Megiddo for more than three years and had absorbed an incredible amount of on-the-job training. It is perhaps a good thing that Guy never saw Smith's letter, for Smith added, almost parenthetically, "I think myself that Guy ought to have a scholar alongside of him in Megiddo and May is just the type of man who ought to be there."[128]

Charles Breasted tried to reassure Guy that it would all work out. Breasted tried to do the same, explaining that May was "a very quiet, modest, and engaging fellow," while again stating that Helen was "an excellent artist." However, May himself was quite worried that his relationship with Guy was starting out awkward and strained.[129] Still, when the Mays finally arrived at Megiddo in late October, they were greeted kindly, and Guy later wrote to Charles (two separate times), saying, "I like May."[130] Unfortunately, that state of affairs did not last long.

Even Lamon was not left out of the three-ring circus that was Megiddo that year, for Guy seems to have taken aim at him as well. Guy told Breasted that there had been a number of incidents involving alcohol over the years, including one summer when Lamon had been left alone at the dig house, with only the servants to see to his needs. Now, Guy reported, he and Charles had had a chat with Lamon. Since then, Lamon had not been drinking, which Guy said was a welcome change.[131]

Perhaps as a result of all this, cables and letters were exchanged between Guy and the Breasteds concerning a transfer of Lamon to one of the other Chicago expeditions, though it is not clear at all whose idea this was—

Lamon, Guy, or the Breasteds. Regardless, the transfer didn't take place—just as DeLoach's hadn't—and it is quite likely that Lamon was never even aware of the fate that might have awaited him.[132] We can be thankful that he did not leave the expedition at that point, for he had much to contribute in the coming years.

All of these personnel sideshows, taking place as they did throughout the entire year, must have affected the team's archaeological work at Megiddo. And yet it seems that they were able to push on. Guy himself must have been buoyed by the fact that his preliminary report on the excavations from 1927 to 1929 was published early in 1931, with copies reaching British Mandate Palestine by late March.[133] It was only the second publication to come out, following Fisher's 1929 initial report.

And yet Breasted remained unsatisfied with the speed of the excavations. In late February, before the season even began, he sent a long letter to Guy in which he said that while he had complete confidence in Guy's plan to go layer by layer, mapping and then peeling off each layer in turn, he was concerned about the slow pace and the fact that, after five years of digging, they still hadn't reached "the monuments of the important age of the Egyptian Empire," by which he meant the Eighteenth and Nineteenth Dynasties, from about the time of Hatshepsut through Ramses II.[134]

He didn't want to upset the general plan of archaeological attack on the mound, Breasted said, but according to his reckoning, "we are near enough to the level of our old friend the King of Megiddo, who fought Thutmose III, to be able to reach his castle soon." He also thought that there was a good chance they might find a palace from this period located on the northern part of the mound, and perhaps even an archive of cuneiform tablets dating to the Amarna Age in the fourteenth century BCE. He also, quite unnecessarily, reminded Guy that archaeological levels are not always actually level, and suggested that the whole idea of horizontal excavation that Guy was pursuing might not be the best way forward. When he had not heard back from Guy by mid-June, Breasted sent another letter, reiterating some of these concerns and opinions.[135]

Guy, who had refrained from replying to Breasted's earlier letter, no doubt because it had infuriated him, finally replied to both of Breasted's letters in late June. In no uncertain terms, Guy let Breasted know he was going as fast as he could while maintaining proper scientific procedures. As he said,

"It is hard to explain to you on paper how very strongly I feel that we should not be tempted to abandon the stratigraphic method . . . I <u>am</u> getting down to earlier strata as fast as I can, you know." His entire plan was to get the stratification as nearly correct as possible; departing from that would invalidate everything that they had been working toward. "People are always saying that archaeology is not an exact science," he wrote. "I am doing all I can to show that more accurate results can be obtained."[136]

Guy concluded his letter by saying, "The complexity of the strata in towns like Megiddo is such that I <u>know</u> that this is the only method of getting things right, and I should be more loath to depart from it than I can tell you." Moreover, he said, there was no way to predict how far beneath their present location would be the layers dating to the Egyptian New Kingdom period—"even supposing I did dig down to look for the palace of Thutmose III, I have not the least idea of its position."[137]

Breasted hastened to reassure Guy that he had no intention of asking him to abandon the method of systematic stratigraphic clearance, level by level, that they were pursuing at Megiddo. He remained optimistic, though, that Guy "might soon find the upper portions of a royal building of the Egyptian imperial period," and if so he "could of course quite safely go down into this earlier building without disturbing your stratigraphic operations."[138]

However, Breasted turned out to be wildly off the mark in predicting that they would soon get to the layers dating to the Late Bronze Age. These turned out to be located well below, in Strata VIII and VII, and Breasted did not live to see them brought to light.

CHAPTER VIII

"The Tapping of the Pickmen"

Despite all the drama, there was actually some digging that took place from 1929 to 1931. In fact, it was in 1930 that they made their next major discovery, the famed water tunnel at Megiddo. Removing the earth that completely filled a wide shaft plunging straight down for 100 feet, and then doing the same in the connecting tunnel stretching out 150 feet more to the water source, consumed most of the team's available time, energy, manpower, money, and ingenuity. It wasn't until mid-June 1931 that Guy sent a long cable to Breasted, although he was so excited at that point that he neglected to translate it into code. It read in part:

> THE MOST REMARKABLE ANCIENT WATER SYSTEM WITH ACCESS FROM SUMMIT OF TELL THROUGH ALL STRATA TO ROCK WHERE ARE SHAFT STAIRCASE AND TUNNEL THE LAST NOT YET FULLY EXCAVATED. SWEET WATER AT DEPTH OF THIRTY-SEVEN METRES. LENGTH OF STAIRCASE BELOW SHAFT FOURTEEN METRES AND TUNNEL TODAY TWENTY-EIGHT METRES BY THREE METRES HIGH BY TWO BROAD.[1]

There was no indication that this lay in store for them when they began the 1929 excavations in mid-April, as soon as the Egyptian workmen arrived at Megiddo.[2] They were able to clear a huge amount of topsoil—some thirty thousand square meters—before taking a break in July. Even though they did not go deeper than fifteen to twenty centimeters anywhere, that nevertheless generated nearly five thousand cubic meters of dirt, stones, and other debris that had to be conveyed to the dump. As a result, quite a bit of time was devoted to laying more track for the small railway, in order to bring the excavated detritus to the chutes, down through which it would tumble to the designated area below. As Guy noted, the dump was looking neat and symmetrical at the moment and, he thought, would "form a good field for agriculture when the excavation is finished." The top of the tell also was now completely gridded, with each of the squares marked by pegs solidly in place.[3]

All of that had taken about thirty-five days to do, which brought them up to 4 June, at which point they were actually able to dig for a month before knocking off for summer vacation. Guy noted that they were able to expose another stretch of City Wall 325, along with what he thought was a level of Sub-II remains, which included a large, well-constructed building that, as he put it, "had been chopped in two by Schumacher."

Perhaps most exciting, Guy said, was the discovery of the back wall of two stable units and an indication that there might be at least four more still buried under the later ruins. They had also, he said, "laid bare the great Tyrian gateway of King Solomon," which reminded him of the gateway at Carchemish where he had dug long ago. Why he called it Solomonic and why he attributed it to "Tyrian" builders remained to be seen, but he was obviously thinking of the biblical verses concerning Hiram of Tyre and his craftsmen working on the temple in Jerusalem, just as he had cited the verses regarding Solomon's chariot cities the previous season.[4]

Even though the "Tyrian" gate was eventually reassigned by Lamon and Shipton to Stratum III and the Neo-Assyrian period, rather than to the Solomonic period in the tenth century BCE, this was an important discovery. It was the first time any of the excavators had located the main entrance to the city, in any period. During the following seasons, they would find ever-earlier versions of this city gate nearby, larger and more complex, dating right back through Stratum VIII and beyond. The configurations of these gates, and the precise periods to which each dated, along with further excavation by both Yadin and then the Tel Aviv excavators, would keep archaeologists busy and arguing for the next century, right up until today.[5] They still play a significant role in the discussions of which level at Megiddo, if any, should actually be dated to the time of Solomon.

Guy took some glee in describing the discovery of the gate to Breasted. As he put it:[6]

As to the main gate, I have always felt that it ought to be in [Square] K9, and in K9 it is. The finding of it was amusing enough. Knowing what I was after, the small indications that I got when we had cleared comparatively little surface soil were sufficient to show me that the plan was going to be like that of the South gate at Carchemish which I had helped Woolley to dig out ten years ago. I waited until I had got a few main points showing, moved the workmen to dig at places nearby for a short time, and set out the plan of the gate with strings and pegs. I then brought the men back and told them to dig for walls along the strings.

I think that some of the locals suspect me of working some kind of magic . . . particularly with regard to the door-pivot sockets: I set a couple of men to look for these, saying that they ought to find stones with holes in them. One was visible after half a dozen strokes of the hoe, and the other a few minutes later—it was rather like bringing rabbits out of a hat!

Guy then described in detail this two-chambered gate, complete with a sketch drawing on the fifth page of his letter. In further describing the excavation of an area next to it, he also hazarded a guess that the level he and Fisher had been calling Sub-II dated to the Neo-Assyrian phase. As he put it, "I have not yet enough material from Sub-II to enable me to determine its date, but I suspect it of being Assyrian."[7] He was completely correct, although when Lamon and Shipton eventually published the results of the excavations, the name of the level was changed from "Sub-II" to "III," as noted above, and so this gate is now assigned to that layer.

Guy also reported that they had unearthed the foundations of a large number of buildings that were so near the modern surface of the tell that the uppermost stones had been scratched by plowshares. Most of these he dated to his Strata II and Sub-II, since Stratum I was absent for the most part. He was impressed in particular with the plaster floors that they came across and with the "quite up-to-date sanitary arrangements" in one of the buildings.[8]

Moreover, he said that it should take no more than a month of work in the spring to finish excavating all of the upper layers across the entire mound, and that when these layers had been removed, the Solomonic city would be revealed "as a complete whole." That would be the most that he could hope to do during the upcoming 1930 season, though, even working as fast as they were able, because he wasn't at all sure how much longer it would take to get down to "Imperial Egyptian strata." However, he was confident that they would be able to present their findings at the next Oriental Congress in 1931, and that they would "be rendering a very real service to near eastern archaeology, and one that will not be forgotten."[9]

In the meantime, Guy also had been engaged since January in arranging for a shipment of thirteen cases of antiquities to be sent to Chicago. This was their portion of the 1925–26 finds from Megiddo after the (supposedly annual) division had been made with the Department of Antiquities. Finally, after many delays, they were sent in mid-May. It was expected to take two months for them to arrive in New York; after their anticipated arrival in mid-July, they would be sent on to Chicago to form the nucleus of what is now an impressive collection of Megiddo artifacts at the Oriental Institute.[10]

Aside from his putting Woolman and Lind to work making a reconstruction of the stables, one of the main innovations that Guy implemented during the season was balloon photography. In his letters back to Breasted, Guy enclosed some of the first aerial photographs that they had taken on top of the mound. In fact, these were among the first that had ever been taken in the entire region.[11]

Guy later published an article about their experimental efforts in the journal *Antiquity*, in which he explained that he had first become interested in the idea of aerial photography way back in 1904. He then reconnected with it during World War I while using air photos "in connexion with the indirect firing of machine-guns," and then again in 1922–23 while with the Palestine Department of Antiquities.[12]

They had already begun discussing the idea of using a balloon back in April 1929. At the time, Charles Breasted was not particularly keen on the idea. He sent Guy some correspondence and a brochure from the Sterling Rubber Company Limited of Canada, writing: "When you have perused this, you will be better able to judge the advisability of investing in an aeronautical department for Megiddo. My own reaction . . . is that by branching out into balloon ascensions, the Megiddo expedition runs a considerable risk of being blown into atoms. However, this again rests with you. Let us know your decision in the matter."[13]

Having evidently decided that it was worth the risk, Guy subsequently asked Lamon, when the latter was headed for America, to procure an electrical release that could be controlled from the ground to trip the camera shutter. As it turned out, the Department of Physics at the University of Chicago was able to make it for them; Guy described it as "light and simple, and it works." Lamon also brought back a small ready-made balloon that was generally used for meteorological purposes, which was lightweight and

Fig. 24. Balloon photography in Solomon's Stables (courtesy of the Oriental Institute of the University of Chicago)

cheap. In the meantime, Lind and DeLoach constructed a camera specifically for this purpose, which Guy describes as a fixed-focus camera made of three-ply wood that would hold one photographic lens and a 5″ × 7″ film holder. Several light steel wires were connected to the balloon, to hold it in place over the desired area as well as to conduct the electric current to the shutter release.[14]

They filled the balloon with hydrogen and sent it up. They were able to take two photographs on the first try, one of which was good and the other poor. However, as they were putting the balloon away in the garage, it burst with a "loudish pop." And with that, as Guy described it, "the balloon, as such, ceased to exist." He remarked that it was perhaps ironic that this had taken place on the fifth of November—Guy Fawkes Day, commemorating the infamous Gunpowder Plot of 1605 and still celebrated in England with fireworks, bonfires, and loud explosions.[15]

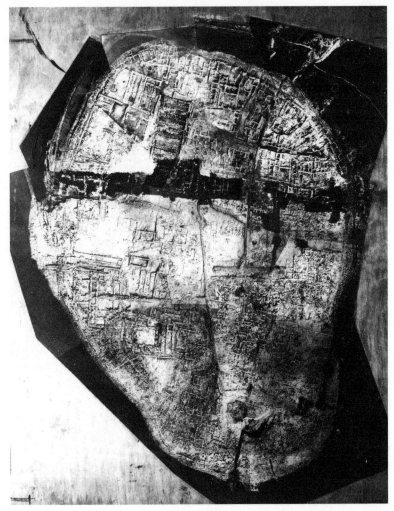

FIG. 25. The first aerial photo mosaic (view looking east) created at Megiddo (courtesy of the Oriental Institute of the University of Chicago)

The importance of this pioneering and innovative work in archaeology cannot be underestimated. It led directly to our current use of drones for taking such aerial pictures today, as well as satellite imagery and airborne LiDAR now being used to record sites that are not easily visible at ground level.[16]

We also know about this entire episode from Janet Woolman's diary as well as letters sent home by both Laurence and Janet Woolman, who were eyewitnesses. Janet confirmed that the balloon was attached to wires controlled from the ground and that a battery powered the camera—it was both complicated and expensive, she said. In her words: "It went off beautifully, took pictures, all well—but when they put the balloon into a shed for future use, bang, it burst for no good reason, wasting the hydrogen, the balloon in shreds. . . . But it could have been worse; suppose it had happened with the camera attached!"[17]

As Guy told Breasted, they had therefore taken the liberty of ordering another balloon, "this time of stouter, non-expanding material," and were hoping that it would arrive soon, so that they could take a complete set of pictures and create a photographic mosaic of the top of the tell as it was at the moment. It did, in fact, arrive soon thereafter, in mid-December, but only after they had stopped digging for the winter. Guy was also seriously considering acquiring a "kite-balloon capable of lifting a man" and made the prescient observation that aerial photography "will be a commonplace before many years are past," concluding, "I feel that the Institute might well lead the way."[18] Eventually, they were able to take aerial photos of the entire summit of the mound and created two photographic mosaics; one was sent to Chicago and the other was kept at the site. Guy also noted, by the by, that they had additionally acquired an "extensible ladder, of the type used for cleaning street lamps," which expanded to a height of nearly ten meters. They were able to use this on days when it was too windy to send up the balloon.[19]

Breasted was optimistic and buoyed by Guy's final letters of 1929. He was elated at the possibility of recovering the entire plan of Solomon's city at Megiddo and then continuing below to get to the Egyptian levels, for both of which he had been impatiently waiting. He was also pleased at the results of the innovative balloon photography and, on a different topic altogether, was curious to know whether beginning a second dump, on the western side of the mound, would speed up the excavation.[20]

Guy was also optimistic, writing back in late January 1930 with some thoughts of his own for the coming season. He didn't think beginning a second dump on the western side of the mound was a good idea, for a variety of reasons, but largely because clearing an area for it would greatly slow them down. However, he too was looking forward to exposing the entirety of what he thought was the Solomonic city, including what might be "the governor's palace" lying underneath the high ground in Squares Q8 and Q9, which he suggested could be "bigger than the great stables."[21]

Breasted also initiated what seems to have been a groundbreaking second innovation for Middle Eastern archaeology. In early February, he instructed Guy to start using the new *Munsell Book of Color*, a copy of which was sent for his use.[22] This is a system for precisely identifying colors, using a combination of hue, value (lightness), and chroma (color purity). First introduced for use in the art world, it was adopted by the Oriental Institute in 1930 for use at all of their overseas excavations as a means of describing and recording the color of the soil as they dug through it—for example, a particular shade of brown soil might be described in an excavation report as 10YR 5/3. This would allow another archaeologist to turn to the relevant page in the Munsell book (though archaeologists most likely already have the numbering system memorized and can picture the color in their mind).[23]

The Munsell color system is now used by almost all archaeological excavations around the world on a routine basis, but since the new version of the book had just appeared the previous year, in 1929, it seems possible that the Chicago teams were among the first in the world, if not actually the first, to use it in the field. The letter sent to Guy as an accompaniment to the book stated that it was being used in art schools across the nation, and that the Art Department at the University of Chicago highly recommended it. The question remains, how did it occur to Breasted to use it for archaeological purposes (or who suggested it to him)? That is not yet clear.

In any event, spring came early that year, with the rains holding off, so already by late April 1930 they had put in twenty-six days of work, clearing the southwest corner of the mound. The later strata were absent there, which meant that they could "get through more quickly to good things below."[24]

The lack of timely detailed reports about their work on the mound began to contribute to Breasted's growing frustration with Guy, although it would take four more years for that to come to a head. At the end of the year, in mid-December, Guy said he was sending a letter "with the details of the season," but it was not until the beginning of the next February, in 1931, that Guy actually got around to sending the one and only full report that he wrote to Breasted with the archaeological details of the 1930 season.[25]

However, it is in mid-May, from a diary entry made by Janet Woolman rather than a report from Guy, that we get an inkling of the most important discovery made that season. "Walked up around Tel before tea," she wrote. "The digging going ahead furiously. Curious things happening, such as a deep pit with rubble pavement at bottom and no walls found as yet."[26]

As it turned out, this was not just a "deep pit." It was a steep entrance leading down to the water tunnel that served the site for more than a thousand years, most likely from the Bronze Age until the end of the occupation of the mound. But it would take much work over the next season to realize this and excavate it fully, long after the Woolmans had left the dig.

As for the actual digging, we have as little information about the fall season as we do about the spring season earlier in the year. In one letter that Breasted received in late November, Guy wrote that they were "putting in as much digging as possible before the rains descend upon us." He reported that they had begun to move some of the latest ruins, so that the plan of everything below would be clearer. Subsequently, writing in mid-December, Guy said that they had ended on the eighth and that he was sending a separate letter on the results (which he did, but not until February, as noted). Here, he said, he would mention only that they had comparatively little in the way of small finds, but that "the whole of the tell is now laid bare . . . and there is a good deal of interesting material to be seen." He concluded, "We have shifted a tremendous amount of stuff in order to get it, and the results of the season may be said to be satisfactory without being thrilling."[27]

Guy finally sent a full report on the season's activities to Breasted in early February 1931.[28] It was a very long letter, but he actually said very little of substance in it, all of which can be boiled down to a few very specific topics or points. First, they had spent most of the season removing the rest of the surface soil across the top of the mound (what we would call "top soil" in today's terminology). He now wanted to take aerial photos of the entire area, layer by layer, but had been held back by a lack of hydrogen for the balloon, which he was hoping would arrive soon. They had also continued to dig on the East Slope of the mound, he said, with the intention of enlarging their dumping area. Furthermore, they had continued to trace an outer defensive wall in that region and even found several more tombs in the area.

Second, they had made modifications to the railway system. The principal modification had been made to the "Great Northern" line, as they called it, which used to go past the stables and across Schumacher's trench. Now it had been reconfigured to run directly from the city gate to the dump, which meant that they didn't have to use the chutes for this line. In turn, this meant that there were only two railway lines using the chutes, which eased up on the congestion that they had previously faced. In addition, by rerouting this line, they had been able to find and clear the approach road to the city gate for some distance down the side of the tell, and now they could walk on what he called the "Solomonic paving stones" of this roadway, right up to and then through the city gate.[29]

Third, he had been thinking about the final publication of the material that had been uncovered during the previous excavation seasons. He envisioned this as providing an introduction to the site and an explanation of their excavation and recording system. It would also contain a consideration of all of the material found in the surface soil as well as all of the objects that they had found in Schumacher's dumps while in the process of removing them. Practically all of the plates for the volume were ready, he said, as well as the descriptive lists of what was pictured on them, so it is certainly bewildering that Guy was not able to find time to write the accompanying text during his tenure.[30] The material was left for Lamon and Shipton to publish as part of their *Megiddo I* volume nearly a decade later, in 1939.

Finally, looking ahead to the upcoming season, Guy was optimistic that they would finish removing the Stratum II material, then turn their attention to Stratum Sub-II and remove that in turn, so that by the time of their summer break they would have their Strata III and IV completely visible all over the mound.[31] This was an ambitious plan in the extreme, and, needless to say, they didn't get anywhere close to achieving these goals during the season.

In fact, it must have been a bit disheartening and demoralizing to consider that by then there had been five full seasons (1926–30) of excavation since Fisher first arrived at the mound, and yet here they were still scrabbling about in the first few levels, which Guy admitted were extremely confusing and difficult to date. Although they must have had their suspicions, given the height of the mound, they did not yet know that there were still many more levels to excavate before they reached the earliest occupation levels of this ancient site.

In the meantime, the intriguing "deep pit with rubble pavement" about which Janet Woolman wrote in her May 1930 diary entry took over center stage as soon as they all returned for the 1931 spring season. It was in early

FIG. 26. Beginning of excavation of water system, with surface soil removed (courtesy of the Oriental Institute of the University of Chicago)

February that Guy told Breasted that they were going to continue digging out the depression that they could see by Squares P4 and Q4. He was "practically certain that this leads to the water supply."[32] They started work on Sunday, 22 March, and by mid-June he was able to send Breasted the long cable quoted above, in which he first announced the enormous dimensions of the water tunnel.

He followed it up with a letter two weeks later, which is notable both for its length (eight pages, of which nearly half were taken up with a description of excavating the tunnel) and its passion. It was the first time that Guy sounded excited about archaeology since they had found the stables several years earlier. A brief account of their findings appeared in the third revised edition of the Oriental Institute handbook later that year, as well as the following year in the newly established journal *Quarterly of the Department of Antiquities in Palestine* (*QDAP*), as part of the report that was now required each year from each ongoing excavation in the region.[33]

It seems that the depression that they had begun excavating had expanded until it measured fully thirty meters wide. It was so large that they had begun digging in Square O5 as well, where they found a stone stairway that led down into what was now clearly the top of a large shaft cut down through the occupation levels, which Guy described as funnel-shaped. The first staircase led down to a second one, which led down farther, spiraling "like a square-cut left-handed corkscrew," along the side of a shaft seven meters across that was cut through solid rock.[34]

In all, the shaft and the staircases went straight down at least 20 meters before connecting to a rock-cut tunnel that sloped down at an angle for another 14 meters; at that point, a connecting horizontal tunnel led southwest for an additional 50 meters (so, all told, about 100 feet down and another 150 feet straight out). The tunnel was 3 meters high and 2 meters wide (about 10 feet by 6 feet), allowing people standing upright to pass through it easily.[35]

At the farthest end of the tunnel was a vast chamber, Guy said, hewn out of the living rock. He was not exaggerating, for they later recorded it as seven meters high and five meters wide. In the floor of the chamber there was a large water hole, with abundant water still present at the bottom. The water, both here and in a few holes in the floor of the tunnel, was "sweet and drinkable," according to Guy. He also noted that the water was immediately replenished if they drew any of it off, so that he identified it, quite properly, as the general subterranean water table.[36]

The chamber extended for a total length of twenty-three meters, at which point the excavators uncovered a blocking wall that was almost perfectly square—four and a half meters wide and five meters high. Guy noted that this was composed of huge stones that had been put in place from the outside, and that its inner face was plastered with mud, in which the "finger-smears" of the workmen "are still plainly to be seen"—thousands of years later.[37]

Just inside the blocking wall, in an alcove up near its top, Guy thought that they had found a guard post, with a little border of stones around its front. There was an area blackened with smoke, perhaps where the guard had placed his lamp, and a big stone with a concave top where he may have sat. The guard himself was also still there, or what remained of him, for he had died at his post, according to Guy. Next to his skeleton they found the head of a fine bronze mace, but Guy said that they couldn't be certain

FIG. 27. Water tunnel (courtesy of the Oriental Institute of the University of Chicago)

whether it belonged to the guard or was part of the weapon that had caused his death.[38]

Lamon also thought that the man, who seems to have been about thirty years old at the time of his death, had been guarding the cave and the water source. He hypothesized that the guard had been the victim of a hostile attack and "met with sudden death 'with his boots on.'" Forgotten, he was

FIG. 28. Skeleton/burial of "guard" in the water system at Megiddo (courtesy of the Oriental Institute of the University of Chicago)

simply left where he fell, possibly even at an early date while access to the water was still only from the southern entrance and before the actual water system had been built to access it from inside the city.[39]

We should note, however, that cold water has recently been poured on both Guy's and Lamon's suggestions, and the story has been deep-sixed, for Anabel Zarzecki-Peleg, of Hebrew University, has recently suggested that the "guard's post" may actually be a rock-cut oval burial niche, and that the body may date to the Middle Bronze Age but was disturbed by the later activities involving the water system.[40] If so, there was no guard who died defending his post and the water system, which is much less romantic but also explains why nobody came back for his body to bury him: he was already buried! However, even this does not explain why the body was left in place in antiquity, rather than being moved, reburied, or thrown out. It is unlikely that it escaped notice during the construction and renovations of the tunnel system, the large chamber, and the blocking wall, so we are left to ponder the mystery, as happens so often in archaeology.

The large chamber also had a stairway running up one side and leading to the outside, meaning that the water had originally been accessible from the other direction as well, or perhaps initially only from that direction. This turned out to be an area located at the southern foot of the tell, as Guy later discovered. However, the blocking wall had been constructed at some point, possibly after the system had been in use for some time, so that entry (or exit) on this end was no longer possible. The only way in to the water source was now through the tunnel inside the city wall.[41] All signs of the other access point were most likely erased, so that the city would be safer in time of siege.

When this was done is unclear, though some scholars suggest that this was at a later stage in the system's history, when the inhabitants were more worried about coming under attack. However, it may have been at the same time as other modifications were made, including further work done to the floor of the tunnel so that it sloped from the large chamber down to the foot of the staircase. This allowed the water to run down the tunnel on its own and fill the vertical shaft so that it was now—for all intents and purposes—a deep well. There are some who suggest that this might have been done right away and that the entire system functioned as a large well right from the beginning, rather than having three separate stages in its history as Lamon thought, but for the moment the debate continues.[42]

Guy said that at one point he took "the gang" outside and positioned them at a point in their Square Q2 where he thought they were immediately above the blocking wall and the chamber. They dug down four meters and, sure enough, reached the outer part of the blocking wall. Jubilantly, he recorded the fact that "from inside the chamber, I have heard the tapping of the pickmen working on the outside, just as it is related in the Siloam Inscription."[43] This inscription, etched in what is now known as Hezekiah's Tunnel in Jerusalem, reads in part:

> While [the stone-cutters were wielding] the picks, each toward his co-worker, and while there were still three cubits to tunnel through, the voice of a man was heard calling out to his co-worker, because there was a fissure in the rock, running from south [to north].[44]

The excavation of this entire water system was exhilarating, as one might imagine, but also a nightmare for Guy and his team. The work was extremely difficult, as Guy noted; at one point he had a chain of ninety to a hundred men passing the newly dug earth from the working face to the surface, but the air was so foul that they could work for only a few hours at a time. It was also "pitch dark past the foot of the stairs," as he put it, and so they decided to install a permanent electrical system, taking advantage of the new 110-volt system to which they had just upgraded. This enabled them not only to have light but also to have fans that "allowed the air to remain fairly good and have made all-day work possible." This meant, though, running heavy electrical wires over a distance of half a kilometer, in order to supply the lamps and fans with the necessary electricity. They also placed railway tracks along the floor of the tunnel, which made transporting the excavation debris much faster and easier, and also cut down on the number of men who were needed in the tunnel.[45]

Parker was invaluable throughout, working "like a Trojan," according to Guy, who no doubt intended it as the highest compliment. He said that Parker invented all kinds of devices to speed up the work and make it run more smoothly, and did much of the carpentry himself. There were also very few accidents, although Reis Hamid (the headman of the Egyptian workmen) was once knocked unconscious when three waterlogged baskets were dropped on him from the top of the shaft. After that, Guy said, workmen were fined whenever they dropped something, which immediately decreased the occurrence of such incidents.[46]

In the end, Guy heaped praise upon Breasted in far-off Chicago, noting that "it is only an expedition with resources such as you have secured that could have done the job." He pointed out, with satisfaction, that Macalister had never completed the excavation of the water tunnel at Gezer, but that he (Guy) had "been determined that there should be no abandonment at Megiddo, and that wherever it led, or whatever obstacles we encountered, we would get to the end of that tunnel."[47]

Intriguingly, we still don't know when the tunnel was first built or when it went out of use. It is clear from Guy's letter to Breasted in 1931 that he thought it was originally dug very early, perhaps during the Bronze Age in the second millennium BCE, though he noted that there had been subsequent alterations, blockings, and reopenings.[48]

However, by the time Lamon published the final report on the water system, in 1935, he observed that the top part of the shaft cut through a Late Bronze Age level, and that an earlier external accessway to the water source (Gallery 629) probably dated to about 1200 BCE, so he suggested that the water tunnel system was first constructed late in the Bronze Age, approximately 1150 BCE or soon thereafter, which would correlate with the time of troubles and the collapse of the Canaanites in the Levant at that time. In a letter that he sent to Breasted a bit earlier, in mid-October 1934, just after they had finished all work in the tunnel, Lamon wrote: "According to my arguments, the water system is fairly definitely dated as having been constructed during the twelfth century, but was used at various subsequent times up to as late as the Greco-Persian period. The original 'cave well' was used before the shaft and tunnel came into existence—during the twelfth century—and probably goes right back to the earliest history of Megiddo."[49]

Yadin, however, writing in the 1960s and 1970s, thought that the construction of the water tunnel dated to Stratum IVA, which would place it during the Iron Age, in the ninth century BCE or later.[50] Many scholars still cite this date, as well as Yadin's arguments, for the construction of the water system,[51] although there have been a few alternative suggestions tweaking the various stages during its lifetime proposed in the interim. Among these is the hypothesis of Norma Franklin, an archaeologist who worked for many years at Megiddo as part of the Tel Aviv team from 1992 onward. She suggests that the system may have been first dug earlier, in the Middle Bronze Age, just as Guy had thought.[52]

In my opinion, the jury is still out. While I do not agree with Yadin and would argue that the shaft and tunnel were most likely in place by at least the twelfth century, as Lamon thought, I would also point to the recently renewed excavations at the very similar water tunnel at Gezer—the one that Macalister did not finish excavating a century ago—which seem to indicate construction in the Middle Bronze Age.[53] If so, and if the system at Megiddo was contemporary, it would mean that Guy was correct about the Middle Bronze Age origins for this one at Megiddo after all.

Guy also noted that there were bees' and wasps' nests in the roof and on the walls of the big chamber, which he thought could only have been made before the blocking wall was built. Without giving a firm basis for his thought process, he tentatively suggested that this—that is, the construction of the blocking wall, the sealing up of the entrance from the south, and the disguising of the location of the water source—would have taken place during the early part of the Iron Age. He also said that they had taken samples of these nests for an entomologist named Buxton to examine and had asked him to determine whether the particular species still existed in British Mandate Palestine. Unfortunately, we do not know the results.[54]

As for when the water system went out of use, Lamon suggested that the system might still have been in use to a certain extent through the time of Josiah, in 609 BCE—that is, during Stratum II—but wasn't sure when it finally went out of use.[55] Guy thought that he detected Hellenistic sherds among the debris in the tunnel and the large chamber. In the brief report published in the 1932 *QDAP* volume, he wrote specifically that he had found "late pottery, including a sherd of black Greek ware, low down in the shaft" of the water system. That, plus the fact that the stairway led all the way up to the surface of the tell (and was not covered over by later strata), suggested to him that the system remained in use "practically down to the latest period of occupation."[56]

Nobody else has really ventured a guess as to why and when the tunnel was finally allowed to silt up. Since water was still present and "sweet" to the taste when Guy and his team cleared out the chamber, it seems likely that the system was still technically functional right up until the end; in other words, the water had not dried up. I would suspect that the system may well have gone out of use toward the end of the Persian period and the abandonment of the site ca. 350 BCE, but it is possible that it took place earlier.

Overall, during the first half of the 1931 season, until digging stopped on 7 July, Guy's efforts were focused on clearing additional squares on the East Slope and removing the latest remains from the top of the tell, as well as working in the water system. They found a number of tombs on the East Slope, some of them apparently dating to the Early Bronze Age, including one that contained forty-eight skulls as well as many other bones. Other tombs yielded scarabs of Thutmose III and Ramses II, so it had been a successful season thus far. When he wrote to Breasted at the end of June, they had already put in eighty-three days of work, which Guy noted was more than during any other season.[57]

A week later, just one day before leaving for their summer break, Guy wrote again, telling Breasted just how much earth they had moved in the past several seasons (40,500 square meters in the last three years alone, of which 37,000 were on the top of the mound), and reiterating: "I have already spoken about getting down to the Thutmose III level in my letter of 30 June. Do please believe that I want to reach it every bit as much as you do, and it is only my knowledge of the tell, and my hatred of archaeological crimes of a type so often committed, that force me to counsel prudence."[58]

Guy planned to return from his summer break on 27 September, and the fall digging season probably began shortly thereafter.[59] However, we cannot be entirely sure, nor do we know what was discovered, for there are very few letters exchanged during the month of October and almost nothing extant from November or December. We do have a cable that Guy sent to Breasted in early December, congratulating him on the dedication of the new building in Chicago for the Oriental Institute. There was also yet another personnel issue that arose, just to put a finishing touch on the season, and so cables were exchanged on 10–11 December regarding permission for Engberg to winter in the Chicago accommodations in Luxor because of an ailment from which he eventually recovered.[60]

When we next have a letter from Guy, it is a full month later, on 10 January 1932. During the fall of 1931, they had been able to dig for much longer than usual, he said, and so the season had only just ended three days earlier. However, he included no news about what they had found, saying only that he had just finally sent his Egyptian workmen home for a well-deserved winter break.[61] Little did any of them know what yet lay in store for them later that year and into the next.

CHAPTER IX

"The Most Sordid Document"

The Megiddo expedition, and Guy's leadership in particular, began to come off the rails (through no fault of the Decauville!) during the 1932 season. The heady days of the previous season, when digging out the water system played a close second to the discovery of Solomon's Stables three years earlier, were now over. Although the team continued to uncover more stables in 1933, Breasted was so unhappy with the excavation and with the publication situation by that point that he stepped in to reorganize things personally, including ordering Guy and Yemima to move out of the dig house. Eventually, by August 1934, the ever-present personnel problems culminated in a lawsuit filed against the expedition. In addition, two staff members threatened each other physically, a young scholar was fined for smuggling antiquities, and, in the end, Guy was fired.

Virtually all of these problems revolved around three people, one of whom was Guy himself. The second was Herbert May, who had just arrived with his wife, Helen, in October 1931. As we have seen in a previous chapter, he had been sent from Chicago to replace Staples, against Guy's wishes. However, after meeting and interacting with May for a few weeks, Guy told Breasted twice in early January 1932 that he liked May, as mentioned. By July, Guy decided that May was an "admirable young man" who was easy to get along with. By that point, Guy said, he had formed "the highest opinion" of May, and his work "has been excellent in every way."[1] However, even if Guy had come around, their relationship subsequently began to sour in 1933, because of Emanuel Wilensky, the third man involved in this interpersonal tangle.

Readers will remember from an earlier chapter that Wilensky had initially worked at Megiddo for a few months during the spring of 1928 as a surveyor, when DeLoach was back in Chicago recovering from malaria (and dating his future wife, Florence). Unfortunately, Wilensky's second stint at Megiddo, from April 1932 through June 1933, was an unhappy one for all concerned, and it was he who eventually filed a lawsuit against the expedition.

But all of that lay in the future in early January of 1932. At that point, Engberg was still in Egypt, recovering from what he finally told Breasted was a bladder ailment, aggravated by chronic kidney problems that had begun in childhood. The problem persisted throughout the year, though doctors in Jerusalem eventually told him there was nothing to be done except to watch his diet, and so forth. He had, however, sufficiently recovered by the summer and was able to tour the museums of Europe with Lamon after they attended an Archaeological Congress in London along with Guy.[2]

It was also at that time, in January, that Guy began asking for permission to hire Wilensky again. He reminded Breasted that Wilensky had worked for them previously, and extolled his virtues. He noted that Wilensky had been trained as an architect, was a very good draftsman, and had worked for four years at Harvard's excavations at the site of Nuzi, in Mesopotamia. Moreover, Guy said, Wilensky could speak Arabic fluently and could "handle men." As Guy put it, "he needs no breaking-in but knows his job and can pull his weight from the first day."[3]

Guy wanted to hire Wilensky as an archaeological assistant this time, rather than as a surveyor, and said that he would put him to work up on the tell, supervising the excavation up there and sharing in writing up the field notes, since he was "a natural excavator," which none of the other team members were, at least in Guy's opinion. He planned to have Wilensky begin in April, commuting to the dig from Haifa, where he lived with his wife, since the road from Haifa to Megiddo was so improved that the journey now took less than an hour each way.[4]

Charles Breasted wasn't particularly in favor of all this, noting to his father that "Wilensky sounds well qualified—but—would we be adding another Semite?" Wilensky was indeed Jewish, a Ukrainian-born immigrant, as noted above.[5] Charles's comment to his father notwithstanding, Guy was granted permission in February to hire Wilensky in time for the start of the spring 1932 season. A three-year contract, ostensibly running through the spring of 1935, was soon signed, although a misunderstanding about a travel allowance dragged on into the fall before being cleared up.[6] However, within a year Wilensky was at odds with most of the other members of the expedition; hiring him was a decision that they would all come to regret.

There are two things to note initially from the 1932 season, both of which had lasting repercussions to differing degrees in coming years. First, there was an ongoing battle for much of the winter and spring, between Guy and the District Commissioner's Office in Haifa, over the proposed location for a new prison—described as a "labour camp"—that was to be built near Megiddo. A site had originally been picked out that was about thirteen hundred meters away from the ancient site, on the other side of what is now called "Megiddo Junction"—where the road leading to Afula crosses the road leading to Jenin.

Guy was okay with this location, but then the commissioner's office decided to move the location to a new area some five hundred meters closer to the site. Guy threw a fit and, eventually, the decision was made to build the prison at the location that had originally been chosen, primarily out of respect for the amount of money that Rockefeller, the sponsor of the dig, had invested in the country to that point, not just at the site, but also in the new museum in Jerusalem, which was just then being completed.[7] Ironically, as was discovered less than twenty years ago, the land on which the prison was built turns out to be directly on top of another ancient site, the town of Kefar 'Othnay or Caporcotani, which contains a mosaic discovered in 2005 that has the earliest occurrence of the name Jesus Christ to be found anywhere.[8]

In addition, Charles Breasted, along with other members of the family, made a highly confidential trip to Megiddo and across much of the rest of the Near East before the spring digging season began. Initially alerted to this by a series of cables, ironically not sent in code, Guy was ready and waiting in late February with an "absolutely reliable closed car with driver."[9]

From then through the first week in March, they filmed all of the activities at Megiddo and then beyond, including aerial shots, and journeying to the other OI excavation sites in Egypt, Turkey, and Iraq. Everyone got into the act—quite literally. In April, Engberg wrote back to the OI that "C.B. and his party have come and gone, but before they left, they succeeded in introducing a rather new vocabulary, the effects of which will probably be with us for some time. All of us are now establishing, shooting, panning, fading, and cutting in all of our daily tasks."[10]

The filming eventually resulted in Breasted's greatest—and only—cinematic triumph. Entitled *The Human Adventure*, it appeared in 1935. The movie explores the history of past civilizations in what was, essentially, an hour-long illustrated lecture given by Breasted for the general public. It was shown three times at Carnegie Hall in New York City and then played to audiences around the United States for years afterward.[11] A reviewer in the *New York Times*, who clearly did not anticipate the popularity of the Indiana Jones movie franchise that lay far in the future, began by saying: "Barring stamp collecting, archaeology would seem to be about the least likely subject matter for a motion picture. It is all the more surprising, then, to discover that even this science can be made into an entertaining film."[12]

Charles Breasted wrote the script and also served as the narrator. The movie opens with James Henry Breasted, clad in his usual three-piece suit and tie, standing in his office behind a table covered with artifacts. He holds up and describes each one in turn, from Neolithic stone tools to a cuneiform clay tablet. A map of the ancient Near East is conveniently set up on a nearby easel, to which he gestures occasionally with a long, old-fashioned wooden pointer.

The air tour, complete with aerial shots of modern Cairo and the ancient pyramids at Giza, starts fifteen minutes into the movie and first takes us the length and breadth of Egypt, describing its history from before the Old Kingdom through the end of the New Kingdom. Action shots at many of the sites that were under excavation at the time serve as a backdrop for the narration. The OI's archaeological headquarters in Luxor, "Chicago House," is highlighted and described in detail before the tour proceeds north to British Mandate Palestine. Flying over Jerusalem and then the Jordan River as if in a biplane with an unencumbered view, we are then treated to a bird's-eye panorama of Haifa followed by the site of Megiddo, almost exactly half an hour after the film has begun. Describing Megiddo as "a layer cake of ancient cities, one built upon another," Charles Breasted dramatically informs the listeners that the Oriental Institute's excavators are stripping off these layers one by one; undoubtedly, he says, "a Stone Age settlement awaits exposure at the very bottom."

The film is not without its problems, of course, not least of which is that much of it is now out of date in terms of the information being presented. Still, for its time, it was an extremely innovative and very daring project that anticipated today's television documentaries on archaeology, and that paid off handsomely in terms of production value and public relations for the Oriental Institute. Moreover, those interested specifically in Megiddo would have found the price of admission more than justified by the scenes of the digging in progress, complete with shots of the Egyptian pickmen and dozens of workers carrying baskets of dirt. There is also an overhead view of the entrance to the water system, a close-up of Engberg excavating skulls in a tomb, the inner courtyard where pottery restoration was in progress, and a demonstration of the balloon being carried up to the top of the mound and sent aloft to film the ruins from high above.

Charles Breasted, as the narrator, takes the time to explain how the digging is actually done, complete with views of the railway system in use. The small cars are filled to the brim with dirt and debris, he says, and are then rolled over the tracks to the chutes, where their loads are released, with the stones "booming and clattering" down to the "ever-growing dump." Even the process of recording and registration back in the dig house is shown, complete with cameo appearances by most of the core staff members, studiously working at their desks, measuring and drawing whole vessels, and so on. Perhaps the best line in the movie is uttered completely deadpan at this point: "Freshly discovered objects are treated much like newly arrested prisoners, brought in to a detective bureau for identification."

The segment on Megiddo stretches for more than eight minutes in all. It ends on a lighthearted note, with a celebration by the workmen, complete with a mock swordfight with sticks, boiled rice and "sweets" for the children, and dancing by the men.[13]

With the filming completed, the 1932 digging season finally started at Megiddo near the end of March.[14] However, once again there was no information about it in any letters sent by Guy back to Chicago during the next few months—not a mention of where on the tell they were digging, what finds they were making, or even when they were stopping for the summer break. It was not until the following January that Guy finally told Breasted what they had been finding.

In the meantime, in late May, Olof Lind was asked to take photographs at the prehistoric site of Atlit, just south of Haifa. The site is located on the slopes of Mount Carmel and is home to what is now usually referred to collectively as the Carmel Caves.

Most of the discoveries at these caves during the 1920s and 1930s were made by an archaeologist named Dorothy Garrod, who later became the first woman to be named a professor at Cambridge University, where she held the Disney Chair in Archaeology from 1939 to 1952. She began digging at Kebara Cave in 1928 and then excavated two other caves, known as Tabun and el-Wad, from 1929 to 1934. The latter two caves had been occupied continuously from about 500,000 years ago until sometime after 40,000 years ago; they became known in particular for Garrod's discovery of the burial of a Neanderthal woman dating to about 120,000 years ago.[15]

However, Lind was being asked to take photographs of skeletons in a different cave, one that lay nearby, known as Skhul Cave. Here, Ted McCown, an American physical anthropologist who had just received his BA degree in 1929 and later went on to a distinguished career at UC Berkeley, was working with Garrod.[16] They had begun to find what eventually turned out to be a series of skeletons, some of which were Neanderthal and others of which were anatomically modern people, that is, *Homo sapiens*. When published, these generated much discussion among scholars, since they provided some of the first evidence that the two groups existed at the same time and seem to have lived side by side, at least here in the Carmel Caves.[17]

McCown suggested that the rest of the Megiddo team might want to come with Lind and visit the site as well. They took him up on the invitation, but disaster struck almost immediately, just twenty minutes after they arrived.

They were standing on a terrace outside the cave, examining the skeletons that were still in situ, when, as Guy later reported, "a stone measuring about a foot across was dislodged, probably by a goat pasturing higher up the hill." It rolled down the slope, he said, and fell "a clear twenty feet onto Mrs. Wilensky's head." It was not a direct blow, for if it had been, her skull would have been crushed "like an egg." Even so, the doctors later said that her skull had been fractured fairly high up in the back, as well as in a double fracture at the base. Moreover, the force of the blow had knocked her facedown onto the terrace, so that she also suffered a terrific bruise and a concussion, although it wasn't clear whether the concussion had been caused by the initial blow from the falling rock or by her striking her face on the rock terrace.[18]

Guy immediately sent the news back to the Breasteds in Chicago, cabling succinctly, "WILENSKYS WIFE TODAY HAD SERIOUS POSSIBLE FATAL ACCIDENT NOT AT MEGIDDO."[19]

They all thought that she would die en route to the hospital, but they did what they could anyway, sending for an ambulance to take her to Haifa as quickly as possible. Remarkably, and apparently in part because the attending doctor decided not to operate but to simply let nature take its course and allow her to heal on her own, she recovered enough to be discharged and to return home just a few weeks later, in late June. She still had trouble with her eyesight and had to learn how to walk all over again, but overall she was already on the mend.[20]

Breasted was incredibly frustrated with Guy by this time, especially since he had been left in the dark all spring as to what was happening at the site. In June, he started right in again, pushing back against Guy's emphatic rejections of the proposal that he change his systematic attack on the mound. He badgered Guy to dig faster and get to the palace dating to the time of "the Egyptian Empire." He pointed out that they had originally been given financing for only five years of digging, but that they were now "well along in a second period of five years."[21]

What Breasted wanted, before this second set of five years was up, was to "find the area of the royal castle with its important monuments of Canaanite or Egyptian period." If they found it, he said, it would be imperative to excavate the royal area entirely. In contrast, he noted, "it will be relatively less important to extend the clearance over the entire mound to regions covered with houses only." While reconstructing a street plan of Megiddo in the Canaanite period would be interesting, of course, Breasted pointed out that "there is every likelihood that the house plans will be roughly uniform throughout." He continued, "After you have excavated a few of them [the houses], you will probably learn very little more by excavating the rest."[22]

Hammering his points home, Breasted said that he found it incredible that they had been working at Megiddo for six years already and had not gotten into the Egyptian or Canaanite levels yet. While he didn't want to disturb the routine of the excavation or "the scientific and systematic execution of the work," the fact remained that they needed to reach those levels soon. Using Guy's own earlier efforts against him, Breasted noted that they had already gone deep into the mound when digging out the water system the previous year, and that the same thing could be done in the north half of the mound, "where the more pretentious buildings seem to have been situated, and where you might be able to locate the castle or palace of the Canaanite rulers."[23] Breasted ended his long letter by saying that he hoped to visit Megiddo during the winter months. In the meantime, he wanted to hear back from Guy, regarding the question of reaching the Canaanite levels in the near future.

Breasted also took the opportunity to bring up again the lack of publications, apart from the two preliminary reports that had appeared in 1929 and 1931. He did concede that there were legitimate reasons why no final publications had yet appeared, although he didn't spell them out, but also said that the time had now come to rectify the situation. He asked Guy, first and foremost, to go back through the letters and reports that he had sent from time to time, pull together the material into one place, and then estimate the length of the text and the number of plates that would go into what Breasted thought would be two volumes—one on the tombs and the other on the discoveries on the top of the mound. His reasoning, he said, was the financial situation in America—that is, the continuing Great Depression—which was making it more difficult for them to complete all of their unfinished tasks. Breasted may well have been anticipating the looming cuts in philanthropy from the Rockefellers, which indeed began soon thereafter.[24]

To all of this, Guy responded in early July with a few proposals of his own. He deliberately ignored Breasted's continued goading and his pleas to get down to the Late Bronze Age levels. Instead, Guy focused on the question of publications. The tombs alone would require two full volumes, he said; they already had 116 plates of tomb material ready to go, along with the plans, complete with captions. As for the material coming from the summit of the mound, that would go into another volume, which could also contain the description and discussion of the water system. For this, he said that twenty-five plates with their captions were already set to go, and that he would want to add a dozen plates concerned with pottery and another twenty or so plates concerned with the Stratum I and surface material from the top of the mound. Thus, rather than two volumes, he proposed three—two of the tombs and one of the material on top of the mound.[25]

However—and it was a big however—Guy said that in order to complete this task as quickly as possible, he would need to cancel the upcoming fall season of excavation and put every team member on the task of pulling together the material for these volumes. As he put it bluntly: "Digging and publication cannot possibly go on at the same time; I tried that this Spring, and had to stop the latter. My whole staff is needed for either piece of work."[26]

If Breasted gave them permission to do this, Guy said, he could have everything ready to hand over for publication when Breasted came to visit

in the winter. And, as for digging quickly and looking for the Egyptian/
Canaanite levels and a palace at the northern edge of the mound, Guy said
he would be happy to discuss that further with Breasted during his visit. As
he put it, that would have the advantage of allowing him "to have the benefit of your views on the mound itself, and you could then give me, on the
ground, your instructions as to how you wanted the remainder of the present five years to be employed."[27] And with that, Guy threw the ball back
into Breasted's court.

Breasted refused to play, however. Writing back at the end of July, just
prior to leaving for vacation himself, he stated with no equivocation that
the fall digging season would absolutely take place. They could not possibly adopt a policy of halting excavations just to publish previous results;
none of their expeditions had ever done anything like that, he said. Decreas-
ing the annual amount of excavation by canceling the fall season would
increase their costs appallingly, as he put it, and so all publication preparations must be done in the intervals between digging periods, as usual—that
is, in the winter months between the ending of the fall campaign and the
beginning of the spring campaign.[28]

To all of this, Guy had no answer, and so in October the team members
began to return, one by one, for the fall season. To their surprise, they found
that over the summer Olof Lind had gotten engaged to a young Swedish lady
named Astrid who was quite literally half his age—he was forty-five, and she
was twenty-two. The wedding was scheduled for September 1933, one year
thence. Guy was not optimistic about their future together, noting, "The
Lord knows how it will turn out." As it happened, it turned out badly, with
Astrid requesting (and getting) a divorce just a few years later, in 1937.[29]

By early October, the full team was in place once again. Among the team
members this time was Breasted's younger son, James Henry Breasted, Jr.,
who was twenty-four years old at the time, and who took part in the excavations for a few weeks.[30]

Toward the end of the season, Lamon received news that his father had
been diagnosed with terminal cancer and was not expected to live much
longer. In early November, Lamon's mother went to see Breasted in Chicago, appealing to him to let Lamon return home as soon as possible, while
Lamon himself did the same at Megiddo, asking both Guy and Charles
Breasted for permission to return home before his father passed away.[31]

Not only was the request granted, but an advance on his summer travel
money was sent immediately, so that Lamon could afford to book passage

home. He left Megiddo in early December, just as they were closing down the dig for the year, and reached the States in plenty of time, for his father did not pass away until June 1933, at the age of fifty-four, having lived long enough not only to see his son again, but to be present when Bob married Eugenia Keefe in early February (though this is getting a bit ahead of our story).[32]

This brings us to the 1933 season, however, which was both a direct continuation of 1932 and a different story altogether. Breasted was no longer amenable to the slow pace of Guy's digging. He mused on the various possible ways to prod Guy to speed things up and then eventually sent a note in late January, informing Guy that he and Mrs. Breasted would be coming out in person this year, rather than simply sending Charles.[33]

As a result, although the Breasteds would not arrive at Megiddo until April, there was an air of anticipation, not to mention anxiety, at the dig house, especially when team members spied an article in the *New York Tribune* published in early February that documented the Breasteds' departure with the headline "Saver of Cities Sailing Today for Near East." Below that, in smaller letters, the subheading read, "Dr. Breasted Off to Review His Armies of Excavation in Ancient Bible Lands." The article began in a similar militaristic tone, "Dr. James Henry Breasted, commanding general of the American army of archaeologists stationed now between the hill at Armageddon and Persepolis in Persia, will start out again at noon today for the Bible lands to review his troops in the field."[34]

At the end of March, Guy notified Breasted that they had been working steadily on the publications for the past several months. While it was still raining at that point, he felt that it was time to begin digging again, so he was planning to send for the Egyptians and begin as soon as they arrived. He also noted that Lamon and his new bride were due to arrive the next day (26 March), and that they would be at full strength in terms of staff by the time that Breasted arrived at Megiddo.[35]

Guy thought he knew what was coming, based on Breasted's previous letters. He planned to go over the yearly budget with Breasted, show him around the site, discuss the remains that had been recently exposed, and find out what was envisioned in terms of excavation for the future. Anticipating these conversations, Guy decided to begin the dialogue before Breasted even arrived, writing to say that he knew both time and money were tight. While he would hate to abandon the stratum-by-stratum method of horizontal excavation that they had been following up to that point, he agreed that it might be advisable to begin working in just one area, rather than across the whole tell, and to dive deep in that area. As he put it, "I do realize that it may be necessary to cut our coat according to our cloth."[36]

This, of course, was exactly what Breasted had been trying to get across to Guy in his letters of the previous year. Perhaps Guy had finally realized that, with the director himself coming to visit again, it might be time to get in line with his wishes. Some of those wishes were made abundantly clear when Breasted immediately replied from Luxor. "It will indeed be necessary to contract the area included in the clearance," he wrote, "and in doing so to make every endeavor to determine the most promising place on which to concentrate the clearance operations." However, Guy did not yet realize that Breasted envisioned the change in excavation strategy as just one piece of a much more substantial reordering that had to be enacted.[37]

In the meantime, in mid-April, the team was visited one morning by the excavators from nearby Samaria—John and Grace Crowfoot, as well as their daughter Joan and two students. One of the students was Kathleen Kenyon, daughter of Sir Frederic Kenyon, the longtime director of the British Museum. Kenyon worked as a team member at Samaria from 1931 to 1934, decades before becoming famous in her own right, in large part because of her excavations at Jericho and Jerusalem.[38]

At the time, Kenyon was already experimenting with the excavation techniques that she had just learned from her mentor and adviser Sir Mortimer Wheeler. These involved digging more slowly and carefully and keeping track of the pottery, walls, and other discoveries "according to the natural layers of soil"—in other words, paying closer attention to the stratigraphy while excavating. Although disparaged by Crowfoot, her method was eventually adopted almost universally by most excavators in this region, after she also used it successfully at both Jericho and Jerusalem. Today it is known as the Kenyon-Wheeler method.[39]

The other student was Betty Murray, who later sent a letter to her mother describing their visit to Megiddo. "It was worth going there," she wrote, "just to see how an expedition can be conducted when money is no object."[40] The dig house was charming and beautifully furnished, and it even had a sun parlor, she said. This is the first such description that we have of the newly renovated accommodations, following the completion of all the improvements that Woolman had suggested a few years earlier.

Fig. 29. Mending pottery at Megiddo, during Guy's directorship ca. 1931–34 (courtesy of the Oberlin College archives)

Fig. 30. Pottery room at Megiddo, during Guy's directorship ca. 1931–34 (courtesy of the Oberlin College archives)

To reach the house, they passed through a courtyard "gay with flowers—bougainvillea and geraniums and shaded by palm trees," Murray said. She was particularly impressed by the hot and cold water and the "palatial bathroom and shower" in each room, as well as the tiled passageways and the marble windowsills. The tennis court also merited a mention.

And, as she put it, "the business part is equally elaborate." There was a special room for photography and a huge room just for drawing the pottery, as well as "rooms and rooms for the pottery fitted with shelves." She was also very impressed by the idea of balloon photography, even though the balloon wasn't working at the moment because they were once again out of the gas that they imported from Marseilles.

After being treated to a picnic lunch and coffee in the courtyard, they were shown around the tell. According to Betty, the top of the mound was "a vast place but uninspiring to look at—foundations of room after room carefully numbered." She was not particularly impressed by the supposed Solomonic stables and walls, but was quite taken by the water system, which they walked through and which she spent quite a bit of her letter describing, calling it "one of the most spectacular finds." Unfortunately, she didn't record Kathleen Kenyon's reaction to any of this.

Breasted and his wife missed the Crowfoots, Kenyon, and Murray by ten days. They finally arrived at Megiddo in late April and proceeded to spend a full three days visiting with Guy and the team.[41] It was only the fourth time that Breasted had been to the site since excavations had begun: the first was in March 1926, following which he fired Higgins; the second was in April 1927, after which he fired Fisher; the third was in March 1929, for the "Great Royal Visit" with the Rockefellers; and now the fourth was in April 1933, when he once again fired someone. There would be only one more trip, in mid-October 1935, but that still lay in the future.

As with several of Breasted's earlier visits, the results of this fourth tour of inspection had repercussions not only for the rest of that season, but for the remainder of the time that the Oriental Institute excavated at the site. The first inkling of what transpired comes from a cable that Breasted sent immediately afterward to Charles, who had stayed behind in Chicago. It reads:[42]

SPENT THREE DAYS MEGIDDO AFTER CONFERENCES WITH ENTIRE STAFF HAVE DISCHARGED WILENSKY AND SERIOUSLY REPRIMANDED CHIEF WHO TOOK IT LYING DOWN WILL LIVE HAIFA WITH WIFE AND IS MEEKLY AC-CEPTING THOROUGH REORGANISATION OF PROGRAM AND STAFF LATTER JUBILANT.

It's not hard to read between the lines and see what happened during the three days that Breasted spent at Megiddo. Simply put, he decided to take command again and reassert control over a dig that he thought had gone rogue, with a field director ("Chief" in the cable) who was digging too slowly, not publishing enough, and in general not listening to the orders coming from far-off Chicago. Somehow Breasted had caught wind of what Woolman had wanted to tell him the previous year but didn't feel that he could; recall that Woolman had said Breasted would have to figure it out for himself, which apparently by now he had.

So, while at Megiddo, Breasted told Guy that Wilensky should be let go at the end of the spring season, with his contract terminated early. He also reprimanded Guy for a variety of perceived misdeeds and banished him to commute from Haifa. If we believe Breasted's cable, the staff members were "jubilant" about these changes.[43]

Leaving nothing to chance, Breasted soon put everything in writing, posting a long letter to Guy in early May. In it, he said that he was taking the first opportunity to recapitulate and elaborate on the main points that they had discussed during their three days together in late April. This may be one of the most important letters written by Breasted in connection with Megiddo since the early days of initial efforts to procure funding and begin excavations at the site, so it is worth spending some time parsing it.[44]

To begin with, Breasted split the contents of his letter into three sections: (I) publications; (II) excavations; and (III) house, equipment, and maintenance. In the first section, Breasted itemized his understanding of the first three volumes that were to appear, which differed from Guy's previous suggestion. The initial volume was to be concerned with the one hundred or so tombs on the East Slope. Since the plates were nearly all ready, he thought that Guy could complete the accompanying text quickly, if he spent at least three hours per day on it, assisted by the others as necessary. The volume was to be finished and submitted no later than 1 October, five months thence, which would also allow Guy to work on it during the summer break. In order to keep track of progress, Breasted asked for monthly reports, to be sent to him on the first of each month.[45]

The second volume would then be a summary of all the upper levels excavated on the mound, Strata I through IV, but would also include discussions of both the stables and the water system. The third volume was left up in the air for the moment but was envisioned as covering the important buildings that presumably would be discovered in the deeper areas of the mound.[46]

As it turned out, the end results deviated from what Breasted envisioned, of course. For example, the book that Engberg and Shipton had been working on, concerning the early pottery from the East Slope—which wasn't even discussed in this letter—was actually the first to appear, in 1934. Moreover, the water system ended up being published separately, written by Lamon and appearing in 1935. And a volume that May had begun working on in 1933, concerning the cult objects and buildings at Megiddo,[47] also appeared in 1935.

The "Volume I" mentioned in Breasted's letter, Guy's long-promised volume on the tombs, was finally published in 1938, fully five years after Breasted's visit to the site. "Volume II" of the original plan appeared one year later, in 1939. Written by Lamon and Shipton and published with the title *Megiddo I*, it covered the seasons of 1925–34, as mentioned previously, and Strata I–V (rather than I–IV, since they renumbered the strata in the interim, during the course of working through the material for publication). That was a good year for Shipton, for he also published a volume that could technically be considered part of the envisioned "Volume III," which was on the pottery that they found in Strata VI–X, in the years after Breasted's visit. Also in 1939, Gordon Loud, who took over as field director after Guy was fired, published a volume on the ivories that they found in 1937—in the palace that Breasted had long been waiting for but didn't live to see discovered. It wasn't until nearly a decade later, in 1948, that Loud subsequently published the other part belonging to "Volume III." Entitled *Megiddo II*, it covered the seasons of 1935–39; we will discuss this later, in one of our last chapters.

Thus the three volumes that Breasted and Guy initially envisioned eventually became eight, published over the course of the next fifteen years. There were also the two preliminary reports that had been published in 1929 and 1931, and two additional volumes published by other scholars more than fifty years later. It is more than a little ironic that Guy published only the single volume on the tombs, albeit with assistance from Engberg, while Lamon, Shipton, May, and Engberg collectively published five of the eight volumes. We hardly need reminding that all of them were junior staff members with whom Guy had problems at one time or another, and that none of them came to the dig specifically trained as a field archaeologist.

However, in May 1933 all of that was yet to come. It would be greatly impacted, though, by the second section of Breasted's letter. This dealt with the changes that were to be made in their excavation strategy, even though by then the season had already started.

First and foremost, Breasted said, the strategy of clearing the entire surface of the mound, stratum by stratum, was to be abandoned immediately. Instead, they would concentrate their efforts on a specific area located on the southern part of the top of the mound, stretching from Squares O to T and 5 to 10—this would henceforth be labeled as "Area A" on their plans.[48] Breasted did not specify why he had suddenly shifted from wanting to dig in the northern half of the site, but simply said that any buildings that were presently exposed in the southern area would be recorded and removed "without hesitation," so that they could get on with their work.

Breasted was at particular pains to stress this point about removing the remains, since the southern stables covered the entire western half of this area. He also, specifically, accused Guy of conferring with the British Mandate government about making the stables a national monument, and permanently preserving them, without having consulted him first. We will see that this point will come up again, a year later, as one of the reasons why Guy was fired.[49]

Breasted also said that at least two hundred workers should be employed at all times, that they should dig at the fastest possible rate, and that, "if necessary, you will employ the entire scientific staff in supervision of the increased force of Field laborers."[50] He reiterated that the entire staff should be on the mound whenever they were needed. When they weren't up there, they should be helping with the registration of finds, which shouldn't take long, he said, and then devote the rest of their time to working on the publications, which could mean several hours per day. Finally, in order to keep track of all this as well, Breasted asked for further monthly progress reports, though he said that they could be sent at the same time as the reports on the progress of the publications; the first one should be sent on 1 June, which was fast approaching.[51]

The third section of Breasted's May 1933 letter ostensibly dealt with the house, equipment, and maintenance, but it was really about something else entirely. The first point he brought up was minor, discussing a glassed-in porch that was to serve as the new social room. Breasted directed that carpets, furniture, hangings, and pictures should be purchased, as much as was necessary to decorate and furnish this room, but it needed to be done promptly, within the current budget year (i.e., by the end of June).[52]

The other two points within this section were both major, and related. Breasted said that the service staff—the cooks and kitchen help, the waiters, the cleaning women, and the like—was to be reduced immediately, in part because it had been too large to this point. However, it was also to be reduced "as a remit of the Field Director's removal to Haifa." In other words, the staff was being reduced because Guy—and Yemima as well—would thenceforth live in Haifa and he would commute to the tell each day.[53]

This is the first time that anything had actually been said about Guy relocating to Haifa, besides Breasted's initial telegram to Charles. It was, quite frankly, unprecedented for the field director not to be living in the dig house. It is hard to believe that this was done with Guy's acquiescence, but apparently it was. Moreover, Breasted said, since the field director (i.e., Guy) had a salary that was three times that of most of the other staff, and since the OI was presently in a difficult financial situation, it would not be possible to give him additional money toward housing expenses or a travel allowance to cover the cost of the daily commute, not "when every piaster is needed on the Mound to retrieve the heavy loss of time incurred during the last five years."[54] Just like that, Guy was responsible for his housing, food, and travel costs, and was basically told that these changes were all imposed because it was his fault that they had been going so slowly during the previous five years.

Guy eventually pushed back again, when he naturally missed the 1 October deadline for the manuscript on the tombs and received an irate cable from Breasted a month later.[55] Regarding the impossibility of trying to prepare publications at the same time as excavating, he wrote, echoing several previous communications, "it is not a good plan to try to publish one thing while one is digging another. Both are full time jobs, and if one tries to carry on both at the same time, one can do justice to neither."[56] To his credit, Guy was absolutely correct in this assertion—it is for this reason that most excavation teams in Israel and Jordan today usually dig for either six to seven weeks every other summer, or only four weeks every summer, and work on their publications in the interim.

Moreover, as Guy pointed out, while the excavation was in progress during the workday, he needed to be on the mound overseeing things; he couldn't be down at the dig house working on plans, plates, and publications. Taking three hours out of each day to do completely different work "makes it impossible to keep fully abreast of digging, particularly with a big gang working among the difficult buildings we get in Palestine."[57] The real problem, Guy said, was that their digging seasons were too long, and that there was not enough time in between to write up the results. He pointed out that their field season at Megiddo was longer than that of any other expedition working in the area—longer, even, than that of any of the other excavations being run elsewhere by the Oriental Institute. "I do beg of you," he wrote, "to allow me . . . to have shorter ones [i.e., digging seasons], with more time for writing up in between."[58] Again, in his favor, Guy was completely correct; this is why nobody digs all year round, or has two dig seasons during each year any more, and it is why dig directors are almost always to be found somewhere on-site while excavation is ongoing.

However, there was no pushback at all from Guy regarding the reduction in service staff or his relocation to Haifa. Only once, more than a year later, does he even mention the fact that he was not living at the dig house between May 1933 and August 1934. It's not clear where in Haifa he and Yemima lived during that period, though we should remember that when Guy was the chief inspector for the Department of Antiquities for five years, from 1922 onward, prior to being hired as field director at Megiddo, he had been stationed in Jerusalem and Haifa.[59] Had he owned a house in Haifa at that time, which is likely, it is by no means out of the question for him to have held on to it during the intervening years, especially so that he could have a place to escape to on the weekends during the dig seasons at Megiddo.

Sadly, at the moment we are also lacking any personal letters or journals from Lamon, Shipton, Engberg, and May dating to this period, so we have no way to separately ascertain how the move and the other changes impacted the rest of the staff members. Apart from the supposed jubilation on the part of the rest of the staff that Breasted wrote about in his earlier cable, the only relevant item that we have is a letter that May wrote to his friend William Graham at the Oriental Institute, in which May said: "Dr. Breasted has arrived and gone. A new program has been arranged for Megiddo, and it has in it possibilities of richer finds and more efficient digging."[60]

In the cable that he sent to his son Charles in late April, Breasted also said that he had discharged Wilensky, but did not elaborate. In fact, he had not done so personally, as it turned out, but instead had left a letter for Guy to deliver to Wilensky, thereby putting it in writing. Dated 28 April 1933, it began: "Dear Mr. Wilensky—I regret to inform you that the Oriental Institute will be unable to continue your appointment beyond September first, 1933. Your last salary check therefore will be for the month of August, 1933."[61]

Wilensky promptly replied, sending his letter to Guy as the official representative of the Oriental Institute. He was "not prepared to accept the termination of my employment before its lawful expiry," he said, "unless the

Oriental Institute is prepared to offer me adequate compensation in respect of the loss that I am only too likely to sustain." After acknowledging that he had received Wilensky's response, Guy forwarded everything to Breasted, who immediately replied in turn, reminding Guy that Wilensky was dismissed <u>for cause</u>, and that the facts could be proven if need be.[62]

By this time, they had a new addition to their staff, a volunteer named Arthur Piepkorn, who had previously sent a letter asking whether he could join them in May and stay until the spring season ended. Piepkorn was twenty-six years old at the time, had a PhD from Chicago with a specialty in Babylonian archaeology, was the American School of Oriental Research (ASOR) annual fellow in Baghdad, and had been digging at Tepe Gawra and Tell Billah in Iraq. He said that their season in Iraq was ending in April and so he would be free after that. Since Piepkorn was also a known quantity to Breasted, on account of his having done his PhD at Chicago, both he and Guy were amenable to this arrangement, and so Piepkorn had arrived at Megiddo in early May.[63]

Guy had also, since Breasted had given him permission to look for two new surveyors, just hired Ernest Forrest (E. F.) Beaumont as a partial replacement for Wilensky.[64] Beaumont was older than most of the other Megiddo staff members. Born in 1871, he had come to Ottoman Palestine in 1896 as part of a group of Americans bent on joining the American Colony religious venture in Jerusalem, to which Lind also belonged.

According to Jack Green, former chief curator of the Oriental Institute Museum, Beaumont was originally the dentist for the American Colony but over the years had also taught himself to be "an artist, draftsman, surveyor, city engineer, and archaeologist"; he had served as a draftsman during the excavations at Beth Shemesh from 1909 to 1911. Some of his artwork, from sketches to lithographs to photographs, was offered for sale by the American Colony from time to time, and there are now twenty-two such pieces at the Oriental Institute, dating to the 1920s and 1930s, which were donated in 2014 by Beaumont's granddaughter.[65]

Like Lind, Beaumont left the American Colony after disagreements with the leaders. According to Green, Beaumont then set up a lodging house in Jerusalem where a number of well-known archaeologists stayed, including Sir William Matthew Flinders Petrie. He also began working again for archaeological expeditions, including at Beth Shean in 1931 and now at Megiddo, where he worked on and off from 1933 to 1935. He left British Mandate Palestine in 1938, after a final season working in Transjordan for Nelson

Glueck and ASOR, and returned to the United States, where he settled in San Diego.[66]

In early June, just a few days after he had been told by Guy that Breasted was remaining firm in his decision to terminate him, Wilensky physically threatened Herbert May. We have a firsthand account of what happened, courtesy of the new arrival, Arthur Piepkorn, who was present when the incident took place. Guy was working in his office at the time, but his second-hand summation also adds another twist to the episode.[67]

May and Piepkorn had gone up to the top of the tell toward the middle of the afternoon, in order to verify the findspot for one of the figurines that May was studying. Unable to determine the answer simply by looking at the proper spot, they asked one of the workmen to dig a little bit in one specific area for them. Wilensky suddenly appeared and demanded to know what they were doing—which he had every right to do, since he was in charge of overseeing the area and the workmen. May and Piepkorn explained why they were there, and asked Wilensky to what stratum the wall that they were interested in belonged. He replied sharply, "That will all come out in due time." When pressed again for an answer, he retorted, "Go and ask Mr. Guy," and then walked away.

After watching them for a while, during which time May and Piepkorn enlisted another workman to help them as well, Wilensky left the tell without speaking. All told, according to Piepkorn, they were on the tell for a total of only about fifteen minutes. Later, while on his way to tea, Piepkorn passed by Wilensky and May standing near the dig house. He overheard Wilensky tell May, "If you ever act that way again, I'll smash your d*** face!" According to Guy's secondhand account, however, May had first told Wilensky that "he had behaved like a damn fool," at which point Wilensky told May that "if he spoke to him like that [again], he would smash his face." Whichever version one chooses to believe, it is clear that Wilensky had physically threatened May. As a result, he was dismissed immediately, rather than at the end of the season.

Two thoughts immediately come to mind. First, Wilensky was undoubtedly already in an extremely bad mood because of the news from Breasted that Guy had given him just a few days earlier. He also knew that a new surveyor—Beaumont—had just been hired and was destined to be one of the two men who replaced him, so he can perhaps be forgiven, or at least granted a little leeway for his actions. Second, such personal incidents between staff or team members are by no means uncommon on archaeological excavations, both in this region and elsewhere, and both then and now. Tempers flare and voices are raised because of stress, the heat, working and living in close quarters for weeks or months at a time, and a myriad of other reasons. However, people usually get over it, albeit sometimes after sulking or stewing for a while.

So was this really sufficient cause to fire Wilensky on the spot? Or was this simply the final straw, on top of everything else? As it turned out, in later statements made under oath, the main complaint against Wilensky actually was much more minor—that he was usually late to work. It was estimated by May, whose office window overlooked the driveway, that Wilensky generally worked at least seven hours less per week than any of the other staff members.

It is likely that there was already bad blood between Wilensky and May, for there would have been no reason otherwise for May to keep a tally of Wilensky's arrival times. However, one could also argue that this is the sort of situation that is found in workplaces the world over and possibly since time immemorial: if the bosses want to fire someone, they will do so, citing a specific action or actions as objectionable; if they don't want to fire that person, they will overlook the very same action. In Wilensky's case, it seems that they were no longer willing to overlook his transgressions.

However, a later letter from Breasted does specify some of the other reasons that they had let Wilensky go <u>for cause</u>. Besides being habitually late, they said, he was also incompetent, having "little or no knowledge of pottery." He had also told the head of the Egyptian workmen, the *reis*, that he was second in command of the expedition. Since they were Muslim and Wilensky was Jewish, this caused serious trouble, not to mention that the other staff members were "also highly indignant and demoralized by it." In fact, Breasted said, when he came for his April visit, he had found the expedition "completely demoralized by this situation," and he had told Guy that the expedition would fall apart unless Wilensky was let go.[68] As Mark Twain reportedly once said, history might not repeat itself, but it does rhyme, and this sounds very much like the situation between Fisher and Higgins all over again, almost a decade later.

Wilensky retaliated, threatening to sue for full salary and damages if he were not reinstated in his position by the end of August. After a flurry of letters and cables, as well as an appeal to the high commissioner in British

Mandate Palestine, Breasted and the university's legal department arranged for a local Jerusalem attorney, Sidney Richardson, to represent them.[69] Both sides were now set.

During their summer break, Guy hired another new surveyor, named Thomas Concannon, so that he now had two people to replace Wilensky: Beaumont and Concannon. Concannon was known as a "PWD architect" and was working at the time under a respected architect named Harrison as a member of the Public Works Department (hence "PWD") in Jerusalem. Later in life Concannon went on to become an esteemed architect in his own right, eventually settling in Jamaica and restoring historic houses. For now, though, Guy hired him at the bargain rate of fifteen pounds per month for the upcoming fall 1933 and spring 1934 seasons, a position in which he served admirably.[70]

Guy returned to the area at the end of September, finding Engberg and his wife, Irene, newly arrived in Haifa. He reopened the dig house on 1 October, and the rest of the team turned up shortly thereafter, including Lind and his new bride, who had just gotten married a month earlier. The Egyptian workmen made their appearance soon afterward, and they all set to work again, on 7 October, "with a gang of 213."[71]

Since it was also growing colder, they installed a new stove in the common room and finished furnishing it, in accordance with Breasted's orders. They now actually had two common rooms; Guy said the upstairs one tended to be used for the morning break and after lunch, while the downstairs one—with the new stove—was used for afternoon tea and in the evenings. He had turned his old sitting room into the expedition library as well, he remarked with some apparent satisfaction.[72]

We should also mention that discussions were ongoing throughout the fall concerning a division of the antiquities that had been found since 1928 or 1929, including where the skeletal material that was assigned to the Oriental Institute should be sent. Breasted had been harping on this for some time, writing in late August 1933: "I need hardly remind you that the Palestine and Megiddo alcove in the exhibition galleries here at the headquarters are the least interesting and least impressive of the Institute's entire display. Yet the Megiddo Expedition has been running since the summer of 1925!"[73] The division was eventually scheduled to take place after the beginning of the new year.[74]

Meanwhile, the legal proceedings with Wilensky also dragged on through the entire fall, with May eventually presenting a letter against Wilensky to Richardson, their attorney, in early December. In it, he made no mention of the incident that had taken place back in early June, when Wilensky threatened him, but instead listed the various deficiencies that he and the other staff members saw in Wilensky. These included "a lack of interest and ability utterly inconsistent with his position and salary"; "unnecessary absences and late arrivals"; "insufficient educational preparation"; "inability to report adequately on work which he undertook"; as well as "unintelligible" writing and a "lack of knowledge of the historical and cultural background of the excavations." He also "knew nothing about the chronological classification of archaeological materials of Palestine." In other words, he was insufficiently prepared, in the eyes of the other staff members, despite his "extreme arrogance and assumption of superiority," and was a liability rather than an asset. Even Guy had acknowledged Wilensky's "relative lack of ability as a surveyor" and confessed that he wasn't sure what he'd be able to find for Wilensky to do during the winter months, according to May.[75]

In all, it was a very damning letter that May wrote. Soon thereafter, when Breasted heard, to his astonishment, that Guy had tried to weasel out of the situation by informing the lawyers that "he would not be prepared to go so far as to state that he found Wilensky actually inefficient in the performance of his duty," he asked Lamon and Engberg to also send letters to the attorneys, which they did.[76] The case continued into the opening months of 1934, which is where we will pick it up again below and finally bring it to a close.

While all of this was going on during the fall, tensions between Arabs and Jews in British Mandate Palestine also rose once again and reached a crescendo beginning on Friday, 27 October. Olof Lind wrote to Charles Breasted, reporting that "there has been a bit of a shootup" in Jaffa, with several British policemen and more than twenty Arab protesters killed. There had been a general Arab strike declared that day, with shops closed throughout the country and demonstrations in Jaffa, Haifa, Nablus, and Jerusalem. As Lind noted, the demonstrators were protesting against the admission of thousands more Jews into British Mandate Palestine. Much of the country was sympathetic to the protesters and there was unrest everywhere, especially in the major cities. He himself was in Jerusalem, Lind said, and had been advised to stay there for the time being, although he hoped to leave for Megiddo the following morning if the police allowed.[77]

Guy sent a cable back to Chicago two days later, saying that everything was quiet at Megiddo and work was proceeding. He followed it up with a longer discussion during his scheduled monthly report in the first week of November.[78] In addition to the problems in Jaffa on the twenty-seventh, there had also been trouble in Haifa that same evening, which continued the next day. A mob tried to rush the police station to seize the rifles that were stored in the armory, according to Guy, and so the police had fired upon them. Two Arabs were killed and more than forty wounded, while a number of policemen were stabbed or otherwise injured. A few cars were also set on fire, though not his, and stone barricades had been built across some of the streets. The troubles in their region were mostly confined to Haifa, though, and did not spread to the adjacent towns or villages, said Guy.

At Megiddo, everything remained peaceful, which was fortunate because the staff members had dispersed for the weekend beginning on the afternoon of the twenty-sixth. Guy was in Haifa for his daughter's twenty-first birthday; May, Lind, and Shipton had all gone to Jerusalem; and the Lamons were visiting Jerash. They all returned safely, mostly on the twenty-seventh, though Lind and May remained in Jerusalem until the thirtieth. The next day, Guy gave the workmen a half holiday to thank them for continuing to come to work and not taking part in the general strike. He said that when they had finished their work at the end of that morning, "they formed a procession on the dig and marched off to their houses with a white flag in front, and singing songs saying they only wanted peace and quietness." By the time that he was writing, a little more than a week after the disturbances, Guy said that "the country, so far as I can gather, now appears to be normal, but I am not certain in my own mind that the episode should be described as closed; there may be more of it."[79] Indeed there would be more, namely, the Arab Revolt of 1936–39.

It is interesting to note that there was something else different about the staff members that fall. With Olof Lind's wedding in early September, for the first time ever, with the exception of Parker and Shipton who were still confirmed bachelors, every one of the core staff was now married and each had his spouse with him—Guy, Lind, May, Engberg, and Lamon. Moreover,

Herbert and Helen May had, for the first time in Megiddo history, added to their family and had a baby girl while at Megiddo, instead of returning to the United States or Canada to give birth, as the DeLoaches and the Stapleses had done previously. Gola Joyce Kina May was born in Jerusalem during July, with "Kina" as a nod to the biblical brook in the Jezreel Valley near Megiddo.[80]

Even Charles Breasted had recently gotten married,[81] and it may be that this event drew his attention to the fact that they were now providing room and board for a number of people—that is, the spouses—who were seemingly not directly contributing to the activities of the dig. Clearly their mere presence was more an asset than a liability, providing a social atmosphere at tea and mealtimes, and leavening the working environment, but it was also costing the expedition quite a bit. As a result, in late September, Charles drafted—but to his credit never sent—a memo stating that, forthwith, all spouses residing at the dig house would be charged a daily rate for food and lodging.[82]

One possible reason why he did not send it, aside from common sense telling him that he would have had a riot on his hands, not to mention a resignation en masse, is that he began hearing rumors that the women were volunteering to help (as no doubt they had done before) and that Guy had finally reversed course and accepted their offer. As a result, for instance, Engberg wrote in late October: "My wife has been highly pleased with Megiddo, not a little of which pleasure as well as interest is due to a new directorial attitude which allows women to work on excavation registration and publication if they prove themselves capable. The ladies have taken avidly to their work, and now I am surprised that I didn't understand until this autumn why a woman wouldn't care to do nothing in her room all day long."[83]

By early December, Guy wrote in his monthly report to Breasted: "You will be interested and, I think, pleased to know that I have lately been having some additional and useful assistance. Mrs. Lamon and Mrs. Engberg volunteered on the work of the expedition, and have been hard at it for some weeks. Mrs. Engberg has chiefly been helping May with his cult objects, and Mrs. Lamon has been at registration as well as assisting with the O.I.P. The arrangement works well, and I am glad about it. Mrs. Lind is also prepared to do something, but she has so far been rather busy with personal matters in connexion with a house they have in Jerusalem, where she spends part of her time."[84] There is no mention, or hint of irony, regarding the fact that

Guy had been previously—and adamantly—opposed to having any of the women helping, though it is not difficult to recall his snide reaction back in July 1931 when, before her arrival, Breasted had suggested that Mrs. May—a skilled artist who had taught drawing—could help with the illustrations.[85]

So far, the first two of these three interconnected seasons, stretching from 1932 to 1934, had been extremely busy, chaotic, and rather tempestuous, we could say, but it was the third one that was to be even more important. It marked a turning point for the Chicago expedition in a number of ways, from a change in the method of excavation to a change of field director (once again). It also determined the authorship of the various final volumes that would eventually be produced by members of the team.

We therefore pick up again with the Wilensky situation, from where we left off in early December 1933. May, Lamon, and Engberg had just sent their statements to the lawyers, while Breasted was angry at Guy for seeming to equivocate in front of those same lawyers. However, it now became clear—in early January 1934—that not all was as it had seemed.

For one thing, we now learn for certain that Breasted had not actually told Wilensky to his face that he was fired during his visit to the site the previous April. Contrary to what he had implied in his cable back to Chicago, Breasted had rejected Guy's suggestion that he speak with Wilensky directly, and had instead simply left the termination letter to be delivered after his departure. Moreover, it became clear that there had not been any prior warnings issued to Wilensky about his behavior, nor were any causes for his termination specified in the letter of dismissal that Breasted had left for him. In other words, although the firing might have been entirely justified, those involved had not gone about it properly.[86]

The subsequent incident between Wilensky and May on the mound was left unaddressed in all of the written documents for some reason, though May told Breasted in mid-January that he and either Lamon or Engberg had met with the lawyers, so it is possible that they related the story in person. The only item of substance that May reported back to Breasted at the time was that "the situation is made extremely difficult through Mr. Guy's insistent refusal to acknowledge Wilensky's patent deficiencies."[87]

Guy subsequently defended himself to Breasted. To be honest, his statements make a certain degree of sense. He said, for instance, that Wilensky was "an efficient excavator," whose architectural knowledge enabled him to "disentangle one building from another."[88] This is an extremely useful trait and is one of the reasons why so many of the earliest archaeologists, like Fisher, had been originally trained as architects.

Guy also pointed out that of course Wilensky didn't know Palestinian pottery, since he had been working in Iraq, and that none of the others had knowledge of any types of Near Eastern pottery either before they had joined the staff, which was certainly true. As for often being late, Guy noted that Wilensky was commuting daily from Haifa and upon occasion had to get his car serviced and, even more often, had to tend to his wife, who was still slowly recovering from her near-fatal accident at the Carmel Caves.[89]

Moreover, Guy reminded Breasted, he had told him back in April that Wilensky could not legally be dismissed, and had strongly suggested that Breasted should talk to Wilensky personally about the situation. "You took a contrary view in regard to his dismissal, and you declined to see him," Guy wrote. "Yet I understand from Richardson that it is in these very points that the strength of Wilensky's case lies."[90]

All of this certainly sounds quite reasonable, but we should also remember that Guy and Wilensky were in similar situations at this point, especially in relation to the other members of the team. Apart from Shipton, they were the only staff members currently present who had not been sent from Chicago. Furthermore, both were Zionists and, for what it's worth, both were living in, and commuting from, Haifa at this point. While they might not have been kindred spirits or soul brothers, it is not too surprising that Guy would defend Wilensky, especially since he had petitioned Breasted to allow him to rehire Wilensky back in 1932.

However, Guy made two grievous errors in his letter to Breasted, the second of which would come back to haunt him several months later. First, he said that Wilensky was "able to handle men," which was patently untrue. Second, he said that he had told Breasted at the time of his visit the previous April that it would be impossible to continue having all three— May, Engberg, and Wilensky—on staff simultaneously, and that he had specifically asked Breasted "to remove the two former and to let me keep the latter."[91] To this astonishing statement, Breasted replied in no uncertain terms: "I have careful notes of our conversation and your memory is decidedly wrong. . . . For the sake of your own judgment I am very glad that you never said any such thing to me, for anybody who would trade May and Engberg in exchange for Wilensky would be demonstrating his complete lack of judgment."[92]

Unfortunately, we are undoubtedly missing some crucial relevant documents at this point, for the next thing we know, Breasted ordered Guy to settle up with Wilensky and close out the matter without further protest. His cable was direct and concise:[93]

FROM INSTITUTE FUNDS PAY IMMEDIATELY TO RICHARDSON AND TURTLE-
DOVE FIVE HUNDRED TWENTYFIVE POUNDS PALESTINIAN FOR WILENSKY
SETTLEMENT CABLE ME WHEN INSTRUCTIONS EXECUTED

We have no idea what happened. Why was Breasted settling without further argument? Had there been a ruling in favor of Wilensky? Did the University of Chicago lawyers, or the lawyers in British Mandate Palestine, advise Breasted to settle before the case went to trial? There must be documents somewhere, but they are not in the files and folders where one would expect them to be in the archives of the Oriental Institute, nor are there any in the Mandate files within the archives of the Israel Antiquities Authority. Undoubtedly, they will show up somewhere one day, but in the meantime, it is enough to note that this settlement brought an end to the legal problems with Wilensky.

So how much was it worth? At the time, the Palestinian pound was tied to the British pound sterling on a 1:1 basis.[94] Accounting for inflation from 1934 until today, 525 British pounds back then would be worth almost £36,000 today.[95] And, given today's exchange rates, that would be worth close to $50,000. In other words, it was quite a substantial sum of money that Breasted paid to make Wilensky and this case go away.

In the meantime, however, Wilensky had apparently also begun working as an intelligence officer for the Haganah and the Jewish Agency from at least 1933, "gathering information about Britons, Jews and Arabs."[96] We do not know whether he was already working in such a capacity while engaged at Megiddo from 1932 on, or if he began spying only after leaving the dig in June 1933. No mention of such activities, or suspicions thereof, is ever made in the letters sent back and forth between Guy and Breasted, although, as we have seen, all sorts of other things about Wilensky were discussed.

Moreover, by 1936, Wilensky was reportedly one of three men who founded the Arab Department of the Haganah. According to some sources, he also served as the head of paramilitary intelligence for the Haganah in Haifa and on at least one occasion compared intelligence work to archaeology: "Archeology, in general, has served, and is serving, as an excellent preparation for intelligence work, because at the core it is similar to such work. In both archeology and intelligence, the researcher has to acquire an image of a distant reality, by piecing together patiently and slowly bits of information and hints, classifying and sifting them, and trying to bring them into an orderly system."[97]

Wilensky, as it happens, was not the only Megiddo staff member to go into intelligence work immediately after leaving the expedition, but we shall revisit that topic below, in one of the final chapters here. For now, it is enough to know that with the settlement payment, the Wilensky situation came to an end. Wilensky does not seem to have worked in archaeology ever again and instead returned to his career as an architect. He published at least one article that we know of, on residential buildings in Haifa in 1946, and lived for another thirty-five years beyond that, eventually passing away in 1981 when he was seventy-eight years old.[98]

While all of the above was taking place, the usual January through March activities were also continuing. Breasted persisted in making Guy's life miserable by sending letters in which he repeatedly ranted about the lack of progress in both publications and digging. Guy continued to defend himself. The others carried on as usual, trying to survive the situation as best they could.[99]

In fact, Breasted did what he could for all of them, at least in terms of salary. During 1933 and into early 1934, President Franklin Roosevelt had instituted a number of drastic economic measures as part of the New Deal, designed to pull the United States out of the Great Depression. These culminated in the Gold Reserve Act, enacted in January 1934, which overnight increased the price of gold from just under $21 per troy ounce to $35 per troy ounce.[100] Although these machinations did eventually have the desired effect and set the United States on the road to recovery, the depreciation of the dollar that went along with it dramatically affected the salaries of all those working at Megiddo (not to mention those back home at the Oriental Institute). Breasted wrote a note to each of them, giving them a substantial salary "supplement," as he called it, in addition to their annual increase, in order to make up for their loss in purchasing power. All of them were extremely grateful, including Guy. Lamon, in particular, wrote to thank Breasted.[101]

However, of them all, May was probably the happiest, and not just because of the salary boost. In early January he sent Breasted a long book manuscript on the religious objects and related finds from Megiddo. He said that Albright had already taken a look at it and approved of it.[102] Breasted was extremely pleased to receive this and delighted in informing Guy that it would appear before the tombs volume, since Guy was still working on that. Indeed, since May sent it in as a complete manuscript, it went through the editorial process quickly and appeared in 1935, three years before Guy's book, as mentioned.

Beyond this, however, May was also offered a job at the Oberlin Graduate School of Theology, back in Ohio, as an assistant professor of Old Testament languages and literature. He wrote to Breasted in late February, telling him of his new position and giving advance notice that he would be leaving. Since his new position called for him to begin teaching at Oberlin in the fall, he and his wife, plus their new daughter, Gola Joyce Kina, would be departing from the expedition at the end of the spring season, in mid-June.[103]

Never one to waste time, Breasted immediately set plans in motion to replace May. By mid-March he had awarded a one-year postdoctoral traveling fellowship to Dr. William A. Irwin, who was a junior professor teaching Hebrew at the Oriental Institute.[104] The fellowship would begin almost immediately, with Irwin leaving for Megiddo just two weeks later, in early April, so that he could learn from May for several months before having to take his place entirely. Breasted cabled Guy to alert him to the impending change, writing:[105]

PROFESSOR IRWIN OF INSTITUTE HEBREW STAFF WILL SERVE TEMPORARILY AS MAYS SUCCESSOR ARRIVING HAIFA APRIL TWENTYSECOND STEAMSHIP EXOCHORDA BREASTED

At the same time, Breasted also sent a notice to Engberg, alerting him that he had been awarded a research assistantship at the Oriental Institute for the coming year (1934–35). This would technically begin 1 July, but they wouldn't need him in Chicago until 1 October.[106] Eventually, because of all these personnel changes, Breasted also promoted Shipton to acting recorder for the expedition, based upon Guy's recommendation.[107]

Breasted, who seems to have been quite busy during this period, sent off a long letter to Guy, assuring him that Irwin not only was Canadian, rather than American, but was "a man of unusually pleasing and attractive personality—courteous, considerate, and easy to get along with."[108] Alert readers will notice that, yet again, Breasted was sending someone out from Chicago without having first consulted Guy.

At the same time, Breasted also informed Guy that Engberg had been awarded a fellowship for the coming year, which meant that both Engberg and May would be leaving the expedition, with Irwin staying on until December. There would be nobody replacing Engberg, Breasted said, which probably came as a relief to Guy; having two new people foisted upon him at the same time from Chicago might have been too much. Finally, Breasted also wrote to May, congratulating him on his new position, informing him of the imminent arrival of Irwin, and expressing the hope that May would be able to train Irwin sufficiently prior to departing.[109]

Needless to say, everyone was happy. Even Guy was probably reasonably content at the prospect of both May's and Engberg's departures. We need only recall, as mentioned a moment ago, that he had been willing to trade both of them for Wilensky at a point in the very recent past.

On the other hand, the animosity between Guy and May seems to have reached a new low by this point, although very little was actually put in writing by either of them. The closest that we get is a statement by May to Breasted in his letter of late February when, in telling him of the job offer at Oberlin, he also asked about housing for the upcoming months, after the rent expired on the house in Jerusalem where his wife and young daughter had been staying. He asked whether they might move into the dig house for that short period of time, but said, "I have not inquired of Mr. Guy, knowing that it would be rejected in view of his attitude towards me."[110] (For what it's worth, Breasted promptly also vetoed the plan.)

During this same period, the long-awaited division of antiquities was finally made in late January. It had been several years since the last division took place, so there was a fair amount of material to consider, coming from the excavations of 1930–32, inclusive. These included the tombs on the East Slope, the surface soil of the mound, Schumacher's dump heaps, and the "early stages" pottery sequence that had been worked up by Engberg and Shipton. Breasted had told Guy that he wanted some material that they could use for study purposes and other material that they could exhibit at the Oriental Institute. He was especially interested in putting together an exhibit that would illustrate the development of pottery forms over time, but since he was aware that there wasn't all that much room available in the display cases at the Oriental Institute, he asked specifically for "only one example of each important type." He also noted that they wouldn't be able to display more than one tomb group (i.e., one tomb with all of its grave goods), so "it should be the best and if possible one left complete and not mutilated by the division."[111]

The representative of the Antiquities Department was John Henry "Harry" Iliffe, a British archaeologist who had previously served as a curator at the Royal Ontario Museum of Archaeology in Toronto until his appointment in 1931 as the very first curator (keeper) of the soon-to-be-built Palestine Archaeological Museum in Jerusalem. He held that appointment until 1948, at which time he moved to England and served as the director of museums in Liverpool until 1959, a year before his death.[112] This was his first time presiding over the division at Megiddo, but he would do so from then on, always aware that the share he was selecting for the government would be going into "his" museum, when it eventually opened in 1938.

In the division, Guy was able to procure much of what Breasted had requested, though Iliffe took the lion's share of the scarabs that had been found, and many of the bronze items. In addition, all of the skeletal material that had been promised to the OI, which seems to have been from about half of the tombs, was also duly handed over, and Guy prepared this for shipment first. It was sent to New York in early April and from there was forwarded on to the Smithsonian Institution in Washington, DC, to be studied by Aleš Hrdlička, one of the leading specialists of the day.[113]

Hrdlička eventually published the skeletal material in Guy's *Megiddo Tombs* volume, as a single page of text, plus one table and sixteen pages of photographs (all of skulls, except for one figure with seven mandibles).[114] He determined that the material, which he complained was very fragmentary and "inadequate for any extensive anthropological study or deductions," was from sixty-eight different individuals. However, he evaluated only their "racial" types, including "Alpine," "Mediterranean," and "negroid," which seems to have been done at the request of Breasted, who specifically asked him for "an intimation of the racial connections or physical characters of the skulls and skeletons which we have deposited at the Smithsonian Institution."[115] The skeletal material is still at the Smithsonian, awaiting a more detailed analysis more than eighty years later; it is not nearly so fragmentary as Hrdlička made it out to be.[116]

The rest of the material from the antiquities division, some three cases' worth—which included a collection of sherds illustrating Engberg and Shipton's seven "stages" of pottery development and the best artifacts from a number of tombs—was packed up and sent two months after the skeletal material, on the SS *Exochorda*, which sailed from Haifa on 17 June.[117] In an odd coincidence, May and his family were scheduled to be passengers on the same ship, departing for his new job at Oberlin.

Speaking of departing, what is now known as the "May affair" took place on the day that May and his family were scheduled to leave from Haifa, on 17 June. It began simply enough but quickly took a turn for the worse. The best way to begin explaining what happened is to simply quote in full the cable that Guy sent to Breasted nearly a month later:[118]

> ON LEAVING PALESTINE MAY WAS PROVED GUILTY OF AND FINED TEN POUNDS FOR SIGNING FALSE DECLARATION WHICH HE ASKED ME TO COUNTERSIGN IN CONNEXION WITH ANTIQUITIES WHICH HE ATTEMPTED TO EXPORT WITHOUT LICENSE STOP LETTER FOLLOWS GUY

Two days after sending the cable, Guy sent Breasted two letters. One was a long report on the season, which he ended by once again suggesting that they should refrain from digging during the coming fall and instead concentrate on their publications.[119] The other letter was marked "Confidential." This missive, which apparently provided further details on the incident involving May, was later said by Charles Breasted to be "the most sordid document ever to reach this office."[120]

Unfortunately, we cannot quote from the "sordid" document itself. In the spot where it should be in the archives of the Oriental Institute, within the folders full of materials relating to Breasted, Guy, and the year 1934, there is now a single pink sheet of paper on which is typed, "Letter from Guy dated July 13, 1934, has been retained by CB for his personal files."[121] Those "personal files" seem to have gone astray, for they cannot now be located, but when the letter comes to light in the future, as it undoubtedly will, it will be interesting to see what it specifically says.

In the meantime, here is what seems to have transpired, as near as we can reconstruct the events, using a combination of other materials from the archives of both the Oriental Institute and the Israel Antiquities Authority. We have no fewer than five points of view, in the form of letters and/or memos from various people: (1) Guy (now missing); (2) Irwin; (3) R. W. Hamilton (acting director of antiquities); (4) an anonymous member of the Department of Antiquities; and (5) K. W. Stead (director of the Department of Customs, Haifa).

May and his family showed up at the dock in Haifa on Sunday evening, 17 June, ready to board the SS *Exochorda* in time for a midnight departure and their journey back to the United States. Engberg was there to see them off, as were Irwin and Parker, and possibly others who are not mentioned in any of the relevant correspondence. However, Guy did not bother to attend.

While going through customs, May signed a declaration stating that he had no antiquities in his luggage. However, when the customs authorities opened his bags, they "found a number of pot-sherds which were antiquities," according to a memo that was filed two days later. Taking a "serious view of the matter," the authorities promptly detained May and refused to let him board the ship until they could investigate further.[122]

According to Irwin, who was an eyewitness for much of the episode, having shown up shortly after the incident began, the custom officers' suspicions "were raised by the size and weight of May's boxes and by the fact that they came in from Megiddo along with the cases of antiquities that were being shipped"—remember that this was the same ship that was to carry the three boxes of antiquities from the division made back in January, which were finally making their way to Chicago.[123]

May promptly called Guy, who was at his home in Haifa, alerting him to the problem, and "stated positively that he had no antiquities." Clearly May did not consider the items in his luggage to be technically classified as "antiquities," as he understood them. However, that wasn't how it appeared to the customs officials, for, according to Irwin, the material that was discovered during the search included "a number of potsherds, a few stones and flints, a couple of Roman lamps to which he was fully entitled having bought them in Jerusalem—and perhaps something more." It was all "quite worthless stuff," as Irwin reported to Breasted, but the customs officials wanted confirmation of that fact.[124]

According to a member of the Department of Antiquities, who filed a detailed memo with an illegible signature two days later, Guy called him at 9:30 p.m., immediately after having spoken with May. Guy asked to be put in touch with Richmond, the director of antiquities, only to be told that Richmond was in Syria. Guy then asked for Hamilton, the acting director, and was told that Hamilton had no telephone, that he might not even be home at that hour, and that there was no way to get a message to him.[125] In fact, the department simply wanted Guy to tell the director of customs that the sherds were not important, and to "take responsibility on behalf of the expedition." However, as the memo notes, "Mr. Guy did not seem to wish to take this responsibility."[126]

In the meantime, May was also busy making phone calls, as was Engberg as well, on May's behalf. Both of them were able to reach Hamilton, either directly or indirectly, according to a memo that Hamilton filed two days later. He said that May had left him a message, reporting that he was being prevented from catching his boat because of "a few discarded sherds collected from the dumps of Megiddo which he was taking with him for study." When Engberg eventually spoke to Hamilton, he confirmed that the sherds were discards and that they were of no value. Moreover, Engberg said, that fact could be verified by Mr. Iliffe, the representative of the Antiquities Department, who had seen the sherds while at Megiddo for the division of antiquities back in late January.[127]

Hamilton said that he was also contacted that evening by Mr. Habash, one of the customs officials, and had, at his request, spoken with K. W. Stead, who was director of the Department of Customs, Excise & Trade in Haifa. Stead informed Hamilton of the following facts, as he understood them:

1. Mr. May, on being asked whether he had anything to declare, had signed a statement that his luggage contained "nothing dutiable."
2. When Mr. May's luggage was opened, however, "a considerable quantity of pottery and other minor objects" was discovered.
3. Mr. May then "admitted that these were antiquities and contraband."

Stead took a serious view of May's perceived offense, despite being told that the items were of no value.[128] Nevertheless, he agreed that May could board the boat at its next stop, in Beirut, after the "antiquities" had been taken from him, and that the customs office should deal with the incident and decide upon any penalties, so that May did not have to appear in court.

As a result, May was able to catch up with the ship in Beirut, and he and his family made their way to Boston, arriving on 9 July,[129] and thence to Oberlin without further incident. He eventually paid a fine of ten pounds as a penalty for attempting "to export antiquities without a licence." While ten pounds does not sound particularly exorbitant, it is the equivalent of £680 today, which comes to just over $900 in today's currency.

That next morning, Hamilton said, Guy finally reached him by phone. Guy said that May had actually called him *before* his luggage had been opened, asking him to send a written statement to the customs officials to the effect that there were no antiquities in May's bags. He said that he had declined to do so, but had offered to say that he had been assured by May that he had no antiquities—in other words, he had not backed up May or offered much help at all. Hamilton concluded his memo by stating that "amongst the objects that Mr. May was exporting were some that were by no means without value, including an alabaster pot, and some bits of bronze."[130]

About two weeks later, as part of the ongoing investigation, Richmond, the director of antiquities, who had been away in Syria at the time of the incident, asked Stead to provide him with a full report, including what had been done with the antiquities that they had seized from May. Stead sent him a copy of the "Seizure Note" (which we do not now have) and included a brief cover letter that read in part, "The case was a bad one in as much as the accused having been working as an antiquarian in Palestine for several years, was well aware that he had to declare the antiquities, that he should have obtained a permit for their exportation, and that in any case he had removed [them] from Megiddo without permission of the Manager of the Megiddo Expedition." He also added, "I felt that in all the circumstances a fine of ten pounds would be sufficient in addition to the confiscation of the antiquities." As for the items themselves, he said, without any apparent trace of irony: "I have issued instructions for the antiquities to be forwarded to your Department at Jerusalem. They are not of any particular value, but this does not affect the offence."[131]

In early September, long after all the fuss had died down, the incriminating objects were forwarded by the Customs Office to the Antiquities Department, in a small box. The attached letter listed the contents:[132]

List of Antiquities.
   93 pieces potsheds [*sic*] fragments.
   95 Flint Flakes.
   2 Pieces Basalt Rings.
   5 Lamps.
   6 Stone Implements.
   3 Jars.
   1 Decorated Stone.

In other words, Engberg and May were essentially correct; for the most part, the objects had little value. It was what we would today call a "study collection," which is used to teach students in the classroom what actual artifacts look like, and is especially important if they haven't participated in an excavation yet. The potsherds and flint flakes were undoubtedly from the discard piles at the dig house, along with a few items (e.g., the Roman lamps and the jars) that May had apparently purchased legally in Jerusalem (according to Irwin). While May certainly should have declared exactly that on the customs form, it also goes without saying that if Guy had simply said as much to the customs officials that evening, this entire incident could have been avoided.

This was certainly the opinion that Irwin held, when he wrote to Breasted immediately afterward, saying, "Possibly we should admit that May's conduct here was in some way deficient; doubtless he should have linked up with his denial of possession of antiquities some mention of these things which he regarded as not worth consideration." As he pointed out, it all hinged on the definition of an "antiquity"; and he felt sure that May did not consider the sherds and bits of flint to be antiquities. In fact, he said that Hamilton had said as much by phone the previous evening, which is why the situation had eased and May was allowed to board the boat in Beirut and then pay a fine, rather than having to appear in court.[133]

Irwin also said that Guy could have avoided all of this at several points. The first was at the time of the actual incident, when Guy refused to confirm that the items were discards and of little value. The second, which Irwin thought was worse, was the next morning, when the officers were going through May's boxes again. Irwin says that it transpired as follows:

> When the searchers got into May's second box and began pulling out a series of sherds and other worthless pieces, Mr. Guy was asked to come down from his house and two questions were put to him. "Are these antiquities?" He answered yes. And "are they valuable?" He shrugged his shoulders and said "Who's to say whether they are or not? I don't know," or words to that effect. If he had given the entirely honest answer, which obviously he was fully competent to give, if he had said no, the affair would have ended right there.[134]

As it was, the Oriental Institute had now been dragged into the mess, for all of the information and copies of the various communications were forwarded to the chief secretary of the Palestine government for his consideration.[135] Breasted and the others were essentially helpless and could only hope that the contretemps would not worsen and would not get reported in the local papers (which it did not).

That, however, was not the end of the episode. Far from it, in fact, for Guy compounded the problem by sending a confidential letter of apology on 4 July to Richmond, the director of antiquities, in which he explained his side of the incident and threw not only May but also Engberg under the proverbial bus.[136]

> Sir, Now that you have returned from leave you will have been informed that on 17 June, when about to leave Palestine, Dr. H.G. May made a false declaration, which he asked me to countersign, in regard to the contents of his baggage; that this baggage, when opened by Customs, was found to contain over two hundred antiquities for which he had obtained no licence to export, and that as a consequence he was fined ten pounds by the Director of Customs. I beg to express to you my most sincere regret that a member of this expedition has been guilty of this offence and to assure you that Dr. May took such of the antiquities as came from Megiddo without obtaining my permission or informing me. I beg furthermore to express my regret that when Dr. May and Mr. R.M. Engberg, who was also at the time a member of this expedition, telephoned to the Acting Director of your Department asking him to help Dr. May in the case they stressed the smallness and unimportance of the collection and omitted entirely to mention the false declaration which had just been brought home to Dr. May.

In the letter, Guy also implied that both May and Engberg had been let go by the expedition as a result of this incident, but in fact they were both departing anyway, with May heading for Oberlin and Engberg heading back to Chicago for his fellowship. According to port records for New York City, the Engbergs sailed on the SS *Excalibur* and arrived back in the United States on 14 July, so they must have left just a few days after May and before Guy sent this letter to Richmond.[137]

Further sealing his own fate, on 11 July Guy sent Breasted the thirty-six-word cable quoted at the beginning of this discussion of the "May affair," and on the thirteenth he followed it up by sending the letter that Charles Breasted called the "most sordid document ever to reach this office." As mentioned, this letter has now gone missing, but it is likely to have read very much like the one that Guy had sent the previous week to the director of antiquities.

In the meantime, having received from Irwin his confidential eyewitness account of the episode, the Breasteds had been in touch with May following his return to the States, including conversations with him in person, presumably when he stopped off in Chicago en route to Oberlin in late July or early August. During these, May apologized profusely, expressing his "deep regret for the Haifa incident, and for any complications it may have caused."[138]

He also refuted several rumors that Guy had spread about him and related further episodes that had transpired at Megiddo of which the Breasteds were unaware, including conversations with the Guys when Helen May first found out that she was pregnant. May told Breasted: "After Guy's own insulting reaction when I told him that we were expecting a family, Mrs. Guy came into the room to see Mrs. May when I was not there. She first stated that Mrs. May should have informed her of her condition before I was told, so that she could have informed Mrs. May of methods of getting rid of the child before I knew anything about it. She also declared that it still was not too late to prevent the birth, and said that I would find it a nuisance and a hindrance, quoting her own experience as evidence."[139]

A decision was reached back in Chicago, and even though Breasted had left for vacation by that time, he sent a cable to Guy, directing him to remain in London pending receipt of a forthcoming letter. He also had Charles send a cable to Parker, telling him to remain in Wales until he received a letter of his own that was being sent. He then directed Charles to send a termination letter to Guy, effective immediately. In this letter, dated 28 August 1934, over the course of more than five single-spaced typed pages, they itemized Guy's transgressions over the years, one by one, beginning with the May affair and his 13 July letter, which they further described as "tardily reporting the May incident with Jesuitical and thinly disguised malevolence," and which "succeeds not so much in discrediting the objects of your criticism as in revealing your own unworthiness of the responsibilities hitherto entrusted to you."[140]

In the remainder of the letter, they worked their way backward through the previous seven years, covering the sins of failing to publish promptly; assigning material to staff members unqualified to do the work; excavating too slowly; ignoring the wishes of the director of the institute; hiring and then defending Wilensky; and proposing to the director of antiquities that Solomon's Stables be made a national monument, without having previously consulted with the Breasteds about this. They ended with specific instructions for what he was to do in terms of vacating his position as field director, right down to removing any of his belongings that might be in the dig house and turning over the checkbooks and bank statements to Parker, following which the Breasteds intended to have certified public accountants examine all of the books for possible financial irregularities.[141]

And with that, Guy's tenure as the field director of the Megiddo expedition ended after seven tumultuous years. However, having learned a valuable lesson from the Wilensky lawsuit of a few months earlier, the Breasteds did not sever ties with Guy completely. They allowed him to finish out his five-year period of employment, which ended one year later, at the end of June 1935, and continued to pay his salary throughout, although it was contingent upon their receiving the remaining parts of his manuscript on the tombs, which was still lacking several crucial pieces.[142]

We do not have to worry about Guy, however, for he was promptly appointed director of the British School of Archaeology in Jerusalem, a position that he filled from 1935 to 1939. After World War II, he operated a stud farm (for horses) near Akko and then, in 1948, was appointed director of excavations and surveys in the newly established Israel Department of Antiquities and Museums. He served in that position until his death in 1952.[143]

May also survived the episode. He went on to have a long and successful career as a professor at Oberlin and an internationally respected biblical scholar, until he was killed in a car crash in Florida in 1977. Moreover, he apparently got his revenge against Guy, through a pointed academic snub. In the preface to May's book, *The Material Remains of the Megiddo Cult*, which is dated almost exactly one year later, 15 June 1935, May thanks by name everyone—absolutely everyone—at Megiddo, in Jerusalem, and even in Chicago for all of their assistance, with the sole exception of Guy, whom he does not once ever mention or thank, despite the fact that he was the field director of the expedition.[144]

In fact, May does not appear to have been alone in this. A quick perusal of the three other volumes that documented work done during the years when Guy served as field director, written together or separately by Engberg, Shipton, and Lamon, shows that they all thank each other and May, as well as Lind, but not one of them thanks Guy by name either.[145]

In contrast, the preface to Guy's volume on the Megiddo tombs, which finally appeared in 1938, thanks virtually everyone by name and contains the most comprehensive list of the team members found in any volume published by the Oriental Institute. One would never have suspected that there was any animosity between any of the team members or even that Guy had parted ways with the expedition four years previously.[146] But since we know of this now, and also know the effort expended by Engberg in terms of completing the volume for Guy (on which see more below), we must take the image of a warmly collegial Guy with a grain of salt: it seems highly unlikely that it was he who wrote the final version of the preface to his volume.

CHAPTER X

"Either a Battle or an Earthquake"

Guy sent a brief note to Breasted in late June 1934, about a week after the "May incident" had taken place but still several weeks before he sent the sordid letter marked "Confidential" that eventually led to his firing. In the note, he said that he was shipping to Chicago a small bronze statue-base that they had found in Stratum "VII lower," as Guy called it, which had Egyptian hieroglyphics inscribed on all four sides. He said that when they showed the statue-base to Alan Rowe, over at Beth Shean, Rowe thought that the cartouches were those of Ramses II.[1]

When the statue-base arrived in Chicago and was carefully cleaned, it turned out that the cartouches actually belonged to Ramses VI, who ruled ca. 1140 BCE. It took until the end of November for the experts in Chicago to determine that reading, but once they did, Breasted sent a cable to the team at Megiddo with the news:[2]

BRONZE STATUE BASE BEARS NAME RAMSES SIXTH MIDDLE TWELFTH
CENTURY LETTER FOLLOWS BREASTED

Breasted was ecstatic. He immediately began researching and writing up the statue-base, musing about it in the letter that he subsequently sent to Lamon.[3] Although his publication of the bronze statue-base did not appear until 1948—in the pages of Loud's *Megiddo II* volume, thirteen years after Breasted's death—it is clear from the similarity of the sentences in the letter to Lamon that Breasted wrote the article almost immediately. Loud simply added a footnote on the object's findspot, stating that it was found under a Stratum VIIB wall in Room 1832, which would indeed be Guy's "VII lower" level. Loud noted that the statue-base was obviously intrusive to its context, which it undoubtedly was, given the difference in dates between the object and the findspot—we now know that Stratum VIIB dates

FIG. 31. Ramses VI bronze statue-base (after Loud 1948: fig. 374; courtesy of the Oriental Institute of the University of Chicago)

to the fourteenth century BCE, while Ramses VI ruled two hundred years later, in the twelfth century BCE.[4]

The most likely explanation for this is that Guy's workmen must have found the statue-base in a pit, which they failed to discern while they were excavating. If so, such a pit would have been dug down into this earlier phase by an inhabitant of Stratum VIIA, just as it was ending ca. 1130 BCE (or perhaps even during the next level, VIA, before it too was destroyed). However, we shouldn't be too accepting of Loud's statement regarding the findspot since he was not yet at Megiddo when it was found back in 1934.

Loud also misstates *when* it was found, saying that it was "autumn 1934," when all of the correspondence clearly indicates that it was found late in the spring and had already been shipped back to Chicago for conservation by midsummer. As a result, tempting as it is, we should be careful about using this particular object to date any of the levels at Megiddo, from VIA back to VIIB, even though it is now one of the most cited objects in the scholarly literature about these periods at Megiddo.

However, all of this is getting ahead of our story about the archaeology during these years from 1932 through 1934, so we'd ideally want to return to 27 March 1932, when the actual digging began for the spring season that year.[5] Unfortunately, it does us no good to return to that specific date, or even to the weeks thereafter, for, as mentioned above, there is no information about the archaeology in any letters sent by Guy back to Chicago during the next few months. They dug at the site until mid-December, but it was not until January 1933 that Guy finally told Breasted what they had been finding.[6]

During both the spring and fall seasons in 1932, Guy said, they had concentrated on the tell itself, removing more of the later remains in the southern portion, between Schumacher's trench and the water system, and then toward the city gate. These remains were "scrappy," as he called them, and reused older walls in many places, which meant that the team had to proceed carefully in order to untangle them properly.[7]

In the end, they managed to retrieve a "definite town-plan over a large area, with four parallel streets." This must be our Stratum III (Guy's Sub-II), since he also says that "there are still some houses later than this overlying it in the northern section." Of the various possibilities, only the plan of Stratum III fits this description of having parallel streets.[8]

While the identity of the inhabitants of Strata II and I at Megiddo remains debated—specifically, whether there were Neo-Babylonians here as well as Persians, as seems most likely, or exclusively Persians[9]—it is now clear from the archaeology that Stratum III belongs to the Neo-Assyrian period, and that it was the last time the site itself was of any importance.

The Neo-Assyrian rulers had been recording their battles and triumphs against the kings of Israel and Judah from the time of Shalmaneser III in the ninth century BCE; we know from their inscriptions (and those of others) that biblical figures such as Omri, Ahab, and Jehu actually existed.[10] By the time of the Neo-Assyrian kings Shalmaneser V and Sargon II in the middle and late eighth century BCE, the northern kingdom of Israel and its capital, Samaria—not far from Megiddo—had been overwhelmed and incorporated as a province of Assyria. The deported Israelites, many of whom were taken away to Assyria in what is now modern Iraq, became known as the Ten Lost Tribes of Israel.[11]

Megiddo itself was likely conquered a decade or so earlier, by Tiglath-Pileser III in about 734 BCE, perhaps rather easily since there are few, if any, signs of destruction at the end of Stratum IVA. By the time of Sargon

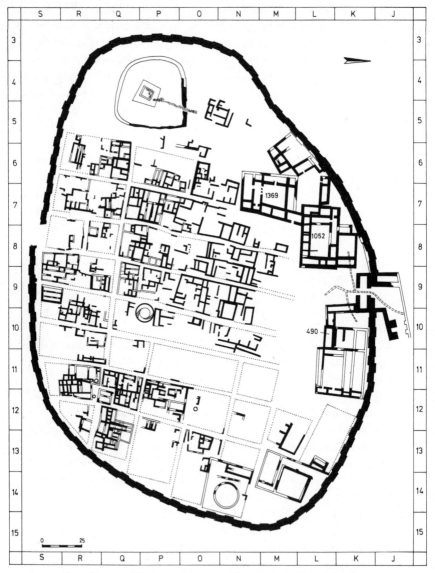

FIG. 32. Plan of Stratum III, view looking west (after Herzog 1997: 256, fig. 5.35; courtesy of the author)

II, a new phase began at the ancient site, namely, Stratum III, which incorporated some of the elements of Stratum IVA, such as the stables, as well as new constructions. The architectural plan, including bathrooms and horseshoe door sockets, reflects the fact that Megiddo now served as one of the Neo-Assyrian regional capitals, when it was known as "Magidu." We even know the name of one of its Neo-Assyrian governors, Issi-Adad-Aninu, who ruled in the year 679 BCE, during the reign of King Esarhaddon.[12]

We can, therefore, finally describe what an actual city at Megiddo—that of Stratum III—looked like, since this was the first layer with a cohesive plan that the Chicago excavators uncovered. There were east-west and north-south streets both separating and connecting well-built blocks of houses, primarily within the central area of the city. The water tunnel was in use at the western edge of the city. There were also two open-court palaces/residencies (Buildings 1052 and 1369) and another large (probably public) building (490) at the northwestern edge of the city, located to either side of the city gate and protected by City Wall 325, which still encircled the city.[13] These palaces/residencies, or perhaps they were simply administrative buildings, look like those built in Mesopotamia, in the heartland of Assyria. The Chicago excavators removed one of the palaces, in an effort to reach deeper levels, but the other is still visible today.

The population of the city at this time most likely consisted of people imported from elsewhere in the empire, as was the practice of the Neo-Assyrian kings, who were known for "de-porting and re-porting" the various peoples whom they conquered.[14] From this point on, from the late eighth century BCE until its demise in the mid-fourth century BCE, Megiddo was incorporated into one large Near Eastern empire after another: first the Neo-Assyrians, then the Neo-Babylonians, and finally the Persians, each of whom dominated the entire region for a century or more, one following the other, as has been noted above.[15]

Guy thought that the "town of the parallel streets," our Stratum III, dated to "roughly 500–700 BC," on the basis of the pottery that the team found.[16] This is, to his credit, quite close to our current thinking, ca. 780–650 BCE. He also noted that they were getting more pottery, from all over the mound now; in some cases, they were collecting as many as thirty to fifty baskets of pottery from a single location. Of course, Guy described almost all of this as being rather dull, but he thought that the other material they were finding—on the East Slope and in the tombs—would be of interest to people.

In particular, Guy remarked upon a lecture that he had heard Dorothy Garrod give at the Prehistoric Congress in London the previous summer, on the material that she was finding in the Carmel Caves. He thought this bore comparison with some of the material that they were finding on the East Slope, and believed that it might date back to the Natufian period, at the very beginning of occupation at the site. He was planning to ask Engberg, since he had some training in anthropology, to take a look at the skulls in consultation with Sir Arthur Keith, who was in charge of studying all of Miss Garrod's skeletal material. He also wondered what Breasted thought of shipping the skeletal material to London so that they could work on it there. As it happened, the material instead went to the Smithsonian Institution in Washington, DC, a year or so later, as already described.

Since that is the extent of Guy's discussion in his letters of the archaeological details from the 1932 season, it is perhaps fortunate that we also have a few additional details in the report that Guy was required to submit to the Department of Antiquities. This was published in 1934, in volume 3 of *QDAP*.[17] Here he reported that more tombs, of various periods, had been excavated on the East Slope, and that these tombs, along with those found in 1927 and in 1930–31, were to be published together in a single volume. He also noted that a number of "habitations—some caves, some houses," as well as pottery belonging to the fourth millennium BCE or even earlier, had been discovered on the East Slope. Seven ceramic stages had been discerned, he said, and would be published in a volume by Engberg and Shipton, which did subsequently appear later in 1934.[18] However, the remainder of his published comments had to do with excavations that were conducted on the top of the mound up through the spring of the next season, in 1933, and seem to have more to do with that year, so we will return to them below.

We also know that Guy provided details for a volume that Breasted had been asked to prepare on the work of the Oriental Institute, which was published in 1933. However, these do not shed any additional light on the work done at the site in 1932, which was one of the least remarkable seasons for the Chicago team at Megiddo.

Guy took to heart Breasted's order to send monthly reports, beginning 1 June 1933. This is the first such report that we have for the year, but since the spring season came to an end six weeks later, in mid-July,[19] it serves as the only information that we have for the entire first half of the year, in terms of archaeology.

Guy said that he had had trouble hiring enough local workmen at the beginning of the spring season because of the harvest, but as of 1 June he had "217 on the pay roll."[20] Even given the fact that Breasted had requested that the labor force always be above 200, this is still an astonishing number compared to today's excavations. Most now utilize college-age students, rather than paid laborers, and few digs today have more than 100 team members at a time. Those who do employ skilled workmen normally hire only a few, and for limited duration, for today such labor can cost upwards of $90 per day per person. Of course, those were different times, and wages are not comparable, but still, imagining the workers lining up to be paid at the end of the workweek in 1933 invokes what must have been a fairly amazing sight.

In any event, Guy said that they had been following Breasted's new commands and had been limiting their work to the new area on the southern end of the mound. They had removed all of the surface remains, which had been categorized as coming from either Stratum I or a catchall "Latest Remains" (which seems to have been anything from the Roman period onward). They had then prepared all of the Stratum II remains and taken an aerial photo, after which many of these ruins had been removed as well. They had also extended the tracks of the "Central Railway", so that they could use it as well as the "Southern Railway" in this area of the mound.[21]

In addition, they had cleared up a large building in Q10 that had been first excavated by Schumacher, and had found another wall belonging to it running off to the west for at least forty-five meters, with no sign of stopping. Since it was "of excellent workmanship," Guy was looking forward to revealing the rest of it. He thought it might connect to two walls located several squares away, in O6, and that it might turn out to be a big palace enclosure.[22]

And, finally, a large circular structure that had been revealed in Square P10 turned out to be a huge grain silo, lined with stone and seven meters deep.[23] This large underground silo is on the stopping point of every tour group that visits the site, since it is at the top of the modern tourist pathway leading up to the current summit of the mound, at the junction where most such groups then turn to the right in order to get to the entrance to the water system and descend the staircase to walk through the water tunnel.

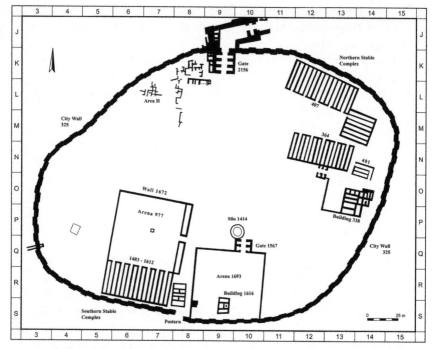

FIG. 33. Plan of Stratum IV (after Franklin 2017: 88, Fig. 1; courtesy of the author)

They had also found a lot of pottery, as perhaps was to be expected, as well as a number of small objects, including fibulae (pins), arrows, beads, amulets, figurines, and stone bowls. There were also a few scarabs, Guy said, but these would have to wait for the Egyptologists to identify them.[24]

In early September, while still on his summer break, Guy sent Breasted the second of the four "monthly" reports that he wrote that year. He spent much of the letter discussing "two great enclosures, each over sixty meters across." These, which were in the same area where he had found the long and well-constructed wall during the spring, could be seen in an aerial photograph that Guy also sent to Breasted. They had well-built walls and floors made of white lime. The western one turned out to be a large court-yard attached to another set of stables, to match the ones that they had found farther to the north back in 1928.[25]

Guy sent two more "monthly" reports back to Breasted that year, one in early November and the other in early December. Both were concerned primarily with the continuation of the clearance of the large western enclosure. By the time of the November report, they had exposed a stable of five units within the southern part of the enclosure, with twenty-eight stalls in each, meaning that it could have held 140 horses. Counting the stables that they had found previously, during the 1928 season, Guy noted that they now had accommodations for well over 400 horses at the site during this period. He interpreted the rest of the enclosure as a "parade ground," which is still considered a possibility, though it is even more likely that it simply functioned on most days as a courtyard for training the horses.[26]

By the time Guy sent his December report, they had removed most of the floor of the "parade ground" as well as the floors of the stables in the western enclosure. Underneath they found a stratum of "pinkish, burnt mud-brick," but Guy noted in passing that "there are also buildings—small rooms intermediate between mudbrick and stables."[27]

There is a little bit more detail in the report that was published in the 1934 volume of QDAP, the official publication of the Department of Antiquities, as previously mentioned. Here, Guy noted that the excavation of the entire mound had continued into the spring of 1933, with the resulting exposure of the town with four parallel streets, remarked upon above. After May 1933, however, he reported that they had restricted excavation to an area measuring 150 m × 100 m, located "on the high ground in the southern part of the city."[28]

He now provided more details about the western enclosure that they had uncovered, which he said measured 90 m × 60 m—consisting of the "parade ground" (60 meters square and covered with white lime) plus the stable of five units at its southern end. The nearby eastern enclosure was simply 60 meters square, because it didn't have the additional stables. Although they still needed to remove some of the later buildings on top of it, they could already see a large area covered by a white lime floor and a gateway in the northern wall. This, he noted, "is the building described by Schumacher as a palace [his "Palast"]."[29]

In his December letter to Breasted, Guy added that they had been working quickly, with over three hundred local workers in the gang at one point, but that now they were down closer to the two-hundred-person mark. Although there had been some rain, they were still digging away, and continued to do so until 22 December, according to the letter that Guy subsequently sent at the end of January.[30]

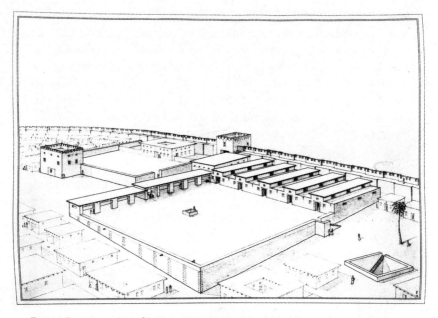

Fig. 34. Reconstruction of Stratum IV structures in Area A from the northwest by Concannon (courtesy of the Oriental Institute of the University of Chicago)

About the same time that the skeletal material was shipped to Washington, DC, the spring 1934 excavation season finally began in early April. Guy had given in to Breasted's repeated pleas and was "going deep in, as you want." He thought that the area of the eastern enclosure, where they had begun digging the previous year, was the most promising, and so they had staked out an area that measured sixty meters on a side in the vicinity of Square R9; this was later dubbed Area CC. We "shall hope to reach Egyptian strata before closing," wrote Guy. Engberg echoed the sentiment, writing optimistically, "I believe we should see the Ramesside level before the end of June." Lamon went even further, writing in early May, "Our slogan for this season is still 'Thutmose or bust.'"[31]

By mid-April, Guy was able to tell Breasted that below the eastern enclosure they had discovered the foundations of a building that measured about twenty-three meters on each side. City Wall 325 passed over part of it and was actually—in this area—built of finished stones that had been taken from the building. Guy noted that the demolition had been almost total,

Fig. 35. Removal of bronze vessel hoard in Locus 1739 from Stratum VIA (after Harrison 2004: fig. 99; courtesy of the Oriental Institute of the University of Chicago)

writing, "This building may well have been a palace, but, as luck would have it, not a single thing remained in it, for the ancient destruction had been thorough except for the foundation course; I am hoping for a foundation deposit under that." These remains are all that are left of what is now known as the Southern Palace, more usually referred to as Palace 1723.[32]

In the 1960s, excavating below the level of the northern stables at Megiddo, the Israeli archaeologist Yigael Yadin found another palace—known as Palace 6000—that dates to the same time as Guy's Southern Palace (1723). This additional palace was later further excavated by members of the Tel Aviv Expedition, including the present author, from 1998 to 2007. These two palaces are now assigned to what is known as Stratum VA/IVB (which will be discussed further below, in our final chapter). At the time, Yadin thought that it was this level that dated to Solomon, rather than Stratum IVA as Guy had believed. However, Yadin's hypothesis has now also fallen out of favor, and most scholars date this level to the time of Ahab and Omri in the ninth century BCE. In part this is because of correlations with the site of Samaria, including masons' marks that Guy first noticed could be seen on the fine foundation blocks of the Southern Palace.[33]

Guy also said that in some places they had dug into the burnt mudbrick layer that lay below the Southern Palace. This burnt city is the level that we now call Stratum VIA. "In this there seem to be more things preserved in situ than in any of the later strata," Guy said, "so I am hoping to get something useful out of it." He also noted that they were working with only 160 laborers at the moment, since there wasn't room for any more in the limited area that they were now excavating, but even these few were producing enough finds to keep the pottery people and the surveyors busy.[34]

Sure enough, just two weeks later, at the end of April, Guy telephoned the Antiquities Department in Jerusalem to tell them that they had come across a group of twenty-seven bronze objects that were in extremely fragile condition. He had ordered paraffin wax to be poured over them all and then surrounded the entire group with plaster of paris, so that they could be moved to Jerusalem for the conservators at the department to work on.[35] A few days later, he sent them off, along with a letter to the director of antiquities, which read in part: "On 25 April we found in locus 1739 (Square R10) a group of about 27 bronzes—bowls, platters, axes, spearheads, etc. They probably belong to a mudbrick stratum, now in course of excavation, which . . . may turn out to be dateable to shortly after 1200 B.C."[36] He was off by more than two centuries, since Stratum VIA is now thought to belong to the tenth century BCE, but he was not wrong about their importance.

Excitement ran high at the dig. May wrote to a colleague, asserting that they had "reached a stratum destroyed by violent siege and fire by the incoming Philistines, probably circa 1190 BC." He described the city as black-

FIG. 36. Crushed skeleton and pottery in Locus 1745 from Stratum VIA (after Harrison 2004: fig. 83; courtesy of the Oriental Institute of the University of Chicago)

ened by the conflagration and noted that they had found the skeleton of a young girl, who still lay where she had been crushed by a falling wall. Of the greatest importance, though, was the large palace that they had found, which was "probably built by David."[37] However, May was conflating two different levels here. First of all, David is unlikely to have built this Southern Palace (1723), which belongs to Stratum VA/IVB. Second, incoming Philistines probably did not cause the destruction of the burnt city (Stratum VIA). In fact, May himself had already helped to determine the most likely cause of the destruction of that level—an earthquake.[38]

Irwin had arrived at the dig by that time—actually more than a month earlier—and he now wrote to Breasted with a detailed description of what they were finding. He seems to have been the first to record the possibility that they were looking at the effects of an earthquake: "The other matter is the interest which May and I are finding in an upheaved course of large stones . . . just north of our present area of excavation and east of Schumacher's trench. It seems inconceivable that it has resulted from anything but earthquake."[39]

Irwin, ever the Hebrew scholar, suggested that it could perhaps be identified with "the great earthquake to which Amos refers" (Amos 1:1), which the Bible says took place during the reign of Jeroboam II. If so, Irwin continued, it could possibly help to solve "the vexed question of the date of Amos' prophecy" and even the date of "the fall of Jehu's dynasty."[40] Would that it were so easy! As Irwin himself admitted, "There are still very weak links in the argument," and indeed there were, in terms of the dating, for Amos's earthquake was probably almost two hundred years later, in the mid-eighth century BCE, rather than toward the end of the tenth century BCE, as this destruction has turned out to be.

Guy expanded on all of this later, in his end-of-the-season report to Breasted, which he sent on 13 July after having stopped for the season on 28 June (and, apparently, having also stopped writing the monthly reports in the interim). It is worth reproducing in its entirety, so that the excitement of the moment is captured:[41]

There had obviously been a disaster of some sort in VI, of which the fire was a culmination, and that disaster may have been either a battle or an earthquake. In the course of it, a number of people had perished. Some skeletons were found crushed under walls in positions of obvious agony . . . but a number of others had been buried. . . . They had, however, been buried very summarily, with no orientation and practically no furniture; the most we found was a bowl over a man's head, and a number of sherds covering the skeleton of a child of perhaps 12. A few people had been stuffed into pots, but not in the Middle Bronze fashion. It looked as if survivors had come back after the catastrophe and had left where they were those bodies which had been hidden by fallen walls but had hastily buried those who were visible.

Guy, like May and Irwin, was also in favor of the earthquake theory for the destruction of the VIA city. He pointed out that several of the walls were cracked, and a few of them had been completely displaced and thrown out of alignment. He also noted that "no weapons, such as arrowheads, were found in any of the skeletons, and very few in the whole of the area excavated." Finally, he—almost casually—mentioned "the presence of quite a lot of burnt wood, some pieces being posts or other structural articles but others almost certainly planted trees," adding that they had kept samples for examination. He ended his description by concluding that "the disaster, whatever it was, had been pretty sudden, for most of the rooms contained very large quantities of pottery <u>in situ</u>, and this gave us a most representative collection of types."[42]

And then, again almost nonchalantly, as if he had nearly forgotten about the earlier excitement, he added: "To return to stratum VI: though we did not get a great number of interesting small finds, we had one real piece of luck. This consisted in digging up a fine collection of bronzes . . . —spear-heads, axe-heads, bowls, plates, jugs and strainers—about thirty pieces in all, stuck together in a pile. It looked as if somebody had made them into a bundle with the view of getting away from the city with them, but had had to drop them in his flight. They were not in a house, but in an open space. I have handed them to the Department for treatment, but this has not yet been completed."[43]

I have to agree with all of them regarding the earthquake hypothesis, after having been a part of the later Megiddo excavation run by Tel Aviv University, where we excavated part of this same layer in 1998, with the same results, including finding crushed skeletons and walls cracked and thrown out of alignment.[44] An earthquake is most likely, in my opinion, especially since (a) there are no arrowheads or other weapons either in or near any of the bodies, nor any cut marks on the skeletons, such as would have been made by a sword; (b) some of the bodies were crushed by falling walls and roofs;

and (c) the walls were moved and misaligned by a force greater than that which is usually caused by humans, even those equipped with a battering ram (which is unlikely to have been wielded inside the city proper).

For those who believe this was caused by enemy attack, on the other hand, it is conceivable that the culprit could be Sheshonq/Shishak, although this seems unlikely. Other recent suggestions have included King David and the Israelites or simply Israelites without David, either before or after his reign.[45] However, none of the arguments for human destruction are particularly persuasive, especially since they cannot account for any of the points just made, and so I think the evidence points more toward an earthquake.

The date of the destruction is also still problematic. While we've seen that Irwin wanted to date it to the mid-eighth century on the basis of the biblical reference in Amos, Guy thought that it fell somewhere between 1100 and 1000 BCE.[46] The recent Tel Aviv excavations of VIA levels in their Areas H and K (Levels H-9 and K-4) have now provided radiocarbon dates that should theoretically help to resolve the dilemma, but the range is still too great, for they suggest that the destruction took place sometime during a fifty-year period between 985 and 935 BCE.[47] This would be either just before, during, or toward the end of Solomon's reign, using the generally accepted dates of ca. 970–930 BCE for his rule. However, David Ussishkin has proposed a slightly earlier date for the destruction of VIA: sometime between 1020 and 950 BCE, basically from just before David's reign until just after (Ussishkin is following the generally accepted dates for David as 1005–970 BCE).[48] In short, the range of dates is wide enough to allow those who want to see VIA destroyed by humans to suggest it could have been done by anyone from David to Solomon to "Israelites" to Sheshonq.

It has been suggested upon occasion that VIA was an Israelite city, but by far the majority of scholars agree that it was actually the last Canaanite city—at least in terms of material culture and, therefore, ethnicity. The most recent exhaustive study, by Eran Arie, now the Frieder Burda Curator of Iron Age and Persian Period Archaeology at the Israel Museum in Jerusalem and formerly a staff member of the Tel Aviv excavations, concludes, "One can safely argue that the bulk of the inhabitants of Megiddo VI were Canaanites."[49]

Forgetting the absolute dating for a moment, and just going with the material culture of the pottery and other artifacts, it appears that Stratum VB, the city of scrappy ruined houses that comes immediately after the burnt city of VIA, is the first undeniable Israelite city.[50] Given its impoverished nature, it seems unlikely that this would have been the city fortified by Solomon, as described in the biblical account, or a city that Sheshonq would have bragged about conquering, and yet, since we have ruled out Strata IVA and VA/IVB so far, we may not be left with much choice. In fact, Ussishkin has recently specifically suggested that VB is Solomon's Megiddo, though this remains unproven.[51]

However, there is another possibility. Already back in 1996, even before all of the new radiocarbon dates became available, Israel Finkelstein had suggested that Megiddo VIA should be dated to the tenth century BCE and the time of the United Monarchy.[52] It is not impossible that the mudbrick city of Stratum VIA was in fact the city that dates to the time of David and Solomon, even if the material culture indicates that the majority of the inhabitants were still primarily Canaanite. It would have been an impressive city, worthy of mention in both the biblical and Egyptian accounts. Alas, the one thing that we know for certain at the moment is that the complete destruction of VIA was an Armageddon for the inhabitants, regardless of whoever or whatever caused it and whether or not it was the city of Solomon.

In any event, below this level, Guy told Breasted, "we came to a stratum of rubble houses . . . and in this begin to appear scraps of Cypriote milk-bowls and [jugs] as well as of Mycenaean pottery." They also found numerous beads and pieces of faience, as well as Egyptian scarabs, perhaps from the time of Ramses III. This they began calling Stratum VII, dating it quite properly to the Late Bronze Age.[53] Deep in this level—"VII lower" according to Guy, which is now interpreted as Stratum VIIB, as mentioned—they also uncovered a Hittite stamp seal originally made in Anatolia, which was inscribed with the name "Anu-Ziti" and his title of "charioteer"—he was perhaps a royal emissary from the Hittite king.[54] It was here that they also found the bronze statue-base of Ramses VI, which Guy first mentioned to Breasted in late June, as he was shipping it back to Chicago.

The team also dug in two other interrelated places that we know of during that spring season. The first area was inside the actual water system itself. In a letter written at the beginning of May, Lamon said that during the previous fall season, in 1933, they had been doing some additional work in the vertical shaft leading down to the tunnel and suddenly realized that the tunnel did not end (or begin, depending upon one's orientation) at the shaft, but rather "extends beyond it in the general direction of the middle of the Tell."[55]

The other area was just inside the city gate, in Square L9, where they dug in order to investigate a sizable depression that they thought might be the top of another vertical shaft. Lamon wrote, in that same letter sent to Breasted in early May, that he had previously thought this "indicated the existence of a second, quite independent and somewhat earlier water system probably not dissimilar to the present, twelfth century water hold; but, since this depression falls on or near the extended line of the newly discovered tunnel, it is not unlikely that the two shafts are connected."[56]

Lamon therefore requested permission from Breasted to conduct further exploration in both areas, though he warned Breasted that this might prove to be fairly expensive. He proposed several different options for conducting the excavations, primarily concerned with how to move the dirt that they would encounter, and thought that the end results would justify the expense.[57] Breasted was intrigued, but hesitant about the cost. He wrote back at the end of May, asking Lamon to send him a memo with the probable expenses listed.[58]

Upon receiving this letter, Lamon put ten men to work in the newly discovered continuation of the tunnel, in order to get some idea of what would be involved in following it out further, so that he could base his estimated expenses in reality. To his consternation, "By noon the same day we reached the end of the tunnel—a 'blind alley' only five meters long!" He attributed the extra portion of the tunnel to an error on the part of the ancient engineer, who had miscalculated the distance necessary to meet the bottom of the shaft, since the tunnel was slightly inclined rather than perfectly horizontal.[59]

He also noted that their related investigations of the "sizable depression" inside the city gate had produced inconclusive results. "If this depression does mark the top of a vertical shaft," he wrote, "it is entirely separate from the present water system." To explore it further would cost approximately twenty pounds, he thought, but in the end, this further exploration was put on hold.[60]

Interestingly, however, in connection with this same approximate area, Irwin wrote to Breasted, also in late May, describing some chats that he had just had with Sir William Matthew Flinders Petrie. He wanted to relay the fact that Petrie was "very anxious that we dig just west of our city gate, or at least run in a trench to see whether we locate thick walls of a palace. He cites his own success by following the principle that the palace would be on the coolest, most breezy part of the tell." Breasted was intrigued, writing back: "I note with interest the suggestion from my old friend Petrie. It shows his old keenness for the practical realities of any situation. There may be something in it, and I shall write Guy about it."[61] In fact, Breasted never did write to Guy about it, for he fired him first, but Petrie was absolutely correct, for it was in this precise location that Gordon Loud, the next field director, found the palace of Stratum VII, complete with its treasures of gold and ivory, which we shall consider in an upcoming chapter.

PART THREE

1935–1939

CHAPTER XI

"A Rude Awakening"

Having finally fired Guy in late August 1934, the Breasteds were faced with two immediate dilemmas. Who should replace Guy as field director at Megiddo? And what should they do about the upcoming fall season, which was fast approaching? Just as they were getting down to the levels for which Breasted had been waiting, it seemed that a rather large monkey wrench had been thrown into the works.

In the end, they decided it would be best to finally adopt the suggestions that Guy had been repeatedly making, and to devote the fall season to getting their publications ready. The excavation season would be postponed until the spring of 1935. But who would be in charge?

Choosing a new field director turned out to be more difficult than they had thought, though they had already been grappling with this since well before they fired Guy. For reasons that are not completely clear, their attention was first drawn to a little-known archaeologist named Lieutenant Commander Noel F. Wheeler, who is mentioned in internal memos exchanged between the Breasteds in mid-August. In these, they proposed putting Wheeler in charge and then—if he did well—promoting him to "acting Field Director" and eventually to field director. They would offer him six hundred pounds as salary for the first year, have him begin 1 October, and allow him the first six months to get up to speed with everything at the site before starting to excavate in April 1935.[1]

So who was Wheeler? He was not related, as one might initially assume, to the more famous archaeologist Sir Mortimer Wheeler, despite their sharing a surname. In fact, he had dug with both Petrie and Reisner in Egypt during the 1920s and had since been working in Cyprus.[2] It is uncertain how, or even whether, the Breasteds knew him personally at the time, but there are letters exchanged between Breasted and Wheeler about six months later, from March through May 1935. These are primarily concerned with a positive review that Wheeler had written for the journal *Antiquity* of Breasted's recent volume *The Oriental Institute*, as well as an article on the pyramids that Wheeler had published in the same issue.[3] The letters give no hint that the two men had ever met prior to this correspondence in 1935 or that the Breasteds had been thinking of offering him the directorship at Megiddo six months earlier, so it clearly didn't come to pass.

Instead, the Breasteds eventually turned to Gordon Loud, their trusted field director at Khorsabad, the Oriental Institute's site in Iraq. Loud, who appears in photographs from this time as a pleasant and well-dressed man, with hair usually parted in the middle and a mustache, was yet another archaeologist who had originally been trained as an architect. Born in Au Sable, Michigan, in 1900, he was the youngest of four children; his brother Harold, older by five years, was killed in France in late September 1918, during the Meuse-Argonne offensive of World War I.[4]

Loud's real first name was apparently Kenneth, but he went by his middle name, Gordon, at all times. He attended the University of Michigan as an undergraduate, graduating in 1922. He then enrolled at Harvard Business School, but after a year transferred into the School of Architecture and received a graduate degree in architecture a few years later, in 1928. Immediately upon graduating from Harvard, he worked as the architect on the University of Michigan's Fayoum expedition in Egypt and then joined the Oriental Institute's excavation at Khorsabad in 1929, eventually being appointed field director of the project in 1932.

It is not completely clear at what point the Breasteds spoke with Loud about transferring him from Khorsabad to Megiddo, but it was before he left the United States in the fall of 1934.[5] Loud later told Breasted that "rumors" about his impending move had already reached the Near East before he arrived. The rumors were correct, and by February 1935 everything had been set in place; Loud would move from Khorsabad to Megiddo and begin work there as field director for the fall 1935 season.[6] He continued in that position through the final season in 1939.

In addition, the Breasteds also turned to Parker, putting everything into his hands except the actual digging. He was now in charge of the bank accounts and all of the finances. He also assumed the role, more than ever, as the manager who kept the day-to-day operations going—maintaining the physical structure of the dig house, keeping the cars running, planning the meals, ordering the supplies, and taking charge of the serving staff—thereby allowing the team members to concentrate on the archaeology and the publications. Up to this point, we could count on one hand the number of

FIG. 37. Gordon Loud ca. 1930 in the courtyard of the expedition house at Khorsabad (courtesy of the Oriental Institute of the University of Chicago)

letters exchanged with Parker since 1927. Now, it seemed that the two Breasteds were writing to him every week, sometimes multiple times.[7]

As for the archaeological activities, in the interim they decided to put Lamon in charge until Loud could take over.[8] At the beginning of September 1934, therefore, Charles Breasted sent Lamon a letter informing him that Guy had been fired, and that they were placing him "in temporary charge of the scientific work of the Expedition." He was also to serve as the institute's official representative in any and all matters related to the excavations but would be acting "without title" for the duration.[9]

However, the Breasteds were clearly not completely happy with this decision, for in the same letter Charles then wrote, "We wish to make absolutely clear that the foregoing assignment of temporary responsibilities means precisely what it says, and is not to be construed as in the slightest degree vesting you with the authority of Field Director. Your position is actually <u>without authority</u>." Without mincing words, he noted further that Lamon's time at Megiddo had been fraught with difficulties over the years, "largely due to your own conduct and apparent immaturity." However, while they had "greatly deplored" some of his past conduct, they had also never lost sight of his "efficient and faithful service" and so had never punished him even when it would have been merited. Therefore, Charles concluded, "The Director considers that you are now in a sense on probation and that the opportunity has presented itself for demonstrating your ability to deal tactfully and efficiently with a situation in which you are not vested with authority."[10]

Later in September, Breasted followed up with detailed letters to Lamon, Shipton, and Lind.[11] He told Lamon and Shipton that they would be the only "scientific staff" at the dig during the fall. He told Lind that, rather than coming to Megiddo, he and his wife, Astrid, would be joining Loud's excavations at Khorsabad in November, where they were to be part of a very small staff consisting of the two of them and Loud, plus Charles and Alice Altman. The Altmans were a young couple, both about thirty years old at the time and both from New York. They had been married for about five years at this point. Charley, as he was usually called, was a trained architect who ended up coauthoring part of the final Khorsabad report with Loud; Alice was the recorder for the expedition.[12]

In the letters to Lamon and Shipton, Breasted also outlined his hopes for the publication program during the fall, including Lamon's own work on the water system volume and the beginning of work by both Lamon and Shipton on the volume dealing with the stratigraphic results on the mound (which would be the *Megiddo I* volume). He ended on a more positive note than Charles had done previously, saying that he was counting on Lamon and Shipton for a successful season, and that their "loyal service . . . will be of great value to science and to the Institute."[13]

As an aside, Charles Breasted's references to Lamon's past conduct seem to invoke those earlier incidents that involved Lamon and alcohol, some of which had been mentioned in a few letters exchanged with Guy over the years. We should also remember, as the Breasteds may or may not have, that Lamon had been only twenty-two years old when he first came over to Megiddo in 1928 and was taking a break from college. Now, six years later, he was still just twenty-eight, but was freshly married.

To his credit, Lamon took the not-so-veiled insults from Charles Breasted in stride. First replying to Breasted's more recent letter, he said that he appreciated being entrusted with the assignment he had been given, even

though it was temporary. He would do his best to "deal tactfully and efficiently with the situation" even though he had no titular authority. Fortunately, as he pointed out, the few of them who were now left at Megiddo,
including him and his wife, were "perfectly congenial," and they probably
wouldn't even notice that there was no field director present.[14]

He replied to Charles a few days after that, restraining himself in simply
remarking, "You have made several rather uncomplimentary statements."
He presented a concise defense of himself, which consisted principally of
copping to an incident that he called "that disgraceful show in Haifa some
four years ago" (an incident, by the way, that is not mentioned in any of the
letters from 1930, when the episode apparently took place). Although he admitted that it—whatever it was—had been "a very serious offence," apparently destined never to be forgotten, he pointed out that it had happened
only once, with no repetition. He also noted that he knew well "the difficulties encountered by a group of people with widely varying personalities
living and working together in close proximity for long periods of time at
a stretch." He concluded by saying, "I honestly believe that you have got me
quite wrong and that at least the strength of your criticism is entirely un-
justified."[15] And with that, he let the matter drop. In turn, Charles Breasted
replied a month later, reassuring Lamon that "the attitude toward you of
the Institute's administration is entirely friendly and that as implied in my
letter of September 1, we hope you will find the new regime at Megiddo a
spur to exceptional achievement, in which we wish you every success."[16]

A few days after he had written to the Breasteds, near mid-October,
Lamon went down to Jerusalem and paid a visit to the Department of Antiquities, to report on the changes at Megiddo. A memo from that meeting,
probably transcribed by the department's director, Richmond, records the
following:

Mr. Lamon called on 12.10.34 and stated that—

1. Mr. Guy is not coming back.
2. He (Mr. Lamon) is taking charge of the work (confined to records, etc.) as representative of the Institute in Palestine (but not
   as Field Director) and that any communications are to be made
   to him.
3. No digging is going on.

I informed Mr. Lamon that the Department only knows (1) the Institute and (2) Mr. Guy, and that it can take no official action on his

verbal communication. We must have a formal delegation from the Institute. Mr. Lamon said he had written to request the Institute to communicate with the Department.[17]

As a result, Breasted wrote to Richmond in early November, informing him that they had reorganized the field staff at Megiddo, that they were focused on publications at the moment, and that Guy would be "superseded as Field Director at Megiddo by another incumbent from the present staff of the Institute elsewhere." After additional letters back and forth, and a confirmation by Breasted that Lamon would be temporarily in charge of the excavation and thus acting field director for all intents and purposes, they were issued a license to continue at the site for 1935, but only to work on the publications and do "local archaeological clearances" if absolutely necessary.[18]

Meanwhile, back at Megiddo, the fall 1934 season was taken up with publication activities, as had been decided back in August.[19] Lamon was very mindful of the trust that they had put in him, and wrote frequently, sending a number of long letters back to Breasted. By the first day, 1 October, he reported that Shipton was busy registering and drawing the pottery and other objects, while Lind—who had not yet left for Khorsabad—was taking new photographs and cataloging the older ones. He himself was finishing up the volume on the water system, Lamon said, and was working half days up on the mound, where he was completing the surveying that needed to be done, and drawing and inking various plans and sections. Although Concannon had returned to Jerusalem and the Department of Public Works, Lamon was hoping that he could persuade him to continue drawing reconstructions of various buildings and areas, such as the Stable Compound, as he called it, on the weekends at Megiddo, in return for room and board.[20]

However, within two weeks, Lamon also asked Breasted whether they could rehire Beaumont, suggesting that he (Beaumont) could take Lind's place as the dig photographer while Lind was away at Khorsabad, and also help him (Lamon) with the surveying. Breasted saw the logic in this and agreed, so that Beaumont became a staff member once again, as of the first week in November.[21]

Overall, Lamon's first priority was working on the volume dealing with the water system, which he completed and sent to Chicago at the end of

October.[22] He also had to quickly write up the annual report for the Department of Antiquities, which he did that same month.[23] He and Shipton then began work on the stratigraphic volume. In it, they made the decision to eliminate "the confusing terms Sub-II and III-IV" that both Fisher and Guy had been using. They also began noticing problems involving the stratigraphy, with instances of a particular locus (findspot) upon occasion listed as belonging to "as many as four different strata," even though by definition a locus can be in only one stratum (layer). They also found other instances where a locus would be listed under one stratum in the Object section but a different stratum in the Pottery section. As he told Breasted: "The confusion in stratification is being put right, and all the cross-references carefully checked. . . . The indefinite headings such as 'Strata II to IV' have been eliminated and the objects put under their proper strata."[24]

They also began to redo many of the photographic plates for the volume, because of the changes that they had made to the various loci and strata. Finally, they decided to remap all of the areas on the mound, so that all the plans would be at the same scale of 1:1000, suitable for publication, and would indicate the various strata that appeared in each area.[25] It was while doing all of this that they discovered an egregious error that needed to be fixed immediately. We will return to this in a moment, for they also tried to save May from publishing related stratigraphic errors in his forthcoming book.

Meanwhile, in London, Guy was slowly finishing the missing sections for his tombs volume, which he finally mailed to Chicago by the third week in November, after a fair amount of additional prodding. Even then, the volume still required much work, for Engberg, Lamon, and others had persuaded Breasted to add in as many as sixty of the tombs that Fisher had found but not published. Engberg was charged with seeing these additional tombs added into the book and through to publication.[26]

Alert readers will notice that Irwin has not yet been mentioned at all with regard to this season, even though he was definitely at Megiddo. This is because, unfortunately for him and through no fault of his own, he was ill for the entire time, with one thing leading to another. The beginning of the season, on 1 October, found him laid up in a Jerusalem hospital, with "gippy tummy," as Parker described it; he had already been there for nearly two weeks by that point. The more technical term was "dysentery," as Lamon put it. Irwin was released from the hospital on 4 October and drove himself up to Megiddo two days later.[27]

That turned out to be a bad idea, for Irwin took a turn for the worse while en route to the site and within just a few days had to be admitted to the hospital in Haifa, ostensibly with "influenza." By that time, his sister had arrived in the country and was able to stay with him. This was fortunate, for he remained in the hospital for four weeks after the diagnosis was changed to "rheumatic fever."[28] According to the Mayo Clinic, rheumatic fever occurs when strep throat or scarlet fever is inadequately treated, or not treated at all.[29] It is rare in the United States today but is still common in "developing nations"—which certainly describes British Mandate Palestine in the 1930s. Antibiotics are effective in treating it, but since Alexander Fleming had discovered penicillin only six years earlier, in 1928, they were not in widespread use yet.

Thus when Irwin was finally discharged from the hospital and returned to Megiddo during the first week of November, he was extremely weak and unable even to make it to the table for most meals. His sister, therefore, booked passage for them to return to the United States just ten days later, and on 18 November they departed.[30] Happily, he subsequently recovered and in March 1935 officially apologized to Breasted for not having been able to do more during the fall season.[31]

Irwin eventually lived to the age of eighty-two, with a full career of teaching at the University of Chicago and Southern Methodist University.[32] In retrospect, his most important contribution to the Megiddo expedition was the eyewitness account that he sent to Breasted on 20 June, reporting on the May affair, for he was the only one of the Megiddo staff members to do so, out of all those who had been present. The second lasting contribution was probably his observations, along with May, about the destruction of Stratum VIA, which he attributed to an earthquake, as mentioned in the previous chapter.

Immediately after the New Year, Parker reported back to Chicago that all was going well. Everyone was working full-time on the *Megiddo I* publication, he said, and it was proceeding quite rapidly though they had a lot of work still ahead of them. It was a good thing that they weren't digging, he added, because they had already had thirteen inches of rain and would not have been able to work on the mound since about the time of Irwin's departure, back in mid-November.[33]

Lamon sent his first full report of the year to Chicago a month later, at the beginning of February. It was extremely long, as were most of his letters during these months; it was almost as if he were trying to prove some-thing to the Breasteds. Lamon said that they were almost finished with the sections on the pottery and objects in the stratigraphy volume and were about to start pulling together the architectural material. It was going fairly quickly, now that they had dealt with a number of initial minor problems, but he estimated that it would take them at least two more months. There-fore, he thought, perhaps they should not dig during the spring season either, so that they could finish all their work on the publication in a timely manner.[34]

Besides which, Lamon said, he had somehow injured his knee and now had some loose cartilage that needed to be removed—he was seriously gimpy and his leg would "go out" on him from time to time. He was trying to decide when to go in for the operation, but, regardless, it would make going up on the mound difficult.[35]

If they did decide to dig, though, Lamon had a few ideas about where they should do so. For one thing, he wanted to uncover more of the stables, since he thought they were "buried only by a foot or two of debris" in one area. They had also uncovered some anomalies in the plans that could bear a bit of investigating, including areas by the city wall, where he now thought they could detect the remains of an earlier wall. However, he was most in-terested in areas that had earlier produced what he described as "the very fragmentary remains of thin rubble walled private houses." Guy had started to find these during the spring 1934 season but had essentially ignored them. Lamon now suggested that these all belonged to a "Stratum V" that seemed to extend over the entire mound and was worth additional investigation.[36]

Lamon wrote again five weeks later, this time much more frantically and in great detail. His frenzy was merited, for what had been a fairly dull and unremarkable stint up to that point, consisting of month after month of working on material and preparing it for publication, had suddenly turned into a crucial appraisal and reassessment of much of their previous work at the mound. He also sent a cable that presented the situation starkly and con-cisely. It read: "FISHER MATERIAL REVEALS SERIOUS STRATIGRAPHIC ERROR INVOLVING MAYS PUBLICATION LETTER FOLLOWS LAMON."[37]

He and Shipton, in preparing new plans for the *Megiddo I* volume, had asked for material from the years that Fisher was in charge to be sent to them from Chicago. In going through those record cards and files, they realized that there were significant problems that had begun with Fisher and con-tinued through Guy's seasons. Fixing the errors would involve "a drastic change in stratigraphy," as Lamon put it. It would also mean having to contradict details that had already been published in both Fisher's and Guy's preliminary reports from 1929 and 1931, as well as portions of May's forthcoming book. However, he and Shipton felt that it had to be done: "The only other alternative, which does not seem to be quite honest, is to suppress the contradictory evidence."[38]

First of all, he said, because of the stratigraphic errors, they needed to combine Guy's Strata III and IV into simply Stratum IV, but then they also needed to split that newly combined stratum back into two parts: an earlier and shorter phase (IVB), which was found only in Area CC, and a later and longer phase (IV), which was found all across the site.[39]

More importantly, though, he said that previously they had all thought that Guy's "Solomonic city," with the stables, had been built immediately on top of the "burnt mud-brick city." However, when they began removing the "Solomonic" buildings in the southern area, it became clear that there was a level in between, namely, the one with the "scrappy" ruins noted above that Guy had basically ignored, but which Lamon and Shipton now said they needed to acknowledge and label as Stratum V. It was these remains that he had just suggested to Breasted in his previous letter that they should investigate further.[40]

In other words, Lamon said, he and Shipton had concluded that Fisher and Guy had missed an entire layer and had left a whole city—and time period—out of their occupation sequence. They now needed to re-create it and put it back together on paper, trying to figure out which of the buildings that they had assigned to other layers actually belonged to this one. Lamon didn't hold back in his letter, in an effort to emphasize the magnitude of the problem to those back in Chicago:

Fisher's material, which arrived yesterday, shows conclusively that my suspicions, based on purely stratigraphic evidence, are definitely borne out by the pottery evidence. A site photo of Room 6 of the "Storehouse" . . . shows typical V pottery in situ and other photos and drawings show that all the pottery from that building and from the building 1A is Stratum V material. With a very sickening feeling I realized that Fisher had published this very site photo and a plate of pottery from the "Store-house" which he describes as his "Stratum III (800–600) pottery"! Of course, during Fisher's time at Megiddo, no pottery of this period had hitherto been excavated—he was not to know.[41]

So, Lamon said, Fisher had completely misidentified these Stratum V remains, and this was but one instance among many. He provided another flagrant example to make his point: "The two buildings 10 and 1A along with the other radial rooms must . . . be erased from the IV plan and if they are to be published at all, they should be assigned to V."[42]

It was imperative to go back through everything again, he said—all of the old plans needed to be redrawn, everything needed to be rechecked, and the various buildings and artifacts needed to be reassessed and reassigned to the proper stratigraphic levels. For instance, in terms of improper attributions and identifications, he pointed out that "the pottery shrine and horned altars which Fisher attributed to the 'Astarte Temple'—according to the note cards just received—were really found in the region of the 'Storehouse.' Practically all the cult material from the 'Sacred Area' which May published as IV is therefore really V and none of it has anything to do with the large building which he describes and illustrates as the 'Temple.'"[43]

Lamon wrapped up his letter by stating that he hoped it was not too late to partially correct May's manuscript that was currently in press, or at least to add a note of explanation so that the reader could be warned about the stratigraphic errors. He concluded in a remarkably understated manner, confiding to Breasted, "Naturally this situation is causing us considerable consternation and we should very much appreciate your help and instructions in the matter."[44]

Breasted eventually sent a reply, but it was to Lamon's letter of early February, rather than his more frantic letters and cable of March. Those latter issues were already being dealt with by the Editorial Department, which came up with the solution for May to acknowledge in his preface that Lamon and Shipton would clarify the stratigraphy and some of the other relevant details in their forthcoming volume, as indeed they did.[45]

Breasted said that Lamon's knee injury, as well as the need to continue working on the publications, had convinced him that they should not dig in the spring, but rather should wait until October. He also mentioned, almost in passing, that they were expecting to appoint Gordon Loud as the new field director. This was the first time that Breasted had put this news in writing to Lamon, since they had only just finalized it, but it was probably not a surprise to him. Undoubtedly, "Who will be the new Field Director at Megiddo?" was a question that had been gossiped about in Jerusalem and elsewhere in the small world of Near Eastern archaeology for months by this point. Breasted said that Lamon should show Loud around the site and point out where he thought they might profitably dig, when Loud stopped by later in the spring while returning home from Khorsabad.[46]

So when Loud came through in mid-May, Lamon showed him around the mound in person, pointing out the areas where he thought they should begin digging in the fall.[47] In the meantime, later that month, Breasted also wrote to the Antiquities Department, to request a real permit. He needed them to grant him a full concession to renew the excavations on the mound under Loud's direction, rather than the limited version that had been issued for Lamon. By late June, the full license had been granted and preparations for the fall season were soon under way.[48]

Unfortunately, Loud had unintentionally created some problems as a result of comments that he made during his visit to Megiddo in mid-May. For one thing, he announced that the Altmans would be coming with him, because the dig at Khorsabad was shutting down. It made sense to shift the Altmans to Megiddo at the same time as Loud moved there, since they worked well together and since Megiddo was so understaffed at the moment. Charley could help Lamon with the surveying and plans, while Alice could assist Shipton with the recording and drawing.

This was actually Charles Breasted's idea,[49] but he had neglected to inform Lamon about any of this. As a result, when Loud casually announced that the Altmans would be coming with him for the fall season, assuming that Lamon and the others already knew about this, it caused a bit of an uproar. In the end, everything was made right, and we have a note from Lamon several months later, in November 1935, in which he says that he "finds them [the Altmans] delightful and very easy to get along with."[50]

As for the house staff, Loud also announced during his stop at Megiddo, in no uncertain terms, that he intended to bring his own staff with him from Khorsabad, including his chauffeur, his cook, and his "personal man," so that they could continue serving him at Megiddo. In theory this sounded fine, but it meant replacing Serge Tchoub, the longtime chauffeur, as well as a local villager named Said who had recently been promoted to cook (after working his way up over the years) and two other local villagers—the houseboy and one of the maids—who had also been with the expedition for years by this point.[51]

Parker went to bat with the Breasteds for all of them, arguing in particular that it would be a very bad show of faith to fire the local villagers in favor of people brought in to replace them. As he put it, "I fear we are treading on very dangerous ground when we sack competent and satisfactory men of the country, and furthermore of the village in the immediate vicinity, in order to replace them with men from another country." And, on an extremely practical note, he pointed out that it would be very expensive to bring the men all the way from Khorsabad, and that the Palestine Mandate Government might well refuse to let them remain in the country after their initial three-month visas expired. Parker also said that it would be especially bad to fire Tchoub and his wife, who had "served the Institute honestly and faithfully for the past nine years." [52]

In the end, everyone agreed with Parker's arguments, and so the Breasteds persuaded Loud to change his plans somewhat. Tchoub would remain as chauffeur, and his wife's position would also remain secure; the Khorsabad cook would come in and take over, while Said would return to his former duties in the kitchen rather than being fired; and Loud's "personal man" would replace the current Egyptian waiter and one of the local houseboys, but both of those would be given new duties instead of being let go. [53]

However, Charles Breasted took the occasion to write a stern letter to Parker. Never mind that Parker had been doing a marvelous job in the year since they had fired Guy, including taking care of all of the finances and the supplies in addition to planting two hundred more trees around the dig house and the ancient mound, [54] many of which can still be seen there today. In his letter to Parker, written before he had received Parker's long letter presenting the arguments for maintaining the current house staff, Charles unloaded what seems to have been years of frustration regarding the dig as a whole and the previous administration—Guy, in particular.

"In terms of time and money expended, the record of Megiddo is far and away the lowest of any of the Oriental Institute's excavational undertakings," Charles wrote. "The history of the Megiddo Expedition has been one of which we have had only intermittent occasion to be proud. Under its previous administration, it was loaded down with a plethora of forms, routine, petty habit, inhibition, and all the impediments of a bureaucratic mind, to an incredible degree which retarded all productivity." Now, he said, changes were coming. Loud had been given instructions to transform the situation immediately. For those on the staff who had become "unduly wedded to the old regime, the reorganization of the entire setup at Megiddo will come as a rude awakening." [55]

CHAPTER XII

"The Director Is Gone"

Loud started things off quickly in early August 1935. He wrote to Lind, who had just been with him at Khorsabad, and asked whether he would serve as photographer for the Megiddo expedition once again. He mentioned that Bob and Jean Lamon had been seen around town (i.e., Chicago), as had Charley and Alice Altman. Lamon was about to go under the knife, he said, having put off the operation on his knee for as long as he could.[1]

Loud also wrote to Breasted, on the very first day of August. This seems to have been preparatory to a face-to-face meeting the next day, for there is a handwritten note scrawled at the bottom of the letter that reads, "oral OK given Aug. 2, '35 JHB." Loud wished to start the season on 10 October, with three soundings or trenches, each in different areas of the mound, so that they could figure out quickly which area was "most worthy of intense investigation," and then plan for the future from there. This must have been music to Breasted's ears.[2]

In fact, what they decided, as Loud later wrote in the *Megiddo II* volume, was to pursue a new strategy of excavation at the site. As he put it, the "original plan of exposing each stratum in its entirety, already partially abandoned, was entirely discarded. While layer-by-layer uncovering of the mound might be most satisfactory in the end, exigencies of time and limitation of funds indicated the need for quicker though less complete examination of the site." They decided to try to reach bedrock in a smaller area and to recover the entire archaeological sequence at the site, back to its earliest beginnings. This would be better, they thought, "than to work over a large area of upper strata and learn nothing of the mound's very early occupations."[3]

Loud thought that one of the soundings should be in the same area where they had been working in the spring of 1934, that is, at the southern end of the mound where they had found the palace and the stables in two sepa-

FIG. 38. Aerial view, looking west, in 1937 (after Loud 1948: frontispiece; courtesy of the Oriental Institute of the University of Chicago)

rate compounds. Another sounding, he suggested, could be placed in the northern part of the site, east of the city gate, while the last one should be in the western part of the mound. In addition, he wanted to do a bit of "exploratory work" to the north of the city gate as well as in the southwestern part of the mound, mostly with an eye toward figuring out the nature of the outer fortification wall.[4]

Of course, it is one thing to sit in an office in Chicago and propose areas to dig at a site thousands of miles away that one has visited only briefly, and quite another to actually put it into practice. Thus when Loud, plus the Lamons and the Linds, arrived in Haifa two months later, just a few days after Parker and Shipton, they all went out on the mound and promptly tweaked the locations of the three areas a bit.

In the 6 October entry in his field diary, Loud noted that the "north dig," as they called it, would be located to the west of the main city gate, rather than to the east of the gate as he had first envisioned. It was to be an exploratory trench five meters wide and fifty meters long. The "east dig" would also be a trench five meters wide but seventy-five meters long. It would cut across the eastern part of the mound, rather than the western part as he had first suggested—they decided to move it in the hopes of catching "something important which may lie in this choicest part of the mound." And, finally, within a week of beginning to dig, they decided to make the "south dig" a five-meter-wide trench also, so that it would be five meters wide by sixty meters long. In the end, "north" became Area AA, "east" became Area BB, and "south" remained Area CC; the areas still retain these designations today. Loud noted that day, "These are so spaced that in one of them we should find the important section of the city."[5] As it happened, they were destined to find interesting remains in two of the three during the coming seasons.

As it also turned out, the reorganization at Megiddo was not so much a rude awakening as it was a welcome relief to those who were still on the staff. There were not many survivors by this point. When the excavations finally resumed in October 1935, only four holdovers were still around to experience the change in leadership: Parker, Shipton, Lamon, and Lind. They were now joined by the Altmans, Charley and Alice, who had come over from Khorsabad with Loud, and two spouses: Jean Lamon and Astrid Lind. In all, there were a total of nine people living in the dig house, with Beaumont coming up for occasional weekends.

Gone by now were Guy, Engberg, May, Irwin, DeLoach, Staples, Woolman, and their wives. Gone also were all of the daily teas and the short workdays favored by Guy. All of the personnel problems and the soap operas of the previous years also vanished, replaced by professionalism and real work done without all the interpersonal scuffles. Even Lamon admitted as much to Charles Breasted by late November: "Contrary to my rather gloomy anticipations concerning the peace of the new Megiddo staff," he wrote, "all has gone smoothly so far, and I now see no reason to think that that condition will alter in the future. . . . [A]ll's well at Megiddo."[6] But by the end of this season, Lamon and Lind would be gone as well.

At Loud's request, a new car was purchased and shipped over for their use. It was a 1933 four-door Ford V-8 and was a welcome addition to the dig, especially for Serge Tchoub, the chauffeur.[7] In addition, the team ordered food supplies in bulk, sufficient to keep them going for most of the season. However, when the crates of food were shipped to Haifa, they were lacking detailed invoices itemizing their contents. The customs officials demanded that the crates be opened on the spot and notes taken of their contents, after which the team was required to leave a hefty deposit pending confirmation from the shipping company as to their exact value, so that the proper amount of duty could be determined. Loud sent such an irate letter back to Howard Matthews in Chicago, who was now in charge of financial matters at the Oriental Institute, that all future shipments came fully invoiced and itemized.[8]

The detailed notes record that, in this single shipment, they received 48 two-pound tins of Scottish Chief Tomatoes; 24 two-pound tins of sweet potatoes; 48 one-pound tins each of asparagus, sweet garden peas, golden bantam corn, lima beans, and extra-small stringless beans; 24 one-pound tins of fancy sliced pineapple; 10 twelve-pound peacock hams; 30 one-pound tins of ground coffee; and fully 384 tins of tomato juice. They also received numerous tins full of chinook salmon, crabmeat, wet shrimp, tuna fish, frankfurters, mincemeat, pimientos, jams, assorted jellies, Santa Clara prunes, yellow cornmeal, cornflakes, bran flakes, shredded wheat, baker's chocolate, maple syrup, crushed pineapple, pork and beans, codfish cakes, cranberry sauce, Ivory soap, and Brill household cleansers. They may no longer have had numerous daily teas, but they were still eating well under Loud's leadership![9] He was probably well aware of the dictum that is still in effect at excavations today—if you want your team members to work hard, you must feed them properly.

In the meantime, there was also a distinct change in leadership style. The easy familiarity and comfortable relations that Loud had with the Oriental Institute administration back in Chicago is noticeable even in the tone of his letters. While James Henry Breasted remained "Dr. Breasted," as was only proper, Loud addressed the others as "Charles" and "John," rather than as "Mr. Breasted" and "Mr. Wilson." Such informality had never happened during all the years when Guy was in charge. Perhaps it could simply be chalked up to chummy Americans with their more relaxed ways, but more likely Loud was much more at ease with the Chicago overlords because he had his own graduate degree from Harvard and an undergraduate degree from Michigan. Unlike Guy, Loud did not have an inferiority complex about his educational credentials. Moreover, Loud was confident in his abilities, having admirably led the excavations at Khorsabad for several years by that point.

Loud introduced somewhat different hours for the digging day, from 6:00 a.m. to 4:30 p.m., with a half-hour break for breakfast at 8:00 a.m. and an hour for lunch at 12:00 noon.[10] He also began the practice of keeping a field diary, with daily entries on where they were digging, what they had found, and how many men had been working that day.

In addition, Loud initiated a different split in the digging year. This very first season under his direction at Megiddo commenced in October 1935 and went straight through to May 1936, without any sort of break at all. He followed this schedule for each of the next four seasons, though beginning more usually in November or December and then continuing through early May of each year. This meant that they put in six months of active digging followed by six months of working on publications, with a bit of time off for vacation during the summer.

Ironically, this is very similar to what Guy had been begging for during his last few years as field director—less time digging and more time for recording and publishing. However, this is not to say that Guy had "loosened the cap on the bottle" for Loud. Instead, unexpected circumstances drove the modifications, especially changes in the financial outlook and expenditures of the Oriental Institute itself.

They finally began digging on 12 October, with their Egyptian workmen and sixty local laborers. The very next day they were honored by a visit from Breasted himself, accompanied by his wife and daughter, but not Charles, who had remained behind in Chicago.[11] They passed through en route to Syria and then again less than a week later while making their way back to Jerusalem and thence to Egypt. For once, Breasted's visit did not culminate in someone being fired; the only other time that someone hadn't been let go as a result of a Breasted stopover was during the "Great Royal Visit" back in 1929. Instead, now he seemed very pleased with what he saw, even though the team was only in the first days of their season. John and Mary Wilson also came through at about the same time, staying for ten days or so.[12]

What was probably unknown to anyone at the excavation at the time is the underlying reason for the visits by both Breasted and Wilson. They had been sent by Robert M. Hutchins, who was now the president of the University of Chicago, at the request of the Rockefeller Foundation (RF) and General Education Board (GEB). As mentioned in a previous chapter, these were two of the philanthropic entities associated with the Rockefellers that, among many other duties, were responsible for approving funding for the Oriental Institute and all of its archaeological activities. The trip to the Near East, to check on the various expeditions and determine how efficiently they were being run, had been requested by the two boards and had been planned by Breasted and Wilson for more than a year at that point.[13]

Why had the request been made? It seems that the devaluation of the dollar and the Gold Reserve Act that had been signed into law the previous year caused sufficient problems that the Rockefeller boards were taking a closer look at some of their expenditures. As a result, just at the time that Breasted was writing to everyone at Megiddo in early 1934 to supplement their salaries because of the damage being done to the dollar, he was called in to meet with a representative from the Rockefeller Foundation.

The meeting was with David Stevens, a former professor of English and associate dean of faculties at the University of Chicago. He had left to join the Rockefeller General Education Board in 1930 and was then appointed the first director of the Humanities Division for the Rockefeller Foundation in 1932. He served in that capacity for the next seventeen years. Stevens and Breasted were quite familiar with each other from the days when Stevens was still teaching at the university, but that did not help matters—according to the Rockefeller Archive Center's own biography of Stevens, he "moved the RF away from its funding of classical studies and archaeology, refocusing the Foundation's efforts on creative fields and international cultural exchanges."[14]

At that meeting, back in mid-February 1934, Stevens asked Breasted about the Oriental Institute's overseas expeditions, since Breasted had asked for fully $370,000 for fieldwork at the various excavations during the 1934–35 season. Later that spring and then in the early fall, Stevens met with Hutchins and then again with Breasted in Chicago. The upshot was that Hutchins agreed to send Wilson and a companion on a foreign tour in order "to gather a detailed record of operations abroad." Not surprisingly, Breasted designated himself as the "companion," and so they set off in the fall of 1935 to tour all of the Oriental Institute's overseas projects, including Megiddo. Far from simply trying to accumulate data that would help him defend their expenditures, Breasted planned to use this tour to collect new facts that he could use in requesting another round of multiyear financial support from the Rockefeller boards.[15]

Immediately after both the Breasteds and the Wilsons had come and gone in October, the dig was hit with torrential rains as well as a labor strike—the local workmen were demanding a seven-hour workday, instead of the current nine hours (including breaks), as well as higher pay. The combination of rain and strike slowed down work considerably for a number of days, but eventually the rain ended and the labor strike was peacefully resolved.[16]

By early November, they had already done a tremendous amount of work. Starting in Stratum III for the most part, they had plunged down through IV, V, VI, and even VII in all three areas—north, south, and east. They were now deep into the Late Bronze Age remains of Strata VIII and IX, with the ulterior motive of searching for evidence of Thutmose III.[17]

However, Loud was unsure which layer would have housed the city that Thutmose attacked in 1479 BCE. He eventually told Breasted that he thought it was likely to have been Stratum VIII, even though it did not impress him as a wealthy city—it "seems a poor show," he said. That meant Stratum IX was "pre-Thutmose," dating to the sixteenth century BCE. He privately confided his doubts to Wilson, writing: "But where oh where is Thutmose III? Was he a liar, or is this not Megiddo?"[18]

The digging proceeded without incident for another month, with between one hundred and two hundred local laborers working each day. They were now down through Stratum IX and into X, moving back into the Middle Bronze Age in all three trenches. However, they had also done some horizontal expansion in places, so they were removing earlier remains as well, from VI and VII, in some areas.[19]

And then the team working in Area BB, the "east dig," made a spectacular discovery. It was a bronze statuette of a seated Canaanite deity, about ten inches tall and covered in gold foil. Loud promptly labeled it "the find of the season." He described the statuette to Wilson, writing: "It is of bronze covered with gold leaf and measures 26 cms from foot to top of crown. It's about as fine a specimen as one could wish for. In the photographs, you see it far from clean, but I don't dare remove any more of the dirt for fear of scratching the gold leaf. It does, of course, suggest north Syria." The workmen had found it within debris from Level VIA, the burnt mudbrick stratum, inside a building that Loud had taken to calling the "big house." Loud thought this might have been a temple, a hypothesis that was now strengthened by the discovery of this object, which he suggested could have served as a cult figure.[20]

In fact, Loud was correct. The "big house" is now known as Temple 2048, or sometimes the "Migdal Temple." It is the largest religious structure dating to the Bronze Age found in Area BB. It also turned out to have several phases, beginning in the Middle Bronze and lasting through the Late Bronze Age. It was just one of many such religious structures that the team discov-

FIG. 39. Canaanite bronze statuette, covered with gold foil (OIM A18316; courtesy of the Oriental Institute of the University of Chicago)

ered as they worked their way down and back through time, for this part of the tell was revealed to have served as the sacred area in city after city, all the way back to the Early Bronze Age. As for the statuette, there is no inscription on its base, or anywhere else for that matter, but it is usually interpreted as a representation of the god El, primarily because of the cap that he is wearing.[21]

F𝐼G. 40. Temple 2048 in Area BB (after Loud 1948: fig. 126; courtesy of the Oriental Institute of the University of Chicago)

Unfortunately, Breasted never got to hear about any of this, for he died one
week before the statuette was discovered, while returning from this latest
voyage to the Near East. According to his biographer, Jeffrey Abt, Breasted
caught a cold on board the ship home, which turned into strep throat complicated by "a latent malarial condition." Doctors in New York City were
able to contain the malaria, but not the strep infection. Breasted died five
days later, on 2 December 1935. He was just seventy years old.[22]

The following day, the *New York Times* devoted three full columns—the
entire left half of the page—to Breasted's obituary, complete with a large
photograph. Lauding him as "one of the foremost archaeologists in the
world," the obituary noted that he had assisted in the exploration of Tutankhamen's tomb and that he had "discovered the site of Armageddon,"

among numerous other achievements. It also mentioned that the physicians had conducted a postmortem exam, in order to eliminate the possibility that his death might be attributed by "superstitious persons to the widely circulated and oft-discredited story of the 'curse of Tut-ankh-Amen'"—though Breasted himself had described the supposed curse as "tommy-rot."[23]

Charles sent cables to the various dig directors as well as to the high commissioner in British Mandate Palestine and to Wilson, who was still traveling in the Middle East and was in Baghdad at the time. The reaction was immediate. "Gloom cast over camp by the arrival of the news announcing the death of the Director in New York yesterday," Loud wrote in his field diary the next morning.[24]

Charles subsequently followed up with personal letters, still in shock several weeks later. "Now he is gone. We simply cannot believe it," he wrote to Lamon in mid-December. He said much the same to Loud the next day: "None of us here can realize that the Director is gone. In meeting the immediate duties and responsibilities which have momentarily devolved upon me, I feel myself merely an automaton moving in a strange new darkness." He did, however, reassure everyone that there would be no changes in their immediate plans. They were to proceed as scheduled for the remainder of the current excavation season. And, said Charles, he would be staying on during the coming year even though he had originally been planning to leave to pursue other opportunities before this sudden development.[25]

However, despite his reassurances, there were large changes already looming that would drastically affect Megiddo. Several weeks before his death, Breasted had sent a letter to Rockefeller, presenting in detail the current financial straits of the institute. The response was unexpected. Rockefeller stated in no uncertain terms that he was not prepared to continue giving money to the Oriental Institute or to Breasted as a constant stream of new revenue. "I have been as enthusiastic as you yourself about the great central purpose of your work," he said. However, he continued, "I cannot but feel, much as I regret to say so, that in your enthusiasm you have been led to expand the scope of your operations far beyond what was prudent or permanently possible to maintain."

Rockefeller made it quite clear that he had never intended to become the sole patron "of the vast enterprise that has since developed," as he described the Oriental Institute. Moreover, he said, there should be "a complete review of the work of the Oriental Institute at an early date having in mind its future," for "the situation which you described . . . is both unsound and precarious."[26] Fortunately, Breasted never saw this letter before he died. As Charles later said to Rockefeller, "the implications . . . would have grieved him deeply."[27]

Thus just two weeks after Breasted died, and during the very same week that Charles Breasted was writing to the dig directors, David Stevens was back in Chicago, like a vulture eying fresh roadkill. He asked Wilson, who would be appointed acting director a few weeks later, to present the Rockefeller boards with a plan in which the overall $700,000 budget of the Oriental Institute was drastically reduced by 50 percent or more and the field projects similarly cut to the bone or shut down completely. With Breasted no longer around to personally defend the various overseas undertakings, Wilson had no choice but to comply.[28]

Meanwhile, unaware of what was happening back in Chicago in the aftermath of Breasted's sudden death, Loud and the others continued to dig through December. More remains of walls and buildings appeared from Levels VI–X, as well as a lot of pottery and a few small bronze figurines of Syrian style, plus one made of black serpentine that appeared to be Egyptian. The "north dig" by the city gate seemed particularly promising, for some of the remains from Stratum VII were beginning to look more and more as if they belonged to a palace such as Breasted had long been hoping they would find in that area.[29]

Since this hypothesized Stratum VII palace would date to the fourteenth century BCE, they also expected to find an archive of clay tablets here. This era was a high point in the ancient Near East and a time when all of the great powers were in contact. Canaan, though, was ruled by a series of small kingdoms or city-states, all of which were vassal to New Kingdom Egypt. In the capital city that the pharaoh Akhenaten built at the site of Amarna, midway between what is today Cairo and Luxor, archaeologists in 1887 found a trove of nearly four hundred clay tablets—the remains of a royal archive of letters belonging to Akhenaten and his father, Amenhotep III. Included among these were six letters sent by Biridiya, the ruler of Megiddo, concerned with various matters.[30] Loud had every right to expect that the Egyptian responses to these letters would be stored in the palace that he hoped to uncover in the northern area at Megiddo.

Loud summarized what they had done so far in a letter sent to Wilson on 21 December. With his letter, Loud included a plan and several photographs, to help Wilson visualize what they were doing. Since Wilson had been at the dig just two months earlier, Loud was able to simply launch right in.[31]

In the southern trench, Area CC, they had found only private houses in each level. Apart from "a good pottery sequence," they hadn't retrieved much that was helpful, so they had stopped once they reached the beginning of the Middle Bronze Age. They were now shutting down the area for the time being, since the other two areas were in the process of being enlarged and thus needed more workmen, whom Loud was planning to take from this area.[32]

In the north trench and the east trench—Areas AA and BB, respectively— they were now enlarging the original trench in each area. In the east, they had excavated down to the same Middle Bronze Age level that they had reached in the south, and had retrieved a good pottery sequence here as well.

They were also continuing to uncover what he would later call Temple 2048, which we have already encountered; it was in this building that the statuette of the seated god had been found. Loud described it as "a building of a type entirely new to Megiddo," with a broad entrance featuring two flanking towers and column bases. He was now certain that it had been built during Stratum X, in the Middle Bronze Age (sixteenth century BCE), but had continued in use through the entire Late Bronze Age, right up until the destruction of Stratum VIA in the early Iron Age (tenth century BCE).[33]

As for the north area, Loud said, there they were running into massive walls, which were up to two meters thick. These he thought were to be dated to Stratum VIII; there was excellent material from the burnt mudbrick VIA level directly above them, with very poor walls from VII in between. In fact, they would later decide to redate these and assign the massive walls to Stratum VII, with the poor walls belonging to Level VIB, which makes much more sense. They were also beginning to think that the walls belonged to a palace—as it turned out, they did.[34]

Summing everything up for Wilson, Loud said that the massive constructions in the east and north trenches probably dated to a single period during the Late Bronze Age, "in which must fall the occupation involved in the battle of Megiddo." He thought that the poorest citizens of the city lived in the southern area, where they had been finding modest houses in each level. He still planned to dig straight down in one area, all the way to bedrock, but this would have to wait until the spring, he said, since the rains were now making it impossible to work in the trenches. However, he was

Fig. 41. (a) Northern Trench (Area AA); (b) Eastern Trench (Area BB); (c) Southern Trench (Area CC) (after Loud 1948: figs. 1–3; courtesy of the Oriental Institute of the University of Chicago)

also at pains to remind Wilson that "most of the information comes only from five-meter trenches and cannot be considered conclusive." He concluded by saying, "I may therefore be forced to change my ideas before the end of the season," adding, "I trust then that you will not let any of this get into print."[35]

The small group at Megiddo then took a brief break for Christmas 1935. They celebrated by going to a dance in Haifa on the evening of the twenty-fourth and opening presents on the morning of the twenty-fifth—"bakshish for the servants and silly presents for staff members," as Loud put it.[36]

A few days later, Albright stopped by, on his way home to Baltimore for a year and a half. Loud was very pleased by the visit, writing in his field diary that Albright "seemed greatly impressed with the dig and our objects, and had nothing to offer in the line of contradicting our current theories concerning them. . . . He confirms my theory that the east building is a Temple beyond a doubt, and thinks, as we hope, that the north building is a palace."[37]

They continued working right into the new year. Then, in mid-January, Loud and Shipton headed up to Iraq and Syria for two weeks, in order to dispose of the Khorsabad property since the Oriental Institute was no longer working there. While they were gone, Lamon and Altman were left in charge of the work, both on the mound and in the dig house.[38]

However, unbeknownst to the rest of the team, Loud received a cable from Wilson just before leaving for Iraq, informing him that the entire Oriental Institute was facing "drastic retrenchment." The impact on Megiddo seemed minimal at that point, though, for Wilson said only that the budget for next season "must unavoidably be somewhat reduced."[39]

In a follow-up letter, Wilson explained that the ten years of funding they had received from the Rockefeller boards back in 1928 for the entire Oriental Institute was due to run out soon. Obviously, given the stock market crash in 1929 and the Great Depression that followed, the world was a different place from what it had been when they received the original grant, and so they had been expecting for some time that they would need to reorganize things. That was why, Wilson now said, he and Breasted had toured the Near East back in the fall; it was, as he put it, "largely for the purpose of collecting information which would be useful in an intensive campaign in New York for refinancing."[40]

Such an intensive campaign was now out of the question, since it had been Breasted's personal relationship with John D. Rockefeller, Jr., that had made all of this possible. With Breasted's unexpected death, the policy of "retrenchment"—a word that Wilson used continually throughout his communications this spring—"has been made virtually a condition of future support." Moreover, that retrenchment was to begin immediately. Some of the Oriental Institute's overseas projects would be marked for an "early and graceful" termination, as Wilson put it, meaning that they would be allowed to continue for a short period, during which they were to wrap up their work.[41]

Megiddo was not yet in this category, however. Instead, Wilson said that their budget for 1936–37 would be reduced somewhat. He also asked Loud to give him an estimate of how many more seasons he would need to complete the excavation, if he were given an annual budget of $40,000. Having worked at the site several years earlier and visited it just recently, Wilson was confident that they could "complete" (his quotes) their work there "without stripping every meter of earth on the tell," adding that "the essential facts can be gleaned through work on certain sections of the mound."[42]

Loud's response was fairly succinct. At an absolute minimum, he would need three more seasons, he said; as a maximum, he would wish for six more. As for the reduced budget for the coming year, it was a blow, as he put it, but understandable under the circumstances. They would make do with whatever they could get. Wilson thanked him for being so understanding, and, with that, the digging continued uninterrupted by such matters for another two months.[43]

In early February, following his return from Iraq, Loud reported that things were going well at Megiddo.[44] The rain was holding off and additional workmen kept showing up; they now had 225 local laborers on their payroll, of whom about 200 came to work each day.[45] In addition, his piano had finally arrived and had been installed in the house. He had also adopted a new dog, an Irish setter.[46]

In the east area, they were leaving the temple alone for the moment, after finding fragments from three Egyptian statuettes there, at least two of which were from the Middle Kingdom period. One of them, portraying a man sitting in a chair, had an inscription that states he is "Thuthotep" (recently rendered as "Djehutihotep"), an Egyptian official known to have been a district governor in Upper Egypt during the Twelfth Dynasty. The other two were of women, each with only the head and upper body preserved. These were definitely heirlooms, since they were too early for the level in which they had been found, but were interesting additional proof that Megiddo had been in contact with Egypt, or under Egyptian influence, during the mid-second millennium BCE.[47]

They had also found the first "liver omen" ever discovered in the region, Loud said, just outside the temple. These were more often found up in Mesopotamia—they were model livers usually made of clay and used by priests to help interpret omens or predict the future.[48]

When they finally began digging in this area later in February, Loud noted that there were two parts to Stratum VII, separated by a burnt layer. This matched what they had earlier noticed in the south area and would be important later in the north area, when it came time to decipher the remains of the palace there.[49]

In the meantime, speaking of the northern area, they were concentrating on the gate area in the north dig. Loud was quite confident that they could see three different phases to the "Solomonic Gate" there, which Guy had first uncovered back in 1928, and hoped to have more data available soon.[50] However, while he was unexpectedly off in Beirut having an emergency appendectomy in March,[51] the team discovered that it wasn't Solomon's gate after all; instead, it belonged to Stratum III and the Neo-Assyrian period of the eighth and seventh centuries BCE.[52] The "true Stratum IV gate exists below," Loud said later, noting that in order to get at this gate they would have to shift their digging area slightly.[53]

He also said that they were still dating the palace in this north area to Stratum VIII and the fifteenth century BCE, but they were beginning to suspect that portions of it might actually date to Stratum VII and the fourteenth century BCE, and that there were two phases to this level here too. In any event, it was turning out to be "colossal," as he put it. There was no way that they would be able to finish excavating the palace this season. They were also finding some fragments of painted plaster in what they thought might be the courtyard of the palace. The plaster was mostly painted blue, but there was also some red and green. In addition, one of the more interesting developments, perhaps related to the palace, was the discovery

FIG. 42. Stratum IV gate, viewed from the north after clearing and before removal of right side (after Loud 1948: fig. 110; courtesy of the Oriental Institute of the University of Chicago)

of a set of huge stairs made of black basalt stone that may have led to the city gate during that period.[54]

These basalt stones can still be seen today, just inside the reconstructed Late Bronze Age city gate. Nearby are the remains of the Stratum IV city gate that Loud now thought was the one that dated to the Solomonic period. Unfortunately, once they had the gate all cleared, they removed half of it in order to continue exposing more of Strata VII and VIII (though this project would not be completed until the following year, in March 1937).[55]

This has created a number of problems for more recent excavators, including both Yigael Yadin and Israel Finkelstein, each of whom have discussed the date of this gate. Yadin, for instance, thought he could link the gate with those built at Hazor and Gezer, and document the existence of a "Solomonic building program" dating to the tenth century BCE.[56]

Finkelstein, on the other hand, as mentioned at the beginning of this book, has been arguing since the 1990s for a lowering of the chronology for the early first millennium BCE across ancient Israel. His arguments for this "Low Chronology," as it is called, are many and varied, based in part on traditional ceramic chronology and in part on cutting-edge scientific research including radiocarbon dating and Bayesian analysis. His suggested redating has a potentially huge impact, including the suggestion that this gate should more likely be dated to the ninth century BCE, perhaps to the reign of Ahab or Omri. The debate continues to the present day.[57]

By the time Loud wrote again to Wilson, in mid-April, he didn't have much to add to his previous report, except to say that they were continuing to work in both the north and east areas, and that they had found some jewelry and the lower part of another Egyptian statue with an inscription within the back chamber of the temple in the east area. They had also been digging a few small trenches to double-check their stratigraphy and dating, so he was pretty confident now that Stratum IX could be dated to the seventeenth and sixteenth centuries BCE—that is, the time of the Hyksos rule in Egypt— and that Levels VIII and VII "fill up the 15th, 14th, and 13th centuries," as he put it.[58]

Loud later filed a mandatory report with the Department of Antiquities on their activities during the season. In it, he mentions that they had also been digging in Levels X, XI, XII, and XIII, which had taken them back to about 2000 BCE and the very beginning of the Middle Bronze Age. He noted further that they now thought the temple in the east area had first been built in Stratum IX, but completely rebuilt in VIII and VII. They now also thought that it was dedicated to the worship of the Canaanite god Resheph, to judge from the number of small bronze "Resheph figurines"— showing the god with one arm upraised and about to "smite" an enemy—that had been found in and around the temple.[59]

Loud also told the department that they had found various "ramps"— probably better described as "roadways"—dating to Levels III, IV, and V in the area by the city gate, all representing approaches to the city over the centuries. In addition to the gates of III and IV, which had caused such stratigraphic problems during the season, they now also had a four-chambered gate dating to Stratum VIII (and continuing in use through Stratum VII) lying just to the west of all the later gates—this is the Late Bronze Age gate that tourists now walk through, mentioned just above. There was also a bit of the ramp from the Stratum XI gate lying even farther to the west. In other words, the main entrance to the city had always been in this northern area but was slowly moving to the east in successive levels.[60]

By mid-April, Loud began to make plans to close up the dig for the season. He sent a cable to Wilson, telling him that their final day of digging would be two weeks thence, on the last day of the month.[61] The digging had been going so well and the stratigraphy and dating were so straightforward that one wonders how things might have been different if Loud had been in charge since the very beginning, instead of Fisher and then Guy. We shall never know.

Loud also arranged for a division of antiquities to be made at the beginning of May, right after they stopped digging, so that they could divide up this season's finds promptly. They had already conducted another division back in February, of items previously excavated from Strata I–V. The Oriental Institute received a fair share both times, and in mid-May Loud shipped back to Chicago seven cases packed full of antiquities plus another case filled with their excavation records.[62]

However, it was at this point, just at the conclusion of the season, from the end of April until mid-May, that cables began to fly back and forth between Megiddo and Chicago once again. Less than a week before they were scheduled to close for the season, Wilson sent Loud the first of these, written in code. When he decoded it, Loud was astonished at the message:[63]

ACTION BOARDS TERMINATES ALL ORINST EXPEDITIONS NOW OR NEXT SEA-
SON STOP MEGIDDO MUST TERMINATE INCLUDING LIQUIDATION NEXT
SEASON

Wilson offered more details in a long letter that he sent the next day. Back in March, he and the others from the Oriental Institute had submitted a budget to the Rockefeller boards that called for a 50 percent cut, as mentioned. That wasn't enough for the boards, however. In mid-April, they simply "appropriated a sum of money for the Oriental Institute, thus closing out their relation to the Institute."[64] In other words, perhaps tired of dealing with the institute and also taking advantage of the fact that Breasted was now gone, the boards had opted to effectively give the Oriental Institute what we would now call a "golden parachute," and terminated their relationship.

We possess the actual details, for the Rockefeller Foundation included them in their Annual Report for 1936, as follows:

> The Foundation has made two grants to the University of Chicago in termination of assistance to the Oriental Institute. The first of these, totaling $1,169,766.01, is for current support of the Institute or for its endowment. The second appropriation, amounting to $1,000,000, has been made with the understanding that this fund shall be held for ten years as endowment for the Institute. These grants are intended to conclude the Foundation's participation in the work of the Oriental Institute.[65]

While these two amounts, totaling more than two million dollars, sound like—and are—a lot of money, Wilson told Loud that the sum would enable only the running of the Oriental Institute on a skeletal basis, without providing for any teaching, fellowships, publications, or fieldwork. In his words, "The Oriental Institute, as it has been established . . . is terminated, even though we may prefer to think of it as suspended." Therefore, he said, they were going to close out most of the projects and expeditions as quickly as possible and concentrate on publishing the material that they had found in Egypt and the Near East during the past decade. After that, they would continue modestly, with less than half their present budget, and eventually hope "to put one small expedition into the field." The Syrian expedition was being closed immediately; the Iranian expedition would close within the calendar year; and Megiddo, Iraq, and Luxor would be terminated before the end of June 1937, with Megiddo allotted only $38,000 for its final season. "By July 1937, the 'Oriental Institute' will not have an expedition in the field," Wilson wrote. "This blow which has hit us is far too great for any wringing of hands and shaking of heads. It is numbing in its violence."[66]

And yet, catastrophic as that all seemed, worse was still to come for the folks at Megiddo. At the end of the first week in May, Wilson sent a second cable, this time in plain English.[67]

REGRET ANOTHER MEGIDDO SEASON IMPOSSIBLE EXPEDITION TERMINAT-
ING NOW STOP CAN YOU REMAIN TO LIQUIDATE HOUSE AND EQUIPMENT
WITH HELP PARKER LIND STOP ADVISE ANTIQUITIES DEPARTMENT OF
TERMINATION

There would be no final season in 1936–37; instead, they were to immediately close up shop, terminate the dig, and sell the dig house and all its

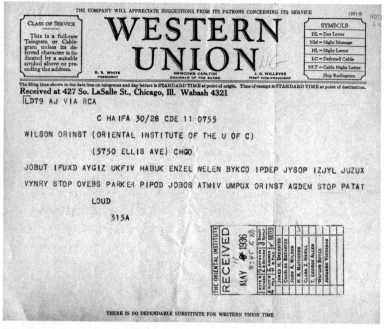

FIG. 43. Coded cable sent from Loud to Wilson on 11 May 1936 (courtesy of the Oriental Institute of the University of Chicago)

contents. The cable went on to say that Altman, Lamon, and Shipton would remain on the payroll, but would be working on publications back in Chicago. Parker and Lind were not being renewed and would be let go at the end of June. A longer letter, sent the same day, explained that the institute administration had been trying for three weeks to figure a way out of the financial dilemma, but had finally concluded that they had to close down all of the excavations immediately, rather than allow them to continue for another year.[68] For the small team at Megiddo, this was the end of the world as they knew it; it was their own personal Armageddon.

More cables flew back and forth across the Atlantic in the next several days—three from Loud to Wilson alone. In them, Loud tersely told Wilson that he, Parker, and Shipton would remain at the site as long as necessary to liquidate everything. He also asked, plaintively, whether they might excavate for one more season after all, on a shoestring budget of $20,000, but Wilson replied that was impossible. And, in one cable, Loud told Wilson that the local conditions were so unsettled that liquidation of the house and all their equipment would be difficult. He followed up almost immediately with another cable, this time in code, stating that the growing disturbances actually made liquidation impossible, and that the government thought the situation could last for weeks. He recommended that they postpone the liquidation until the fall, if things had calmed down by then.[69]

What was Loud talking about? As it turned out, the "disturbances" lasted for a full six months; they marked the beginning of what is now known as the 1936–39 Arab Revolt in British Mandate Palestine. Loud recorded some of the events in his field diary. On 19 April, he noted: "The Garstangs drop in for five minutes after tea . . . but all are whisked away in a hurry by police. Riots are under way in Jaffa and Tel Aviv, and the police are taking precautions in keeping people off the roads here. So far Haifa remains quiet." The next day he wrote that it remained to be seen what effect the riots would have on them locally. By 22 April, he noted that the riots were quieting down and had not affected their local work situation.[70]

What Loud and the others were experiencing at the time was just the opening stage, which soon morphed into a general strike that lasted from May to October 1936. A second, more violent and deadlier, phase would begin a year later, in the fall of 1937, after the Peel Commission released its findings in July of that year, concluding that British control of the area could not be sustained, and proposing a partition—dividing the land between the Arabs, who would receive 80 percent, and the Jews, who would receive 20 percent. The Peel report led to an escalation of the protests, which lasted until 1939 and resulted in an eventual death toll estimated at 150 British soldiers, 500 Jews, and more than 3,000 Arabs. However, that still lay a bit in the future at this point.[71]

On 12 May, having exhausted all avenues with Chicago, Loud made his way down to Jerusalem, accompanied by Parker. The next morning he went to see Richmond, the director of the Department of Antiquities. Since Richmond was unavailable, Loud met with Hamilton instead and told him that they were finished, not just for the season, but forever. The message certainly resonated with Hamilton—remember that he had once been a member of the Megiddo team for a few weeks back in 1929. A handwritten note that Hamilton penned to Richmond later that same day captures Loud's reluctant message: "The Oriental Institute has officially closed down the expedition

to Megiddo. They are packing up everything except pictures, plants, etc. Mr. Parker will return in the autumn to wind up their affairs. . . . Mr. Loud wishes to keep the matter of the closing of the dig confidential for the present."[72]

And then Loud broke the news to the rest of the team, who had been—seemingly—blissfully unaware until this point. Reaction was immediate—Shipton wrote expressing his "sense of shock and great disappointment" at hearing the sad news that "Megiddo must go the way of all field expeditions." He was especially disappointed since he felt sure that the next season was destined to have spectacular results. On that point he was remarkably prescient, as we shall see.[73]

Olof Lind took it hardest of all. Loud recorded in his field diary that Olof and Astrid stormed off on 15 April, just after the Altmans and Lamons had departed a bit more ceremoniously for Haifa.[74] The next day, from Jenin, Lind sent a handwritten letter to Wilson in Chicago, commencing a series of increasingly bitter exchanges that continued throughout much of the summer. "We are stranded in Jenin with all our worldly possessions," he began in this first letter. "I shall join the escorted convoy to Jerusalem, but am obliged to leave everything here. It does seem ridiculous to be ordered out on so short a notice and I should be glad to hear what you intend to do with me after these ten years of services."[75]

In the end, after much back-and-forth, including veiled threats of a lawsuit and a plaintive handwritten line, "I was promised a future with the Institute," at the bottom of one letter, Lind was paid for the months of July and August as a severance package and shown the door.[76] Had he played his cards differently, Lind could probably have remained a part of the expedition, but as it was, he proved so aggressive and obnoxious in his interactions with Wilson that when the team regrouped and returned to the field after all, in December 1936, Lind was no longer welcome.

CHAPTER XIII

"You Asked for the Sensational"

In fact, the expedition reversed course from potential termination so quickly that Lind was still fighting for his severance pay when Wilson met once again with Stevens of the Rockefeller board in mid-July. Wilson informed Stevens, somewhat defiantly, that they were allocating $28,000 toward a field season at Megiddo for 1936–37. He said that they might even be able to raise more money, if necessary, before they headed for the field again.[1] Stevens had no objections; the institute was free to do with their money as they pleased, just as long as they understood that they weren't going to get any more from the Rockefeller boards beyond what had just been approved for them.

With that, Wilson and Loud began thinking about how to approach the next season in terms of staffing. There weren't many team members from whom they could choose, actually. Lind would never be hired by the OI again, while Engberg and Lamon were busy with publications in Chicago—Engberg was working on fixing Guy's tombs manuscript at the same time as finishing up his PhD dissertation on the Hyksos, while Lamon was working on the stratigraphy volume that would become *Megiddo I*. Even though Shipton was also working on the publications, they were going to need him at the dig; they also needed the Altmans and Parker.

First, though, they had to make certain that they could get permission to dig again. In early September, Loud sent letters to Richmond, in his role as the director of antiquities, and to the chief secretary in Jerusalem. He explained that recent developments had made another season at Megiddo possible after all, and that they would like to postpone the liquidation and instead dig again beginning in November or December.[2]

Richmond replied positively, so the only thing that Loud had to do now was wait to see whether the general strike would eventually come to an end, allowing them to begin work. He sent cables to Richmond inquiring about the conditions in mid-October and then again in late October, finally receiving a positive reply: "AS AT PRESENT ADVISED WORK RESUMEABLE DECEMBER."[3]

Loud told Shipton and Parker to get ready for an imminent departure. He then told Richmond that Parker would show up in late November, and he himself would arrive in mid-December. He also requested a license to excavate for the coming season. Richmond replied positively for a third time and enclosed a license for Loud and the OI to dig, valid through the end of December 1937.[4]

One of the last things that they did before leaving for Megiddo—and which actually had to be continued from the field—was to hash out some of the archaeological terminology that they had been using, which was now about to be put into print for the rest of the world to see. George Allen, in the Editorial Department at the Oriental Institute, had real problems with some of the terms that Guy was using for the relative dates in his tombs volume—not the absolute chronological dates like 1479 BCE, but his system of archaeological classification that involved overlapping periods, including something called "Middle-Late Bronze" (abbreviated "M-LB"). As Allen put it fairly bluntly, Guy's classification system "does not seem to agree with the facts nor with the way he has actually used it." Allen was also insistent that they needed to work their way through this now, so that the new terminology could be used consistently throughout the volumes that were about to appear.

Allen proposed that they should follow a new scheme, which Albright had introduced just four years earlier when publishing his excavations at Tell Beit Mirsim in 1932. The various phases would be labeled as Early Bronze, Middle Bronze, Late Bronze, and Early Iron Age, for instance, with subdivisions in Roman numerals, so that one could talk about the EB I period or the LB II period and other scholars would know exactly what was meant. In the end, after much wrangling, primarily between Shipton and Allen, with Loud stepping in when needed and Guy essentially informed after the fact, they agreed to follow Allen's suggestion. This ultimately proved to be a wise decision, since Albright's cultural chronological scheme was subsequently adopted by everyone else as well and is still in use today by all archaeologists working in the ancient Near East.[5]

Loud sailed from New York on the RMS *Queen Mary* in early December, arriving at the port of Cherbourg in northern France less than a week later.

After spending the night in Paris, he caught the train to Brindisi in Italy and from there took the SS *Galilea*, reaching Haifa and then going straight on to Megiddo, "arriving in time for a late breakfast" on 14 December. Parker and Shipton had already been there for two weeks by that point, so the house was in order with everything ready to go for the season, though the Altmans wouldn't be arriving for another ten days.[6]

And thus, with the Altmans still to come, the dig officially began a few days later, on 19 December, less than six months after it had been scheduled for termination and liquidation.[7] It was later in the year than they had ever begun before—in previous years they would have been closing down around this time for the winter break, but now they were just getting started. It was also a very small staff: Loud as field director, and then Shipton and Parker as always, plus Charley and Alice Altman. That was it. The Megiddo expedition was back down to the same small size that it had been during the very first season a decade earlier, in the spring of 1926, when Fisher and Higgins were at each other's throats, watched by DeLoach, Kellogg, and Fisher's nephew Stanley. As Loud told Wilson a few weeks later, "The five of us fairly rattle about in this large house."[8]

On the bright side, they found themselves with a plethora of local labor and were soon overseeing more than two hundred workers each day, in large part because the locals had been driven to the edge of poverty by the general strike, which had only just ended in October.[9] Loud said that there were still bitter feelings throughout the country, but their property had suffered no damage while they were away, and the local villagers had been looking after it of their own accord. It was now dangerous to travel at night, for fear of being held up by bandits, and trips to Jerusalem could be done safely only in broad daylight. As it turned out, although Wilson continued to be concerned about the political situation, Loud and the others seem to have had no problems during the entire season—or at least none that they reported.[10]

They began work immediately in the north and east areas again, leaving the south area untouched. Loud's goal was to get all of the north area that was lying to the west of the city gate down to Stratum VIII, so that they could finish clearing the "big house"—that is, the palace. They were only in Stratum VI at the moment, however, so it was going to take a while, especially since they knew that Levels VII and VIII were very complicated in that area. Over in the east area, though, they were already down in Stratum IX, which Loud was still confident dated to the Hyksos period, toward the end of the Middle Bronze Age.[11]

As Christmas approached, they began finding some strange burials in the east area, relating to houses that had been built in Stratum VIII near the temple. One burial, underneath the corner of a room, contained the bones of a man with a metal piece lying across his nose and eyes for some reason and his head lying on the jawbone of an animal.[12] Another burial, located neatly under the floor of a nearby house, contained an alabaster jar, a shell, a piece of yellow pigment, and a single human foot. No other bones; just a foot. Loud wrote in his field diary that he wondered about the significance of the yellow pigment, but surely we must wonder (tongue-in-cheek) whether the ancient Canaanites talked, as we do, about "having one foot in the grave."

Ironically, he also noted that even though they had already found a gold pendant with the goddess Astarte on it, overall "the objects to date cannot be considered sensational. No stela nor tablets have made an appearance, and the burials have so far been without the crown jewels." Little did he know that they were about to make two separate discoveries that would certainly be considered "sensational" and covered worldwide, but that was still a few months away.[13]

Just in time for Christmas, on the afternoon of the twenty-fourth, Charley and Alice Altman finally arrived. The groceries and other supplies for the season had shown up the day before, so there was plenty of food for Christmas Eve dinner. Unfortunately, Loud's piano had somehow been damaged "by force and by water" while in storage, so that when they unpacked it along with the groceries, they found that the case was split on both sides and the finish had been ruined. However, the strings and the sounding board were intact, and so there was undoubtedly also music that evening. A week later, having been unable to work because of rains every day since the twenty-fourth, they went to Haifa for a Toscanini concert and the New Year's celebration at the club, so one could say that the year ended on a high note.[14]

By early January, they had more than two hundred men working full-time on the tell, and by mid-February they were already clearing Stratum XI in the east area and encountering XII. Loud's plan was to keep going down in this area, so that they could be certain of the cultural and ceramic sequence all the way back to about 2000 BCE. Eventually, they did exactly that over the course of the season, reaching down to Stratum XVII. Along the way they found a level with "mammoth walls, colossal stairways, [and] a curving enclosure wall (perhaps the parapet wall of a terrace overlooking the plain)." Loud thought these were from what he called "interlocked" Strata XIV and XV, but said that they would have to wait until the next season to figure out where it all fit into the general sequence.[15]

In the meantime, Wilson had not been having any success in his initial attempts to persuade the Rockefeller boards to give them additional money. In a letter sent in late January, he wrote to Loud that this definitely would be the last season at Megiddo: "A trip to New York last week failed to change our financial picture . . . it now seems improbable that any future work will be done at Megiddo next season or in the indefinite future." He closed by saying: "All this is very depressing, but you may have built up an immunity to it by this time. At any rate, you are in the field and I rather envy you that. Make the most of it and have a very successful season."[16]

Just four days earlier, Loud had sent a long missive to Wilson, which began with his blatantly stated desire that they would find something sensational soon: "Your desire for the sensational from Megiddo is no greater than mine," he wrote. "Something startling would certainly be a big help. My greatest desire for the moment, however, is for a break on the weather so that we might dig to the pot of gold, whatever form it may take."[17]

Loud wrote again in late January 1937, saying that they had been rained out and prevented from digging for more than a week at that point—the amount of rainfall so far had exceeded the usual average for the entire winter. That did not mean they remained idle, however, for they took the opportunity to record and register the tremendous number of pottery vessels that were coming from all of the burials they had uncovered during the previous weeks. A few days later, he said they had been rained out again—"surely these rains can't go on forever," he wrote.[18] One can only point out that this is why neither Fisher nor Guy ever excavated during the winter months.

As it turned out, Loud's letter wishing for the "sensational" was prophetic. The clouds eventually parted, the sun came out, birds started singing, and so forth, and toward the end of February, Loud was able to write to Wilson saying that the north area, which he had previously perceived as dull and troublesome, "now takes its full share of interest." As he described it, the palace was proving to be both extensive and magnificent, with walls standing as high as four meters in some places and covered with painted mud plaster. There was also a "floor of shells which gives the appearance of a mosaic pavement." Further, the team began finding pieces of carved ivory, some with incised Egyptian hieroglyphics and others decorated with elaborate designs. Soon these initial pieces would be joined by a host of additional artifacts, in the form of a hoard of gold objects followed immediately by a treasure trove of ivory objects. All were found within just a few rooms of the palace in the north area and made this "a most successful season," as Wilson later put it.[19] In early March, Loud wrote, "There can no longer be any doubt of the importance of this mound."[20]

They found the first pieces on the first day of March. In his field diary entry the next day, Loud wrote: "Full work the past three days, but so many extras to attend to that non-essentials must slide. All this largely due to what is probably the find of the season—a hoard of gold jewelry, vessels, etc in 3100—an outer room of the north palace. So rich, so varied, and so fragile are the finds that there is infinite work in removing and cleaning them. It began yesterday morning when a shell-shaped dish in which was a green stone jar capped with gold first appeared."[21]

Four days later, he sent a coded cable to Chicago, announcing the find. When decoded on the other end, the message read:[22]

Fig. 44. Stratum VIII gold hoard under floor of Room 3100 (after Loud 1939: fig. 58; courtesy of the Oriental Institute of the University of Chicago)

STRATUM EIGHT PALACE PRODUCES MAGNIFICENT EGYPTIAN GOLD HOARD:—FLUTED SHELL-SHAPED BOWL, PERFUME JARS, JEWELRY, ETC. 18TH DYNASTY CONTEXT [BUT] STYLE SUGGESTS PARTLY MIDDLE KINGDOM ORIGIN. UNPARALLELED THIS COUNTRY.

Just as with Guy's discovery of the stables almost a decade earlier, the cable sent back in reply consisted of a single word. "CONGRATULATIONS."[23]

Loud also sent a much longer letter later that same day, with all of the details. It began: "Dear John: In one of your letters, you asked for the sensational. If I'm not very much mistaken, I think this is now a fait accompli." What they had been calling for some time the "big house" in the northern area by the city gate was now, beyond all doubt, "a grand palace full of no mean treasure." Specifically, they had found a hoard of gold and ivory treasure deliberately buried under the floor in the southwest corner of a small room (3100) located at the northern end of the palace. The pieces were amazing, "a magnificent collection, absolutely unique in Palestine."[24]

Neither Loud nor the other members of the team were clear on the function of some of the objects they were finding, or to when they dated. Other archaeologists who came to see them, including Iliffe and the revered Petrie, were similarly "stumped," as Loud put it. Although most of the objects were made of gold, there were also items of ivory, lapis lazuli, serpentine, and other materials.

According to Loud, they were found in two layers. The pieces in the top layer included what he called an ivory "wand," but which looks more like a horn of some sort, with three bands of incised gold around it and a woman's head on the narrow end. There was also a fluted shell-shaped gold bowl in which was lying a perfume bottle made of serpentine with a gold rim; fifteen gold granular beads and a number of round lapis lazuli beads; a Mitannian lapis lazuli cylinder seal from North Syria; three conical paste medallions in gold mountings; a possible whetstone; and burnt bones—possibly human—"scattered all over the place."

Underneath this group was another layer of objects, which included a large gold scarab ring, with the scarab so disintegrated that they were not able to read the hieroglyphics on it. There was also a second perfume jar, this one probably made of hematite and with gold on its rim and base; two ivory disks and several "disk crowns"; a gold mesh chain with two unidentified objects attached to it; and a double item of gold that Loud labeled "Egyptian Siamese twins, beautifully modeled of thin gold filled with paste." These are now thought to be representations of the Egyptian goddess Hathor, joined at the ear, with a spoon for cosmetics or ointment attached at the top of each of the heads.

Finally, there was also part of a face from an ivory figurine, a second Mitannian cylinder seal of lapis lazuli with gold caps on the ends, and a gold headpiece, as well as a number of additional beads. These last few pieces, Loud said, were found two weeks after the other objects and were slightly apart from them—underneath the northern wall rather than next to it.[25]

Loud noted in his field diary that there was no evidence to suggest that this was a burial, despite the presence of what seemed to be burnt human bones. Instead, at first he thought it seemed more like a "robbers cache," but by the time he actually published everything more than a decade later, in the *Megiddo II* volume, he suggested that it was simply a hoard dating to the time of the original Stratum VIII palace, "buried beneath the floor apparently in the hope that it would escape detection by threatening attackers."[26]

Most recently, David Ussishkin has suggested that the hoard was actually hidden in a pit that was dug into the floor of the later Stratum VIIA palace, which went all the way down into the Stratum VIII level, and that Loud's workmen had failed to detect this pit. If so, all of these objects will most likely have been hidden at the time of the destruction of the VIIA palace, sometime in the twelfth century BCE. This does make more sense, since there is no indication that the Stratum VIII palace was destroyed, or that there was a significant episode involving "threatening attackers" back in the later fifteenth or early fourteenth century BCE. Regardless, whenever it was buried, the hoard evaded detection until 1937, a span of well more than three thousand years.[27]

A similar type of gold hoard, consisting primarily of golden earrings and numerous beads, was found in 2010 by the Tel Aviv Expedition to Megiddo, in their Area H, which is located just to the west of this palace. That hoard had been hidden inside a jar, which had then been buried beneath a floor of the building.[28] It probably dates to about the time of the final destruction of the palace or a bit later, which means, if Ussishkin is correct about redating the hoard that Loud found, the two treasure troves would have been buried at about the same time and for the same reason—the very real threat to the VIIA city that resulted in the destruction of the palace and the rest of the level.

Loud joyfully described Megiddo as becoming "the Tut's tomb of Palestine," because of the quantity of gold and the fact that the majority of these objects dated to the Egyptian Eighteenth Dynasty. He cautioned, though, that some might be heirlooms dating back to the Middle Kingdom. On this he was quoting both Iliffe and Petrie; the latter said that the perfume jars were definitely "middle 18th dynasty," but Loud also noted that Petrie had never seen anything like the shell-shaped gold bowl: Petrie "thinks it more Asiatic than Egyptian."[29]

Loud later sent photographs of the gold objects to Wilson and asked whether he should request a loan of the entire group, so that they could put it on exhibit in either Chicago or New York, or both places.[30] Wilson was in favor of such an exhibit, of course, in part because of the potential for attracting future donors to both Megiddo and the Oriental Institute as a whole. However, he noted that although newspapers "are waiting with tongues hanging out for feature pictures of the gold objects and an imaginative story to go with," they would have to postpone such an exhibit until after the division of objects had been made at the end of the season, and then put in a loan request for any that had been taken by Iliffe for the museum.[31]

In the meantime, though, Wilson put out a press release, and articles about the discovery soon appeared in papers around the country. The *St. Louis Post-Dispatch*, for instance, breathlessly reported that "Egyptian Gold of 1400 B.C." had been dug up in Palestine, and quoting Wilson as saying that it had been found "in the palace of the Prince of Megiddo." It appeared on the front page, right next to an article about Adolf Hitler, who had floated a promise not to go to war against France, though the proposal (Hitler's, not Wilson's) was being seen as an effort to "scuttle" the League of Nations, as the newspaper phrased it.[32]

Later, in early August, the gold treasures did finally go on display, after Iliffe took only a few pieces for the museum (the fluted gold bowl, the serpentine perfume jar, and three gold beads). The same St. Louis paper then ran a full-page article on them, complete with pictures of the gold objects as well as some of the other artifacts.[33]

However, all of that was just the appetizer. The main course was yet to come, for it subsequently turned out that there was more than just the gold hoard in this palace. In fact, what they found next eclipsed the hoard almost

FIG. 45. The Treasury (3073) viewed from the south (after Loud 1939: fig. 3; courtesy of the Oriental Institute of the University of Chicago)

entirely, at least in terms of discoveries that are today most frequently cited and discussed when it comes to Megiddo.

In the same letter that he sent to Wilson in early March, Loud reported that they were clearing three other rooms, which were turning out to be "veritable mines" of ivory objects. In just one corner of one room, they found "combs, spoons, plaques, medallions, etc. all helter skelter with skeletons of a child and a young camel plus another human skull, and more camel skull!" One of the nicest pieces was still half-buried, he said, but seemed to be part of a cup or goblet with an exquisitely carved design of pomegranates and scrolls.[34]

Loud rarely used exclamation marks in his letters, so he must have been truly excited when he wrote all of this. He later explained to Wilson that he had been tempted to send a cable about the discovery of the ivories as well but had refrained "less the shock of so much from Megiddo might be too much for you."[35] He also told Howard Matthews that since sending his cable about the gold, which Matthews had been the one to decode back in Chicago, the ivories "have so far surpassed the original find that they, rather than the gold, now take first place."[36]

FIG. 46. Complete animal skeleton and ivories in the western half of the northern room of the Treasury, looking east (after Feldman 2009: fig 3; courtesy of the Oriental Institute of the University of Chicago)

On that same day, Loud wrote in his field diary that "in N=3073 whence so many ivory fragments have come, in the NW corner, is a strange burial [—] a camel's head (?), probably a complete camel—head, neck, and forelegs now cleared—, two human skulls and some human ribs, etc. Mixed in with this strange assortment of bones are quantities of ivory . . . the entire burial must be cleared for photographing before we can remove any of the objects."[37]

On the next day, he wrote, "The amount of ivories appearing in N=3073 becomes alarming." He also noted again the two skeletons and two additional skulls that they were uncovering: "Skeletons number two, one child and one young camel, with two additional skulls, one human and one camel. What a strange assortment it all is." And, two days after that, he wrote again: "Ivories of every size, shape, and description coming forth in both N=3073 and 3073 itself. They will make a fine varied collection <u>after</u> proper treatment which will take months."[38]

In fact, it took them more than a month of work, from 6 March until 7 April, just to carefully excavate and remove all of the ivories, all the while entertaining visitors who came to see their finds, including some of the best-known archaeologists working in the area, from Petrie to Nelson Glueck (later president of Hebrew Union College), Eliezer Sukenik (later renowned for purchasing and translating the first three Dead Sea Scrolls), Olga Tufnell (who was excavating at Lachish with James Starkey), and Gerald Lankester Harding (director of the Department of Antiquities of Jordan at the time). Removing the ivories was an elaborate and time-consuming process that involved using celluloid to harden or piece together the fragments; applying solvent to soften the dirt that remained attached; and occasionally sticking paper to the fragments, again using copious amounts of celluloid, which could later be easily peeled off.[39]

The ivories were all definitely from the palace of Stratum VIIA. They were found in the destruction layer of the three rooms, dating to the twelfth century BCE. Together these three interconnected rooms formed what Loud later termed the "Treasury," which was semisubterranean and thus situated a few feet lower than the rest of the rooms. It was a new addition that had not been present in the earlier phase(s) of the palace. There was also no obvious access to it from the rest of the palace; Loud hypothesized that there had originally been a ramp or a staircase leading down to the rooms, but as he noted, there was no actual evidence for this.[40]

Loud gave the center room the number 3073. The room to the north—which had almost all of the ivories—became N=3073, while the room to the south became S=3073, according to the terminology that they were using at the time. Later, in the *Megiddo II* volume, Loud renamed these 3073 A, B, and C, with A being the southern room, B the middle room, and C the northern room.

Loud also noted that there were fragments from broken items that were found in the separate rooms and yet went together when mended—as he put it, "Often, however, fragments from one room fit those from another room." This was a clear indication that the rooms were all related, but it was still not at all clear how or why such trauma to the items could have occurred.[41]

Loud later sent a brief report to Iliffe, reporting on the findspots of the various ivory pieces. As noted, the vast majority of the ivories were found in the western half of the northernmost room (3073C, originally known as N=3073). There were so many here that Loud subdivided the room into one-meter squares, each one labeled with a Roman numeral from I to IX, in order to keep better track of where the various ivories were found. We now call this "fine gridding" or "micro-gridding," which is a procedure that is frequently done today in exactly such situations. Loud included a sketch, which never made it into the final publication, but that clearly depicts the rooms and the subdivided sections of the northern room.[42]

Early on, Loud estimated that there were more than a hundred "first-class pieces." In fact, there are closer to four hundred pieces all told, including items that Loud thought had "Egyptian, Syrian, Cretan, and Assyrian motives." He was correct—later scholars have confirmed the international nature of this collection, detecting Hittite, Mycenaean, Egyptian, Ugaritic, Canaanite, and Assyrian motifs.[43] They found so many ivories that Loud told Wilson he had hired a photographer named G. Eric Matson, from the American Colony in Jerusalem, to help out with all of the documentation.[44] No doubt he now regretted that they had parted ways with Lind less than six months earlier.

In addition to the combs, spoons, plaques, medallions, and various other items that Loud had mentioned in his original letter to Wilson back in early March, there was also a box, measuring fifteen centimeters square and ten centimeters high, that was carved in deep relief on all four sides. Two sides had a pair of sphinxes and two sides had "as good representations of the Lion of Babylon as you could wish to find." Loud needed help with this object, so Iliffe came with his ivory expert to assist in removing it without undue damage during the process. Iliffe also agreed to have his conservators work on all the fragmentary ivories at no cost to the Chicago expedition, and to allow for an immediate loan of the pieces that were still complete and could survive the trip to the United States, both of which were incredibly generous offers.[45]

Fig. 47. Ivory pen case with cartouche of Ramses III (after Loud 1939: plate 62; courtesy of the Oriental Institute of the University of Chicago)

Another piece, one of the last to appear but possibly the most important, was another box, long and rectangular, that is usually identified as a "pen case," that is, a receptacle for the writing implements used by Egyptian scribes. This particular one belonged to an Egyptian official named Nakht-Amon, who was a "king's messenger." To the excavators' delight, the inscribed text on the case included the cartouche of Pharaoh Ramses III, thereby allowing them to date the case, the ivory deposit as a whole, and the destruction of the palace as well, for Ramses's dates of rule during the first half of the twelfth century are well known (1184–1153 BCE).[46] It is perhaps worth noting in passing that this is exactly the sort of discovery for which Breasted had been waiting—if only it had happened two years earlier.

When Loud later published the ivories, he used some of the same phrases that he had written earlier in his private letters and field diary: "The helter-skelter arrangement of the ivories as they were discovered is astonishing," he wrote in 1939. "The great majority of the pieces were found in the western half of the outermost room [N=3073]. They were in close confusion, mingled with occasional fragments of gold jewelry and alabastra and with scattered animal bones, the whole mass topped with a complete animal skeleton." He went on to note that the ivories were not found lying in clear-cut layers; instead, "one piece might overlap another, often in actual contact. They were found in all positions, in oblique planes as often as horizontally."[47]

Both Loud and later scholars have suggested that the "helter-skelter" distribution of the ivories was the result of looters and thieves who had broken into the Treasury, perhaps as the palace was undergoing its final destruction, and that they ripped apart wooden furniture, and the like, leaving these ivory pieces lying on the floor. However, Loud emphasized the fact that many of the pieces had been broken before being buried—implying that they were not broken at the final moment, but rather at some earlier point. He also suggested that the ivories were stored on wooden shelves, which had long since disintegrated, a hypothesis that many other scholars accept. In the end, he concluded that perhaps these pieces, even the broken parts, constituted a collection that belonged to a prince of Megiddo whose hobby was collecting pieces of ivory.[48]

However, later scholars have taken issue with this suggestion. Richard Barnett, a longtime keeper at the British Museum, most definitely did not like the "weak" suggestion offered by Loud that the "eccentric lord" of Megiddo had a hobby of "ivory collecting." Instead, Barnett and others, including most recently Marian Feldman and David Ussishkin, have pointed to the real commercial value of the ivories, along with the fragmentary alabaster jars, gold beads, and other items that were scattered among them, and have thought that all this actually represents the tangible wealth of the prince—and the royal family—of Megiddo. Feldman suggests that the pieces may have been deliberately buried as a hoard rather than merely a group of items collected as part of a hobby. Still others have suggested that this might have been an ivory workshop.[49]

The conundrum of the skeletons continued to puzzle Loud and is still an enigma today. After all of the ivories had been safely removed, Loud wrote to Wilson: "The late date for the ivories which Ramses III attaches to them was at first startling, but the ivory rooms are clearly of the last phase of the palace, the earlier walls having been ruthlessly cut away for this one unit, the floor level of which is below the earliest palace. The whole thing suggests to me a treasury of cellar-like construction from which the objects of intrinsic value were removed in haste while the ivories were simply chucked aside. But I still can't account for the child and camel skeletons unless they were caught in the act of thieving and paid the extreme penalty on the spot."[50]

In the final publication of the ivories, he wrote further: "Even if such a theory of ivory collection be accepted, we are still at a loss to explain the presence among the ivories of the animal bones and of the complete skeleton."[51] Note that he here mentions only "animal bones" and the "complete [animal] skeleton." There is no mention of the skeleton of a child, or even simply "the two human skulls and some human ribs," either here or in his *Megiddo II* volume, despite the fact that they were quite specifically mentioned in two of his letters and two field diary entries.[52] Did the "two human skulls and some human ribs" or the "skeletons of a child and a young camel plus another human skull, and more camel skull" later become simply "animal bones"? This seems extremely unlikely—one does not usually mistake human skulls and ribs for animal bones.

So how does one account for the full or partial child(ren) and animal skeletons, especially since there is no such thing as a "thieving camel"? Most scholars don't even try—they ignore the fact that even in his book on the ivories, Loud included a picture that clearly shows the animal skeleton still in situ, directly on top of the spot where he would later remove the ivories using the fine grid system. An even better photograph is also in the Oriental Institute archives and was first published by Marian Feldman (see fig. 46).[53]

However, there is one explanation that can account for everything Loud found in these rooms and for the confused, and confusing, state in which he found it all. In 1993, Rolf Hachmann, subsequently followed by other scholars, proposed that these three interconnected rooms at Megiddo are actually a built royal tomb, specifically placed in a semisubterranean level of the palace. Hachmann had previously published an excellent parallel from his site of Kamid el-Loz, located near Damascus in what is now Syria, where there is a built tomb associated with the Late Bronze Age palace. He noted that there were other possible parallels as well, found in Bronze Age levels at the sites of Byblos and Alalakh.[54]

Interestingly, the tomb at Kamid el-Loz was also dubbed the "Treasury" by the site's excavators. It contained the skeletons of a child and an adult in one room and a second child in another room, apparently interred at two different times. The grave goods included pottery, gold ornaments, and a number of ivory objects that were already broken when they were placed in the tomb, as well as others that apparently were scattered when the tomb was reopened for the second burial(s).[55]

If these rooms at Megiddo are also a tomb, perhaps with two interments made at different times, it would explain the presence of the two children and the two animals, as well as the scattered and broken objects.[56] According to this scenario, the ivories would belong to the earlier interment, to which would also be assigned the partial skeletons, that is, the skulls (and perhaps the ribs) of one of the children and the other animal. In preparation for the later interment, all of the earlier material, including the ivories, would have been pushed to the back of the tomb, as frequently happens in such cases. If the ivories had been carelessly shoved into a pile in the back room in order to create space for the second burial, it would explain why they were found lying "helter-skelter" and in disarray, "in oblique planes as often as horizontally." It could also explain why broken pieces from the different rooms fit together, since they may have been shattered and fragmented during this process.

Furthermore, such a situation would also explain the other items that were found scattered among the ivories, including gold pomegranate beads, gold jewelry, scarabs, fragmentary alabaster jars, and pottery sherds,[57] which might now be identified as grave goods. Moreover, if the two children had been interred at different times, this might explain why the complete animal skeleton was found directly on top of the ivories, for it and the other grave goods that accompanied the later interment of the second child may simply have been placed on top of, and/or next to, the earlier material.

While all of this must remain a very tentative hypothesis, it does seem to better account for all of the items present, and for their specific locations within the rooms, than any of the other suggestions that have been made to date. Moreover, it is worth noting again that in his initial diary entry, Loud himself referred to all of the skeletal material as a "strange burial," although he seems to have promptly forgotten that fact.[58]

As for the complete animal skeleton, Feldman suggested that the animal was more likely some sort of bovid: a cow, rather than a camel.[59] More recently, however, Haskel and Tina Greenfield have suggested that it is actually much more likely to be an equid (i.e., a horse, a donkey, or an onager).[60] Since the bones were discarded by Loud long ago and we are reduced to looking at fuzzy, low-quality photographs now, we cannot decide for certain what type of animal it was, nor what type of animal the other "camel" skull was from. However, if it is an equid, then there are a number of parallels and other examples of tombs in Canaan in which equids were buried alongside the human remains, including at Tell es-Safi in the Early Bronze Age and Tell el-Ajjul during the Middle Bronze Age.[61]

The other detail to consider is when all of this took place. The fact that the pen case was inscribed with the cartouche of Ramses III meant that the destruction of the palace could not have happened before his reign, but did it take place during his reign or sometime afterward? This is a question of great importance, for this is the approximate time period when most of the great civilizations, and some of the minor ones, in the ancient Near East came crashing down, in what is usually referred to as the "Collapse" at the end of the Bronze Age.[62]

The final destruction of the VIIA palace at Megiddo fits right into this context. Radiocarbon dates seem to indicate that it took place sometime after the reign of Ramses III, no earlier than approximately 1130 BCE and perhaps a few decades later, rather than during his actual reign.[63] However, there is another aspect to consider, for there is also a destruction of an earlier phase of the palace, about which we haven't yet spoken, namely, the palace of Stratum VIIB.

Alert readers will recall Loud's observation in the east area from a year earlier, during spring 1936, when he noted that there seemed to be two parts to Stratum VII, separated by a burnt layer. This matched what they had seen in the south area as well, and they had already begun to suspect at the time that the same was true in the north area. Now they were able to confirm that this was indeed the situation here in the palace.

This phase of the palace lay in between the edifices of VIII and VIIA, meaning that the entire history of the palace lasts from sometime in the fifteenth century to sometime in the twelfth century BCE. Loud does note that some of the western portion was altered, while a later construction in Stratum VI destroyed most of the eastern wing. However, the VIIB palace was also violently destroyed, at least in part, such that Loud noted the following in his *Megiddo II* volume: "The Stratum VIIB palace obviously suffered violent destruction so extensive that the Stratum VIIA builders deemed it more expedient to level off the resulting debris and build over it than to remove it all as was the procedure in previous rebuilding undertakings. When excavated court 2041 and room 3091 of Strata VIII–VIIB were filled with fallen stone to a height of about a meter and a half . . . over which a new, Stratum VIIA pavement must have stretched." As the late Itamar Singer noted, that means that the floor of the Stratum VIIA palace was almost two meters above the floor of the VIIB palace.[64]

Back in 1995, David Ussishkin suggested that this is not a separate destruction, but that the palace simply had two stories, both of which were destroyed at the same time in the twelfth century BCE. He has since doubled down on this suggestion, even though it has not found much favor with other scholars.[65]

Mario Martin, currently one of the codirectors of the ongoing Tel Aviv Megiddo Expedition, has recently proposed a different scenario, which seems more logical to me. He suggests that the VIIB phase of the palace was destroyed in the early twelfth century BCE, which is in line with the destructions at other sites. He then dates the final destruction of the VIIA phase of the palace, and the entire city, to a few decades later.[66]

In any event, this miraculous season, so unexpected back in January—and which almost didn't come to pass in the first place, given the events at the end of the previous season—finally wrapped up when digging stopped in mid-April.[67] Among the last things that they did was to begin removing the remains of the palace that they had just painstakingly spent all season excavating. In his field diary entry for 7 April, Loud noted that they had started "breaking down the walls of the ivory unit to get its connection with the real palace." A week later, he wrote, "The ivory rooms [are] gradually being wrecked in order to trace the walls of earlier periods which run underneath and form quite a different plan."[68]

They ended up, over the course of the next seasons, removing every bit of the VIII and VII palaces that they had found, leaving nothing standing. They took out the walls that stood fully four meters tall and had painted plaster on them, as well as the mosaic shell pavement, to see what lay beneath. Unfortunately, there was nothing nearly as spectacular underneath, and today there is nothing to be seen at the site of this once-magnificent palace. For that I personally mourn, and I agree with Ussishkin's recent assessment that it was "a totally superfluous action."[69]

There is, however, still a part of the palace remaining, because Loud and his team did not get to it. This is the continuation of the palace to the south, which is now tantalizingly partially visible in the forty-foot-high balk that the Chicago team created in this area. The current Tel Aviv excavators began to dig here in the early 1990s but later moved away from this sheer drop. Since then, they have been excavating immediately to the west of this space, in their Area H, with excellent results, and are now down into Middle Bronze Age levels, but they will miss recovering the rest of the palace by a few dozen feet at the most.

The division of the artifacts found during the season, with the exception of the ivories, was made on 1 May.[70] Two days after that, Loud wrote to Wilson, saying that "the division was really astonishing." He and Iliffe had already agreed to leave the division of the ivories for the next year, after they had all been conserved and repaired, so they had been splitting the rest of the objects. Loud told Wilson that perhaps Iliffe was "lying in wait for the ivories," but he actually thought "it is because Iliffe likes this expedition and hopes for the future from us." Iliffe had taken a lot of the pottery and scarabs, "but not at all unfairly." And, as for the rest of the objects, "he scarcely took a thing," according to Loud.[71]

In addition to everything that they had acquired in the division, Loud said, he was also going to be shipping to Chicago more than a hundred pieces of ivory from the "Treasury" as well as the two gold artifacts from the hoard in room 3100 that Iliffe had taken for the museum but was loaning them for the coming year. All of these they were allowed to put on exhibition, which Loud hoped would take place in October, if all went well.[72]

Loud then sent all of the ivories down to Jerusalem for initial conservation and renovation. Along with them went several pages of a detailed inventory list, so that they would know which came from each of the separate rooms.[73]

And with that, Loud and the other members of the team began packing up the dig house and prepared to head off in various directions for well-deserved vacations. They would all reconvene in Chicago for the fall, including Shipton (who was eagerly anticipating his first visit to the States), in order to work on the publications. Lamon would not be joining them, though, for back in March he had taken a job in Ibagué, Colombia, working as a petroleum geologist—he continued in that career for the rest of his life, as mentioned previously.[74]

Loud closed a late April letter to Wilson with the words "Thus ends the 1936/37 Megiddo season." He left Megiddo in mid-May, sailing for London via Trieste, and then a week later for New York, on the SS *Aquitania*, arriving on the first day of June. The others left a few days later, for a well-deserved vacation in Jordan, at Petra and Aqaba, before heading back to the States as well.[75]

CHAPTER XIV

"A Miserable Death Threat"

The gold hoard and the ivory treasure found during the spring of 1937 turned out to be the high point of Loud's four seasons of excavation, in terms of glittering items that would catch the public's imagination. However, his final seasons proved to be just as important to the overall aims and goals of the expedition. It was now that they were able to finish digging all the way down to bedrock in Area BB—their east dig—and to complete their reconstruction of the entire occupational sequence of Megiddo, from the earliest indications of inhabitation in Stratum XX to the final abandonment of the mound after Stratum I.

Along the way, though, in these final seasons, they had to deal with the dangers that came with living in British Mandate Palestine during the Arab Revolt, which had begun with the general strike in 1936 and was now entering its final and most violent phase. For the team at Megiddo, this included a death threat against Loud, the attempted assassination of their good friend Iliffe, and the murder of an archaeological colleague who was en route to the opening of the Palestine Archaeological Museum.

But all of this still lay in the not-too-distant future, and they knew none of it when Loud and the others—the Altmans and Shipton—all left together from New York in mid-November 1937, heading once again for Megiddo.[1] Their exciting discoveries during the spring had guaranteed them another season. In fact, even though Wilson had been pessimistic at first, unexpected returns from investments had already allowed him to budget $25,000 for 1937–38 back at the end of February, even before all of the gold and ivory treasures began to come to light. Even though it was $3,000 less than they had just had for the 1936–37 season, it would still be enough for another year of digging, given the skeleton staff at the site.[2]

There was also a new member of the team with them—a young Harvard-trained architect named George Preston Frazer, known to all simply as "Preston." He had been hired to serve as the new architectural assistant. However, this turned out to be his only season at Megiddo, because he was subsequently offered a job as an assistant professor of art at Virginia Tech and taught there for his entire career—from 1939 to 1974, with a break to serve with the Second Armored Division during World War II. He had volunteered to join the Megiddo staff after Loud, back at the end of the last digging season, sent a letter of inquiry to Harvard University asking for interested applicants, and was now happily on board with the others as their ship steamed out of New York harbor.[3]

They reached Haifa on the afternoon of 25 November. Despite spending what seemed like an eternity getting their belongings through customs, they were at the Megiddo dig house in time to enjoy Thanksgiving dinner with Parker, who had arrived ten days earlier. The following day, Loud sent a letter to the director of antiquities, alerting him that they were back and asking whether they could once again renew their license to dig for the coming year.[4]

The reply came back positive, of course, and they began digging again in early December, supervising 160 local men and boys by themselves for nearly a week before the Egyptian workmen arrived for the season. Once again they were digging in the north and east areas, but initially it was a season more of destruction than of exploration, for they were removing the palace in the one area and what they were calling the "East Temple" (now Temple 2048) in the other: "demolishing our best architectural specimens," as Loud put it, in order to see what lay below.[5]

Soon thereafter, Olof Lind stopped by, twice in a single week, to see how things were going and to reach an arrangement about some items that he had left behind at the dig house. It was the first time they had seen him in more than a year; he was far friendlier than he had been at the time that they had all parted ways. In the interim, he had bought an orchard located half an hour south of Haifa and was busy tending to fruit trees, for he was now a "citrus export agent" for the Pan Arab Corporation of London and the proud owner of five thousand apple trees and another five thousand plum, peach, pear, and assorted other trees.[6]

By mid-December, Loud told Wilson that he hoped "cablegrams announcing stupendous finds will be keeping Western Union busy" soon, but it was not to be. Instead, as he told Matthews at about the same time,

"Two weeks of digging leave us minus most of the architecture we so carefully dug out last season but with few objects." By the end of December, the temple in the east area was gone, but they were still pulling the palace apart in the north, "piece by piece." Loud reported sadly that it was presently "about as dull on the dig as any day could be." His only consolation lay in remembering that the previous season had started off just as bereft of finds before they literally struck gold.[7]

Loud later had little to say about what they found underneath the Strata VIII–VII palace. He noted only that they were in Middle Bronze Age levels there, looking at possible Hyksos-period remains, and that their findings confirmed the stratigraphic sequence that they had determined from the east area.[8]

However, he did say that they were also clearing an area in which stables had been previously exposed, and were removing one of them so that they could dig deeper in this region.[9] Although he does not specify a precise location, a bit of detective work reveals that this stable (5082) was the westernmost of five within the northern stables on the mound, which Guy had originally found back in 1928. The easternmost (407) of these five stables had already been removed during Guy's seasons, while the middle three were excavated by the Tel Aviv Expedition from 1998 to 2007, but during this season and the next, Loud's men removed this one stable in order to see what lay beneath.[10]

In addition, they were continuing to work in the area of the various city gates. They had found the Middle Bronze Age city gate belonging to Stratum XIII, which lay directly underneath the palace that they had just destroyed, and finished excavating the city gate that belonged to the period of the palace itself.[11]

They also opened a new area, which was called "K-10" at first, after the grid square in which they put the initial trench. It was at first only eight meters long (and presumably five meters wide, as usual), but was soon expanded and eventually became their Area DD. It was located east of the Stratum III and IV gates—that is, between their north and east areas—and was intended to connect Schumacher's original Great Trench with their own excavations in the gate area (i.e., Area AA).[12]

In this new area they went down through the upper levels quickly until they reached "the best VII walls we have ever encountered with the exception of the palace." Loud noted that this was a promising area for the future if they were looking for more remains dating to what he called "the Egyptian levels." Removing these in turn, they reached Stratum XIII in that area too and were poised to go farther below in the next season.[13]

Toward the end of December, Wilson sent a coded cable with good news, just in time to make it a Christmas present for the team. The International Education Board of New York had just given him a $50,000 donation toward the excavations at Megiddo. This entity had formerly been associated with the Rockefeller Foundation but was now going out of business and was looking to disburse their remaining capital. Even though the General Education Board and the Rockefeller Foundation had said they wouldn't fund the Oriental Institute any longer, this third entity was not bound by that decision for some reason, and so an agreement was reached with them to fund Megiddo for two additional seasons at $25,000 each.[14]

This gift was all Wilson's doing—he had sent a letter to the board in early November, extolling the magnificence of the ivory and gold treasures that the team had found and including two multipage articles that Loud had published in the *Illustrated London News*. He pointed out the tragedy of having lost the funding for the Megiddo expedition just as it was reaching "fruitful" levels, and therefore requested money to cover the $50,000 cost for two further seasons, to be conducted in 1938–39 and 1939–40, and another $12,500 toward publication of their results. He ended with the estimate that it would cost a total of $62,500 "to fight the battle of Armageddon." Within a month, the board had voted to award them $50,000—enough money to cover the two additional digging seasons, but not publication.[15]

Therefore, to all of Loud's gloomy talk about the dearth of finds, Wilson replied that he personally was unconcerned, particularly now that they had enough funding to see them through the spring of 1940, and could properly wrap up what would be a total of fifteen years of work at the site. Besides which, as he quite wisely said, "even negative information about a site . . . is an addition to our knowledge. . . . We will get more objects in the future. There is no pressure upon you to get some every month or even every season."[16]

The team celebrated with a nice Christmas dinner, together with Robert and Linda Braidwood, a pair of University of Chicago archaeologists who had shown up at the dig house unexpectedly, accompanied by their architect Carl Haines. The Braidwoods would later go on to rank among the most famous archaeological couples of all time, but at this point they were just getting started, were recently married (as of 1937), and were digging at Tell Tayinat in Syria, as part of the master plan that Breasted had put into place several years earlier. Haines would also go on to prominence later, in particular as the field director for the Nippur expedition to Iraq beginning in the late 1940s.[17]

In the meantime, Howard Matthews, who by now had taken Charles Breasted's place as the executive secretary of the Oriental Institute, was making plans to visit Megiddo in March 1938, as part of a larger tour of the Middle East that Wilson had asked him to undertake. It would be the first such official visit from an Oriental Institute administrator since both Breasted and Wilson had come through two and a half years previously, just before Breasted's sudden death.[18]

Writing in mid-December, Loud hastened to assure Wilson that it was safe for Matthews to come visit them, despite the recent reports that were appearing in the media both in British Mandate Palestine and back home. As he put it, "Our local press tells of bombs, shootings, and mischief going on not far away, but as far as we are concerned they do not exist." This is actually similar to situations often found on digs today, for life on an excavation can be like living in a bubble, essentially unaffected by events taking place even fairly close by, especially if one does not venture away from the excavation. As Loud put it, "A curfew along the railroad track closes our road to Haifa during the night, but as we stay home evenings anyway it doesn't bother us any."[19]

Moreover, as he said a few days later, their own area remained quiet, although more than forty bandits had recently been killed in the region of Tiberias during a combined attack of police, air force, and troops, with the rest of the large gang rounded up. He also advised Matthews not to get too alarmed about what he read in the newspapers concerning the conditions in British Mandate Palestine. It was true, he said, "there is a lot of lawlessness," but "with reasonable precaution it can be avoided."[20]

However, things soon began to change for the worse. In early January, James Starkey, the excavator of Lachish, was murdered while on his way to Jerusalem to have dinner with Iliffe and attend the preview before the official opening of the Palestine Archaeological Museum.[21] Thereafter, Loud was in constant touch with the district officer for Haifa, a Mr. Bailey, regarding what he called "precautionary guarding" for the site and the dig house. As Loud noted in his field diary, "Altho I am not apprehensive of any great danger, still we must recognize the fact that there are brigands in the hills back of us and should be prepared for a possible attack."[22]

In fact, on the last day of January, those "brigands," as Loud called them, but who were actually part of the Arab Revolt of 1936–39 rather than simple highway bandits, fired upon troops in the village of Umm el-Fahm, which is located not far from Megiddo in the Wadi Ara pass leading into the Jezreel Valley—the same route that both Thutmose III and General Allenby had taken thirty-four hundred years apart. As Loud again noted in his field diary, this led to a full-fledged battle between the "brigands" and the troops. Reinforcements were sent by the British, who also ordered bombs dropped from planes flying above the rebel gang. Loud reported that they could hear bombing and machine-gun fire throughout the afternoon and evening, but by the next morning the ongoing battle appeared to have moved farther away from them.[23]

In the meantime, in the area of the "east dig"—Area BB—by the third week in February they had already hit bedrock. This was a huge accomplishment, since they now had the entire sequence of occupation, from beginning to end, at the mound. In fact, in the final report that Loud submitted to the Department of Antiquities, he said that their primary achievement for the season had been "the establishment of the complete range of occupation of the site by clearance to bedrock of the large east area."[24] He then went through the various levels, in detail.

Starting at the bottom, he noted that Stratum XX, the earliest building period at the site, lay immediately upon the bedrock. The architecture consisted mainly of crudely built stone walls, while the pottery was a mixture of Neolithic and Chalcolithic shapes—primarily bowls made of very coarse gray ware and with decoration similar to that on bowls that had been found not too far away at Neolithic Jericho. They weren't certain of the exact date for this earliest evidence of occupation at Megiddo, which we now think started about 5000 BCE, but Shipton thought the pottery indicated that the mid-fourth millennium (i.e., ca. 3400 BCE) seemed to be about right for the end of this period.[25]

Intriguingly, while tracing the bedrock down the eastern slope of the mound, they happened upon a huge cave in which there was no pottery but a "considerable quantity of flints and bones."[26] This may well have been the original "Ground Zero," as it were, where humans first settled down for any length of time at Megiddo and perhaps began tending domesticated plants and animals.

FIG. 48. City wall of Megiddo Stratum XVIII (after Loud 1948: fig. 154; courtesy of the Oriental Institute of the University of Chicago)

The next level, Stratum XIX, was much more interesting to Loud. He thought that the pottery was still primarily Chalcolithic, though some Early Bronze Age forms were beginning to show up; the level is now more usually dated simply to the beginning of the Early Bronze Age (EB IB). In this level, "architecture suddenly appears fully developed," he said. Here they found a portion of a large building constructed of mudbrick on a stone foundation, which had a wall three meters wide that ran across their entire excavation area. This formed one side of a room in which there appeared to be some sort of altar. There were also two superimposed temples found in this area, including one that Loud identified as Temple 4050.[27]

Down below these buildings, and leading to the eastern edge of the mound, Loud had begun unearthing already in late December a pavement of stones, on many of which were scratched drawings of humans and animals. The Tel Aviv Expedition reexamined this area in 2008 and found more such etchings on these stones, which has now been dubbed the "Picture Pavement."[28]

The next level, Stratum XVIII, also contained both Chalcolithic and Early Bronze pottery, but now the Early Bronze forms dominated, so it appeared that the site was firmly in the Early Bronze Age by this point, meaning a chronological date in the third millennium BCE. Here they uncovered 150 feet of an absolutely tremendous city wall (Wall 4045). It stood five meters high and was originally four meters thick but was then doubled in width later in the period, so that it measured fully eight meters thick. This may have been the largest city wall ever built at Megiddo, but Loud and his team removed it completely after taking pictures, in order to proceed down to bedrock.[29] I would hope that future archaeologists, when they get down to this level in an adjacent area, will have the common sense to leave it in place.

Fortunately, the Chicago excavators did leave untouched the other major architectural find from this season within this area. This is the now-famous round stone altar (4017) that is currently the most prominent structure within the deep trench that Chicago left in Area BB, readily seen from the tourist lookout point at the Northern Observation Platform at the site. First built in Stratum XVIII, it continued in use during the next few levels. Loud initially mentioned it in his field diary entry on 11 January: "The temple area holds the center of interest for the day with the appearance at the west end of the cut of a strange stone structure—circular in plan with diameter of about 8 meters, with battered sides, and with a stairway at the east. . . . All about it the earth is full of EB sherds and bones, but no complete vessels or skeletons."[30]

The large number of bones discovered in this area has led some present-day tour guides to assert that child sacrifice was performed on this altar by the Canaanites during the Early Bronze Age. However, when the Tel Aviv Expedition reexcavated this area, the excavations yielded thousands of bones from this area, which were mostly from sheep and goats, as well as from cattle, and even from a lion and an ostrich or two, but none were the bones of children.[31]

Loud was correct that the next stratum, Level XVII, was fully situated in the Early Bronze Age. The pottery forms included serving platters, bowls, and vessels with handles that formed small ledges for holding and carrying. There was also a large-scale building that continued beyond their excavation area, and which Loud thought might be another temple.[32]

To all of this, we should append Loud's report from the previous season, which continued the description of these levels in Area BB.[33] Here he said that Strata XVI through XIII showed very little change throughout the period. The characteristic pottery found in these levels was made of a red burnished fabric. Loud thought that these levels dated to the Middle Bronze Age, but in fact Strata XVI–XIV are now considered still to be in the Early

FIG. 49. Stone Altar 4017 in Area BB (after Loud 1948: fig. 165; courtesy of the Oriental Institute of the University of Chicago)

Bronze Age and the Intermediate Bronze Age, while it is Stratum XIII that is considered to be the beginning of the Middle Bronze Age, ca. 2000 BCE (see table 1 in the preface). Perhaps most impressive was a large city wall, made of mudbrick, which completely encircled the mound during Stratum XIII; the current Tel Aviv Expedition has recovered more of this impressive mudbrick wall in their Area K in recent years.[34]

In his 1937 report, Loud says that "there is no hiatus between the pottery of XII and XIII, the one is the natural development of the other." He did correctly date Stratum XII, stating, "There is little doubt, however, that Stratum XII must have its inception somewhere in the middle of the 18th century B.C." The pottery here was similar to that of the previous periods, frequently made of a red burnished fabric that seemed to have parallels with ceramics found at sites up in Syria.[35]

Strata XI and X fell into what Loud properly identified as the Hyksos period. This was the final period of the Middle Bronze Age; it was during this time that invaders from the general region of Canaan descended upon Egypt and took over as rulers from ca. 1720 to ca. 1550 BCE.[36]

These levels at Megiddo, and the tombs from the period, are full of Hyksos scarabs as well as daggers and spearheads known to have been associated with them. This was a period of warfare, sustained in part by innovations in weaponry including a new type of chariot and the introduction of the composite bow, which could shoot farther than earlier types; both contributed to the Hyksos conquest of Egypt at this time. It was also during this period that Loud thought Temple 2048 had first been constructed,[37] with periodic rebuilding and renovation throughout the next few levels. Now it was gone, for they had just spent much of this season removing it completely.

Stratum IX saw the beginning of the Late Bronze Age. Loud dated it from 1550 to 1479 BCE and thought that it was the city which Thutmose III had conquered. He may well be correct; it will probably have been either Stratum IX or VIII that the Egyptians captured, but IX seems more likely, since there is no real break between VIII and VII, as mentioned.[38]

Instead, Stratum VIII saw the beginning of the construction in Area AA of what would become the elaborate palace with the gold hoard and the ivory treasures of level VII. It also is the period in which consistent international trade begins with Cyprus and the Aegean, including imported Cypriot and Mycenaean pottery. There are also substantial buildings from this period in Area BB, such as Temple 2048, as just discussed.[39]

Stratum VII, Loud said, had two distinct building or rebuilding phases: VIIB and then VIIA. Together they cover the period from 1350 to 1150 BCE or a bit later (i.e., the time of the Egyptian Eighteenth and Nineteenth Dynasties as well as part of the early Twentieth Dynasty).[40] This will have been the time that Biridiya ruled Megiddo, during the mid-fourteenth century BCE, and was in communication with the Egyptian pharaohs Amenhotep III and his son Akhenaten.

And that brought them to Stratum VI, the burnt mudbrick city belonging to the early Iron Age, about which much had already been written. Above that lay Strata V through I, which Lamon and Shipton were publishing, and which covered the periods from the flourishing of the Northern Kingdom of Israel through the Neo-Assyrians, Neo-Babylonians, and Persians.

By the time Matthews's visit drew near, Loud's attitude had changed even further, for at the beginning of March he received a death threat. While going to the village for milk early in the morning, one of the house staff discovered a letter that had been left next to the path that led across the tell.

The contents announced that the letter was from the "Black Hand Gang," and that all excavation work should be stopped immediately or Loud would die. It was signed with six blood stains.[41]

Although Loud was convinced that there was no real danger, he had the letter read out loud to the workmen at the end of the day and told them there would be no more digging until they had resolved this matter. He also notified Bailey, the district commissioner for Haifa, who in turn notified the district commissioner for Nablus, with the end result that two policemen were assigned to sleep in the entrance hall of the dig house each night. The letter itself was sent down to Jerusalem for analysis.[42]

Then they began working with the local villagers to find out whether this was a serious threat. Several days of meetings, with both the workmen and the other villagers, resulted in the consensus that the letter was probably the work of children rather than of bandits. Nevertheless, Loud subsequently alerted the consul general in Jerusalem and sent several cables to Wilson, apprising him of the situation.

Loud also wrote to Matthews, who was by that point in Egypt. "Welcome to these parts!" he began. "I write you all this just as tho you will find us normally carrying on. Actually all work has stopped upon receipt of a miserable death threat which I have every reason to believe will turn out to be nothing but a harmless piece of mischief. Until I have such proof, however, we shall continue to comply with the terms of the threat by keeping the work stopped."[43] Loud said further that he was certain by the time Matthews and his wife, Dagmar, arrived, it would all be resolved. It had been raining every day anyway, he said, so they hadn't lost any digging time because of the death threat.[44]

After ten days, and with the assurance of the local district officer from Jenin that there was probably nothing to fear, Loud sent out a notice to the workmen that work would begin again on 12 March. All of them showed up for work early that morning, but so did a second letter. This one was tied to a square marker next to the main path leading to the tell—and it stated that this would be the last warning. Loud also noted in his field diary that some of the workmen had received a similar warning while on the road the previous evening, but he didn't give any further details.[45]

The next day a squad of policemen showed up, with a police dog that promptly picked up the scent and traced it to the village of Lejjun, only to lose it in the stream there. Nevertheless, two men and four boys were brought in as suspects. Although, as Loud put it, "all fail[ed] to confess after beating," they recognized three of the boys as having been recently fired from the dig.[46]

As it turned out, those three were innocent; it was a different set of three boys who were responsible. They were finally turned in by one of their companions to whom the letter writer had made the mistake of bragging about what they had done. All three were subsequently interrogated and confessed to writing the letters, after their fathers were called in as well.[47]

Although the sentencing explicitly called for five years in reform school, Loud and the others didn't want to pursue the matter, so the boys were released "on bond of good behavior." By this point, however, it was nearly the end of March, so the boys' actions had cost the workmen who came from the village almost a month's worth of wages each. As a result, when they were brought home by their fathers, they were punished by their neighbors, including being beaten and spat upon for what they had done.[48]

That same day, 24 March, the Matthewses arrived at the dig, along with the Braidwoods again, so the timing was perfect. Excavation started up a day or so later, and since the Matthewses stayed until the last day of the month, they were able to see the dig in action after all.[49]

Despite feeling that the mystery had been solved, and that the threat had indeed turned out to be a prank by a few boys, several of the workmen were hired to serve as night guards from then on. This was in addition to the two policemen who were still sleeping in the entrance hallway of the dig house.[50]

Amusingly, on the last day of March, two letters arrived from an actual local bandit leader, "written on official stationery." In the letters, which were identical (one had apparently been delayed), the bandit leader was at pains to assure Loud that he had had nothing to do with the death threats. In fact, he said, the dig had nothing to fear from them, since they considered the archaeologists "their countrymen" who were kind to the local Arab villagers.[51]

Moreover, the bandit leader said, Loud was to notify him personally if there were any future threats, so that the bandits could locate and punish "any trick players." He closed by adding that only letters written on official stationery should be considered genuine.[52]

Undoubtedly, Loud was as surprised as any of us would be to find out that bandits have "official stationery." Nevertheless, he was relieved to receive these two letters of reassurance and wrote in his field diary, "All in all I think we have from this source far greater protection than from the police." The bandit leader followed up by sending a letter to the villagers, telling them that they needed to go back to work on the mound; a few days later, he showed up at the dig house in person to reassure Loud that they had nothing to fear from him or his gang.[53]

With the exception of the work stoppage during most of the month of March, the team was able to continue working pretty much straight from late November through the end of April, a normal dig season for Loud. However, they did require some $2,000 in additional advance money sent by Matthews toward the end of the season. This was in part because they had an extra team member for the entire season, Preston Frazer, as well as another new member for the second half of the season.[54]

This second additional staff member was Gustavus Debrille Pope, Jr., a twenty-six-year-old budding archaeologist from Detroit, Michigan, who was called simply "Tony" by his friends. He is listed in the official Megiddo records, as well as on various websites, as having been a member of the staff during the final season, 1938–39, but in fact Loud's entries in his field diary indicate that Pope was present from mid-February through the end of this penultimate season as well. About ten years later, Pope went on to receive his PhD from Yale and became an archaeologist working primarily in Connecticut and Massachusetts for most of his career.[55]

The last day of digging was on 27 April, and the Egyptians left for home the next day. Iliffe came up, as usual, for the division of the artifacts, which took place over the course of several days in early May. Included in the division this year were all of the 386 ivories from the previous season, counting those that had been on loan for exhibition in the States during the past year. Loud noted that the objects sent back from the States had unfortunately been badly packed for the return journey to British Mandate Palestine, and nearly a third of them—39 out of 113 pieces—had to be mended again before the division could take place.[56]

The dig officially shut down on 15 May. Loud wrote to Matthews the day before, noting, "We're closing up tomorrow and I'm not sorry."[57] As it turned out, the 1937–38 season went down in the books as the year that they finished compiling the occupation sequence of Megiddo—it was a successful season despite the problems swirling about them in British Mandate Palestine at the time.

CHAPTER XV

"The Stratigraphical Skeleton"

When the team reassembled for the 1938–39 season, yet another new member joined them, for Loud had gotten married just before the season began. His bride was Honor Merrell, a young lady active on the social and philanthropic scene in Chicago. The ceremony was held in early November at the Fourth Presbyterian Church, an imposing neo-Gothic edifice on East Chestnut Street in the Magnificent Mile neighborhood of Chicago. Loud looked quite dashing in his top hat, while the *Chicago Tribune* described the bride as wearing "a cream-colored satin dress with a high neck, long sleeves and a long train." Charley Altman served as an usher, while Hal Noble, a close friend of Loud's (whom we will meet again) served as the best man.[1]

Following the small ceremony, and a larger reception at her parents' house nearby on Lake Shore Drive, they departed a few days later on the SS *Conte di Savoia*.[2] The Italian ocean liner was just six years old at the time and was the first ever fitted with gyroscopic stabilizers designed to create a smoother trip across the Atlantic.[3] They headed to Sicily for a honeymoon and then directly to British Mandate Palestine, arriving at Megiddo by mid-December. Parker was already there, and the Altmans, Pope, and Shipton showed up a week later. As usual, Loud immediately wrote to Hamilton, who had been recently promoted to director of the Department of Antiquities and was awaiting news of their arrival. Loud requested a license to dig for the year and, also as usual, Hamilton replied promptly and positively.[4]

Work began five days later, with scheduled workdays that now lasted from 6:45 a.m. to 3:55 p.m. Loud wrote to Matthews a few days later that it was "a great joy to have work under way again." He was pleased to report that everything was peaceful at Megiddo—he hadn't received any threatening letters yet; the workmen were delighted to be back at work again; and the local bandits were equally pleased that the villagers now had money which they could steal. He also thought that it was "only a matter of days" before the bandits were all either rounded up or driven off.[5]

Since they had excavated down to bedrock during the previous season, most of the 1938–39 season was spent tying up loose ends. As Loud wrote in his final report, submitted in May, "With the twenty strata and their sub-periods already established, the aim of the 1938/39 season . . . and of all future seasons is to add flesh to the stratigraphical skeleton and to tie together the several areas which have been excavated in the past."[6]

In addition to continuing their efforts in K-1 (Area DD), they also resumed excavations a bit farther north and east, in the stable area that they had begun during the previous season. In addition, they opened up a new area immediately adjacent to Area BB, fifty meters long from north to south, which connected their east area to Schumacher's Great Trench. By the end of the season, they had already gone down to Stratum XV in this area.[7]

However, things started off slowly. By the end of January, Loud confessed to Wilson that it had been "an extremely dull month, both from the standpoint of science and of outside events." The latter was good; the former not so good.[8]

Loud mentioned that they had found a second liver omen in the area of the original temple within the east area.[9] They had also exposed more remains dating to VII and VIII in K-10, including part of a central courtyard and rooms to the west and north; as he put it, the architecture "is so similar to that of the three main phases of the palace that it is not funny." As in the palace, there were few objects above floor level, but he was hoping to get some "buried treasure" once they got below the floors.[10]

In the meantime, Wilson wrote to float the idea that he might make a final trip to the Near East in the fall and come to visit them at the beginning of their season, if the political situation and the institute's finances permitted. Loud replied that he thought it was "a very swell idea," but the trip never came to pass.[11] In part this was because of something to which Wilson referred in his letter—"the London conference"—which he expected would eventually reach "some point with which one party or another will disagree." This would be followed immediately by fresh disturbances in British Mandate Palestine, he thought, which might affect his planned trip to the Near East. In his response, Loud was a bit more optimistic: "Unless the

London conference completely upsets the applecart, I feel we have nothing to fear."[12]

What were they talking about? These are the first references to this particular conference in their correspondence, and they continued to mention it several times more over the course of the next few months. Now known as the London Conference of 1939, or, alternatively, as the St James' Palace Conference, this took place between 7 February and 17 March 1939. During this time, the British government held a series of meetings in London with separate delegations of Arabs and Jews, in an attempt to plan an end to the Mandate and decide how the region was to be governed in the future.[13]

These resulted in what is now called the "1939 White Paper," which was issued in mid-May. Among other things, it proposed a limit to Jewish immigration—a maximum of seventy-five thousand new immigrants over the next five years—and restrictions on where Jews could buy land. If no violence erupted in Palestine during the ensuing ten years, power would be transferred to a representative government and the British would withdraw.[14]

Of course, upon publication of this white paper, which some promptly nicknamed the "Black Paper," renewed violence broke out in British Mandate Palestine, just as Wilson—and much of the rest of the world—had feared. According to the historian Tom Segev, David Ben Gurion wrote in his diary, "Satan himself could not have created a more distressing and horrible nightmare."[15] Fortunately for Loud and the rest of the team at Megiddo, the issuance of this white paper came a few days after they had closed up the site for the season and left the country, as we will see in a moment.

Meanwhile, the team received word in late January that Lind and his wife, Astrid, had gotten divorced, apparently at her parents' urging. She was now back in Sweden while he remained on his new orchard south of Haifa.[16] At the dig house, things were still peaceful, although there was some consternation when a local rebel leader—not the one we've met who possessed official stationery—sent Loud two chickens. It eventually became clear that the chickens were meant as a gift, rather than a threat, and an indication that the brigand wished to come chat with Loud.[17]

Even though he showed up "armed to the teeth," as Loud described it later to Wilson, it turned out that the rebel was indeed friendly, and that he had an ulterior motive as well: his younger brother was one of the workers at the dig, and the leader wanted to make certain that the young man was protected from potential harm, since he was not a member of the gang. As an aside, Loud made the very interesting observation that the "rebel friendliness is clear from the fact that this is the only expedition house in all Palestine which was not destroyed during the past summer."[18]

At about the same time, the team was visited by a group from the American School of Oriental Research in Jerusalem. The group was led by Nelson Glueck, who was now the director. Glueck's account of their visit is worth quoting in full:[19]

> Arriving near Megiddo, we stopped on the road, and had [a] picnic lunch, photographed the great mound, and then drove up to the house of the Oriental Institute of the University of Chicago, which has for years now been conducting remarkably productive excavations at Megiddo. The present Director of the excavations is Mr. Gordon Loud, and this is, I believe, now his third season there. We were warmly received by him, and Mrs. Loud, and the rest of the staff, and were promptly served with delicious Turkish coffee. I am glad to report that all is well with them. The excavations are proceeding apace. Mr. Loud spent several hours with us showing us around, and explaining in detail the course of the excavations, where during the two previous years some phenomenal finds have been made. I also had a particularly satisfactory conversation with Geoffrey Shipton regarding Bronze Age ledge-handles found in Palestine, and their relationship to those found by our School during the course of the archaeological survey of Transjordan. He and Robert M. Engberg had previously published the Notes on the Chalcolithic and Early Bronze Age of Palestine, which has become of basic importance for the study of Palestinian pottery, and in which a large section is devoted to ledge-handles. We left Megiddo at about 4 P.M.

Fisher was on the trip too, as Loud noted in his field diary that day, although Glueck didn't mention him in his newsletter account. Loud took the opportunity to show Fisher a copy of Guy's *Megiddo Tombs* volume, which had finally been published and had just arrived a day or so before. Although Loud noted that the volume set "a high standard for us to live up to in our future publications," he also reported that Fisher wasn't too enthusiastic about it.[20] Small wonder, since it included the sixty tombs that he had excavated back in 1925–26 but had never published.

Loud also received a rather surprising notice in late January, from the district officer in Jenin, informing him that one of the local landowners, Feiz Saad, the son of Hassan Saad with whom Fisher had dealt back in 1925, was now demanding that the team pay him rent going all the way back to 1928. He had retained a lawyer named Asfour, who had filed papers and was demanding action. It seems that this was a saga that kept popping up from time to time, with never any final resolution to the matter, but this time its reemergence had been prompted by a land court decision handed down the previous November that had somehow affected the expropriation of their land in particular. Loud therefore informed Wilson of the new developments and then contacted the government's representative, a man named Wadsworth.[21] Although it took a while, Wadsworth eventually informed Loud that the team need not worry; even if rent were owed, the government would handle it, since they had never finished expropriating the land. In fact, as previously mentioned, the case eventually simply ended when the new Israeli government took control of the land following the 1948 War of Independence.

Meanwhile, the British military had been doing roundups periodically in Lejjun—usually on payday, as Loud noted. In the first roundup, back on 1 January, two men had been killed while trying to escape. In the second roundup, four days later, Loud reported that planes "were flying all around the village and us, some actually firing on the path between Lejun [*sic*] and the mound while the workmen were on their way over, this apparently because leaflets had been dropped on the village saying that all who ventured out of doors would be shot." Eight of their workmen were taken off to prison, reportedly for three months.[22]

During the third such roundup, which took place in the middle of January, Loud said that the planes came in firing again, "this time . . . so close to the house that it was decidedly unpleasant." This was because more than thirty local men were hiding in and around the dig house, including in the chicken coop and various other locations. In the end, their local foreman, Fareed, was detained, despite the fact that Loud needed him.[23]

In spite of all this, on the digging side things were still proceeding as planned, well into February. The weather was unusually good, with little rain, and they were continuing to remove quantities of earth, revealing nu-

merous walls and routine objects. Nothing spectacular had yet been uncovered, Loud said, but "everyone is well, no one has been robbed or shot
at, and military operations seem to avoid our area." By now they had finished the initial K-10 area and had moved slightly to the east and south, in
order to enlarge the area. They unearthed more stables in this area, connected to others that Guy had previously excavated, and then quickly removed them. They had also gone deeper in the area where Stable 5082 had
been; Loud thought that they were by now in Strata IX–XI at this point and
included photos in his letters to demonstrate his points.[24]

Then, toward the end of February, Loud said that one day at noon a truck
driver from Haifa brought a false report that the London conference had
resulted in Arab demands being fulfilled, and that Arab independence would
be coming soon. The resulting impromptu celebration by their workmen
led to a cancellation of work, both that afternoon and the following day.
However, just a day after that, two bombs went off in Haifa, one in the railway station and the other in the marketplace.[25] Unrest was heating up
again, this time not so far from them.

By March, when it rained for an entire fortnight straight, Loud reported
that work had continued in both K-10 and the stable area, but that their digging "still fails to produce anything to get excited about." Also, the military
still hadn't released their foreman and had in fact sentenced him to three
months' detention. "Maybe he did associate with the brigands," said Loud,
"but after all who hasn't?" They had about two hundred workers at the time,
of whom about half were young boys, who were probably acting as the
bucket runners—taking the full buckets and emptying them into the railway cars. Loud also attached a sketch plan, to better show Wilson and Matthews where they had been working.[26]

To all of this, Wilson replied—much as he had the previous season—that
despite their not finding many "goodies," it was extremely valuable that
Loud had tied together the north, east, gate, and stables areas and connected
them as much as possible to Schumacher's Great Trench. As he put it: "From
the standpoint of objects, Megiddo has already given brilliantly. We need
such work as you are doing at present to make a closer control."[27]

At about the same time as he wrote to Wilson, in early March, Loud also
wrote to Matthews, saying that conditions were tense in the area, while
"Arabs and Jews are speculating on the outcome of the London doings." He
predicted that there was a fresh wave of terrorism coming, but he hoped it

wouldn't last long and wouldn't affect them. Ten days later he mentioned the situation again, writing, "Everyone still awaits the outcome of the London conference, hoping that something will be settled soon."[28]

He also told Wilson that "the air has been tense throughout the country since the first intimations of Arab independence were announced." Since his letter to Matthews at the beginning of the month, there had been fresh outbreaks of terrorism in the towns, and "there doubtless will be more and worse to come," he said. However, he didn't think that they had anything to fear at Megiddo, for they were in good standing with the villagers, and the local rebel leader had called on them several more times, for coffee and a chat. Loud did ask Wilson to keep that last bit of information under his hat, "for the military's attitude apparently is that anyone not out to get the brigands is cooperating with them."[29]

In response, Wilson noted: "You still seem to operate despite rumors and alarms originating from the negotiations in London. I wonder what will happen in your region when Britain imposes a settlement. I hope that, as in the past, it need make no difference to you in your relations to the locals."[30] In fact, although the announcement of the 1939 White Paper was still more than a month away at the time, the violence was already beginning to increase. Just a few days after Wilson wrote in early April, news arrived at Megiddo that their good friend Iliffe had been shot and severely wounded by a would-be assassin in Jerusalem.

Glueck recounted the events a few days later.[31] It seems that Iliffe had come to pick up his wife at the American School late on a Monday afternoon. Glueck and Iliffe spent some time talking together about various archaeological matters, and so the Iliffes finally left at about 7:15 p.m., driving to their house, which was only about three blocks away. Not three minutes later, Glueck heard two shots fired, followed by a phone call from Mrs. Iliffe, who was screaming, "My God, my husband has been shot. Help!" Iliffe had been the victim of a targeted attack, in which the assassin(s) hid outside their house and waited for him to come home.

Accompanied by two policemen, Glueck dashed to Iliffe's house and found him lying on the couch, bleeding from a gunshot wound to his chest. The first bullet had missed, but the second punctured his right lung before exiting his body. They rushed Iliffe to the hospital, where he immediately received intensive medical care that saved his life.

Loud recorded in his field diary that he had heard on the radio that Iliffe had been shot. The news also reached Chicago; Matthews wrote to Loud that they had been shaken "to learn almost simultaneously of the shooting of Iliffe, the death of King Feisal of Iraq, and the murder of the British Consul at Mosul." As he noted, it was reassuring to later learn from Loud's letters that things were quiet at Megiddo, "but we shall feel more relieved when we know you have embarked for the return journey to America."[32] As for Iliffe, it took him several long months of convalescence, but eventually he recovered enough to resume his duties at the Palestine Archaeological Museum.

Despite the increasing violence, April produced some of their best results of the season, at least in terms of architecture. They did also find a bone "magic wand," as they called it, with an Egyptian inscription upon it, which they were unable to translate right away. More importantly, they had reached Stratum XV below the stable area and had revealed three separate buildings all with essentially the same ground plan—a portico with two columns in front, a large central room, and then a smaller room at the back. This is usually called a "megaron" type plan. Such buildings are found primarily in the Aegean and Eastern Mediterranean, first as stand-alone buildings, as at Megiddo, and then later—for instance, at the site of Mycenae in Greece during the Late Bronze Age—often incorporated as the main part of a king's palace.[33]

In his letters to Wilson and in his field diary, as well as in the final report that he submitted to the Department of Antiquities, Loud first called these "hilani" buildings, but those are more specifically North Syrian in origin and more usually later in time, that is, Iron Age. Already by August, Loud had caught this and asked the department to change "hilani" to read "megaron" before the report was published, which they did. In the final publication, he specifically noted that such megara (the plural) were "usually associated with but not confined to the Mycenaean Aegean world" and cited in particular a similar grouping of such buildings from the second city at Troy, which dated to about 2400 BCE. Here at Megiddo, these megara in Stratum XV, which dated to about the same time, seem to have served as temples. In fact, the large round stone altar that Loud had found the previous season could now be seen to go with one of the three buildings (Temple 4040), standing immediately behind it and obviously related to it in this level.[34]

Toward the end of April, Immanuel Ben-Dor, who would later become the deputy director of antiquities after 1948, was sent to conduct the division

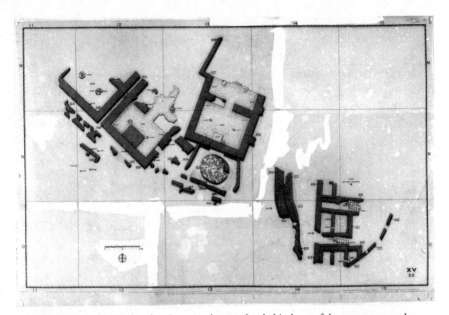

FIG. 50. Stratum XV plan showing round stone altar behind one of the megaron temples (after Loud 1948: fig. 384; courtesy of the Oriental Institute of the University of Chicago)

of the antiquities at Megiddo, since Iliffe was still in the hospital at the time. The digging had ended a week earlier.[35] In making the arrangements, Loud mentioned to Hamilton that Ben-Dor might want to stay in Haifa rather than at Megiddo. Although they were happy to house him at Megiddo, Loud wrote, "I regret to admit that we are absolutely at the mercy of the 'hill men'"—that is, the rebels. He hastened to add that the "hill men" had been nothing but friendly so far, and that "we ourselves are safe enough and our guests probably are too, providing a Government representative isn't too tempting."[36]

Perhaps not surprisingly, given what had just happened to Iliffe, albeit in Jerusalem, Ben-Dor opted to stay in Haifa and make his way to and from Megiddo during daylight hours. In fact, Loud recorded in his field diary that Ben-Dor arrived in a taxi as part of a larger convoy and then returned to Haifa escorted by an armored car that had been specifically sent to accompany him back.[37]

The division didn't go as smoothly as it usually did, since Ben-Dor didn't have the authority to act on his own initiative as Iliffe was able to do. However, later, after filing a complaint that the government had taken all of the best finds from the season, rather than splitting them as usual, Loud made a personal trip to Jerusalem to pursue the matter further. In the end, both parties agreed to a fair division, and Loud ultimately arranged for an additional set of crates full of "antikas," as they called them, to be sent back to Chicago in mid-May.[38]

The team then split up for the summer, unaware that it would be for the last time. After visiting Iliffe in the hospital in early May, Loud and his wife, Honor, along with Tony Pope, headed for Athens and a brief vacation and then on to New York, eventually arriving in early June. The Altmans sailed directly to the States on 11 May, while Parker closed up the dig house two days later and then stayed on in Haifa with Shipton for a month, after which Shipton was due to head for Chicago once again, to work on the publications.[39]

The Americans thus all left British Mandate Palestine just days before the British released the 1939 White Paper on 18 May. Within a week, the anticipated violence began, with shootings and bombings lasting into early June. Loud had written to Matthews several weeks before, "I don't think any of us . . . will be sorry to get out when the time comes." He later similarly told Wilson, "I shan't . . . be sorry to leave the tense atmosphere of Palestine behind." However, they must have despaired when they read the headlines while vacationing in Greece, knowing that Parker and Shipton were still in Haifa at the time.[40]

That was not the end of the story, though, for less than three weeks later Shipton wrote with an unexpected announcement. While he knew that Loud and Chicago had assured him of employment for the next two years, he said that, effective immediately, he was taking a job with Spinney's, the provisioning and distribution company that is still active as a supermarket chain in the Middle East today. He would not be coming to Chicago after all but instead would remain in Haifa, working at the company offices. He also would not be available for the final season at Megiddo.[41]

Shipton's letter and its surprising contents arrived like "a Haifa market bomb," Loud later told him, "blowing to pieces" their publication plans for the remainder of the summer and beyond. It also created obvious personnel problems for their upcoming excavation season, which would have to be dealt with.[42]

Shipton said that he knew full well this would be a blow to them, and he felt sick at letting them know so suddenly, but although his heart was really in archaeology, he literally couldn't afford to pass up this employment offer. "If I had private means, it would be a horse of a very different color," he wrote, but such was not the case. Moreover, he believed that his lack of schooling meant that archaeology would eventually be a dead end for him, and it would prove impossible to "have made a mark."[43]

Little did Shipton realize that he would make quite a lasting mark in archaeology anyway, with his two major Megiddo publications. In fact, his book on the pottery from Strata VI–XX had just seen the light of day and may have crossed in the mail with this letter, while the *Megiddo I* volume that he coauthored with Lamon would be out before the end of the year.[44]

Shipton's sudden resignation from the team threw everything into disarray, from the publication plans to the upcoming 1939–40 season. Loud wrote to Shipton in early August, saying that they had decided not to replace him on either the publications or the project, but were hopeful that he would be able to join them once the excavation season started, perhaps on Sundays and on Wednesday afternoons as well, since he would be off work both times. They had also decided not to have a *Megiddo II* and a *Megiddo III* volume, but to condense all five seasons (1935–39) into a single volume.[45]

Shipton replied at once, saying that he would be "more than delighted" to help out with the pottery during the coming season, and that "it will be great fun coming out to Megiddo of a Sunday—and Wednesday afternoon if necessary." However, he warned Loud that the situation in British Mandate Palestine was extremely tense, as a result of the nonaggression pact between Germany and Russia, and that he was sure "the next few days will bring war." He had just been sent his officers' reserve papers and had committed himself to the air force—if war did come, he said, "I may yet be dropping bombs on some unfortunate German towards whom personally I hold no animosity."[46]

He also said that while his work at Spinney's so far was both fun and very interesting, "it does not make up for archaeology by a long shot." However, he did have a couple of secretaries and was kept busy from 7:30 a.m. until 2 p.m. dictating letters, which made him feel tremendously important, "but it appears I am the only person that thinks so!"[47]

The summer of 1939 then saw something unprecedented from Megiddo— the beginning of regular letters, from July onward, sent in perfect English and legible handwriting, from Serge Tchoub, the chauffeur whom Loud had almost let go back in 1936. Throughout the coming years, Tchoub and Parker would maintain a steady flow of letters and information sent first to Wilson and then to his successor at the Oriental Institute, Carl Kraeling, as the two of them maintained the dig house and the vehicles in preparation for another field season that never materialized. At the moment, Tchoub said, Parker and Shipton were in Haifa, where he saw them occasionally. Everything was quiet in the vicinity of Megiddo, with no real rebels in sight, though there were still some small local gangs that were occasionally active.[48]

On the last day of August, Tchoub wrote again to say that everything was still okay at Megiddo, if one ignored the malaria that was troublesome during the summer, and that was currently affecting both himself and his wife. Everyone was getting anxious about the very real possibility of war, which was not surprising since Hitler invaded Poland the very next day, on 1 September. Tchoub said that they were all practicing air raid defense, and that some pricing regulations on food had been imposed by the authorities.[49]

Wilson and Loud did not yet fully realize that the coming excavation season at Megiddo was not to be, nor that there would never be another one for them. Loud sent a cable to Parker in early September: "STILL HOPE RETURN CABLE YOUR PLANS WHEN DEFINITE." He then wrote to Tchoub later that month, saying that they had been planning to depart in mid-October and to begin work at Megiddo in mid-November, though the war had put those plans on hold. He also wrote to Parker in October and then again in November, pushing the date for their departure back each time.[50]

However, none of Loud's letters were making it through to Tchoub, who wrote again in mid-October asking about their plans for the season and requesting that all future letters be sent as registered mail, so as to guarantee delivery. The workmen, he said, "still hope and expect the beginning of work this season," and he himself was "anxious to hear from you about the future of Megiddo." In addition, he said, Parker had moved all of his personal belongings, and those of Shipton, to their apartment in Haifa, located near the sea.[51]

In mid-November, Loud tried to locate just one more full-time team member—for he rightfully believed that he and Charley Altman would not be able to handle the entire tell operation, even if Shipton were able to make it every Wednesday afternoon and all day on Sundays to look at the pottery. Using as an intermediary his good friend Hal Noble in Philadelphia, who had been the best man at his wedding, Loud contacted Arthur J. Tobler.

Tobler had worked on the University of Pennsylvania excavations at the site of Tepe Gawra in northwestern Iraq, near the ancient site of Nineveh, for a number of seasons from 1936 onward. Interestingly—and a testament to the small interconnected world of archaeology, especially in those days— both Arthur Piepkorn, who had been at Megiddo from May through July 1933, and Immanuel Ben-Dor, who had just come to oversee the division of the 1938–39 finds, had participated as staff members at Tepe Gawra during the 1932–33 season. In fact, Piepkorn had come directly from Tepe Gawra to Megiddo that year, after their season ended in April (as mentioned in a previous chapter).[52]

However, after an initial series of exchanges, which looked promising at first, Tobler ultimately turned Loud down flat. His final cable to Loud read simply, "REGRET CANNOT ACCEPT AT THIS TIME GOOD LUCK."[53]

Having postponed their departure for British Mandate Palestine three times already, Loud finally capitulated in late November.[54] He wrote to Tchoub, "For several weeks now we have been making plans to return to Megiddo, but it was only last week that we found it will be impossible to come this season." They were all very disappointed at having to miss a season, he said, and he was especially sorry to disappoint the workmen who would have no work this year. But—ever the optimist—they had "the satisfaction of knowing that we shall return next year." In the meantime, he said, they were all very busy working on the publication of the material that they had excavated during the previous seasons.[55]

It was ironic that they were unable to assemble a staff, Loud told Parker, for "conditions are probably more favorable for digging than during the past two years yet no staff is available." They would, however, Loud promised, continue to pay Parker's salary (as they would Tchoub's), albeit at one-quarter of the previous amount, in return for his looking in on things at the dig house once in a while.[56] Shipton, replying on behalf of both himself and Parker in early December, confirmed that it was indeed now "quiet at the dig—so much more so than it has been for years."[57]

In a follow-up letter to Tobler, after receiving his final cable turning down their offer, Loud said much the same thing about the irony—it was rather incongruous to be sitting in Chicago, "struggling with publication," instead of digging in British Mandate Palestine, where all reports were favorable and the country was "far more peaceful than during the past three years."[58] Still, he was hopeful that they'd be able to get a team together and dig for one final season. As it turned out, they did not.

PART FOUR

1940–2020

CHAPTER XVI

"Instructions Had Been Given to Protect This Property"

Just as the very first season of the dig almost ended a week after it began, back in 1926, so the last scheduled season actually did end before it could begin. Despite having enough money for a final season, the team had to shut down the dig for good before they could properly wrap up the entire project, for World War II brought a sudden halt to their efforts.[1] The team members, or many of them at least, joined the war effort in various capacities and put the skills they had learned on the dig and in British Mandate Palestine to a different use—trying to stop the modern world from heading down the road toward a new Armageddon.

In early 1940, however, Loud was still optimistic and was hopeful that they would be able to start digging again in the fall. He began again to try to put together a team, months ahead of when they would be needed.[2] In addition, as of early January 1940, Loud reported hearing rumors that Engberg had been nominated to succeed Nelson Glueck as the director of the American School of Oriental Research in Jerusalem. Already by the end of that month, his appointment was "now a fact beyond rumor," as Loud put it, with the Engbergs scheduled to sail over to British Mandate Palestine in June or July to assume their new role. Having Engberg in charge of the American School would be immensely beneficial to the Megiddo excavations, if they ever got back in the field again.

However, the war got in the way here too, and by the time that they were supposed to leave, the Engbergs' departure had been postponed indefinitely. Ironically, Clarence Fisher, who was still in Jerusalem working on his pottery volumes, was asked to serve as interim director of the school until such time as the Engbergs were able to sail over, and he did so until his sudden death in late July 1941.[3] Engberg never did take up his appointed position in Jerusalem; instead, Glueck took over again after Fisher died.

Fɪɢ. 51. Megiddo car overturned and totaled in collision in Iraq (courtesy of the Oriental Institute of the University of Chicago)

Meanwhile, Loud was never able to seriously pursue the possibility of getting a team back together for a season in the fall, and so he eventually authorized Parker to begin selling off bits and pieces of the Megiddo equipment and to transport whatever furniture he could to Haifa for use in his own apartment. The piano, Loud's pride and joy, was sent down to Jerusalem and given to the Vesters at the American Colony. The Megiddo car was sold to the British Army, which sent it to Iraq where it was promptly totaled in a collision with an oil truck. Loud learned of this later and quite by accident, when an unknown officer sent him photographs of the smashed car lying upside down on a desert road. Soon they also began to get requests from various organizations, such as the "Medical Authorities," according to one letter from Parker, asking whether the expedition house could be used for various purposes, such as the storing of supplies.[4]

The two big pieces of Megiddo news in 1941 both involved Shipton. First was the fact that he was asked by the Department of Antiquities to write a *Guide to Megiddo* for the many tourists who were coming to visit the site.

He agreed to do this, after receiving approval from Chicago, and the guide eventually appeared in late 1942.[5]

Possibly more important, though, at least to him, was his sudden marriage to Miss Hester Wood, who had apparently originally come to British Mandate Palestine to teach at the Girls' College in Jerusalem but was now working in the governmental hospital in Haifa. According to Parker, she was "a jolly nice girl," about the same age as Shipton. They had met back in February, had gotten engaged within six weeks, and were married in mid-May. The wedding itself was small, with only fourteen people invited to the ceremony in Haifa, but the engagement party that was held at Megiddo beforehand was huge, with 120 people present, including the Iliffes, Hamilton and his wife, and Clarence Fisher. Serge Tchoub reported that the saloon, the dining room, and even the Ping-Pong room of the dig house had been crammed full of guests. Shipton's job was also going well; by now he had been promoted to a senior position—"Secretary of Spinney's" was his official title, according to Parker (who continued to live with the newlywed Mr. and Mrs. Shipton in Haifa).[6]

By 1942, both the dig house and the site had been taken over by British forces. In his 1991 book on the battle for Crete during World War II, Antony Beevor describes the training for British paratroopers that was held at the Ramat David airbase near Megiddo. More specifically, he also notes that "some students, especially those destined for intelligence gathering, would do another course afterwards on secret procedures—they included disguises, codes and dead-letter drops—at the American School of Archaeology in the valley of Megiddo." Since there is no "American School of Archaeology" in the "valley of Megiddo," this can only be the Megiddo dig house. This is confirmed by an obituary for one Ian Macpherson, published in the *Telegraph* for 12 January 2011, which states that, sometime prior to 1944, he had attended the "agents' training course at Megiddo, near Haifa, where he was instructed in explosives, sabotage, and the dissemination of 'black propaganda.'"[7]

It is at this same time that Loud himself either volunteered or was called up to serve in the US war effort. In early May 1942, he requested a leave of absence from the Oriental Institute.[8] His request was duly approved and then subsequently renewed each year through 1945. During those years, he worked for the Office of Strategic Services (OSS), the forerunner to the CIA, which was then run by "Wild Bill" Donovan. As part of his duties, Loud served as Nelson Glueck's primary contact, for Glueck was also working for the OSS, but was stationed in the Middle East rather than in Washington, DC.[9]

As the war came to an end, Loud was offered a position with the Atlantic Refining Company—the same company for which DeLoach had been working since 1935. It was a job that he couldn't pass up, he told Wilson, especially since he would be based in Cairo. With Wilson's reluctant consent, and with the proviso that Loud would see the *Megiddo II* volume through to completion, Loud submitted his resignation from the Oriental Institute in January 1946, noting that he would "always look back on my affiliation with the Institute as one of the happiest associations for which one could ever wish."[10]

Loud never returned to work at Megiddo, although he was relatively close geographically, living and working for Atlantic Refining in its Cairo office for the next decade. He thus joined Lamon and DeLoach as Megiddo alumni who went to work for oil and gas companies following their departure from the expedition.

However, in Chicago, there still remained some small hope that a return to the site would eventually be realized. Back in November 1942, when Loud took his first leave of absence, Harold Nelson, who was serving as the acting director of the Oriental Institute at the time, had sent a letter to Hamilton, the director of antiquities. In it he had written that they intended to resume the excavations when conditions permitted, and requested "an official recognition" of their claim to the site, with a concession that would last through the war and then for an additional "period of one year after the cessation of hostilities." Hamilton was happy to oblige, and actually did them one better—sending a note in February 1943 saying: "I am very glad to learn that it is the intention of the Oriental Institute to resume excavations at Megiddo as soon as conditions permit. You may rest assured that no license to excavate at Megiddo will be granted, within two years of the cessation of hostilities in Europe, to any other person or institution without the consent of the Oriental Institute."[11]

That hope, however, was never fulfilled. By the end of World War II, the site was in bad shape, despite the maintenance efforts of Parker and Tchoub. A visit to the site in the spring of 1946 by Parker and Hamilton revealed damage to the city gate, the city wall, the stables, the water shaft of the tunnel, and one of the buildings with standing stones. Some of the damage was due to erosion, but some was caused by the local villagers using the exposed remains as a quarry and removing large stones, for instance from the stables, for their own building projects.[12]

The Chicago team itself also removed some stones from the site, for Shipton told Hamilton in 1944 that three Masonic lodges had asked whether they could have "some of the foundation stones belonging to the Solomonic period at Megiddo and which have Masons' marks inscribed." The lodges in question were the Grand Lodge of Scotland, the Grand Lodge of England, and the King Hiram Lodge, Shipton said. Permission was eventually granted, and although we now know that the stones with such markings most likely belong to the period of Omri and Ahab rather than Solomon, by 1952 the stones had been sent to Chicago, where they were received in good order and presumably delivered to the lodges.[13]

All of this, however, paled in comparison to what happened in 1948, during and immediately after the Israeli War of Independence. Three separate incidents involving Megiddo and the dig house occurred during that year: the battle that was fought on 30–31 May, looting that took place sometime between late June and late July, and a fire that destroyed most of the dig house in mid-October.

The year had begun with Olof Lind facing a crossfire of bullets, from both Arab and Jewish forces, on his orchard property just south of Haifa in January. His servants escaped to Athlit and then to Deir Yassin, only to be swept up in (and to survive) the events there in early April, while Lind himself eventually fled to Sweden in late May.[14] He left just five days before the battle that was fought at Megiddo, when Israeli forces from the Golani Brigade charged up the ancient mound, using the cut made at the southeast by the Chicago excavators that they called Area CC.

The Israelis took control of the site without firing a shot as the Arab forces beat a hasty retreat. They then used its height to provide covering fire for their own forces, who raced across the fields to take the police station at the Megiddo crossroads some thirteen hundred meters away. This was located where the prison stands today, complete with its recently discovered Jesus mosaic mentioned in a previous chapter. They also posted soldiers, reportedly to protect the dig house and the exposed remains on the site, but more to guard against possible Arab attacks. Serge Tchoub and his wife were taken into custody at first but then later released, according to Parker.[15]

Remnants from these military actions were recovered in 2008–14 by the Tel Aviv Expedition in their Area Q, located at the southeastern edge of the mound, in the form of hundreds of spent cartridge cases from machine-gun fire. They also discovered that several Neo-Assyrian rectangular rooms from Stratum III in this area, which had been exposed by Fisher during the

1925–26 season and thereafter left untouched by the Chicago excavators, had been rearranged by either the Arab or Israeli forces to create foxholes for the soldiers and firing platforms for the machine guns.[16]

Following the battle, several prominent archaeologists, including Immanuel Ben-Dor, whom we have met previously, as well as Shemuel Yeivin and Benjamin Maisler (later to become much better known as Benjamin Mazar), stopped by Megiddo during a tour of the north in late June 1948. They reported that the dig house hadn't suffered any damage and that some of the artifacts, plus the Chicago dig library, had been transported for safekeeping to the museum in Haifa. Other items were still present in three rooms and a storeroom; the archaeologists recommended that these should be "removed to a place of safety at Haifa" as well.[17]

Unfortunately, their suggestions were not followed. Within a month, the dig house was severely ransacked and many of its furnishings stolen, reportedly by individual soldiers or groups from within the Israel Defense Forces searching for supplies. The three archaeologists returned at the end of July to assess the damage; their subsequent report was somber.[18]

In their report, they noted that there was now a camouflaged area for wounded soldiers in the middle of Schumacher's Great Trench, and defensive trenches had been dug into the slope of the tell. However, they said that the damage to the actual site was minimal, and that it was the dig house that had suffered the most. Shocked by what they now saw, they wrote that "in general the offices look as if after a real 'pogrom.'" They noted that "files and papers were thrown down on the earth, torn, and ruined; closed cupboards were broken open, glasses shattered, objects piled into heaps upon each other without order." Condemning what had happened in the strongest possible terms, they concluded, "In this case the private property of a scientific team from a friendly country was molested and robbed in a vandalistic, irresponsible way." In response to the filing of their account, a government committee was immediately formed and an investigation commenced. This committee eventually issued two reports in April 1949.[19]

In the meantime, however, the misfortunes continued. In mid-October 1948, a soldier decided "to burn out a hornet's nest situated in the roof of one of the outside buildings" and instead burnt down the entire dig house, according to Parker. It was impossible to estimate the cost of the damage, he said, for "the house and outside buildings are completely wrecked."[20] Both he and Serge Tchoub compiled lists of their own personal items that had been lost, as well as much longer list covering ten full pages of items that had been in the house. They sent the lists to the insurance company, which balked at paying, since they had not been occupying the house at the time. Instead, the insurance company suggested that the Israeli military or government should reimburse the Oriental Institute for all of the losses.[21]

Parker eventually wrote to the Ministry of Foreign Affairs, in early June 1949. In his letter, he documented what he had personally witnessed while visiting the site and the dig house the day before, on 1 June, in the company of the consul and vice-consul of the United States of America. It is worth quoting in full, for it is an accounting of the damage done during both the looting in July 1948 and the fire in October 1948:[22]

Sir,

I desire to place on record that I, representing the Oriental Institute of the University of Chicago, in company with the United States of America Consul, Mr. Bloodworth, and the Vice Consul, Mr. Crosby, visited and inspected the Megiddo Expedition House and premises yesterday, the 1st June, and found:—

1. The whole house and premises completely abandoned.
2. The whole place in a complete state of chaos.
3. That everything movable (absolutely) has been removed.
4. That every fixture, including bathroom, sanitary, electric, down to the last glazed tile has been removed.
5. That all internal doors of rooms, built in cupboards, etc. have been removed.
6. That more than half of the windows including the anti-malaria appliances have been removed.
7. That all the light railway, except a few containers, has been removed.
8. That the power station and battery room has been completely destroyed, with all valuable materials, such as switchboards, dynamos, etc., removed.

I would refer to your letter F.O./H/173/6263, addressed to the Director of the Oriental Institute, para 2, sub para 3, in which you stated that instructions had been given to protect this property. I regret to inform you that judging by what we saw yesterday, such instructions have been completely ignored.

I shall be most grateful if for the purpose of my report to the Oriental Institute I could be informed as to what steps are being taken to protect the Megiddo site and what remains of the property.

Parker followed this up a week later with a shorter, but just as specific, letter to Wilson back at the Oriental Institute. In it he noted that when he and the American officials arrived at the site, they found it "abandoned and open to anyone who wished to enter." Furthermore, everything was in chaos; Parker wrote that he had never before seen "such willful destruction; the whole house interior and exterior has been stripped of everything moveable. All interior fixtures, baths, ablution basins, lavatory appliances, electric fittings, refrigerator, etc. etc., have been removed. They even took away all glazed tiles from bathrooms, bed rooms, and kitchen, and you know what beautiful bathrooms, etc., we did have. Well, the whole place is a shamble[s]." He concluded by saying: "It all makes me very sad when I think of the efforts the Oriental Institute has made to preserve the site equipment and house for further research. To restart again we would have to go back to the position and conditions prevailing, as far as equipment etc. is concerned, to 1926."[23]

In the end, the insurance company refused to admit any liability and suggested again that the military or government should be held responsible, so Parker continued his efforts with the Ministry of Foreign Affairs.[24] Eventually, years later and after yet another committee had deliberated, a substantial amount in damages was paid to the Oriental Institute. Yeivin later said that the amount was "more than 10,000 Lira" in compensation, which the Israeli government paid in order to avoid a huge public scandal. That was the equivalent of nearly half a million dollars today.[25]

In late 1954, Parker was given a supplementary retirement bonus as thanks for his nearly thirty years of service and finally parted ways with the Oriental Institute. He moved to Cyprus for a few years, as mentioned, and then finally returned to England, where he died in London in December 1979.[26] The same sort of retirement bonus was given to Serge Tchoub at about the same time. When last heard from, also in about 1954, he was living in Haifa and still working as a chauffeur, despite being sixty-five years old at that time.[27]

On 18 January 1955, the Oriental Institute quietly signed over the Megiddo dig house to the government of Israel (specifically the Israeli Department of Antiquities and Museums) for the nominal sum of "One Dollar ($1.00)." The Chicago excavations at Megiddo were officially over, three decades after Clarence Fisher and his small team first arrived at the site in 1925.[28]

"Certain Digging Areas Remain Incompletely Excavated"

By way of conclusion, I should note that, prior to writing this book, I had always wondered why Chicago didn't resume their excavations at Megiddo after World War II. Now we know the answer: they fully intended to. As we have seen, Hamilton agreed to extend their claim until two years after the hostilities ended. By that time, though, Loud was out of archaeology and working in the petroleum industry. And before the Oriental Institute could find someone else to lead the renewed excavations, it was 1948 and the dig house was looted, with all the equipment stolen, and then accidentally set on fire. As Parker wrote, they were back to where they had been in 1926. So, rather than begin all over again, the Oriental Institute simply started digging elsewhere in the Middle East. The Chicago years at Megiddo thus came to an end, but the site was by no means exhausted.

Lamon and Shipton's *Megiddo I* volume, on the 1925–34 seasons, appeared in 1939. Loud's *Megiddo II* volume, on the 1935–39 seasons, was completed three years later, in 1942. However, because of the war it was not published until six years later, finally appearing in 1948.[1]

Loud himself admitted that the *Megiddo II* volume was less than satisfactory. He began the foreword by saying: "This is not the exhaustive publication of the earlier strata at Megiddo anticipated by the staff during the years [that] the excavation of this material was in progress. It falls short of its intended comprehensiveness on two counts, both due to World War II."[2]

He gave as one reason the fact that the final season had never come to pass, which meant that "certain digging areas remain incompletely excavated." They had intended, for example, to excavate more than twice the area in the earliest levels that they had actually done—while the upper strata had been removed, the team had not investigated the lower levels. They also had not been able to completely connect the various digging areas, resulting in numerous loose ends.[3]

In addition, Loud said, the presentation of the material in the volume was incomplete because "one by one the members of the staff . . . were called to serve in one capacity or another the war emergency." They had been faced with a choice: to either suspend work on the volume for the duration of the war or "to publish it in catalogue form, thereby making the facts at least available to the scientific world with the least possible delay." They had opted for the latter, Loud said, and therefore his opening words were a warning that the volume "pretends to be no more than a catalogue of the architecture and artifacts recovered primarily in the seasons of 1935–39." Although a "certain amount of descriptive text is included," he was well aware that the volume as a whole was insufficient, and therefore specifically invited future scholars "to take up the task where the excavators have been forced to lay it aside."[4]

Each of these volumes received pushback from colleagues right away. The most important feedback was the questioning by others of the dating and assignations of buildings and artifacts to various strata, especially Strata IV and V, made by Lamon and Shipton in their *Megiddo I* volume. John Crowfoot, the excavator of Samaria, started things off with a review published in the *Palestine Exploration Quarterly* in 1940, in which he disagreed with their dating of these levels, arguing instead that the stables of Stratum IV were to be dated to the time of Ahab, and that it was Stratum V which dated to the time of Solomon.[5]

Even Herbert May, the former team member whose volume entitled *Material Remains of the Megiddo Cult* had been published in 1935, got into the act. In early February 1940, he wrote to Albright, saying he had been looking again at Fisher's "Astarte temple" and wondering "whether Fisher did or did not see . . . two building periods when there were really only one." He continued, "I find it difficult to follow Lamon's reasoning at many points . . . and find myself in considerable disagreement with the conclusions of Lamon."[6]

Albright's initial review of the volume, which included his review of Shipton's pottery volume as well, appeared in 1940 in the *American Journal of Archaeology*. It was a fairly positive review, on the whole. However, by 1943, quite likely influenced in part by the letter sent to him by May, Albright suggested that Lamon and Shipton had indeed erred in some of their assignations. He also renamed their Stratum IV as IVA, since they had already created IVB.[7]

In addition, in his *Megiddo II* volume, Loud subsequently subdivided Lamon and Shipton's Stratum V into VB and VA, although only in his Area DD (and noting that he didn't actually know which one came first, chronologically). Albright's former student G. Ernest Wright, who was a professor at the McCormick Theological Seminary in Chicago at the time, promptly and specifically proposed in no uncertain terms that even more buildings had been misassigned by the excavators than had originally been thought, and that the strata to which they belonged therefore needed to be revised and renumbered yet again.

Wright suggested specifically that Stratum IVB in Area CC and Stratum VA in Area DD went together and should be referred to as Stratum VA/IVB, as it has been ever since. And, most impactfully for some scholars, it was this level that he and others said should be identified as the "city of Solomon," based upon the reworkings and suggestions made by Crowfoot, Albright, and Wright over the years.[8] This is the layer to which Palaces 1723 and 6000 are now assigned, and which Yigael Yadin also thought dated to the time of Solomon. However, that did not settle the matter, for Finkelstein and others would now date this level to the time of Omri and Ahab instead, on the basis of comparisons to buildings and stonemasons' marks at the site of Samaria (which was built by Omri and Ahab).

The debate, which is admittedly very confusing even to those integrally involved, has continued apace.[9] Normally, none of this would be of interest to anyone but archaeologists, and even just a small fraction of those. However, since we are still trying to figure out which level at Megiddo might be attributable to Solomon, this has remained a discussion of interest to a great many people. In fact, in terms of finding Solomonic Megiddo, it seems that the Chicago excavators were far less successful than Guy had initially thought, when the stables were first discovered back in 1928.

To put it plainly, it seems fair to say that what were once identified by Guy in that June 1928 cable as "Solomon's stables" soon became "Ahab's stables" and now are possibly "Jeroboam II's stables." So too the various excavators (and other scholars) have so far attached the moniker "city of Solomon" to at least four different levels at Megiddo. Guy was convinced that Stratum IVA was Solomon's Megiddo (but it might actually be Jeroboam II's); Crowfoot, Albright, Wright, and Yadin thought it was Stratum VA/IVB (but that is probably Ahab/Omri's); and now Ussishkin has tentatively suggested that it is Stratum VB (despite the fact that that stratum is less than impressive). However, as mentioned, in 1996, Finkelstein suggested that Stratum VIA could date to the tenth century and the time of the United Monarchy,[10] and I would agree that this burnt mudbrick city should still be considered a contender, perhaps almost by default since most of the others have been ruled out. This, of course, is assuming that there even is a Solomonic city to find at the site. The one thing that we can all agree upon is that Solomonic Megiddo has been extremely difficult to find; we may never have a definitive identification.

Enough questions remained after the end of Chicago's excavations at Megiddo that, as noted at the beginning of this book, Yigael Yadin came with his graduate students from the Hebrew University of Jerusalem for several seasons in the 1960s and early 1970s.[11] Twenty years after that, there were still enough questions remaining, and new ones that had emerged, for Israel Finkelstein and David Ussishkin of Tel Aviv University to begin their renewed series of excavations at the site in 1992. This most recent set of excavations has now continued every other summer for fourteen seasons—the same number as the Chicago excavators put in.[12]

And yet, even with all that digging, beginning with Schumacher in 1903, we have barely scratched the surface of this ancient site of Armageddon and have plumbed its depths down to bedrock in only one area. Much still remains to be discovered. Moreover, despite the best efforts of the Chicago excavators, as well as Schumacher before them and two additional expeditions that came after them, there is still no clear answer to the specific questions that led Breasted to undertake the excavations at Megiddo in the first place: which city was the one fortified by Solomon, and which one was captured by Thutmose III?

Perhaps those questions will finally be resolved by the current Tel Aviv Expedition or by a future archaeological expedition, whenever that occurs. Or perhaps they are destined never to be answered. We now know that we cannot place such demands on archaeology; we can only interpret what we happen to uncover, to the best of our abilities. That has not changed since the days of Fisher, Guy, and Loud.

Cast of Characters: Chicago Expedition Staff and Spouses (alphabetical and with participation dates)

Altman, Alice S.: recorder; wife of Charles Altman (October 1935–1939)

Altman, Charles (Charley) B.: architect and photographer; husband of Alice Altman (October 1935–1939)

Beaumont, E. F.: surveyor (June–October 1933, November 1934–February 1935, and April 1935)

Breasted, Charles: executive secretary to his father, James Henry Breasted (1925–1935)

Breasted, James Henry: director of the Oriental Institute and of the Megiddo Excavations (1925–November 1935)

Breasted, James Henry, Jr.: team member (September–October 1932)

Concannon, T.A.L.: architect (September 1933–June 1934)

DeLoach, Edward L.: cartographer and surveyor (September 1925–March 1930); assistant field director (July–September 1927)

DeLoach, Florence: wife of Edward DeLoach (May 1929–March 1930)

Engberg, Irene (Jean): wife of Robert Engberg (October 1930–June 1934)

Engberg, Robert M.: topographic assistant (October 1930–June 1934)

Fisher, Clarence S.: field director (September 1925–May 1927); advisory director (May 1927–June 1929)

Fisher, Clarence S. ("Stanley"): accountant (September 1925–November 1926)

Frazer, George Preston: assistant architect and artist (November 1937–April 1938)

Gad, William: assistant surveyor (September 1925–May 1927)

Guy, Philip Langstaffe Ord (P.L.O.): field director (May 1927–August 1934)

Guy, Yemima: wife of P.L.O. Guy (May 1927–August 1934)

Hamilton, Robert W.: assistant (24 June–10 July 1929)

Hassan, Hassan: draftsman (April–October 1927)

Higgins, Daniel F., Jr.: surveyor and assistant field director (August 1925–June 1926)

Hucklesby, C. M.: surveyor (June–July 1931)

Irwin, William A.: recorder (April–November 1934)

Kellogg, John P.: assistant (May–October 1926)
Kent, Charles: draftsman (March–June 1929)

Lamon, Eugenia: wife of Robert Lamon (February 1933–April 1936)
Lamon, Robert S.: draftsman and surveyor (September 1928–April 1936);
    acting field director for fall 1934 and spring 1935 seasons
Lind, Olof E.: photographer (August 1926–August 1936)
Little, Charles: draftsman (April–July 1928)
Loud, Gordon: field director (October 1935–April 1939)
Loud, Honor Merrell: wife of Gordon Loud (December 1938–April 1939)

May, Helen: wife of Herbert May (October 1931–June 1934)
May, Herbert G.: epigrapher and recorder (October 1931–June 1934)

O'Neill, J. G.: assistant (April–May 1927)

Parker, Ralph B. ("Harry"): superintendent (June 1927–April 1939 [actually
    1954])
Phillips, Dudley W.: assistant (October 1930–January 1931)
Piepkorn, Arthur C.: assistant (May–July 1933)
Pope, Gustavus D., Jr.: assistant (February–April 1938 and
    November 1938–April 1939)

Shipton, Geoffrey M.: draftsman and recorder (January 1928–June 1939)
Sorial, Labib: assistant surveyor (September 1925–May 1927)
Staples, Margaret Ruth: wife of William Staples (September 1928–July 1931)
Staples, William E.: epigrapher and recorder (September 1928–July 1931)

Tchoub, Serge: chauffeur (January 1927–April 1939 [actually 1954])
Terentieff, Ivan: surveyor (June–September 1928)

Wilensky, Emmanuel: surveyor and archaeological assistant (April–June 1928
    and April 1932–June 1933)
Wilson, John A.: surveyor and team member (April–June 1927)
Wilson, Mary: wife of John Wilson (April–June 1927)
Woodley, Ruby: recorder/registrar (August 1926–August 1928)
Woolman, Janet: wife of Laurence Woolman (September 1929–June 1930)
Woolman, Laurence C.: architect (September 1929–June 1930)

Year-by-Year List of Chicago Expedition Staff plus Major Events

Year	Personnel at Megiddo	Personnel Details	Major Events (internal and external)
1925 (Fall)	Clarence Fisher Stanley Fisher DeLoach Higgins	Arrival of initial team members in September	Albright is denied admission to site in October
1926 (Spring)	Clarence Fisher Stanley Fisher DeLoach Higgins Kellogg	Kellogg arrives in May; Higgins fired in June	Dig house completed; Breasted visits in March
1926 (Fall)	Clarence Fisher Stanley Fisher DeLoach Lind Woodley	Lind and Woodley hired in August; Kellogg leaves before the season, in October; Stanley Fisher leaves in early December	Digging finally begins
1927 (Spring)	Guy (× 2) DeLoach Lind O'Neill Parker Tchoub (× 2) Wilson (× 2) Woodley	Tchoub joins in January; Fisher reclassified at end of April and Guy takes over as field director; Wilsons present from April to June; O'Neill arrives in April and is fired in May; Parker arrives in June	Breasted visits in April
1927 (Fall)	Guy (× 2) DeLoach Lind Parker Tchoub (× 2) Woodley	DeLoach appointed assistant field director for July–September, to temporarily assist Guy	Earthquake hits region in July, Megiddo not affected

Year	Personnel at Megiddo	Personnel Details	Major Events (internal and external)
1928 (Spring)	Guy (×2) Lind Little Parker Shipton Tchoub (×2) Terentieff Wilensky Woodley	Shipton arrives in January; DeLoach remains in Chicago; Wilensky present April–June; Terentieff present June–September; Little leaves at end of season, in July; Woodley fired in August	Stables discovered in early June
1928 (Fall)	Guy (×2) DeLoach Lamon Lind Parker Shipton Staples (×2) Tchoub (×2)	Lamon and the Staples arrive in September; DeLoach also returns at same time	Excavators realize that Mrs. Rosamond Templeton owns much of the site
1929 (Spring)	Guy (×2) DeLoach (×2) Hamilton Kent Lamon Lind Parker Shipton Staples (×2) Tchoub (×2)	DeLoach gets married in late April; Kent present only for March–June; Hamilton present only for June and July	Breasted visits in March, with Rockefellers
1929 (Fall)	Guy (×2) DeLoach (×2) Lamon Lind Parker Shipton Staples (×2) Tchoub (×2) Woolman (×2)	Woolmans arrive in September	Arab Riots in August, just before start of season at Megiddo; US stock market crash on "Black Tuesday," 29 October; first experiments with balloon photography
1930 (Spring)	Guy (×2) DeLoach (×2) Lamon Lind Parker Shipton Staples (×2) Tchoub (×2) Woolman (×2)	DeLoaches leave in March; Woolmans leave in June	Higgins dies in Tennessee, in March; foundation stone laid for the new Palestine Archaeological Museum in June

Year	Personnel at Megiddo	Personnel Details	Major Events (internal and external)
1930 (Fall)	Guy (×2) Engberg (×2) Lamon Lind Parker Phillips (×2) Shipton Staples (×2) Tchoub (×2)	The Engbergs and the Phillipses arrive in October	Oriental Institute buys Mrs. Templeton's portion of the site in December for $3,500
1931 (Spring)	Guy (×2) Engberg (×2) Hucklesby Lamon Lind Parker Shipton Staples (×2) Tchoub (×2)	Phillips fired in January; Hucklesby present only for June and July; the Stapleses leave at end of season, in July	Excavation of water tunnel begins
1931 (Fall)	Guy (×2) Engberg (×2) Lamon Lind May (×2) Parker Shipton Tchoub (×2)	The Mays arrive in October	Excavation of water tunnel continues
1932 (Spring)	Guy (×2) Engberg (×2) Lamon Lind May (×2) Parker Shipton Tchoub (×2) Wilensky	Wilensky returns in April; Wilensky's wife fractures skull in May, in freak accident	Filming at Megiddo and elsewhere in February and March, for Breasted's movie, *The Human Adventure* (appeared in 1935)
1932 (Fall)	Guy (×2) Breasted (son) Engberg (×2) Lamon Lind May (×2) Parker Shipton Tchoub (×2) Wilensky	Breasted (son) present September–October	Guy asks to have a study season, but Breasted refuses and digging continues

Year	Personnel at Megiddo	Personnel Details	Major Events (internal and external)
1933 (Spring)	Guy (×2) Beaumont Engberg (×2) Lamon (×2) Lind May (×2) Parker Piepkorn Shipton Tchoub (×2) Wilensky	Lamon gets married in February; Wilensky fired in June; Piepkorn present May–July; Beaumont present June–October	Breasted visits in April; dig house renovations completed by this time; Wilsensky problems
1933 (Fall)	Guy (×2) Concannon Engberg (×2) Lamon (×2) Lind (×2) May (×2) Parker Shipton Tchoub (×2)	Lind gets married and Concannon arrives, both in September	Arab general strike affects Megiddo in November
1934 (Spring)	Guy (×2) Concannon Engberg (×2) Irwin Lamon (×2) Lind (×2) May (×2) Parker Shipton Tchoub (×2)	Irwin arrives in April; Engbergs, Mays, and Concannon all leave at end of season, in June; Guy fired in August	May accused of smuggling antiquities, resulting in a fine; Guy fired in fallout
1934 (Fall)	Lamon (×2) Beaumont Irwin Lind (×2) Parker Shipton Tchoub (×2)	Lamon appointed acting field director; Beaumont returns and Irwin leaves, both in November	Staff all working on publications; study season, with no excavation
1935 (Spring)	Lamon (×2) Beaumont Lind (×2) Parker Shipton Tchoub (×2)	Lamon continues as acting field director; Beaumont present through February and then again in April	Work continues on publications; stratigraphic errors discovered and corrected

Year	Personnel at Megiddo	Personnel Details	Major Events (internal and external)
1935 (Fall)	Loud Altman (×2) Lamon (×2) Lind (×2) Parker Shipton Tchoub (×2)	Loud appointed new field director; brings Altmans with him	Breasted visits in October; dies in early December, while returning from visit
1936 (Spring)	Loud Altman (×2) Lamon (×2) Lind (×2) Parker Shipton Tchoub (×2)	Lamons leave at end of season, in April; Lind let go in August	Arab Revolt of 1936–39 begins; affects expedition from April onward; dig nearly terminated at end of season for lack of funds
1936 (Fall)	Loud Altman (×2) Parker Shipton Tchoub (×2)	Late start to season	Arab Revolt of 1936–39 continues; dig season funded after all
1937 (Spring)	Loud Altman (×2) Parker Shipton Tchoub (×2)	Team members continue, with no changes or additions	Arab Revolt of 1936–39 continues; gold hoard discovered in March; ivories discovered in April
1937 (Fall)	Loud Altman (×2) Frazer Parker Shipton Tchoub (×2)	Frazer arrives in November	Arab Revolt of 1936–39 continues
1938 (Spring)	Loud Altman (×2) Frazer Parker Pope Shipton Tchoub (×2)	Pope arrives in February; Frazer leaves at end of season, in April	Arab Revolt of 1936–39 continues; Starkey murdered in January; Loud receives death threat in March
1938 (Fall)	Loud (×2) Altman (×2) Parker Pope Shipton Tchoub (×2)	Loud gets married just before beginning of the season	Arab Revolt of 1936–39 continues

Year	Personnel at Megiddo	Personnel Details	Major Events (internal and external)
1939 (Spring)	Loud (×2) Altman (×2) Parker Pope Shipton Tchoub (×2)	Pope leaves at end of season, in April; Shipton resigns after the season, in June	Arab Revolt of 1936–39 continues; Iliffe shot in April; "1939 White Paper" issued in mid-May
1939 (Fall)	Parker Tchoub (×2)	Unable to find replacement for Shipton	Season canceled; dig comes to an end after fifteen years
1940–54	Parker Tchoub (×2)	Shipton gets married in mid-May 1941; Tchoub and wife stay in dig house after final season never materializes; Parker also looks after things, but from Haifa	Dig house and mound occupied and used by various entities during World War II; battle fought at site in May 1948; dig house looted in July and then burnt down in October 1948

Acknowledgments

It is a great pleasure to acknowledge that I was one of the thirty-six inaugural recipients (2015–16) of a Public Scholar grant from the National Endowment for the Humanities to work on this book; I hope that they will overlook the fact that it took far longer to complete than I had originally anticipated. That grant allowed me to spend the spring 2016 semester researching and writing full-time, in conjunction with a leave granted by a very understanding administration at George Washington University (GWU).

I had previously received a Collections Research Grant from the Oriental Institute of the University of Chicago and a sabbatical leave from GWU during the spring 2015 semester, which allowed me to take the first preliminary steps toward tackling the material. The final push was subsequently made possible by a Dean's Research Chair fellowship from GWU, which allowed me to do additional research and writing during the summer and fall of 2018, as well as to be on leave during the spring 2019 semester in order to put the final touches on the manuscript and begin to see the project through the publication process.

I am grateful to all of the above, as well as to the student participants in my undergraduate seminar on Megiddo, taught at GWU during fall 2016. They allowed me to try out numerous ideas and provided me with their feedback and insights in return.

The vast majority of the archival material cited and quoted here comes from the archives at the Oriental Institute Museum of the University of Chicago, primarily filed under "Megiddo Collection" or "Director's Correspondence." This archival material is, however, not currently digitized and must be accessed in person. Much of the additional cited material appears courtesy of the archives of the Israel Antiquities Authority (available online at http://www.iaa-archives.org.il/default.aspx under "Megiddo, Tell").

Further material comes from the Rockefeller Archive Center in Sleepy Hollow, New York (http://rockarch.org/about/); the Olof E. Lind papers at the Library of Congress (https://www.loc.gov/item/mm2014085935/); the Aleš Hrdlička Papers in the National Anthropological Archives of the Smithsonian Institution (https://anthropology.si.edu/naa/fa/Hrdlicka_Ales.pdf); the National Archives in Washington, DC (https://www.archives.gov); the Herbert G. May Papers at Oberlin College (http://www2.oberlin.edu/archive /archon_pdfs/May_Herbert_Inventory.pdf); the archives of the University Museum at the University of Pennsylvania (https://www.penn.museum /about-collections/archives); the archives of the Palestine Exploration Fund (https://www.pef.org.uk); the archives of the American Schools of Oriental Research (http://www.asor.org/initiatives-projects/asor-archives/); and various personal collections.

Overall, I am extremely grateful to all those who made this archival material and other relevant items available to me for observation and publication, and who have allowed me to quote liberally from their holdings. These include the following (in no particular order and with sincere apologies in advance to anyone whom I may have accidentally omitted).

Gil Stein (former director), John Larson and Anne Flannery (successive archivists), Kiersten Neumann (curator and research associate), Helen McDonald (registrar), Susan Allison (associate registrar), Catie Witt (intern), and Charles E. Jones (former research archivist—bibliographer) at the Oriental Institute of the University of Chicago, as well as Jack Green (former chief curator) and Jean Evans (current chief curator) of the Oriental Institute Museum; Silvia Krapiwko, head of the Archives Branch at the Israel Antiquities Authority; Lee R. Hiltzik (senior research associate), Amy Fitch and Tom Rosenbaum (archivists), and the rest of the incredible staff at the Rockefeller Archive Center; Alessandro Pezzati, archivist at the Penn Museum; Felicity Cobbing, executive director at the Palestine Exploration Fund (PEF); Ken Grossi (archivist) and Ed Vermue (special collections and preservation librarian), as well as Louisa Hoffman (archival assistant), at Oberlin College; Daisy Njoku of the National Anthropology Archives at the Smithsonian Museum Support Center, Smithsonian Institution; the various archival assistants in the Manuscript Reading Room of the Library of Congress (Madison Building); Aaron J. Brody (director) and Tara Lewandowski (collections manager) at the Badè Museum of Biblical Archaeology, Pacific School of Religion; Cynthia Rufo-McCormick, archivist and website manager at the American Schools of Oriental Research; Sue Richter (director) and Alan Woodrum (volunteer coordinator) at the Lamon House in Danville, Illinois; Ryan Rikicki (director), as well as Rose Overton and Linda Warrum, at the

Working Men's Museum in New Harmony, Indiana; Patricia Sides, archivist at the Willard Library; Dan Elliott, web manager for the Maple Hill Cemetery in New Harmony, Indiana; David Woolman, son of Laurence and Janet Woolman, who allowed me to see and cite his unpublished manuscript about his parents' time at Megiddo and Luxor; Barbara A. Keller, who provided material and photographs from the estate of Stanley Fisher; Steven R. Fisher, grandson of Clarence S. Fisher; Michael Stanner, grandson of Yemima Guy; Annabelle Redway Dunn and Merrell Redway Cherouny, granddaughters of Gordon Loud, as well as cousins Susan Gordon Kern and Gordon S. Loud; and Carol DeLoach Fletcher, daughter of Edward and Florence DeLoach, who went far beyond the call of duty to provide material from the letters, diaries, and photographs of her parents. Quotations or citations of archival and other material in this book appear courtesy of the above-named institutions, museums, and individuals, to all of whom I am most grateful.

I also owe thanks to a number of other individuals for providing information about a variety of topics, as well as assistance in searching for and procuring various documents, including Herb Somers of the GWU Jacob Burns Law Library; Shmuel Ben-Gad of the GWU Gelman Library; Ruth Levush of the Global Legal Research Center at the Law Library of Congress; Jennie Ebeling of the University of Evansville; Edhem Eldem of Bosphorus University; Yasar Ersoy of Hitit University; Zeynap Kiziltan, director of the Istanbul Archaeological Museums; Nazan Ölçer, director of the Sabanci Museum; Sabine Böhme of the Vorderasiatisches Museum in Berlin; Anat Kidron and Yaron Perry at the University of Haifa; Eran Arie, the Frieder Burda Curator of Iron Age and Persian Period Archaeology at the Israel Museum, Jerusalem; Raz Kletter of the University of Helsinki; Shimon Gibson of UNC Charlotte; and Israel Finkelstein and David Ussishkin (emeritus) of Tel Aviv University and the Tel Aviv Megiddo Expedition. As with my other books, I could not have written this without the assistance of many other people as well; they are too numerous to mention by name here, but they know who they are and that I am immensely grateful for their efforts on my behalf.

For their labors and permissions regarding the photographs and other illustrations reproduced in this book, I would like to specifically thank Anne Flannery and Susan Allison at the Oriental Institute of the University of Chicago; Ed Vermue and Ken Grossi at Oberlin College; Cynthia Rufo-McCormick at the American Schools of Oriental Research (ASOR); Felicity

Cobbing at the Palestine Exploration Fund (PEF); Daisy Njoku at the Smithsonian Museum Support Center; and Barbara A. Keller, Jack Green, Michael Stanner, Zeev Herzog, Norma Franklin, and Dan Elliott. I would also like to thank Eisenbrauns and Pennsylvania State University Press for permission to republish the material pertaining to Rosamond Templeton and her ownership of Megiddo.

As for additional thanks and expressions of gratitude, once again I would like to single out my intrepid editor, Rob Tempio, and all of the hardworking people at Princeton University Press, for their belief in me, their patience, and for helping me turn this book into reality. In particular, however, I would like to especially thank Norma Franklin, who knows all the details about Megiddo past and present, and without whose tremendous store of knowledge this book could not have been written. Both Mitch Allen and Jill Rubalcaba helped make my wordsmithing inestimably better than it would have been otherwise; I am also grateful to a number of additional people who read through parts or all of the manuscript while it was in draft form, including Bill Dardis, Jean Evans, Steve Fisher, Anne Flannery, Norma Franklin, Rachel Hallote, Randy Helm, Michael Howell, Barbara Keller, Raz Kletter, and Sarah Parcak.

Finally, I would like to respectfully dedicate this book to the memory of James Henry Breasted and all of the staff members and their spouses who took part in Chicago's excavations at Megiddo, as well as to my Megiddo family, including all of the staff and team members of the Tel Aviv Expedition past and present. I would also like to thank once again my real family—Diane, Hannah, and Joshua, as well as the cats—who put up with me being away at Megiddo every other summer for as long as they can remember.

Notes

Note: As mentioned in the acknowledgments, the vast majority of the material consulted during the writing of this manuscript comes from the archives at the Oriental Institute Museum of the University of Chicago; other material is in the archives at the Israel Antiquities Authority, Oberlin College, the University Museum of the University of Pennsylvania, the Rockefeller Archive Center, the Smithsonian Institution, the National Archives in Washington, DC, the Library of Congress, the American Schools of Oriental Research, and the Palestine Exploration Fund. Unless otherwise noted, the material cited comes from the archives at the Oriental Institute.

EPIGRAPH

1. As quoted in Charles Breasted 1947: 394.

PREFACE

1. The book of Revelation describes the penultimate battle as being fought at Megiddo; it is not the final battle between good and evil, as is commonly misstated, for that will be fought a thousand years later, in or near Jerusalem. For more discussion, see Cline 2000 with further references. Regarding the mentions of Megiddo in the Bible, see Josh. 12:21, 17:11; Judg. 1:27, 5:19; 1 Kings 4:12, 9:15; 2 Kings 9:27, 23:29, 23:30; 1 Chron. 7:29; 2 Chron. 35:22; Zech. 12:11, and see also Chris McKinny's blog post at: http://seekingahomeland.blogspot.co.il/2009/08/megiddos-identification-in-historical.html.
2. The earliest versions of the New Testament had a rough breathing at the beginning of the word, manifested as an "H" sound, so that it was originally pronounced "Harmageddon." But the rough breathing is merely represented in Greek writing by what looks like an apostrophe (thus 'Armageddon), and over time and much recopying, that little initial sign was lost, so that we now simply say "Armageddon."
3. For detailed discussions of the battles that have been fought at Megiddo or in the Jezreel Valley during the past four thousand years, see Cline 2000. See now also overview article of the battles and recent excavations at Megiddo by Weintraub 2015.
4. Niemann and Lehmann 2006a: 694, 2006b.
5. Schumacher 1904b: 33, 36, Abb. 5; later Schumacher 1908: 4–6, fig. 4 and plate II.
6. Besides Megiddo, the site of Hazor also influenced Michener (I have often said that Megiddo + Hazor = Makor, both in terms of sounding similar and in terms of the archaeology), as did other sites that Michener visited; see Silberman 1993: 314; May 2005: 173–75; Brocker 2006; Magness 2012: 8; Glatt 2016; also http://www.biblewalks.com/files/LookingForTheSource.pdf.

7. See, e.g., Yadin 1960, 1970, 1980; also Ussishkin 1966, 1973, 1980.

8. See Finkelstein and Ussishkin 1994; Silberman et al. 1999. Baruch Halpern was the third member of the original triumvirate of codirectors but departed after several seasons of involvement. The present author served as associate director from 2006 and then as codirector from 2010; upon my own retirement from the dig in 2014, Matt Adams and Mario Martin became codirectors with Finkelstein. For a full list of staff members over the years, see Ussishkin 2018: 13–14 and https://megiddoexpedition.wordpress.com/past-seasons/. For an overall summary, see now Ussishkin 2018: 79–105.

9. See, e.g., in just the recent past, Toffolo et al. 2014; Forget and Shahack-Gross 2016; Sapir-Hen et al. 2016, Sapir-Hen, Martin, and Finkelstein 2017; Cradic 2017; Finkelstein et al. 2017a, 2017b; Shahack-Gross et al. 2018.

10. See, e.g., Finkelstein 1996a and 1999 for some of the earliest articles in which he presents his arguments for the "Low Chronology." See now Finkelstein 2013, summarizing his more recent thinking and with further reference to additional articles that appeared in the interim; see also Balter 2000; Ussishkin 2018: 323–26; Richelle 2018: 82, 85–88.

11. A quick search on JSTOR on 8 July 2018 yielded 7,783 results for articles and books that mention Megiddo. Of course, many of these are concerned with its connection to biblical Armageddon, but a very substantial portion are concerned with the actual archaeology of the site. Even in this book, with more than a thousand endnotes and hundreds of entries in the bibliography, I have room to include only those books and articles that are the most germane to the topics being discussed; other detailed scholarly publications pertaining to specific buildings, for instance, can be found, e.g., in Ussishkin 2018.

12. As it turned out, this was an extremely fortuitous decision, for in 2018, David Ussishkin published a very detailed book that focuses almost entirely on the architecture of the site, layer by layer. I have been able to cite that book where appropriate in this volume.

PROLOGUE

1. Cables of 4 June 1928, exchanged between Guy and Breasted. See now also Franklin 2019a.

2. Letter from Breasted to Rockefeller dated 30 July 1928, with reply from Rockefeller dated 8 September 1928; both in the Rockefeller Archive Center (filed under Educational Interests, RG III 2G: Box 111, Folder 802).

3. *New York Times*, 9 August 1928, p. 22, and 26 August 1928, pp. 71 and 76.

4. Letter from Charles Breasted to Guy dated 11 June 1928.

5. *St. Louis Post-Dispatch*, 9 August 1928, p. 1.

6. The scripture quotations contained herein are from the New Revised Standard Version Bible, copyright 1989 by the Division of Christian Education of the National Council of Churches of Christ in the U.S.A. Guy later quoted these in full, in his publication of the stables; see Guy 1931: 46.

7. The debate about these buildings has been continuing ever since their first discovery by the Chicago excavators—see, e.g., Guy 1931: 37–48; Lamon and Shipton 1939: 32–47, 59; Holladay 1986; Pritchard 1970; Yadin 1976; Kempinski 1989: 96–97; as well as now Cline 2006, 2009: 37–38; Cantrell 2006, 2011: 87–113; Cantrell and Finkelstein 2006; Cline and Samet 2013; Franklin 2017; Ussishkin 2018: 399–407; Richelle 2018: 54–55.

CHAPTER I

1. Cable from Fisher to Breasted dated 22 April 1926. The excavation had officially started on 18 April, according to a subsequent cable sent on 24 June 1926, which mentions this date.

2. Cable from Breasted to Fisher dated 25 April 1926.

3. Quotation from Robinson and Smith 1856: 116–18; see also Robinson and Smith 1841: 3:177–80; Ussishkin 2018: 22–23, 443. See Kempinski 1989: 1; Harrison 2004: 1; Hallote 2006: 9–11; also detailed discussions in Tepper and Di Segni 2006: 8–11 and Ussishkin 2018: 22–23. The *New York Times* reported on this incident exactly one hundred years later, in an article published on 15 April 1938 (p. 21).

4. See Conder and Kitchener 1882: 65–66, 70. They visited the region on 14 October 1872.

5. Conder and Kitchener 1882: 49.

6. Conder 1879: 2:68. He had first made this claim two years earlier, in 1877, in the pages of the *Palestine Exploration Fund Quarterly Statement* (Conder 1877: 13–20). See also previously Conder 1873: 5–7, where he discusses the plain of Jezreel/ Esdraelon and its suitability for battles/fighting. See also the discussion in Ussishkin 2018: 23.

7. See Smith 1894: 380, 385–90, and see further Smith 1931: 386, where Smith conclusively identifies Mutesellim with Megiddo. See also the statements made by the Megiddo excavators themselves in Lamon and Shipton 1939: xix and Guy 1938: 1. For a good discussion and references, see the blog post entitled "Megiddo's Identification in Historical Perspective," posted on 19 August 2009 by Dr. Chris McKinny at http://seekingahomeland.blogspot.co.il/2009/08/megiddos -identification-in-historical.html. See also the discussion in Ussishkin 2018: 23.

8. On both Allenby and Thutmose III at Megiddo, see full discussion, with further references, in Cline 2000: chap. 1.

9. On the riots, see, among many others, Sachar 1979: 123; Armstrong 1996: 374–75; Gilbert 1996: 82–84; Smith 1996: 70–71; Segev 2000: 127–29, 132–39; also brief discussion with references in Cline 2004: 251–52.

10. Larson 2010: 261–62; see also Breasted 1920: 285, 1922: 272; Wilson 1936: 108; Hallote 2006: 172–73; Abt 2011: 230, 246; Cline 2014: 4–5; Ussishkin 2018: 44. Breasted began writing the letter on 23 May and sent it on 10 June; the attempted visit took place on 2 June.

11. As I noted in Cline 2000, however, I have never been able to confirm that he actually said this.

12. For a detailed discussion, see chap. 1 in Cline 2000. See now also discussion in Ussishkin 2018: 221–35.

13. Wilson 1936: 108. On the funding for the Oriental Institute, which began with a letter from Breasted to Rockefeller dated 16 February 1919 and culminated in the pledge from Rockefeller on 2 May 1919, with follow-up letters and documents dated 12 May 1919, 25 October 1920, and 9 and 26 July 1921, see the original materials in the Rockefeller Archive Center (filed under Educational Interests, RG III 2G: Box 111, Folder 802 and Box 112, Folder 812).

14. Breasted received the permit despite the fact that—back in late February—the American School of Oriental Research in Jerusalem had already requested a one-year option to dig at either Ta'anach or Megiddo. Nevertheless, Breasted's application was approved on 16 November 1920 by the Archaeological Advisory Board,

as documents in the Israel Antiquities Authority Archives show (British Mandate Administrative Files ATQ_169/12 [58/58])—see, e.g., the letter from Breasted to Garstang dated 13 October 1920; the minutes of the 4th Ordinary Meeting of the Archaeological Advisory Board dated 16 November 1920; the letter sent by W. J. Phythian-Adams on behalf of Garstang to Breasted on 23 November 1920, as well as Breasted's response to Phythian-Adams dated 4 January 1921; and the wording of the actual permit when it was finally issued on 9 July 1925. See also Worrell 1920: 35; Running and Freedman 1975: 71–72; Hallote 2006: 170; Hallote 2011: 166.

15. On the history of archaeology, including Schliemann and Carter, see now Cline 2017a; on Schliemann at Troy, see Cline 2013, with further references; on the history of biblical archaeology in particular, see Silberman 1982; Davis 2004; Hallote 2006; Cline 2009.

16. Hallote 2006: 101–2, 108–18.

17. See Cline 2009: 21–23, with additional references.

18. Letter from Breasted to Judson dated 7 March 1921, in the Rockefeller Archive Center (filed under Educational Interests, RG III 2G: Box 112, Folder 824).

19. Letter from Judson to Rockefeller dated 10 March 1921, in the Rockefeller Archive Center (filed under Educational Interests, RG III 2G: Box 112, Folder 824). Surprisingly, especially given the trip that Breasted had promptly undertaken, Judson states that this request is being made even though "excavations were never intended to be included" as an integral part of the Oriental Institute. More likely he meant to say that excavations had not been explicitly mentioned in the original agreement, rather than that they were never intended at all.

20. Fosdick 1956: 360. Note that Rockefeller subsequently also contributed to the American School of Classical Studies in Athens—including the excavations of the Agora and the reconstruction of the Stoa of Attalos—and the American Academy in Rome; see Fosdick 1956: 365–68 and 1962: 236–37.

21. Pledge made in a letter from Rockefeller to Judson dated 19 April 1921, with a subsequent letter from Judson dated 28 June 1921; see the original materials in the Rockefeller Archive Center (filed under Educational Interests, RG III 2G: Box 112, Folder 824). See also Fosdick 1956: 360; Abt 2011: 359.

22. *New York Times*, 2 July 1921, p. 5 (copy of the article in the Rockefeller Archive Center, filed under Educational Interests, RG III 2G: Box 112, Folder 824).

23. Letter from Breasted to W. S. Richardson (assistant to Rockefeller) dated 5 August 1924, with a subsequent letter from President Burton (successor to Judson) to Richardson dated 17 November 1924; see the original materials in the Rockefeller Archive Center (filed under Educational Interests, RG III 2G: Box 112, Folder 824).

24. Letter from Fisher to Breasted dated 14 July 1924.

25. The group visited Megiddo on 9 April 1921. Information from Cynthia Rufo-McCormick, ASOR archivist, based on material contained in "Fisher, Box 6, Folder 35."

26. Vogel 1993: 209; Kuklick 1996: 84; Pickett 2013: 14. For the relevant passport applications and other official documents, see Ancestry.com (searching for "Clarence S. Fisher").

27. Vogel 1993: 109; Kuklick 1996: 150–52, 161–62, 186; Davis 2004: 57–61. See also Cline 2009: 13–39.

28. Letter from Fisher to Gordon dated 27 June 1924, quoted in full within a later letter from Gordon to Fisher dated 6 January 1925, in the archives of the Penn Museum (UMA/Fisher/Box 1: 6/27/1924 and 1/6/1925). Other letters dealing with similar complaints from Fisher to Gordon were sent on 17 October and 20 No-

vember 1924; there is also a reply from Gordon dated 21 October 1924 (UMA/Fisher/Box 1: 10/17/1924, 11/20/1924, and 11/21/1924).

29. After sending his letter, Fisher actually received a raise and continued to negotiate about getting an assistant; see initial letter from Fisher to Harrison dated 7 December 1924, in the archives of the Penn Museum (UMA/Fisher/Box 1: 12/7/1924), and subsequently a letter from Fisher to Gordon dated 5 January 1925, with a reply from Gordon dated 6 January 1925 (UMA/Fisher/Box 1: 1/5/1925 and 1/6/1925). See also a letter from Gordon to Fisher dated 5 December 1924, in which he discusses Fisher's complaints about salary and the matter of his assistant, as well as a reply from Fisher to Gordon dated 9 December 1924 (UMA/Fisher/Box 1: 12/5/1924 and 12/9/1924).

30. Letter from Breasted to Fisher dated 22 December 1924.

31. Letter from Breasted to Garstang dated 18 December 1924, in the Israel Antiquities Authority Archives (British Mandate Administrative Files ATQ_169/12 [58/58]).

32. Letter to Breasted from Guy, acting director of the British School, dated 12 January 1925 and sent in the absence of Garstang, in the Israel Antiquities Authority Archives (British Mandate Administrative Files ATQ_169/12 [58/58]). Note that this is the first time we meet Guy, who will eventually become the field director at Megiddo in 1927.

33. When Harrison finally received Fisher's letter, he immediately accepted the resignation. The Board of Managers then reviewed and confirmed the decision to release Fisher in mid-January 1925. Copies of the articles from the *Philadelphia Record*, the *Evening Bulletin*, the *Evening Ledger*, and numerous other newspapers that ran articles on Fisher's resignation on 12–13 January 1925 are in the archives of the Penn Museum (UMA/Fisher/*Evening Ledger, Evening Bulletin*, and *Philadelphia Record* 12–13 January 1925). See also Davis 2004: 61; Pickett 2013: 14.

34. See the newspaper articles, from which this information and the quote come, in the archives of the Penn Museum (UMA/Fisher/*Evening Ledger, Evening Bulletin*, and *Philadelphia Record* 12–13 January 1925). See again also Davis 2004: 61; Pickett 2013: 14.

35. Letter from Gordon to Rowe dated 10 September 1925, in the archives of the Penn Museum (UMA/Beisan/Box 1: 9/10/25). See also Davis 2004: 61 and Pickett 2013: 14, who both quote Gordon's remarks in part, although Pickett incorrectly attributes them to William F. Albright.

36. Reply from Fisher to Breasted dated 3 February 1925.

37. Letter from Gordon to Rowe dated 10 September 1925, in the archives of the Penn Museum (UMA/Beisan/Box 1: 9/10/25); see also Davis 2004: 61 and Pickett 2013: 14.

38. See comments in letter from Luckenbill to Breasted dated 23 June 1925, after he had met with Fisher in person.

39. https://rockfound.rockarch.org/biographical/-/asset_publisher/6ygcKECNI1nb/content/raymond-b-fosdick.

40. Letter from Breasted to Fosdick dated 15 May 1925, in the Rockefeller Archive Center (filed under Educational Interests, RG III 2G: Box 112, Folder 824).

41. Letter from Breasted to Fosdick dated 15 May 1925, in the Rockefeller Archive Center (filed under Educational Interests, RG III 2G: Box 112, Folder 824).

42. Letter from Breasted to Fosdick dated 15 May 1925, in the Rockefeller Archive Center (filed under Educational Interests, RG III 2G: Box 112, Folder 824).

43. Letters from Higgins to Luckenbill and from Luckenbill to Breasted, both dated 4 February 1925; Breasted to Luckenbill dated 22 March 1925; Luckenbill to Breasted dated 15 May 1925; Breasted to Luckenbill dated 18 May 1925; and

Breasted to Fisher dated 25 June 1925. See also information available on Ancestry .com, searching for Daniel F. Higgins and Daniel Franklin Higgins, as well as for Eleanor Ruth Higgins Garraway and Mary Elizabeth Higgins.

44. Letter from Fosdick to Rockefeller dated 2 June 1925, in the Rockefeller Archive Center (filed under Educational Interests, RG III 2G: Box 112, Folder 824).

45. Letter from Rockefeller to Fosdick dated 4 June 1925, in the Rockefeller Archive Center (filed under Educational Interests, RG III 2G: Box 112, Folder 824). See also a subsequent letter from Trevor Arnett (vice president and business manager of the University of Chicago) to Richardson dated 6 July 1925, a letter from Fosdick to Harold Swift (chairman of the Board of Trustees of the University of Chicago) also dated 6 July 1925, and a letter from Arnett to Richardson dated 6 August 1925, all in the Rockefeller Archive Center (filed under Educational Interests, RG III 2G: Box 112, Folder 824). See also Abt 2011: 359, 464n15 and details in the *New York Times*, 9 August 1928, p. 22: "Armageddon Bared by Exploring Party; Well-Laid-Out Town Revealed by the University of Chicago Excavations." Conversion to today's dollars based on http://www.dollartimes.com/inflation/inflation.php?amount=1000&year =1925 and http://www.carinsurancedata.org/calculators/inflation/215000/1925.

46. See Wikipedia entry "RMS Homeric."

47. Cable from Breasted to Luckenbill dated 5 June 1925.

48. See again letters from Higgins to Luckenbill and from Luckenbill to Breasted, both dated 4 February 1925; Breasted to Luckenbill dated 22 March 1925; Luckenbill to Breasted dated 15 May 1925; Breasted to Luckenbill dated 18 May 1925; and Breasted to Fisher dated 25 June 1925.

49. Letter from Breasted to Luckenbill dated 11 June 1925.

50. Cable from Breasted to Fisher dated 13 June 1925; cables from Luckenbill to Breasted dated 20 June and 23 June 1925; letter from Luckenbill to Breasted dated 23 June 1925, with a related letter from Breasted to Luckenbill dated 25 June 1925; letter from Fisher to Breasted dated 15 July 1925. There is also what appears to be a draft of a cable from Breasted to Luckenbill dated almost a full month earlier, on 18 May 1925, in which Breasted wrote, "Find Fisher offer him field directorship MEGIDDO excavations. Cable me result."

51. Letter from Luckenbill to Breasted dated 23 June 1925.

52. Letter from Breasted to Fisher dated 25 June 1925.

53. Letter from Breasted to Garstang dated 24 June 1925 in the Israel Antiquities Authority Archives (British Mandate Administrative Files ATQ_169/12 [58/58]).

54. Letter from Breasted to Luckenbill dated 11 June 1925; see also letter from Breasted to Luckenbill dated 6 July 1925, in which he states that someone named Titterton whom they had been considering had decided instead to take a job on the editorial staff of the *Atlantic Monthly*. This meant that the Megiddo team had no epigrapher on their team at the start of their project.

55. Letter from Luckenbill to Breasted dated 23 June 1925; letter from DeLoach to his mother dated 10 July 1925 (courtesy of Carol DeLoach Fletcher). Biographical information courtesy of Ancestry.com, including birth, marriage, and census records for DeLoach (searching for Edward DeLoach and Edward Lowell DeLoach).

56. Letter from Breasted to Fisher dated 25 June 1925.

57. Letter from Breasted to Garstang dated 29 September 1926.

58. Letters from Fisher to Luckenbill dated 6 and 8 July 1925; there is also a detailed letter from Fisher to Garstang dated 27 July 1925 in the Israel Antiquities Authority Archives (British Mandate Administrative Files ATQ_169/12 [58/58]). See also

letters from Higgins to Breasted dated 4, 11, and 14 August 1925, with a reply from Breasted on 13 and 15 August.

59. Re official permit: see letter from Garstang to Breasted, plus official permit (No. 26), both dated 9 July 1925, with reply from Breasted dated 6 August 1925, all in the Israel Antiquities Authority Archives (British Mandate Administrative Files ATQ_169/12 [58/58]). Re Fisher's arrival at Megiddo and related matters: see letters from Fisher to Breasted dated 15 July 1925 and from Fisher to Luckenbill dated 21 and 24 July 1925; see also Harrison 2004: 2, who notes that the expedition was "launched in the summer of 1925."

60. Letter from Fisher to Luckenbill dated 8 July 1925. See also Fisher 1929: 17.

61. Letters dated 5, 6, 7, and 13 August 1925, sent between Fisher, Luckenbill, Breasted, and the OI secretary. See also Fisher 1929: 17, 24.

62. Biographical information for Fisher and his family courtesy of Ancestry.com, including birth, marriage, and census records; I thank also his grandson Steve Fisher, author of a novel (Fisher 2016) that is based in part on the life of his grandfather. Higgins was born in either 1882 or 1884 (see further below).

63. Letter from Breasted to Garstang dated 6 August 1925; see also a letter from Fisher to Garstang dated 27 July 1925; both in the Israel Antiquities Authority Archives (British Mandate Administrative Files ATQ_169/12 [58/58]).

64. Cable from Higgins to Breasted dated 21 September 1925; letters from Higgins to Breasted and Luckenbill, both dated 14 October 1925 (see further below on these letters from Higgins, which did not reach the recipients until late April or early May 1926).

65. http://www.brynmawr.edu/library/exhibits/BreakingGround/index.html; see write-ups on these and other early women archaeologists in the edited volume by Cohen and Joukowsky 2004.

CHAPTER II

1. *St. Louis Post-Dispatch*, 16 July 1925, p. 15, and 13 September 1925, pp. 1–2 of the Sunday Magazine supplement.

2. Fisher 1929: 17; letter from Fisher to Luckenbill dated 24 July 1925; letter from Higgins to Breasted dated 29 August 1925; letter from Fisher to Breasted dated 14 September 1925; letters from Higgins to Breasted and Luckenbill, both dated 14 October 1925. See also Wikipedia entry "RMS Aquitania" and a letter from De-Loach to his mother dated 2 October 1925 (retrieved from the Olof E. Lind papers in the Library of Congress <lccn.loc.gov/mm2014085935>).

3. In the Israel Antiquities Authority Archives, a cable from Fisher to the Department of Antiquities dated 21 September 1925 requests that a representative be sent to help "in settling land claims at Megiddo"; see also a letter sent in reply that same day (British Mandate Administrative Files ATQ_169/12 [58/58]). In the archives at the Oriental Institute, there is another copy of the letter sent in reply to Fisher as well as a further letter dated 10 October 1925, which reports that a "commission" had been set up, which consisted of Hassan Saad, representing the landowners, Fisher (or a representative) from the dig, and Mr. L. Andrews, chairing the commission on behalf of the District Commissioner's Offices in Haifa. There are also letters from Higgins to Breasted and Luckenbill, both dated 14 October 1925, which give similar details, including complaints about the steep rent to which Fisher had agreed. See also now discussion in Ussishkin 2018: 51–52.

4. Fisher 1929: 18; the lease documents in the archives of the Oriental Institute are dated 24 October and 1 November 1925.

5. The description of this argument, along with other complaints about Fisher, especially about the high rent for the land, is, as noted, in the letters from Higgins to Breasted and Luckenbill, both dated 14 October 1925, which didn't reach them until late April or early May 1926.

6. Letter from DeLoach to his mother dated 11 November 1925, now in the possession of his daughter, Carol DeLoach Fletcher, and cited here with her permission.

7. Memo from Fisher to Breasted, dated only "1926."

8. Letter from DeLoach to his mother dated 2 October 1925 (retrieved from the Olof E. Lind papers in the Library of Congress <lccn.loc.gov/mm2014085935>).

9. Fisher 1929: 17–19; letter from DeLoach to his mother dated 2 October 1925 (see above).

10. Fisher 1929: 17–19; letter from DeLoach to his mother dated 2 October 1925 (see above). See also Ussishkin 2018: 48–50.

11. Letters from Breasted to Fisher and Breasted to Higgins, both dated 13 December 1925, and from DeLoach to Breasted dated 24 January 1926.

12. Letter from Garstang to Breasted dated 26 January 1926.

13. Breasted in Fisher 1929: ix–x.

14. Letter from Albright to Breasted dated 1 March 1926.

15. Anonymous note sent from Nazareth to Chicago dated 12 January 1926.

16. Letter from DeLoach to Breasted dated 24 January 1926; see also Fisher 1929: 20.

17. See, e.g., Benzinger 1904; Schumacher 1904a, 1904b, 1905a, 1905b, 1905c, 1906a, 1906b, 1906c, 1906d, 1908; Kautzsch 1904; Erman and Kautzsch 1906; Macalister 1906: 62; Watzinger 1929. See also the discussion in Ussishkin 2018: 29–41.

18. Fisher 1929: ix–xii, 12–15, figs. 7–9; 60–61; see also Guy 1931: 44, fig. 17; Lamon and Shipton 1939: 60–61, fig. 70; Ussishkin 1990: 71–74, figs. 1–2, 2018: 326–31; Chapman 2009: 4–17, figs. 1a–b, also 2015.

19. Schumacher 1908: 7, Tafel 1; Harrison 2004: 1; Tepper and Di Segni 2006: 11–12; Fisher 1929: 26. See also the PEF biography of Schumacher (http://www.pef.org .uk/profiles/gottlieb-schumacher).

20. Schumacher 1908; Watzinger 1929. Böhme 2014: 41–43 notes that Schumacher sent fourteen crates of material from his Megiddo excavations to Berlin in 1908. See discussion of Schliemann at Troy in Cline 2013, with further references.

21. Fisher 1929: ix–xii, 12–15, 60–61, figs. 7–9; see also Guy 1931: 44, fig. 17; Lamon and Shipton 1939: 60–61, fig. 70; Ussishkin 1990: 71–74, figs. 1–2; Chapman 2009: 4–17, figs. 1a–b, 2015. Sagrillo 2015: 69–70 notes that the museum number is Rockefeller Archaeological Museum I.3554. Sheshonq is frequently also spelled Sheshonk and sometimes Shoshenq/k.

22. See previous discussions in Ussishkin 1990: 71–74; Cline 2000: 75–82, Cline 2009: 25, 81, and Cline 2017a: 223–24. See also Chapman 2009, 2015; Levin 2012; and Sagrillo 2015, with further references.

23. Letter from Higgins to Luckenbill dated 19 May 1926.

24. Handwritten letter from Breasted to Fisher dated 25 March 1926 (though misdated 1925).

25. Letter from Breasted to Luckenbill dated 29 March 1926.

26. Letter from Breasted to Garstang dated 29 March 1926.

27. Letter from Breasted to Rockefeller dated 24 March 1926, with reply from Rockefeller dated 18 April 1926.

28. Letter from Garstang to Breasted dated 29 March 1926.

29. Cable from Guy to Breasted dated 2 May 1928; according to a letter sent by Guy to Breasted on 28 June 1928, the division of antiquities had taken place on 27–28

April, and he took the objects to Jerusalem himself on 5 June, returning on 7 June. Sagrillo 2015: 69–70 notes that the museum number is Rockefeller Archaeological Museum I.3554.

30. Many have discussed this topic previously; see now Ussishkin 2018: 328–29. See also the numerous papers in the conference volume edited by James and van der Veen 2015.

31. See Breasted in Fisher 1929: xi. See also Breasted 1926: 164–65. Quoted also by Ussishkin 2018: 329.

32. *St. Louis Post-Dispatch*, 20 June 1926, p. 2 of Sunday Magazine section.

33. *St. Louis Post-Dispatch*, 20 June 1926, p. 2 of Sunday Magazine section.

34. Fisher 1929: 60–61; Guy 1931: 44.

35. Harrison 2004: 7–8; see further discussion in Chapman 2009: 6–7 and passim.

36. Letter from Breasted to Luckenbill dated 29 March 1926.

CHAPTER III

1. Letter in the Chicago archives from Fisher to Breasted dated 5 April 1926; also relevant letters in the Israel Antiquities Authority Archives written variously by Fisher, Garstang, and Guy (as inspector of the region), dated 16 and 20 February, 4, 28, and 29 March, and 1, 7, and 28 April 1926. The discussion about the import duty and refunds requested by the Chicago team continued throughout the remainder of the calendar year, as attested in numerous additional letters from June through December 1926; the matter was ultimately resolved in Chicago's favor, at least for most of the items in question.

2. Breasted 1928: 20.

3. Letters from Breasted to Luckenbill dated 29 March and 3 May 1926.

4. The letters, written to Breasted and to Luckenbill, were dated 14 October 1925; first referred to by Breasted in a letter to Luckenbill dated 3 May 1926. See also letter from Garstang to Breasted dated 17 August 1926, with reply from Breasted to Garstang dated 29 September 1926. Fisher was also aware that Garstang had been sent a copy of Higgins's letter to Luckenbill; see letter from Fisher to Breasted dated 26 September 1926. Eventually both letters found their way to Breasted, and thence into the Oriental Institute archives, but only long after the fact.

5. Breasted in Fisher 1929: x–xi. Harrison 2004: 2 notes that the area where Fisher dug on top of the mound was later designated Area C by the Chicago excavators who followed him.

6. Letter from Breasted to Luckenbill dated 3 May 1926.

7. Letter from Kellogg to Luckenbill dated 7 May 1926.

8. Letter from Luckenbill to Breasted dated 22 April 1926; cable from Breasted to Fisher dated 25 April 1926; letter from Breasted to Fisher dated 24 May 1926.

9. Handwritten copy of cable from Breasted to Higgins dated 25 April 1926 (I have taken the liberty of reproducing it in ALL CAPS, as the final version would have appeared); also mentioned in a letter from Breasted to Luckenbill dated 3 May 1926.

10. Information from Ancestry.com (searching for John P. Kellogg, John Payne Kellogg, and John Kellogg). See also letters exchanged between Kellogg, Breasted, and Luckenbill in 1925 and 1926, some to and from Kellogg himself and others in which he is simply mentioned and/or quoted. According to the registrar at the University of Chicago (personal communication, 21 May 2018), Kellogg was registered as a student at the university from 1 October 1925 through 20 December 1938 but did not receive a degree of any kind.

11. Letter from Luckenbill to Breasted dated 22 April 1926; letter from Kellogg to Luckenbill dated 7 May 1926.

12. Letter from Kellogg to Luckenbill dated 7 May 1926.

13. Letter from Luckenbill to Breasted dated 27 May 1926; also letter from Breasted to Luckenbill dated 1 June 1926.

14. Cable from Fisher to Breasted dated 26 April 1926.

15. Letter from Higgins to Breasted 19 May 1926; many of the points are repeated in a letter sent from Higgins to Breasted on the same day, 19 May 1926.

16. Letter from Kellogg to Breasted dated 19 May 1926; cable from Fisher to Breasted dated 12 May. The following information comes from Fisher's letter to Breasted dated 29 May 1926, which also independently confirms the material contained in Kellogg's letter of ten days earlier.

17. Letter from Fisher to Breasted dated 29 May 1926.

18. Letter from Kellogg to Luckenbill dated 2 June 1926.

19. Letter from Fisher to Breasted dated 26 September 1926.

20. Cable from Breasted dated 16 June 1926.

21. The draft of the cable to Higgins on 16 June 1926 was sent from Chicago by J. Spencer Dickerson, secretary of the Board of Trustees, rather than by Breasted. There are also two other copies of the cable to Higgins, dated 21 and 23 June.

22. Letters from Kellogg to Breasted dated 26 June and 17 July 1926; cables from Higgins to Chicago dated 25 and 27 June 1926.

23. Letter from Higgins to Breasted dated 19 May 1926; letters from Breasted to Higgins dated 29 May and 16 June 1926.

24. Letter from Breasted to Higgins dated 16 June 1926.

25. Letter from Kellogg to Breasted dated 17 July 1926; later quoted by Breasted in a letter to Luckenbill dated 17 August 1926.

26. Note that most of this information is dependent upon the narrative in Running and Freedman 1975: 130–31, as none of the letters exchanged between Luckenbill and Albright pertaining to this specific episode can be located in the Oriental Institute archives.

27. Letter from Higgins to Luckenbill dated 19 May 1926.

28. Running and Freedman 1975: 130.

29. Letter from Luckenbill to Breasted dated 23 June 1925. In a letter from Breasted to Luckenbill dated 6 July 1925, Breasted thanked Luckenbill for clarifying this point with Fisher, stating, "I'm [e]specially glad that you told Fisher clearly our position with regard to Albright. We shall not be in need of any of his assistance."

30. Running and Freedman 1975: 131.

31. Cable from Breasted dated 19 June 1926.

32. Cable from Fisher dated 24 June 1926.

33. Sworn statement by Fisher dated 25 July 1926.

34. Sworn statement by Fisher dated 25 July 1926.

35. Cable from Breasted to Higgins dated 29 June 1926; subsequent cables back and forth between Higgins and Breasted dated 17 July 1929; final cable from Higgins to Breasted accepting the offer dated 22 July 1926; letter from Breasted to Luckenbill dated 17 August 1926; memo dated 18 August 1926 is attached to Fisher's sworn statement dated 25 July 1926.

36. According to entries on Ancestry.com and the inscription on his tombstone in Browns Church Cemetery, Manhattan/Joliet (Will County), Illinois, Higgins was born in 1882 and died in 1930. However, his obituary, which was published in the

AAPG Bulletin for June 1930 (p. 819), gives his birth year as 1884; it also specifically gives his death in Knoxville, Tennessee, as occurring on 21 March 1930.

37. Letter from Fisher to Breasted dated 6 August 1926; see also Fisher 1929: 24. A note in her file at the Oriental Institute says that she officially resigned as of 31 December 1928. However, she is included on a UK incoming passenger list, on which her profession is listed as "archaeologist" and her age as thirty-seven (with a birth year noted as "abt. 1891"), which records that she arrived by ship in England on 24 August 1928 (see Ancestry.com, searching for "Ruby Woodley").

38. There are four boxes of archival files of Olof E. Lind now kept in the Manuscript Records Room of the Library of Congress (Olof E. Lind papers <lccn.loc.gov /mm2014085935>), which contain much relevant information on Lind's life both before and after his time at Megiddo. See also https://www.loc.gov/collections /american-colony-in-jerusalem/about-this-collection/.

39. Letter from Fisher to Breasted dated 6 August 1926; see also Fisher 1929: 24.

40. Letter from Fisher to Breasted dated 26 September 1926.

41. Letter from Fisher to Breasted dated 26 September 1926.

42. Letter from Fisher to Breasted dated 7 October 1926.

43. Letter from Fisher to Luckenbill dated 6 August 1925; letter from Breasted to Fisher dated 7 August 1925; letters from Fisher to Breasted dated 29 May 1926, 6 August 1926, and 17 August 1926.

44. Letter from Fisher to Allen dated 26 February 1927.

45. Letter from Fisher to Breasted dated 26 September 1926.

46. Letters from Breasted to Fisher dated 21 and 30 October 1926.

47. Letter from Breasted to Fisher dated 29 December 1926.

CHAPTER IV

1. Letter from Kellogg to Breasted dated 10 July 1926.

2. Letter from Kellogg to Breasted dated 17 July 1926.

3. Letter from Fisher to Breasted dated 17 August 1926; see also Fisher 1929: 24, 28.

4. Letter from Fisher to Breasted dated 17 August 1926.

5. Letter from Fisher to Breasted dated 17 August 1926; see also Fisher 1929: 28; Guy 1938: 2; Lamon and Shipton 1939: xxiii. See also Davis 2004: 62; now Ussishkin 2018: 52.

6. Fisher 1929: 28. See also now Ussishkin 2018: 52–55.

7. Fisher 1929: 28. See also now Ussishkin 2018: 52–55.

8. Fisher 1929: 29–30.

9. Fisher 1929: 30–31.

10. Letter from Guy to Breasted dated 13 August 1927.

11. Letter from Fisher to Breasted dated 26 September 1926.

12. Letter from Fisher to Breasted dated 17 August 1926.

13. Letter from Fisher to Breasted dated 26 September 1926.

14. Letter from Fisher to Breasted dated 17 August 1926.

15. Fisher 1929: 66; see also the final publication of Stratum I in Lamon and Shipton 1939: 88–91, fig. 98.

16. See Lamon and Shipton 1939: 83–87, figs. 95–97, and more recent discussion in Kempinski 1989: 103–5; Singer-Avitz 2014: 124.

17. Fisher 1929: 61; Barag 1966: 10; Kempinski 1989: 103–7; Stern 2002.

18. Fisher 1929: 16, 59–75; Guy 1931: 9–10, 19–20; Lamon and Shipton 1939: 91; Albright 1940: 549; Barag 1966: 10; Kempinski 1989: 107; Harrison 2004: 2; Ussishkin 2018: 440–41.

19. Suggested by Ephraim Stern, according to Kempinski 1989: 107, as well as by Kempinski himself.
20. See detailed discussions in Cline 2000, with further references.

CHAPTER V

1. Letter from Breasted to Guy dated 29 December 1926.
2. Details from the PEF Profile of P.L.O. Guy: http://www.pef.org.uk/profiles/lt-col -philip-langstaffe-ord-guy-1885-1952.
3. Details from Green 2009: 167–71 and from the PEF Profile of P.L.O. Guy: http:// www.pef.org.uk/profiles/lt-col-philip-langstaffe-ord-guy-1885-1952. See also now Ussishkin 2018: 55.
4. Details from Green 2009: 167–71 and from the PEF Profile of P.L.O. Guy: http:// www.pef.org.uk/profiles/lt-col-philip-langstaffe-ord-guy-1885-1952.
5. Details from Green 2009: 167–71 and from the PEF Profile of P.L.O. Guy: http:// www.pef.org.uk/profiles/lt-col-philip-langstaffe-ord-guy-1885-1952.
6. Letter from Fisher to the director of antiquities dated 26 March 1927, in the Israel Antiquities Authority Archives (British Mandate Administrative Files ATQ_7/6 [56/56]).
7. Letters from Breasted to Fisher and from Fisher to Breasted dated 6 April 1927; letter from Stefanski to Fisher dated 7 April 1927; cables between Breasted and Fisher dated 12 April 1927.
8. Letter from Breasted to Fisher dated 19 April 1927 and from Breasted to Guy dated 20 April 1927.
9. Letter from Breasted to Montgomery dated 25 May 1927.
10. Breasted in Fisher 1929: xii.
11. Guy 1931: 9.
12. Letter from Breasted to Montgomery dated 25 May 1927.
13. Letter from Alan Rowe to Miss McHugh, secretary at the University Museum in Philadelphia, dated 23 April 1927, in the archives of the Penn Museum (UMA/ Beisan/Box 2: 4/23/27); see also Davis 2004: 63 and Pickett 2013: 14.
14. Kuklick 1996: 83–89. One must, however, also take into consideration the source cited by Kuklick, which was the dig director Hilprecht, who was first Fisher's champion but then turned against him (as Hilprecht eventually did with most of his students and colleagues).
15. Ousterhout 2010: 12.
16. Geere 1904.
17. I am indebted to Norma Franklin for suggesting the possibility that Guy may have resented some of his more educated colleagues who were sent to him by Breasted.
18. Letter from Guy to Breasted dated 21 April 1927 and response from Breasted to Guy dated 23 April 1927.
19. Letter from DeLoach to Breasted dated 20 May 1927.
20. Information from Ancestry.com, searching for "Ralph Bernard Parker"; see also letter from Guy to Breasted dated 13 August 1927.
21. Letter from Guy to Breasted dated 13 August 1927.
22. See the folders containing letters and documents to, from, and concerning Parker in the Oriental Institute at the University of Chicago, which go through 1954. See also Ancestry.com, searching for "Ralph Bernard Parker."
23. Letter from DeLoach to Breasted dated 20 May 1927.
24. Letter from DeLoach to Breasted dated 4 July 1927.

25. Letters from DeLoach to Breasted dated 20 May and 5 June 1927.
26. See a report submitted by J. C. Carter dated 18 July 1927, entitled "Summary of Activities during Quarter Ending June 20, 1927," for the Department of Health, Malaria Survey Section, Jerusalem; copy in the Rockefeller Archive Center (filed under Rockefeller Foundation International Health Board/Division [IHBD], RG 5, Series 3 [3.825/3.825I], Box 250, Folder 3030).
27. Wilson 1972: 68–69.
28. Wilson 1968–69: 8.
29. Letter from Guy to Harold H. Nelson dated 10 May 1927, with copy to Breasted; cable from Guy to Breasted on 11 May 1927; reply from Breasted to Guy on 18 June 1927. DeLoach also wrote to Breasted, with his version of the events, on 20 May 1927. See also two confidential letters sent to the chief immigration officer in Jerusalem by Guy dated 14 May 1927, in which he states that the Egyptian workmen whom he lists had "broken faith with their employers" and "should, without exception[,] be returned to Egypt"; both are in the Israel Antiquities Authority Archives (British Mandate Administrative Files ATQ_7/6 [56/56]).
30. Letter from O'Neill to Guy dated 3 June 1927.
31. Letters from Guy to Breasted dated 13 August 1927 and 26 September 1927, with response from Breasted to Guy dated 18 October 1927.
32. https://vault.sierraclub.org/history/bade.aspx. The Wikipedia entry for Badè is quite good: https://en.wikipedia.org/wiki/William_F._Badè.
33. Letter from Badè to Breasted dated 6 June 1927.
34. Letter from Badè to Breasted dated 6 June 1927.
35. Letter from Badè to Breasted dated 6 June 1927.
36. Cables sent between Fisher and Breasted dated 25 May 1927.
37. Letter from Badè to Breasted dated 6 June 1927.
38. Letter to Breasted from "An Observer," dated 15 June 1927.
39. Letter from Breasted to Guy dated 18 June 1927.
40. Letter from Breasted to Guy dated 24 June 1927; also letter from Breasted to Guy dated 5 August 1927.
41. Letter from Breasted to Badè dated 25 June 1927.
42. Guy 1931: 9.
43. See the letters exchanged between DeLoach and Breasted on 5, 11, and 24 June 1927.
44. Letters from Breasted to Guy dated 14, 18, and 24 June and 6 July 1927; also cables from Breasted to Guy on 17 and 25 June 1927. Breasted informed DeLoach of his promotion in a letter dated 24 June and a cable dated 25 June 1927; acknowledged by DeLoach in a reply to Breasted dated 4 July 1927.
45. Letter from Guy to Breasted dated 15 July 1927; see also the letter from DeLoach to Breasted dated 4 July 1927.
46. Letter from DeLoach to Breasted dated 4 July 1927.
47. Cable from DeLoach to Breasted on 12 July 1927 and letter from DeLoach to Breasted on 19 July 1927; also letter from Lind to Breasted on 16 July and reply from Breasted on 15 August 1927.
48. Cables between Breasted and Guy on 9 and 10 August 1927 and a letter from Breasted to Guy dated 11 August 1927.
49. Letter from DeLoach to Guy dated 19 July 1927.
50. Letter from DeLoach to Breasted dated 19 July 1927. It is in a letter to Breasted dated 24 February 1927 that Fisher first described Serge Tchoub as "our Russian chauffeur."
51. Letter from DeLoach to Breasted dated 3 August 1927.

52. Letter from DeLoach to Breasted dated 3 August 1927. See also the responses thanking him for the reports, sent on 11 August and 21 September 1927 by Breasted and on 25 August 1927 by Charles Breasted.

53. Cohen 2014: 107; Guy 1931: 9; letter from Guy to James Henry Breasted dated 13 August 1927 and to Charles Breasted dated 22 September 1927.

54. Letter from Badè to Guy dated 3 October 1927.

55. Letter from Charles Breasted to DeLoach dated 25 August 1927.

56. Letter from Guy to James Henry Breasted dated 13 August 1927 and from Guy to Charles Breasted dated 22 September 1927.

57. Letter from Breasted to Guy dated 9 January 1928.

58. Letter from Breasted to Guy dated 24 June 1927; cable from Breasted to Guy dated 25 June 1927. See subsequent letters from Breasted to Guy dated 24 January, 11 and 30 June, and 30 July 1928. See also a letter concerned specifically with De-Loach's malaria sent by Breasted to Dr. Flexner of the General Education Board (GEB) dated 28 January 1928, in the Rockefeller Archive Center (filed under General Education Board, RG 2324.2, Series 1, Box 659, Folder 6852).

59. See https://www.harvardartmuseums.org/art/311394 for a painting by Wilensky from Nuzi. See also https://archive.org/stream/in.ernet.dli.2015.106111/2015.106111 .Excavations-At-Nuzi-Vol1-texts-Of-Varied-Contents_djvu.txt.

60. Two letters from Breasted to Guy dated 22 March 1928 and a letter from Guy to Breasted dated 28 June 1928; also the list of personnel in Guy 1931: vii.

61. Letter from Breasted to Guy dated 22 March 1928 and letters from Guy to Breasted dated 28 June, 8 July, and 28 July 1928; letter from Guy to Hurst dated 28 July 1927; see also the list of personnel in Guy 1931: vii.

62. Letter to Breasted from J.M.P. Smith dated 8 July 1931 (in the Oberlin College archives: Herbert G. May Papers, IV. Correspondence, Box 2, Letters to University of Chicago).

63. There are a number of documents recording the efforts of Shipton, and of those around him, to get him admitted to the University of Chicago; see letter from Engberg to Miss Jean Roberts (assistant to Breasted) dated 9 January 1934 and reply from Miss Roberts dated 26 January 1934; letter from Breasted to Engberg dated 21 March 1934; letter from Mr. Walter Jones (former headmaster of Shipton's school in Wales) to Charles Breasted dated 13 August 1934 and reply from Charles Breasted dated 31 August 1934; letter from Charles Breasted to Shipton dated 6 September 1934 and reply from Shipton dated 2 October 1934; letter from Irwin to Charles Breasted dated 16 January 1935. Shipton finally actually applied in January 1936, after Breasted's death, only to be denied both admittance and a fellowship—see letters from Shipton to Wilson dated 1 January 1936; from Wilson to Shipton dated 28 January and 1 April 1936; from Shipton to Wilson dated 17 May 1936; from Shipton to Wilson dated 4 January 1937; from Wilson to Loud dated 26 January and 10 March 1937.

64. Letters from Guy to Breasted dated 14 January 1928 and 4 April 1928; replies from Breasted to Guy on 24 January 1928, 3 March 1928, and 30 July 1938. See also the budget for 1928–29 dated 20 June 1928; the list of personnel in Guy 1931: vii; Braund 1975: 94–98; and Shipton's obituary (Braidwood and Esse 1988). On Shipton's resignation in June 1939, see letters to John A. Wilson from Gordon Loud dated 23 and 29 June 1939; replies from Wilson to Loud dated 26 and 29 June and 5 July 1939; also letter from Loud to Shipton dated 28 June 1939 and from Howard Matthews (the executive secretary of the Oriental Institute at the time) to Shipton also dated 28 June 1939.

65. Letter from Charles Breasted to Guy dated 27 August 1928. See also previous letter from Lamon to Charles Breasted dated 13 August 1928. Re his "fine family," including his grandfather who was a judge and served in the Department of the Interior during Grover Cleveland's administration, see http://lamonhouse.org/Lamon_Tree/lamon_tree.html; http://lamonhouse.org/Lamon_Tree/RBL_0001.html.

66. See information on Ancestry.com, searching for "Robert Scott Lamon"; also Finch 2002: 19.

67. Engberg and Shipton 1934; Lamon 1935; Lamon and Shipton 1939; Shipton 1939; Shipton 1942. Fisher, Guy, and Loud were separately responsible for Fisher 1929; Guy 1931; Guy 1938; Loud 1939; Loud 1948. The other publications are May's 1935 volume on cult worship at Megiddo and two short popularizing articles by Engberg in 1940 and 1941.

68. According to the list of personnel in Guy 1931: vii; letters from Charles Breasted to Guy dated 13 and 27 August 1928. See also https://archive.org/stream/jstor-1354727/1354727_djvu.txt, from a notice posted in the *Bulletin of the American Schools of Oriental Research* (*BASOR*) regarding a scholarship that Staples had won several years earlier, when he held the Thayer Fellowship at the American School in Jerusalem.

69. Letter from Guy to Breasted dated 28 June 1928.

70. Letter from Breasted to Guy dated 30 July 1928.

71. Letter from Guy to Breasted dated 28 June 1928.

72. Letter from Guy to Breasted dated 28 June 1928.

73. Letter from Guy to Breasted dated 28 June 1928.

74. Letter from Badè to Breasted dated 6 June 1927.

75. Letter from Guy to Breasted dated 28 June 1928.

76. Miss Woodley's last day is recorded as 13 August 1928, according to Guy 1931: vii, and she is listed on a ship's passenger list as having arrived in England on 24 August, as noted above.

77. See Waterhouse 1986: 34–37, 78–79, 142, 144, 160; also details on pp. 16, 21, and 30 in the publication *L'École Britannique à Athènes de 1919 aux années 1980*, posted online at: https://www.academia.edu/27029614/L_ÉCOLE_BRITANNIQUE_A_ATHÈNES_De_1919_aux_années_1980.

78. See, e.g., the letter from Guy to Breasted dated 28 June 1928, in which he complained about Fisher, and the letter from Fisher to Breasted dated 12 July 1928, complaining about how he has been treated by Guy.

79. Letter from Guy to Breasted dated 28 June 1928.

80. Letter from Guy to Breasted dated 28 June 1928.

81. Geere 1904: 89, 196.

82. Letter from Guy to Breasted dated 28 June 1928.

83. Letters from DeLoach to Breasted dated 19 July and 3 August 1927.

84. Letter from Guy to Breasted dated 7 July 1928.

85. Letter from Guy to Breasted dated 7 July 1928. The inquiries by Guy began with a letter that he sent to Richmond dated 13 April 1928, with subsequent replies back and forth through June 1928. In it, he broaches this same topic and says that he is writing about it to Breasted; see the Israel Antiquities Authority Archives (British Mandate Administrative Files ATQ_7/6 [56/56]).

86. Letter from Guy to Breasted dated 18 July 1928. Guy had begun the conversation with Breasted in two previous letters: a handwritten note at the bottom of a letter dated 28 June 1928 and a letter dated 7 July 1928. For the continuance of the conversation, see letters from Guy to Breasted dated 18 July, 10 September, and 1

November 1928; letter from Breasted to Guy dated 10 October 1928; and cables exchanged between Guy and Breasted on 26 September and 1 October 1928. A longer version of the following events was first published as a contribution to a festschrift in honor of Israel Finkelstein (Cline 2017b); the material below, which has been both shortened and updated in places, appears courtesy of Pennsylvania State University Press, to whom I am most grateful.

87. See Templeton 1929; Wilson 1964: 206–8; Taylor 1982: 242–47; Tornede 1992; Casey 2015: 248, 253–62; Goldman 2009: 47–56; Oren 2012.

88. Wilson 1964: 206–8; Taylor 1982: 254; Tornede 1992: 111–12; Goldman 2009: 75–76, 81–85; Casey 2015: 253.

89. Tornede 1992: 107–8; "Armageddon Battlefield Bought for $3,500 from an American Widow for Exploration," *New York Times*, 1 December 1930, p. 1.

90. "Armageddon's Owner. Interview with Mrs. R. Templeton," *London Daily News*, 13 November 1903, p. 3; "English Lady Owns Armageddon," *Edinburgh Evening News*, 12 December 1903, p. 5. The interviews appear to have taken place upon the publication of a small pamphlet that year, entitled *The Mediators* (Templeton 1903).

91. Oliphant 1887: 178–80; Henderson 1956: 234–35; Taylor 1982: 222–23; Tornede 1992: 109; Casey 2015: 228–33, 241, 253, 261–62, 278.

92. Oliphant 1887: 178–80; Henderson 1956: 234–35; Taylor 1982: 222–23; Casey 2015: 228–33, 241, 253, 261–62, 278.

93. "Armageddon's Owner. Interview with Mrs. R. Templeton," *London Daily News*, 13 November 1903, p. 3; see also the briefer version in "English Lady Owns Armageddon," *Edinburgh Evening News*, 12 December 1903, p. 5. See also Tornede 1992: 107n228; Trombetta 2009.

94. See again "Armageddon's Owner. Interview with Mrs. R. Templeton," *London Daily News*, 13 November 1903, p. 3; see also the briefer version in "English Lady Owns Armageddon," *Edinburgh Evening News*, 12 December 1903, p. 5.

95. Templeton 1929.

96. Templeton 1929: 242–43; cited and quoted also in Goldman 2009: 84.

97. Letter from Rosamond Templeton dated 26 December 1928, containing a copy of the letter that she had sent to A. Abramson, Esq., on 19 December 1928.

98. Newton 1948: 98; Tornede 1992: 107–8, 120.

99. Letter from Guy to Breasted dated 10 September 1928.

100. Letter from Guy to Breasted dated 10 September 1928.

101. Cable from Guy to Breasted dated 26 September 1928. See also letter from Breasted to H. C. Luke, acting high commissioner, dated 4 September 1928; letter from Richmond to the chief secretary dated 20 September 1928; letter from Luke to Breasted dated 25 September 1928; letter from Guy to the chief secretary dated 8 October 1928; and various other relevant documents from October and November 1928, all in the Israel Antiquities Authority Archives (British Mandate Administrative Files ATQ_7/6 [2nd Jacket: 122/120]). See also another copy of the letter from Luke to Breasted dated 25 September 1928 and Breasted's reply dated 12 October 1928, both in the Israel Antiquities Authority Archives (British Mandate Administrative Files ATQ_7/6 [5th Jacket: 132/126]). Similar expropriation actions were begun ten years later at the site of Lachish, far to the south, so that the excavators there could excavate on the top of the mound; see now Garfinkel 2016, with references.

102. Cable from Breasted to Guy dated 1 October 1928; letter from Breasted to Guy dated 10 October 1928.

103. Letters from Guy to Breasted dated 1 November and 24 December 1928.

104. Letter from Guy to Breasted dated 24 December 1928.
105. See the English summary published in *International Law* Reports (5 *ILR* 183–184) and the French original in *Recueil des decisions des tribunaux arbitraux mixtes institués par les traités de paix* 9: 239–41. I am indebted to Herb Somers of the GWU Jacob Burns Law Library and Shmuel Ben-Gad of the GWU Gelman Library for their help in procuring these documents.
106. *New York Times*, 1 December 1930, p. 1; see also "The Field of Armageddon," *New York Times*, 2 December 1930, p. 24, and "Ancient Armageddon Plain Comes into American Hands," *New York Times*, 14 December 1930, p. 165. See also "Armageddon Bought for £700. Archaeologist's Treasure House Near By," *Nottingham Evening Post*, 12 December 1930, p. 7; also "Armageddon Bought for £700," *Hartlepool Northern Daily Mail* (Durham), 12 December 1930, p. 9. Note that Tornede 1992: 119–20 mistakenly says that she sold only "half an acre" to the Oriental Institute. The monetary conversion is based on http://www.dollartimes.com/inflation /inflation.php?amount=1000&year=1925.
107. See the new final chapter in the revised edition of Templeton 1929; see also the relevant letters in the Oriental Institute archives and the archives of the Israel Antiquities Authority. I am indebted to Alex Joffe for drawing my attention to the additional relevant documents that now may be found posted online in the Israel State Archives website (https://www.archives.gov.il/en/).
108. Inscription on the plaque for Rosamond Templeton at Maple Hill Cemetery at New Harmony, Indiana. I am grateful to Dan Elliott, who maintains the website for the cemetery, for a high-resolution photograph of the tombstone.
109. Letters from Breasted to Guy dated 11 and 30 June, as well as 30 July, 1928.
110. Letter from Guy to Breasted dated 12 December 1928.
111. Letter from Guy to Breasted dated 12 December 1928.
112. Letters from Guy to Breasted dated 1 November and 12 December 1928.

CHAPTER VI

1. Guy 1931: 9.
2. Letter from Breasted to Guy dated 30 April 1927.
3. Letter from Guy to Breasted dated 13 August 1927. See also, e.g., the letter from DeLoach to Breasted dated 5 June 1927, which contains similar assorted details.
4. Letter from Guy to Breasted dated 23 May 1927.
5. Letter from Guy to Breasted dated 13 August 1927; Guy 1931: 10–17; Harrison 2004: 2. DeLoach's letter to Breasted dated 4 July 1927 also describes the excavations on the lower slope, along with some of the tombs and the grave goods found there, including some scarabs, two cylinder seals, and part of an Egyptian statuette.
6. Letter from Guy to Breasted dated 13 August 1927.
7. Letter from Guy to Breasted dated 13 August 1927.
8. Letter from Guy to Breasted dated 13 August 1927; see also Harrison 2004: 2.
9. Letter from Guy to Breasted dated 28 June 1928; Harrison 2004: 2. The city wall that they were clearing lay within their Squares M–N 15 and O–P 14.
10. Letter from Guy to Breasted dated 28 June 1928.
11. Letter from Guy to Breasted dated 28 June 1928. On the division of finds, conducted on 27 April 1928, see letters from Richmond to Guy dated 20 January and 3 May 1928; letters from Guy to Richmond dated 27 January and 13 April 1928; all in the Israel Antiquities Authority Archives (British Mandate Administrative Files ATQ_7/6 [56/56]).

12. Letter from Guy to Breasted dated 28 June 1928. See also, later, his comments in Guy 1931: 42–43.
13. Letter from Guy to Breasted dated 28 June 1928.
14. Letter from Guy to Breasted dated 28 June 1928.
15. Letter from Guy to Breasted dated 7 July 1928. See the final publication in Guy 1931: 37–48; Lamon and Shipton 1939: 32–47, 59.
16. *New York Times*, 9 August 1928, p. 22, and 26 August 1928, pp. 71 and 76.
17. See now also Cline 2006; Cantrell 2006; Cantrell and Finkelstein 2006; Cantrell 2011: 87–113; Cline and Samet 2013; Franklin 2017; Ussishkin 2018: 399–407.
18. Letter from Guy to Charles Breasted dated 7 July 1928 and letter from Charles Breasted to Guy dated 13 August 1928.
19. Letter from Guy to Breasted dated 28 June 1928. See Guy 1931: 37–48; Lamon and Shipton 1939: 32–47, 59. See also additional references for the ongoing "stables debate" given above.
20. I had the great good fortune to help excavate this area; see Cline 2006; Cantrell 2006; Cantrell and Finkelstein 2006; Cline and Samet 2013.
21. Letter from Guy to Breasted dated 28 June 1928.
22. Albright 1943: 2–3n1, 29–30n10; Wright 1950a: 42, 1950b: 59–60, 1959: 14–15. See also Albright 1940, 1949; Yadin 1976; Cantrell 2006; Cantrell and Finkelstein 2006; Franklin 2006, 2017, 2019a,b; Richelle 2018: 54–55. On the Monolith Inscription, see Miller and Hayes 2006: 292, 294, 297.
23. Letter from Guy to Breasted dated 28 June 1928.
24. Letter from Guy to Breasted dated 7 July 1928.
25. Letter from Guy to Breasted dated 7 July 1928.
26. Letter from Guy to Breasted dated 7 July 1928.
27. Letters from Guy to Breasted dated 1 November and 12 December 1928.
28. Letter from Guy to Breasted dated 1 November 1928.
29. Letter from Guy to Breasted dated 1 November 1928.

CHAPTER VII

1. For a quick summation on the stock market crash, see, e.g., http://content.time.com/time/nation/article/0,8599,1854569,00.html and http://www.history.com/topics/1929-stock-market-crash. On the "Wailing Wall Riots" of mid to late August 1929, which began in Jerusalem and spread across the country, see further below.
2. Letter from Guy to Breasted dated 1 November 1928; see also response from Breasted to Guy dated 4 December 1928.
3. Letters from Guy to Breasted dated 16 January and 12 February 1929.
4. Letter from Breasted to Guy dated 4 February 1929.
5. Letters from Charles Breasted to Guy dated 4 and 17 February 1929.
6. See letters from Breasted to Guy dated 12 and 14 March 1929. See also the schedule for 4–12 March 1929, the itinerary for "Palestine Trip," and the entry for "Fri. Mch. 8" in Rockefeller's personal diary; all are now kept among the personal papers of John D. Rockefeller, Jr. in the Rockefeller Archive Center (filed under Rockefeller Family; RG III 2Z (2, OMR); Series II; Box 42, Folders 376 and 377).
7. Letter from Breasted to Guy dated 9 April 1929.
8. Wilson 1936: 108–9.
9. Diary entry by John D. Rockefeller III, on pages marked "Thursday 7—Friday 8 March 1929"; see also newspaper articles reporting on the proxy fight in the *Daily Tribune*, the *New York Herald*, and the *New York Times*, all dated 8 March 1929. All of the above are in the Rockefeller Archive Center, filed under Office of the Messrs.

Rockefeller records; the diary is in the John D. Rockefeller III papers, Series 1, Subseries 1: Personal Papers, Box 4, Folder 41 (FA108), while the newspaper clippings are on microfilm in the John D. Rockefeller, Jr. Personal Papers, Series Z, Subseries 9 (9, OMR); Volume 11–12, Reel M26 (FA335).

10. Rockefeller diary entry for 8 March 1929, in the Rockefeller Archive Center (filed under Rockefeller Family; RG III 2Z (2, OMR); Series II; Box 42, Folder 376). Also letters from Charles Breasted to Guy dated 4 and 17 February 1929 and from Guy to Charles Breasted dated 4 March 1929.

11. Rockefeller diary entry for 8 March 1929, in the Rockefeller Archive Center (filed under Rockefeller Family; RG III 2Z (2, OMR); Series II; Box 42, Folder 376).

12. Letters from Rockefeller to Nobel and to Chancellor dated 8 March 1929; both in the Rockefeller Archive Center (filed under Rockefeller Family; RG III 2Z (2, OMR); Series II; Box 41, Folder 367).

13. Letter from Breasted to Guy dated 12 March 1929.

14. Cable from Abby Rockefeller to Nelson Rockefeller dated 12 March 1929, in the Rockefeller Archive Center (filed under Nelson Rockefeller Papers, Family and Friends; RG III 4H; Series H; Box 28, Folder 361).

15. Letter from Guy to Charles Breasted dated 4 March 1929, which set on record the substance of their conversations at Megiddo, as Charles had requested be written and sent to him.

16. Letter from Rockefeller to Breasted dated 8 July 1929, with reply from Breasted dated 16 July 1929; both in the Rockefeller Archive Center (filed under Rockefeller Family; RG III 2H (2, OMR); Series II; Box 49, Folder 363), as well as in the archives at the Oriental Institute. See also letter from Breasted to Charles Breasted dated 15 July 1929, informing him of the gift, and a further letter from Rockefeller to Breasted dated 25 July 1929, acknowledging that (at Breasted's request) Rockefeller would hold on to the money and send only the quarterly interest to Breasted (which was an interesting arrangement).

17. Letter from Lamon to Charles Breasted dated 7 March 1929, written and sent at Charles's request, so that he could take it to the dean of the university. See also reply from Charles Breasted to Lamon dated 8 April 1929, a letter from Guy to Charles Breasted dated 10 April 1929, and cables exchanged between Charles Breasted and Guy on 20–21 April 1929.

18. See published obituaries, now available on the internet at:
    https://www.britac.ac.uk/pubs/proc/files/94p491.pdf
    https://web.archive.org/web/20150617040611/http://www.britac.ac.uk/fellowship/directory/dec.cfm?member=2147
    https://www.independent.co.uk/voices/obituaryrobert-hamilton-1576224.html

19. Letter from Breasted to Fisher dated 11 February 1928.

20. Letters from Guy to the director of antiquities in Jerusalem dated 20 February and 29 April 1929.

21. Personal communication from Carol DeLoach Fletcher, 7 May 2018, to whom I am most grateful for providing material that helped to clear up the questions surrounding this episode, and additional material that shed light on both Edward DeLoach and Florence Burnham DeLoach, including letters and postcards sent between the two of them as well as photographs and selections from Anita Willets-Burnham's book *Round the World on a Penny* (1946).

22. Letter from Guy to Charles Breasted dated 11 October 1929.

23. Willets-Burnham 1946: 196–97.

24. Cable from Guy to Breasted dated 13 April 1929 and reply from Charles Breasted also dated 13 April 1929.

25. Willets-Burnham 1946: 198–202.
26. Letter from Guy to Charles Breasted dated 11 October 1929.
27. Letter from Charles Breasted to Guy dated 15 April 1929.
28. Cable from Charles Breasted to DeLoach dated 27 August 1928.
29. See especially a letter from Charles Breasted to Guy dated 10 August 1929 and the reply from Guy dated 11 October 1929.
30. Letter from Guy to Charles Breasted dated 11 October 1929.
31. Letter from Charles Breasted to Guy dated 10 August 1929. Original letter from James Henry Breasted to Guy dated 24 June 1927.
32. Letter from Charles Breasted to Guy dated 10 August 1929. In his letter to Guy dated 15 April 1929, Charles had made a similar statement to the effect that "the present staff at Megiddo is an unusually convivial and happy one," and that he hoped that the addition "of a new and to me unknown person will merely serve to accentuate this pleasant state of things." Apparently, in the interim, he had decided that the addition of Flo had not accentuated the pleasant state of things. Janet Woolman's statements in her letters and diaries from September 1929 through March 1930 probably present a more realistic picture.
33. Letters from Charles Breasted to Guy dated 15 April and 10 August 1929.
34. Information from obituary for Anita Willets DeLoach Haines in the *Houston Chronicle*, 2–4 June 2006: https://www.legacy.com/obituaries/houstonchronicle /obituary.aspx?n=anita-willets-de-loach-haines&pid=17961996.
35. Letter from Charles Breasted to Guy dated 10 August 1929, though in his reply dated 11 October 1929, Guy said that was the first he had heard of the transfer request and that DeLoach had never said anything to him about it. See also the letters sent by Janet Woolman to her parents dated 5 March and 1 April 1930. Additional information about DeLoach and his intention to resign is courtesy of Carol DeLoach Fletcher (personal communication, 14 September 2019).
36. See David Woolman's unpublished manuscript (pp. 5–6 and 37). I would like to again thank David, son of Laurence and Janet Woolman, for letting me see and cite his unpublished manuscript written about their time at Megiddo. Relevant discussions below are based on the letters and diaries of Laurence and Janet Woolman that he donated to the Oriental Institute archives and which also form the basis of his unpublished manuscript. Please note that I should also have cited his manuscript in virtually every note below dealing with the Woolmans and their time at Megiddo, but in the interest of space I have referenced it only in the cases where the manuscript contains information not in the archival material or that differs from my understanding of that material.
37. See, e.g., letter from Charles Breasted to Guy dated 1 May 1929; letter from Woolman to Charles Breasted dated 3 May 1929 and a reply to Woolman dated 6 May 1929; cable from Charles Breasted to Guy dated 9 May 1929; a letter from Charles Breasted to Woolman also dated 9 May 1929, with a cabled acceptance from Woolman in return on the same day; cables from Guy to Breasted dated 17 May 1929 and from Guy to Charles Breasted dated 30 May 1929; letter from Charles Breasted to Guy dated 31 May 1929.
38. Cable from Guy to Breasted dated 17 May 1929, with a cabled reply from Breasted and a longer letter from Charles Breasted, both dated 18 May 1929.
39. According to David Woolman's unpublished manuscript (p. 20), the marriage took place at noon on 17 August, in Harrisburg, Pennsylvania, following which they immediately rushed to the station and caught a train to Philadelphia.

40. Letter from Charles Breasted to Guy dated 18 May 1929; a further lengthy justification was subsequently made in a letter that Charles Breasted sent to Guy dated 10 August 1929.
41. Cable from Guy to Charles Breasted dated 30 May 1929; letter sent in reply from Charles Breasted dated 31 May 1929. Letter from Charles Breasted to Guy dated 6 July 1929.
42. Cables exchanged between Guy and Breasted dated 27–31 August and 2 September 1929. Details regarding the Woolmans' departure date come from a letter sent by Laurence Woolman to his parents dated 30 August 1929 as well as from David Woolman's unpublished manuscript (p. 21).
43. See, among many others, Sachar 1979: 173–74; Armstrong 1996: 381–82; Gilbert 1996: 120–26; Smith 1996: 89–90; Segev 2000: 309–10, 314–27; Wasserstein 2001: 324–27. See also brief discussion in Cline 2004: 253–54, with further references.
44. Letter from Laurence Woolman to his parents dated 18 September 1929.
45. Letter from Laurence Woolman to his parents dated 18 September 1929.
46. E.g., letters from Laurence Woolman to his parents dated 18, 19, and 25 September 1929, as well as 20 October and 26 November 1929.
47. David Woolman, unpublished manuscript (pp. 43–44).
48. See, e.g., letters from Laurence Woolman to his parents dated 19 and 28 September and 1 and 6 October 1929.
49. Cables from Guy to Breasted dated 31 August and 3 September 1929, with additional cables exchanged between Breasted and Guy dated 3–4 September 1929. See also letter from Guy to Breasted dated 11 October 1929.
50. Letters from Laurence Woolman to his parents dated 21 and 25 September 1929.
51. See David Woolman, unpublished manuscript (p. 58).
52. Letter from Laurence Woolman to his parents dated 19 September 1929.
53. Letter from Laurence Woolman to his parents dated 6 October 1929.
54. Letter from Laurence Woolman to his parents dated 2 November 1929.
55. Letter from Yemima Guy to Breasted dated 9 October 1929. See also subsequent letter from Guy to Breasted dated 11 October 1929.
56. Letters from Guy to Breasted dated 11 October and 1 November 1929. Regarding the Chicago World's Fair, see letter from Guy to Charles Breasted dated 4 March 1929.
57. Letters from Guy to Breasted dated 11 October and 1 November 1929.
58. Letter from Laurence Woolman to "Aunt Marie" dated 9 October 1929; letters from Laurence Woolman to his parents dated 12, 16, and 23 October and 4 November 1929.
59. Letters from Laurence Woolman to his parents dated 10 November and 16 December 1929.
60. Letter from Guy to Charles Breasted dated 11 November 1929; also cable from Charles Breasted to Guy dated 12 November 1929 and a subsequent letter dated 27 November 1929, sent after Charles reached Cairo. See also letter from Guy to Breasted dated 8 December 1929.
61. Letters from Laurence Woolman to his parents dated 3, 6, 12, 16, 23, and 26 October and 20 and 23 November 1929. Charles Breasted, in his letter to Guy dated 27 November 1929, said that he was eager to see the blueprints of the proposed expansion, but was also somewhat anxious about the costs involved. Further details about the construction are contained in Guy's letter to Charles Breasted dated 3 December 1929.
62. Letter from Laurence Woolman to his parents dated 23 October 1929.

63. Letters from Laurence Woolman to his parents dated 8 December 1929 and 5 March 1930. See also quotes and discussion in David Woolman, unpublished manuscript (e.g., pp. 87, 100, 118, 198).

64. Janet Woolman diary entries dated 19 and 25 September as well as 3 October 1929.

65. Letter from Laurence Woolman to his parents dated 19 September 1929.

66. Letter from Laurence Woolman to his parents dated 8 November and 12 December 1929.

67. Letters from Laurence Woolman to his parents dated 2, 4, and 14 November and 8 December 1929.

68. Letter from Janet Woolman to her sister Peg dated 18 September 1929. See also letters from Laurence Woolman to his parents dated 21 September and 2 November 1929.

69. Letter from Janet Woolman to her sister Peg dated 18 September 1929; letter from Laurence Woolman to his parents dated 6 November 1929; also a letter sent from Laurence to "Aunt Marie" dated 9 October 1929.

70. Letters from Laurence Woolman to his parents dated 28 September and 16 October 1929.

71. Letter from Laurence Woolman to his parents dated 6 November 1929; letter from Hurst to Guy dated 29 November 1930, concerning the renewal of these magazines.

72. Letter from Laurence Woolman to his parents dated 14 November 1929.

73. Letters from Laurence Woolman to his parents dated 28 September and 3 October 1929.

74. Letter from Laurence Woolman to his parents dated 1 October 1929.

75. Letter from Laurence Woolman to his parents dated 20 November 1929.

76. Letter from Laurence Woolman to his parents dated 12 December 1929.

77. Letter from Laurence Woolman to his parents dated 1 October 1929.

78. Letter from Laurence Woolman to his parents dated 23 October 1929.

79. Letter from Laurence Woolman to his parents dated 13 December 1929. Note that it is not clear what the "Specialist" was.

80. Letter from Guy to Charles Breasted dated 3 December 1929 and from Guy to Breasted dated 8 December 1929.

81. Letters from Laurence Woolman to his parents dated 16 and 30 December 1929.

82. Letter from Laurence Woolman to his parents dated 1 January 1930; see also David Woolman's unpublished manuscript (p. 142).

83. Letter from Laurence Woolman to his parents dated 19 February 1930; see also David Woolman, unpublished manuscript (p. 156).

84. Letter from Laurence Woolman to his parents dated 5 March 1930; see also David Woolman, unpublished manuscript (p. 142).

85. Cable from Guy to Charles Breasted and reply, both dated 29 January 1930.

86. Letter from Laurence Woolman to his parents dated 5 March 1930.

87. Letters from Laurence Woolman to his parents dated 5, 9, and 11 March 1930; see also letter from Janet Woolman to her sister Peg dated 10 March as well as Janet's letter to Laurence's parents dated 12 March and her diary entries for 4, 5, and 10 March.

88. See https://www.britannica.com/topic/Mauretania-ship-1906-1935.

89. Letter from Janet Woolman to her sister Peg dated 10 March 1930.

90. Letters from Laurence Woolman to his parents dated 5 and 9 March 1930; see also letter from Janet Woolman to her sister Peg dated 10 March 1930. Information about the later details courtesy of Carol DeLoach Fletcher.

91. Cable from Guy to Breasted dated 16 March 1930; see also letter from Guy to Hurst dated 12 March 1930.

92. Letter from Laurence Woolman to his parents dated 18 May 1930, citing a letter that Janet had just received from Flo DeLoach, sent from Chicago.

93. The 1930 excavations began on 23 March and ended on 8 December, according to letters from Guy to Breasted dated 26 March and 16 December 1930. See also letters from Laurence Woolman to his parents dated 25 and 31 March 1930.

94. Letter from Laurence Woolman to his parents dated 25 March 1930. For a much more recent reassessment of the potential reconstruction of the stables, see now Belkin and Wheeler 2006.

95. Letters from Laurence Woolman to his parents dated 23 and 27 February 1930.

96. Letter from Laurence Woolman to his parents dated 31 March 1930; also notes dated to February 1930 from Guy, currently in the Oriental Institute archives, which mention a "field director's suite," a screened-in porch, a new dining room, and renovations to the old dining room, the old common room, and the pantry, kitchen, and various other rooms. See also David Woolman's unpublished manuscript (pp. 203–4).

97. Letter from Laurence Woolman to his parents dated 31 March 1930; see also David Woolman, unpublished manuscript (pp. 183–84).

98. Cable from Charles Breasted to Guy dated 19 May 1930 and subsequent letter sent to Guy dated 23 May 1930.

99. Letter from Charles Breasted to Staples dated 22 January 1930; also letters from Staples to Charles Breasted dated 13 March and 2 July 1930; letters from Breasted to Staples dated 7 July and 20 and 22 November 1930; letter from Charles Breasted to Guy dated 7 July 1930; letters from Staples to Breasted dated 26 October and 11 December 1930; letter from Breasted to Guy dated 22 November 1930; cable from Guy to Breasted dated 14 June 1930; and letters from Guy to Breasted dated 13 June, 6 November, and 14 December 1930.

100. Letter from Breasted to Staples dated 7 February 1931 and response from Staples dated 6 March 1931.

101. Letter from Breasted to Guy dated 18 January 1930.

102. Letter from Charles Breasted to Guy dated 27 May 1930, followed by a cable from Breasted to Guy dated 27 September 1930, a cable in reply from Guy dated 5 October 1930, a more detailed letter from Guy dated 9 October 1930, and a confirmation letter from Breasted dated 29 October 1930.

103. Letter from Laurence Woolman to his parents dated 18 May 1930. See also David Woolman, unpublished manuscript (pp. 205 and 302).

104. Cable from Guy to Breasted dated 19 June 1930.

105. Remarks sent by Breasted to be read at the ceremony held at the Palestine Archaeological Museum on 19 June 1930. See Fosdick 1956: 362–63 on Rockefeller and the funding of the museum.

106. Information from David Woolman, unpublished manuscript (pp. 221, 299, and n483).

107. Letter from Charles Breasted to Guy dated 22 January 1930; Fox 1955: xxv; Ward 2013: 179.

108. Letter from Charles Breasted to Guy dated 22 January 1930.

109. Letter from Breasted to Phillips dated 18 April 1930, extending the original invitation to begin work on 1 October 1930. Re the sudden departure, see letters from Guy to Breasted and Hurst, both dated 14 January 1931.

110. Information derived from "News of the Schools," as published on p. 41 of the *Bulletin of the American Schools of Oriental Research* 71 (October 1938). Note that Irene Lamon signed her name "Jean Lamon" on 31 May 1934 in an autograph book

kept by Olof Lind (retrieved from the Olof E. Lind papers in the Library of Congress <lccn.loc.gov/mm2014085935>).

111. Letter from Breasted to Guy dated 25 September 1930; reply from Guy received on 22 November 1930.

112. Letter from the editorial secretary to Staples dated 17 December 1930. Cf. Staples 1931.

113. Letter from Guy to Charles Breasted dated 31 December 1930; letter from Charles Breasted to Guy, also sent on 31 December 1930.

114. Letter from Robert J. Barr to Guy dated 27 December 1930.

115. Letters from Guy to Hurst and to Charles Breasted, both dated 14 January 1931; letter from Charles Breasted to Guy dated 27 January 1931 (sent from Cairo).

116. Letter from Guy to Charles Breasted dated 14 January 1931.

117. Letter from Guy to Breasted dated 6 November 1930.

118. Letter from Guy to Charles Breasted dated 15 January 1931.

119. Letters from Guy to Charles Breasted dated 15 January 1931 and from Guy to Breasted dated 3 February 1931; letter from Charles Breasted to Guy dated 27 January 1931; letter from Ruth Staples to Charles Breasted dated 12 March 1931.

120. Letter from Breasted to Staples dated 30 June 1931; letter from Charles Breasted to Staples dated 1 July 1931. Prior to receiving the job offer, Staples had also been offered another year of financial support in the form of an OI fellowship in early April and had accepted it in mid-May, just two days before his new daughter, Elizabeth Marion Staples, greeted the world back in Canada; he then declined the fellowship when he accepted the job (letter from Charles Breasted to Staples dated 3 April 1931, offering him the fellowship; letter from Staples to Charles Breasted dated 14 May 1931, accepting the fellowship; birth announcement dated 16 May 1931).

121. Separate letters from Staples to Breasted and to Charles Breasted, both dated 11 June 1931; letter from Guy to Charles Breasted dated 22 June 1931; and letters sent back and forth between Staples and Charles Breasted on 1 July, 22 July, 7 August, and 13 August 1931.

122. On Staples's teaching career at Victoria College, see http://www.csbs-sceb.ca/A_History_of_CSBS.pdf. On an award sponsored by Elizabeth Staples McLeod, class of 1953, see http://nmc.utoronto.ca/undergraduate/awards/.

123. Cable from Guy to Breasted dated 6 May 1931; return cable from Charles Breasted to Guy dated 7 May; letter from Guy to Charles Breasted dated 22 June 1931; letter from Guy to Breasted dated 7 July 1931.

124. Letter from Guy to Breasted dated 7 July 1931.

125. Letter from Guy to Charles Breasted dated 22 June 1931; see also letter from Guy to Breasted dated 7 July 1931.

126. Cable from Breasted to Guy dated 1 July 1931.

127. Cable from Guy to Breasted dated 6 July 1931 and letter from Guy to Breasted dated 7 July 1931.

128. Letter from J.M.P. Smith to Breasted dated 8 July 1931 (copies are in both the Oriental Institute archives and the Oberlin College archives—at Oberlin, see the Herbert G. May Papers, IV. Correspondence, Box 2, Letters to University of Chicago).

129. Letter from Charles Breasted to Guy dated 16 July 1931; letter from J.M.P. Smith to Breasted dated 8 July 1931; letter from Breasted to Guy dated 13 August 1931; letter from May to Charles Breasted dated 26 October 1931.

130. Two letters from Guy to Breasted, both dated 10 January 1932.

131. Letter from Guy to Breasted dated 7 July 1931 (the second one with that date); also previously letter to Charles Breasted dated 31 December 1930, reporting the earlier incidents.

132. Cable from Breasted to Guy dated 18 September 1931; letter from Breasted to Guy dated 20 October 1931.

133. Guy 1931; see letters exchanged between the director of the Palestine Department of Antiquities and Robert J. Barr at the University of Chicago, regarding the dispatch of a requested second copy of the publication.

134. Letter from Breasted to Guy dated 28 February 1931.

135. Letters from Breasted to Guy dated 28 February and 12 June 1931.

136. Letter from Guy to Breasted dated 30 June 1931.

137. Letter from Guy to Breasted dated 30 June 1931.

138. Letter from Breasted to Guy dated 13 August 1931.

CHAPTER VIII

1. Cable from Guy to Breasted dated 13 June 1931.

2. Letters from Guy to Breasted dated 11 April and 8 December 1929.

3. Letter from Guy to Breasted dated 8 December 1929.

4. Cable from Guy to Breasted dated 13 July 1929; Letter from Guy to Breasted dated 8 December 1929.

5. See detailed discussion of this specific Stratum IVA gate in Ussishkin 2018: 422–27 and additional discussions with references below, especially Yadin 1960, 1970, 1980; also Ussishkin 1966, 1973, 1980. On the Stratum VIII gate, see Loud 1948: 16, figs. 39–45.

6. Letter from Guy to Breasted dated 8 December 1929.

7. Letter from Guy to Breasted dated 8 December 1929.

8. Letter from Guy to Breasted dated 8 December 1929.

9. Letter from Guy to Breasted dated 8 December 1929.

10. Letter from Charles Breasted to Guy dated 25 June 1929. See also previous letters from Guy to Breasted dated 16 January 1929 and from Guy to Charles Breasted dated 17 January 1929, as well as letters exchanged between Richmond and Guy dated 3, 16, and 19 January 1929, as well as 10, 13, 15 March 1929, and 10 and 13 May 1929—all in the Israel Antiquities Authority Archives (British Mandate Administrative Files ATQ_7/6 [2nd Jacket: 122/120]).

11. Ussishkin 2018: 20 notes that the first aerial photograph of Megiddo was actually taken in 1917 by German aviators during World War I, more than a decade earlier. See also further discussion in Ussishkin 2018: 58–61.

12. Guy 1932a: 148.

13. Letter from Charles Breasted to Guy dated 15 April 1929.

14. Guy 1932a: 149.

15. Guy 1932a: 150. See also letter from Guy to Hurst dated 7 November 1929.

16. See, e.g., Parcak 2009; McNeil 2015; Dunston 2016; Parcak et al. 2016; and further brief discussion in Cline 2017a: 82–87, with additional references. See now also Parcak 2019.

17. Janet Woolman diary entry dated 5 November 1929; see also her letter to her sister Peg dated 6 November 1929; also letters from Laurence Woolman to his parents dated 4 and 6 November and 16 December 1929.

18. Letter from Guy to Breasted dated 8 December 1929; letter from Laurence Woolman to his parents dated 16 December 1929.

19. Guy 1932a: 154–55.

20. Letter from Breasted to Guy dated 3 January 1930.

21. Letter from Guy to Breasted dated 28 January 1930.

22. Letter from Charles Breasted to Guy dated 5 February 1930.

23. See, e.g., http://munsell.com; https://www.nrcs.usda.gov/wps/portal/nrcs/detail/soils/edu/?cid=nrcs142p2_054286; http://munsell.com/color-blog/brown-soil-color-chart-archaeology/; http://munsell.com/about-munsell-color/how-color-notation-works/how-to-read-color-chart/; https://extension.illinois.edu/soil/less_pln/color/color.htm. Note that, in a similar manner, Lamon and Shipton provided a color plate with pictures of thirteen sherds "illustrating the colors used in describing the pottery" throughout their *Megiddo I* volume—the colors ranged from yellow to sepia (Lamon and Shipton 1939: plate 116).

24. Letter from Guy to Breasted dated 26 April 1930; also a much later letter from Breasted to Guy dated 25 September 1930, with a reference to Guy's letter of 26 April.

25. Letters from Guy to Breasted dated 16 December 1930 and 3 February 1931.

26. Diary entry by Janet Woolman for 17 May 1930; see also David Woolman, unpublished manuscript (p. 207).

27. Letter from Guy to Breasted received on 22 November 1930; letter from Guy to Breasted sent 16 December 1930.

28. Letter from Guy to Breasted dated 3 February 1931.

29. Letter from Guy to Breasted dated 3 February 1931.

30. Letter from Guy to Breasted dated 3 February 1931.

31. Letter from Guy to Breasted dated 3 February 1931.

32. Letter from Guy to Breasted dated 3 February 1931.

33. Letter from Guy to Breasted dated 30 June 1931; Breasted 1931: 43, 46–47; Guy 1932b: 161–62. Breasted also described the water system at length in a letter to Rockefeller dated 25 September 1931, with reply from Rockefeller dated 23 October 1931, both in the Rockefeller Archive Center (filed under Educational Interests, RG III 2G: Box 111, Folder 802).

34. Letter from Guy to Breasted dated 30 June 1931.

35. Letter from Guy to Breasted dated 30 June 1931.

36. Letter from Guy to Breasted dated 30 June 1931.

37. Letters from Guy to Breasted dated 30 June and 5 July 1931.

38. Letters from Guy to Breasted dated 30 June and 5 July 1931; cable from Guy to Breasted dated 8 July 1931 (also not sent in code).

39. Lamon 1935: 9–10.

40. Zarzecki-Peleg 2016: 176–77; see previously Zarzecki-Peleg 2005 (in Hebrew). See also Yadin 1970: 90–91.

41. Letters from Guy to Breasted dated 30 June and 5 July 1931.

42. Lamon 1935: 10–36; Yadin 1970: 89–93; Kempinski 1989: 129–31; Franklin 2000: 515–23; Zarzecki-Peleg 2016: 178–80; Ussishkin 2018: 409–15.

43. Letter from Guy to Breasted dated 30 June 1931.

44. http://bibleodyssey.org/en/places/related-articles/siloam-inscription-and-hezekiahs-tunnel; translation by Christopher Rollston.

45. Letter from Guy to Breasted dated 30 June 1931; letter from Guy to Charles Breasted dated 22 June 1931.

46. Letter from Guy to Breasted dated 30 June 1931.

47. Letter from Guy to Breasted dated 30 June 1931.

48. Letter from Guy to Breasted dated 30 June 1931.

49. Lamon 1935: 10–12, 26, 36; Ussishkin 2018: 415; letter from Lamon to Breasted dated 13 October 1934.
50. Yadin 1970: 89–93.
51. Zarzecki-Peleg 2016: 167–80, esp. 178–80; Ussishkin 2018: 409–15.
52. Franklin 2000: 515–23; See also Franklin 2013: http://www.asor.org/anetoday /2013/10/who-really-built-the-water-system-at-megiddo/.
53. See, e.g., Warner and Yannai 2017: 26–27, 56–57.
54. Letter from Guy to Breasted dated 5 July 1931.
55. Lamon 1935: 37; see also now Franklin 2000: 517–21.
56. Letter from Guy to Breasted dated 30 June 1931; Guy 1932b: 162.
57. Cable from Guy to Breasted dated 12 June 1931; letters from Guy to Breasted dated 22 and 30 June 1931.
58. Letter from Guy to Breasted dated 7 July 1931.
59. Letter from Guy to the director of antiquities dated 6 July 1931, in the Israel Antiquities Authority Archives (British Mandate Administrative Files ATQ_7/6 [3rd Jacket: 277/271]).
60. Cable from Guy to Breasted dated 5 December 1931; cables exchanged between Guy and Breasted dated 10 and 11 December 1931.
61. Letter from Guy to Breasted dated 10 January 1932. A letter sent by Guy to Breasted one year later, on 3 January 1933, confirms that the 1931 season had ended late, on 7 January 1932, and that the 1932 season subsequently began on 27 March 1932, which was a shorter break than usual.

CHAPTER IX

1. Letters (two) from Guy to Breasted dated 10 January 1932 and letter from Guy to Charles Breasted dated 3 July 1932.
2. Letter from Engberg to Breasted dated 1 January 1932; letters from Engberg to Charles Breasted dated 12 April and 27 May 1932; letter from Guy to Charles Breasted dated 9 October 1932.
3. Letter #2 (multipage) from Guy to Breasted dated 10 January 1932.
4. Letter #2 (multipage) from Guy to Breasted dated 10 January 1932.
5. Handwritten note from Charles Breasted to James Henry Breasted dated 28 January 1932; re Wilensky's origins and religion, see Black and Morris 1991: 7; also http:// cosmos.ucc.ie/cs1064/jabowen/IPSC/php/authors.php?auid=44197.
6. Cables exchanged between Charles Breasted and Guy dated 2 and 9 February 1932; letter from Guy to Wilensky dated 1 May 1932; cable from Charles Breasted to Guy dated 23 May 1932, with follow-up letter dated 28 May 1932, reply from Guy dated 29 June 1932, and final cable and letter from Charles Breasted to Guy both dated 23 July 1932, with response from Guy dated 9 October 1932.
7. See letters and documents dating to 1932, including from 9 and 23 February, 16, 17, and 19 March, 6 April, and 9 May, with final letters and confirmation of the site dated 21 and 31 May 1932; all in the Israel Antiquities Authority Archives (British Mandate Administrative Files ATQ_391 (33/33).
8. See Tepper 2002, 2003a, 2003b, 2007; Tepper and Di Segni 2006: 5–15; McGreal 2005; Myre 2005; Wilson 2005; Tzaferis 2007; Ashkenazi 2009; Pincus et al. 2013; Adams, David, and Tepper 2014; Ben Zion 2015; Ussishkin 2018: 441–43. See also the brief note on the Megiddo website, available at: https://sites.google.com /site/megiddoexpedition/additional-information/an-early-christian-prayer-hall; and "Archaeologists Unveil Ancient Church in Israel," NBC News, 6 November 2005,

available online at: http://www.nbcnews.com/id/9950210/ns/technology_and
_science-science/t/archaeologists-unveil-ancient-church-israel/#.VoWd_jbFpbk.

9. Cables exchanged between Guy and both Breasteds dated 2, 9, and 22 February 1932; also letter from Guy to Charles Breasted dated 12 March 1932.

10. Letter from Engberg to Hurst dated 7 April 1932.

11. Abt 2011: 382–83; letter from Charles Breasted to Loud dated 25 October 1935. The movie has now been uploaded to YouTube, on the Oriental Institute's channel, and can be found and watched at https://www.youtube.com/watch?v=yysHJk0v5XA.

12. The 1935 review, which appeared in the *New York Times* on the occasion of the film's screening at Carnegie Hall, can be accessed at https://www.nytimes.com /1935/10/30/archives/at-carnegie-hall.html, although it is behind a paywall. Credit goes to Daniel Shoup who, in an August 2009 post on his "Archaeopop" blog (http://archaeopop.blogspot.com/2009/08/insult-to-archaeologists-and-stamp .html), rather gleefully noted that the "dour" reviewer "was obviously not gifted with a prescience for future motion picture trends in the vein of Indiana Jones and Lara Croft." See also the post at http://oihistory.blogspot.com/2009/09/review -of-review-of-human-adventure.html, by Charles E. Jones, former research archivist–bibliographer at the Oriental Institute, with a reference to Shoup's post.

13. The present version of the film, as posted online by the OI, ends the Megiddo segment with a statement by the narrator that we would now head to the OI excavations at Alishar in Anatolia. Instead, after being shown the route northward via a dotted line on the map, we veer abruptly and head for modern Mosul and then the ancient sites of Nineveh and Khorsabad in Iraq, without first hearing any discussion or getting a sense of the work being done at Alishar. I thank Charles E. Jones for pointing out this glitch to me and for suggesting the hypothesis that one of the original reels of the film must now be missing; I believe that he is likely to be correct.

14. Letter from Guy to Breasted dated 3 January 1933.

15. See brief discussion in Cline 2017a: 103–4, with further references.

16. McCown's father and brother were also both well-known archaeologists, working in Jordan and Iran, respectively; see http://anthropology.iresearchnet.com /theodore-d-mccown/. See also further re McCown's father in a note below.

17. See again brief discussion in Cline 2017a: 103–4, with further references.

18. Letter from Guy to Charles Breasted dated 29 June 1932.

19. Cables from Guy to Charles Breasted dated 26 and 30 May 1932; cabled condolences from Charles Breasted to Guy dated 27 May 1932, followed by longer letter to Guy dated 28 May 1932 and a response from Guy a month later, dated 29 June 1932.

20. Letter from Guy to Charles Breasted dated 29 June 1932; see also reply from Charles Breasted to Guy dated 23 July 1932 and letter from Guy to Charles Breasted dated 9 October 1932.

21. Letter from Breasted to Guy dated 4 June 1932.

22. Letter from Breasted to Guy dated 4 June 1932.

23. Letter from Breasted to Guy dated 4 June 1932. He was later proven correct; the palace of Strata VIII/VII was indeed found at the northern edge of the mound, by the city gate, as we shall see.

24. Letter from Breasted to Guy dated 4 June 1932.

25. Letter from Guy to Breasted dated 3 July 1932.

26. Letter from Guy to Breasted dated 3 July 1932.

27. Letter from Guy to Breasted dated 3 July 1932.

28. Letter from Breasted to Guy dated 27 July 1932.

29. Letter from Guy to Charles Breasted dated 9 October 1932. See letters from the summer of 1937 in the Olof E. Lind papers in the Library of Congress (lccn.loc .gov/mm2014085935).

30. Breasted Junior is listed in the *Megiddo I* volume as being present at the dig from September through October 1932, but since everyone was away on vacation during September, it seems unlikely that he arrived that early; moreover, when Guy returned and wrote on 9 October, he said that there was a stack of mail waiting for the young man, and that he was expecting him to arrive the next day. According to Abt (2011: 182 and 434n27), this younger son of Breasted, who was ten years younger than Charles, was born in 1908; he later attended Princeton as an undergraduate and then received an MA in art history from the University of Chicago, eventually serving as the director of the Los Angeles County Museum (see also the obituary in the *New York Times*, 6 May 1983, D15).

31. Letter from Lamon to Charles Breasted dated 28 October 1932; letter from Breasted to Guy and memo dictated by Breasted in the OI files, both dated 8 November 1932; cable from Breasted to Guy dated 23 November 1932; cable from Guy to Breasted dated 30 November 1932.

32. On the passing of Lamon's father, Judson A. Lamon, see https://www.findagrave .com/memorial/84750095/judson-alexander-lamon; on his passing as well as on the marriage between Bob Lamon and Eugenia Keefe, see http://www.lamonhouse .org/Lamon_Tree/RBL_0003.html.

33. This 25 January letter is not extant but is mentioned in another letter, sent from Guy to Breasted dated 25 March 1933.

34. Article in the *New York Tribune* dated 4 February 1933; copy in the Rockefeller Archive Center (filed under Rockefeller Family; RG III 2H (2, OMR); Series II; Box 49, Folder 362).

35. Letter from Guy to Breasted dated 25 March 1933.

36. Letter from Guy to Breasted dated 25 March 1933.

37. Letter from Breasted to Guy dated 31 March 1933.

38. Letter from Betty Murray to her mother dated 17 April 1933 (currently in the archives of the PEF).

39. Davis 2008: 65–66. The title of the present book pays tribute to Kenyon, mirroring the titles of her books *Digging Up Jericho* and *Digging Up Jerusalem* (Kenyon 1957, 1974).

40. Letter from Betty Murray to her mother dated 17 April 1933 (currently in the archives of the PEF). Davis 2008: 59 also mentions several trips that the team took to Megiddo. See also Davis 2004: 62, with a similar description of the Megiddo dig house by Chester McCown (1943: 173); McCown, who was dean of the Pacific School of Religion and served as director of the American School in Jerusalem for a short while, was also the father of Ted McCown, who was the physical anthropologist digging at Skhul Cave when the Megiddo archaeologists visited and Mrs. Wilensky was seriously injured (see above).

41. Letter from Breasted to Guy dated 5 May 1933.

42. Cable from Breasted to Guy dated 29 April 1933.

43. Cable from Breasted to Guy dated 29 April 1933.

44. Letter from Breasted to Guy dated 5 May 1933.

45. Letter from Breasted to Guy dated 5 May 1933.

46. Letter from Breasted to Guy dated 5 May 1933.

47. Letter from May to Breasted dated 20 November 1933; reply from Breasted dated 15 December 1933.

48. See Lamon and Shipton 1939: xxiii and fig. 3. In Breasted's letter, he mistakenly wrote "Q" instead of "O," but it is clear what he meant, given the later outlines of "Area A" on the various topographical maps. See also Harrison 2004: 2, where he confirms that the excavations during the spring of 1933 were "confined to Area A, which covered most of the southwest part of the site."
49. Letter from Breasted to Guy dated 5 May 1933.
50. Letter from Breasted to Guy dated 5 May 1933.
51. Letter from Breasted to Guy dated 5 May 1933.
52. Letter from Breasted to Guy dated 5 May 1933.
53. Letter from Breasted to Guy dated 5 May 1933.
54. Letter from Breasted to Guy dated 5 May 1933.
55. Cables between Breasted and Guy dated 11 and 13 November, in which Breasted noted that the manuscript was seriously overdue, and asked when it would be submitted, to which Guy said it would be in by the end of November (which, of course, it wasn't).
56. Letter from Guy to Breasted dated 8 November 1933 (his third monthly report of the season).
57. Letter from Guy to Breasted dated 8 November 1933. As promised, Guy kept Breasted continually updated on the status of the publication throughout this year, sending reports on 1 June, 12 September, 8 November, and 9 December 1933.
58. Letter from Guy to Breasted dated 8 November 1933.
59. Green 2009: 169; letter from Fisher to Breasted dated 26 September 1926.
60. Letter from May to William C. Graham dated 5 May 1933 (in the Oberlin College archives: Herbert G. May Papers, IV. Correspondence 1933, Box 1).
61. Letter from Breasted to Wilensky dated 28 April 1933.
62. Letter from Wilensky to Guy dated 4 May 1933; letter from Guy to Wilensky dated 7 May 1933; letter from Guy to Breasted dated 7 May 1933; letter from Breasted to Guy dated 23 May 1933; letter from Guy to Wilensky dated 3 June 1933.
63. Letter from Guy to Breasted dated 25 March 1933. Piepkorn was already ordained in the Lutheran Church, as of 1930, and later was known professionally as Rev. Dr. Arthur C. Piepkorn. After first serving in a number of pastorates and then as a chaplain (and colonel) in the US Army from 1940 to 1951, during both World War II and Korea, he began teaching at Concordia Seminary in St. Louis, Missouri, in 1951. He died in 1973, at the age of sixty-six. See http://pdf.oac.cdlib.org/pdf/gtu /piepkorn.pdf, http://cyclopedia.lcms.org/display.asp?t1=p&word=PIEPKORN .ARTHURCARL, and https://www.findagrave.com/memorial/112154314/arthur -carl-piepkorn.
64. Letter from Guy to Breasted dated 3 July 1933.
65. Green 2015: 15–19.
66. Green 2015: 15–19.
67. The incident took place on 7 June 1933. Letter from Guy to Wilensky dated 8 June 1933; letter from Piepkorn to May dated 2 July 1933; letter from Guy to Breasted dated 3 July 1933.
68. Memorandum from Breasted to Charles Breasted dated 23 July 1933.
69. Letter from Guy to Breasted dated 3 July 1933; memorandum from Breasted to Charles Breasted dated 23 July 1933; memoranda from Charles Breasted to Breasted dated 27 July, and 5 and 7 August 1933; cables from Charles Breasted to Breasted and to Guy dated 9 August 1933.

70. Cable from Guy to the Oriental Institute dated 2 September 1933; letter from Guy to Breasted dated 12 September 1933. On Concannon's later career, see, e.g., Millar 2014: 175.
71. Letters from Guy to Breasted dated 12 September and 8 November 1933.
72. Letter from Guy to Breasted dated 9 December 1933.
73. Memorandum from Breasted to Charles Breasted dated 29 August 1933.
74. Memorandum from Breasted to Charles Breasted dated 29 August 1933; letter from Guy to Breasted dated 12 September 1933; letter from Charles Breasted to Guy dated 19 September 1933; letter from Guy to Breasted dated 6 November 1933; letter from Breasted to Guy dated 10 November 1933; letter from Guy to Breasted dated 9 December 1933; letter from Guy to director of antiquities dated 17 December 1933 (in the Israel Antiquities Authority Archives [British Mandate Administrative Files ATQ_7/6 (3rd Jacket: 277/271)]).
75. Letter from May to Richardson dated 7 December 1933 (in the Oberlin College archives: Herbert G. May Papers, IV. Correspondence 1933, Box 1).
76. Letters from Breasted to Guy dated 11 and 12 December 1933; letters from Breasted to Lamon, Engberg, and May dated 12 December 1933.
77. Handwritten letter from Lind to Charles Breasted dated 28 October 1933.
78. Cable from Guy to OI dated 29 October 1933; letter from Guy to Breasted dated 8 November 1933.
79. Letter from Guy to Breasted dated 8 November 1933.
80. Letter from May to William C. Graham dated 5 May 1933 (in the Oberlin College archives: Herbert G. May Papers, IV. Correspondence 1933, Box 1); birth announcement from Herbert and Helen May dated 29 July 1933; wedding announcement from Olof and Astrid Lind dated 1 September 1933; congratulations from Breasted and Charles Breasted dated 3 October and 18 September 1933, respectively. I thank Norma Franklin for reminding me about the connection to the Kina brook.
81. Handwritten letter from Lind to Charles Breasted dated 28 October 1933.
82. Letter from Charles Breasted to Guy dated 28 September 1933, but not sent.
83. Letter from Engberg to Charles Breasted dated 25 October 1933.
84. Letter from Guy to Breasted dated 9 December 1933. In his response, Breasted said that he was glad to hear this, and that he thought it would be "a most helpful arrangement"; letter from Breasted to Guy dated 5 January 1934.
85. Letter from Guy to Breasted dated 7 July 1931.
86. Letter from Guy to Breasted dated 12 January 1934; undated letter from Guy to Breasted stamped by the OI "received 29 January 1934."
87. Undated letter from May to Breasted stamped by the OI "received 19 January 1934."
88. Undated letter from Guy to Breasted stamped by the OI "received 29 January 1934."
89. Undated letter from Guy to Breasted stamped by the OI "received 29 January 1934."
90. Undated letter from Guy to Breasted stamped by the OI "received 29 January 1934."
91. Undated letter from Guy to Breasted stamped by the OI "received 29 January 1934."
92. Letter from Breasted to Guy dated 15 March 1934.
93. Cable from Breasted to Guy dated 19 April 1934.

94. Mitter 2014: 136.
95. https://www.officialdata.org/1934-GBP-in-2017?amount=525.
96. Black and Morris 1991: 7; also http://cosmos.ucc.ie/cs1064/jabowen/IPSC/php/authors.php?auid=44197.
97. Quotation from Eyal 2002: 664, translating from the original Hebrew publication by Lephen 1987: 99. See also Black and Morris 1991: 7; Kahana 2006: xix.
98. Aleksandrowicz 2015: 60.
99. Letter from Breasted to Guy dated 5 January 1934; letter from Guy to Breasted dated 31 January 1934; letter from Breasted to Guy dated 15 March 1934. See discussion in Harrison 2004: 2–3.
100. See https://www.federalreservehistory.org/essays/gold_reserve_act; https://www.forbes.com/2008/12/09/dollar-devaluation-gold-pf-ii-in_fb_1209soapbox_inl.html#8dbcbc619687; http://library.cqpress.com/cqresearcher/document.php?id=cqresrre1934013000; https://www.nytimes.com/2013/10/11/business/at-risk-the-dollars-privilege-as-a-reserve-currency.html.
101. Letter from Breasted to Guy dated 15 March 1934; letter from Lamon to Breasted dated 1 May 1934; letter from Guy to Breasted dated 19 May 1934; cable from Charles Breasted to Guy dated 5 June 1934.
102. Letter from May to Breasted dated 8 January 1934.
103. Letter from May to Breasted dated 22 February 1934.
104. Letter from Breasted to Irwin dated 14 March 1934.
105. Cable from Breasted to Guy dated 15 March 1934.
106. Letter from Breasted to Engberg dated 14 March 1934. Engberg immediately accepted, in a handwritten letter to Breasted dated 5 April 1934.
107. Letter from Guy to Breasted dated 19 May 1934; letter from Charles Breasted to Guy dated 8 June 1934 but not sent until 18 July 1934.
108. Letter from Breasted to Guy dated 15 March 1934.
109. Letter from Breasted to May dated 21 March 1934.
110. Letter from May to Breasted dated 22 February 1934.
111. Letter from Breasted to Guy dated 5 January 1934; letter from Hamilton to Guy dated 9 January 1934; letter from Guy to Breasted dated 31 January 1934. The division took place from 28 to 30 January 1934. See also subsequent letters, including from Hamilton to Guy dated 2 February 1934 with reply from Guy dated 19 February 1934, and letter from Guy to Hamilton dated 8 March 1934 with reply from Hamilton dated 10 March 1934.
112. There are a number of boxes of Iliffe's papers and other items relating to his career at the University of Queensland in Australia. See https://www.library.uq.edu.au/fryer-library/ms/uqfl514.pdf. See also Donaldson 2015: 7–11 (available online at http://www.friendsofantiquity.org.au/documents/novas/2015/2015-07.pdf).
113. Letter from Guy to Hrdlička dated 10 March 1934; letter from Richmond to Guy dated 23 March 1934; letter from Guy to Breasted dated 15 April 1934. The related initial correspondence includes a letter from Breasted to Hrdlička dated 12 May 1934 with a reply from Miss Heckler (Hrdlička's secretary) dated 16 May 1934; a letter from Charles Breasted to Miss Heckler dated 31 July 1934; letter from Hrdlička to Breasted dated 20 September 1934 with a reply from Breasted dated 26 September 1934; and a letter from Hrdlička to Breasted dated 1 October 1934 with a response from Breasted dated 9 October 1934. All of these letters and the related correspondence, cited here and below, are located among the Aleš Hrdlička Papers in the National Anthropological Archives of the Smithsonian Institution. They were first brought to my attention by Jonathan D. Greenberg, who con-

sulted and cited them for a senior honors thesis in archaeology at George Washington University conducted under my supervision (Greenberg 2005). I thank Daisy Njoku for permission to cite and quote from these letters.

114. Guy 1938: 192, table VI, figs. 187–203.

115. Letter from Breasted to Hrdlička dated 5 December 1934. See also letters from Hrdlička to Breasted dated 8 and 19 December 1934 with a response from Breasted dated 22 December 1934 and acknowledgment from Hrdlička dated 31 December 1934; letter from Hrdlička to Breasted dated 28 February 1935, with a response from Breasted dated 6 March 1935; letter from Wilson to Hrdlička dated 26 June 1935; also a similar letter from George Allen to Hrdlička dated 8 July 1935, with responses from T. D. Stewart, Hrdlička's assistant, dated 28 June and 10 July 1935; letter from Wilson to Hrdlička dated 23 December 1935; letter from Hrdlička to Wilson dated 27 December 1935, with response from Wilson dated 2 January 1936 that included an original letter from Engberg to Guy dated 18 June 1933; letter from Wilson to Hrdlička dated 6 January 1936, with response from Hrdlička dated 17 January 1936; subsequent reply by Wilson dated 24 January 1936 and response from Hrdlička dated 28 January 1936; letter from Wilson to Hrdlička dated 3 February 1936 and responses from Hrdlička dated 5 and 21 February 1936; letter from Wilson to Hrdlička dated 25 February 1936, with response from Hrdlička dated 27 March 1936; subsequent exchanges concern the layout and final proofs of the pages in question.

116. Courtney Prutzman, also a GWU student at the time, took some preliminary measurements of the skeletal remains, which are included as an appendix to Greenberg's 2005 senior honors thesis; in 2014, Laurel Poolman also wrote a senior honors thesis for the archaeology BA at GWU, involving stable isotope analysis on teeth from eleven of the individuals (Poolman 2014); and Cecilia Chisdock worked on stress and hyperplasia related to the Megiddo skeletons for her senior honors thesis. As far as I know, these undergraduate senior honors theses represent the only work done to date on this skeletal material at the Smithsonian since the time of Hrdlička. Note that letters in the Israel Antiquities Authority Archives (British Mandate Administrative Files ATQ_7/6 [5th Jacket: 132/126]) dating to 1946 involve the request for, and repatriation of, either thirty-seven or thirty-nine skeletons (there was some confusion as to the number) from the Oriental Institute to the Department of Antiquities. Five boxes of skeletal material, weighing several hundred pounds, were apparently sent back, but these seem to have been different from the skeletal material that is still at the Smithsonian; see letter from Hamilton to Wilson dated 5 April 1946; letter from Wilson to Hamilton dated 1 June 1946, with reply from Hamilton dated 4 July 1946.

117. Letter from Guy to director of antiquities dated 5 June 1934 with replies from Hamilton dated 9 June and 16 June 1934, all in the Israel Antiquities Authority Archives (British Mandate Administrative Files ATQ_7/6 [3rd Jacket: 277/271]); letter from Guy to Breasted dated 13 July 1934.

118. Cable from Guy to Breasted dated 11 July 1934.

119. Letter from Guy to Breasted dated 13 July 1934.

120. Letter from Charles Breasted to Guy dated 28 August 1934. See also Harrison 2004: 3.

121. Place-marker sheet for original letter from Guy to Breasted dated 13 July 1934. There is only one other potential clue, which is a note sent by Breasted's personal secretary, Miss Jean Roberts, to Charles Breasted, dated 30 July 1934. She writes, cryptically, "Did Dr. Breasted leave with you the GUY matter—and the folders of

correspondence which he had at hand the last few days before he left Chicago?" A handwritten response from Charles Breasted is scrawled below this typed message, reading simply, "He took this material with him, will mail us reply etc from Havana."

122. Memo filed by unknown member of the Department of Antiquities dated 19 June 1934, in the Israel Antiquities Authority Archives (British Mandate Administrative Files ATQ_7/6 [3rd Jacket: 277/271]).

123. Handwritten letter from Irwin to Breasted dated 20 June 1934.

124. Handwritten letter from Irwin to Breasted dated 20 June 1934. See also belated letter of thanks from Breasted to Irwin dated 26 September 1934 and handwritten acknowledgment from Irwin dated 31 October 1934.

125. Memo filed by unknown member of the Department of Antiquities dated 19 June 1934, in the Israel Antiquities Authority Archives (British Mandate Administrative Files ATQ_7/6 [3rd Jacket: 277/271]).

126. Memo filed by unknown member of the Department of Antiquities dated 19 June 1934, in the Israel Antiquities Authority Archives (British Mandate Administrative Files ATQ_7/6 [3rd Jacket: 277/271]).

127. Memo filed by Hamilton dated 19 June 1934, in the Israel Antiquities Authority Archives (British Mandate Administrative Files ATQ_7/6 [3rd Jacket: 277/271]).

128. Memo filed by Hamilton dated 19 June 1934, in the Israel Antiquities Authority Archives (British Mandate Administrative Files ATQ_7/6 [3rd Jacket: 277/271]).

129. See records in Ancestry.com, searching for "Herbert G. May."

130. Memo filed by Hamilton dated 19 June 1934, in the Israel Antiquities Authority Archives (British Mandate Administrative Files ATQ_7/6 [3rd Jacket: 277/271]).

131. Letter from Richmond to Stead dated 29 June 1934; reply from Stead dated 3 July 1934; acknowledgment from Richmond dated 11 July 1934, in the Israel Antiquities Authority Archives (British Mandate Administrative Files ATQ_7/6 [3rd Jacket: 277/271]). There is also a copy of Stead's letter in the Israel State Archives: https://www.archives.gov.il/en/archives/#/Archive/0b07170680050224/File/0b07170680720b44.

132. Letter from Department of Customs, Excise & Trade, Haifa to Richmond as director of antiquities dated 3 September 1934, with acknowledgment from Richmond dated 8 September 1934, both in the Israel Antiquities Authority Archives (British Mandate Administrative Files ATQ_7/6 [3rd Jacket: 277/271]).

133. Handwritten letter from Irwin to Breasted dated 20 June 1934.

134. Handwritten letter from Irwin to Breasted dated 20 June 1934.

135. Letter from Richmond to the chief secretary dated 11 July 1934, in the Israel Antiquities Authority Archives (British Mandate Administrative Files ATQ_7/6 [3rd Jacket: 277/271]).

136. Letter from Guy to Richmond as director of antiquities dated 4 July 1934 and undated response from Richmond, probably 11 July 1934, both in the Israel Antiquities Authority Archives (British Mandate Administrative Files ATQ_7/6 [3rd Jacket: 277/271]). There is also a copy of Guy's letter in the Israel State Archives: https://www.archives.gov.il/en/archives/#/Archive/0b07170680050224/File/0b07170680720b44.

137. In a letter to Breasted dated 19 May 1934, Guy said, "I understand that May expects to leave Haifa in the Exochorda on 17 June, and that Engberg proposes to sail somewhat later." See also specific port arrival record courtesy of Ancestry.com, searching for "Robert M. Engberg" and specifically for immigration records.

138. Letter from May to Charles Breasted dated 8 August 1934.

139. Letter from Charles Breasted to May dated 6 August 1934 and two responses from May both dated 8 August 1934.
140. Cable from Breasted to Guy dated 20 August 1934; cable from Charles Breasted to Parker dated 25 August 1934; letter from Charles Breasted to Guy dated 28 August 1934.
141. Letter from Charles Breasted to Guy dated 28 August 1934. Guy sent detailed responses on 18 and 23 September 1934, reacting to each of the criticisms in turn and requesting a number of things that would allow him to complete his manuscript, but his protests were countered in turn by the Breasteds, who agreed only to pay for a typist to help him finish in a timely manner. See internal memos from Breasted to Charles Breasted dated 27 September and 6 October 1934; letter from Breasted to Guy dated 13 October 1934; and letter from Charles Breasted to Guy dated 19 October 1934.
142. Letters from Charles Breasted to Guy dated 28 August 1934 and 3 January 1935; also Harrison 2004: 3.
143. Green 2009: 167; see also the entry for Guy, written by Green in 2008, posted on the website of the PEF: http://www.pef.org.uk/profiles/lt-col-philip-langstaffe-ord-guy-1885-1952.
144. Ussishkin 2018: 62; see May 1935: vii.
145. Engberg and Shipton 1934: vii; Lamon 1935: vii; Lamon and Shipton 1939: vii (here they do thank "the two successive Field Directors," but do not actually name either one).
146. Guy 1938.

CHAPTER X

1. Letter from Guy to director of antiquities dated 25 June 1934, requesting permission to send the statue-base (M 6014) to Chicago for treatment; letter from Guy to Breasted dated 28 June 1934, alerting him to the fact that he was sending the statue-base under separate cover, for a loan not to exceed one year, for the purposes of cleaning. See also the report subsequently filed with the Department of Antiquities written by Lamon dated 10 October 1934—with copies in both the Oriental Institute and the Israel Antiquities Authority Archives (British Mandate Administrative Files ATQ_7/6 [3rd Jacket: 277/271]).
2. Cable from Breasted to Lamon dated 28 November 1934; also longer letter from Breasted to Lamon dated 5 December 1934 and reply from Lamon dated 28 December 1934.
3. Letter from Breasted to Lamon dated 5 December; see Breasted's publication in Loud 1948: 135–38, figs. 374–75.
4. See brief discussion in Cline 2014: 116–18 about this findspot; for the initial mention, see Loud 1948: 135n1. See also discussion in Singer 1988–89: 106–7; Ussishkin 2018: 271–72.
5. Letter from Guy to Breasted dated 3 January 1933.
6. Letter from Guy to Charles Breasted dated 9 October 1932; letter from Guy to Breasted dated 3 January 1933.
7. Letter from Guy to Breasted dated 3 January 1933.
8. Letter from Guy to Breasted dated 3 January 1933; see plans published in *Megiddo I* (Lamon and Shipton 1939) and Kempinski 1989: fig. 35 and plans 13–14. On Stratum III, see Lamon and Shipton 1939: 62–83, figs. 71–94, and also now more recent discussions in Peersmann 2000; Reich 2003; Zertal 2003; Singer-Avitz 2014.

9. See, e.g., Zertal 2003.
10. On these inscriptions, see, for example, Miller and Hayes 2006: 291–335.
11. I have discussed this in greater detail in Cline 2007.
12. Albright 1943: 3; Kempinski 1989: 13, 98–100; Halpern 2000: 565–68; Peersmann 2000; Stern 2000, 2002; Blenkinsopp 2002; Singer-Avitz 2014: 124, 137–39; Ussishkin 2018: 419–20; also Franklin 2019b.
13. See Lamon and Shipton 1939: 62–83, figs. 71–94; more recently Kempinski 1989: 98–100, 154, 166; Joffe, Cline, and Lipschitz 2000: 140–60; Finkelstein and Ussishkin 2000: 601–2; Halpern 2000: 563; Peersmann 2000; Reich 2003; Franklin 2019b. See now Ussishkin 2018: 422–34.
14. On Neo-Assyrian deportation practices, see also the discussion in Cline 2007, chap. 7, with further references.
15. See, e.g., discussion in Halpern 2000.
16. Letter from Guy to Breasted dated 3 January 1933.
17. Guy 1934: 178–79.
18. Engberg and Shipton 1934.
19. Letters from Guy to Breasted dated 3 July and 12 September 1933.
20. Letter from Guy to Breasted dated 1 June 1933.
21. Letter from Guy to Breasted dated 1 June 1933.
22. Letter from Guy to Breasted dated 1 June 1933.
23. Letter from Guy to Breasted dated 1 June 1933. See now Franklin 2006, 2017; Ussishkin 2018: 407–8, figs. 18.1 and 18.19.
24. Letter from Guy to Breasted dated 1 June 1933.
25. Letter from Guy to Breasted dated 12 September 1933. See Franklin 2006, 2017; Ussishkin 2018: 399–408, fig. 18:13.
26. Letter from Guy to Breasted dated 8 November 1933. See again the discussion in Ussishkin 2018 cited above and the discussions in Cantrell 2006 and Cantrell and Finkelstein 2006 as well as now Cantrell 2011: 87–113 and, most recently, Franklin 2017.
27. Letter from Guy to Breasted dated 9 December 1933.
28. Guy 1934: 178–79.
29. Guy 1934: 178–79.
30. Letter from Guy to Breasted dated 9 December 1933; letter from Guy to Breasted dated 31 January 1934.
31. Handwritten letter from Engberg to Breasted dated 5 April 1934; letter from Guy to Breasted dated 15 April 1934; letter from Lamon to Breasted dated 1 May 1934. See discussion in Harrison 2004: 2.
32. Letter from Guy to Breasted dated 15 April 1934; see also letter from Guy to Breasted dated 13 July 1934 and discussion in Harrison 2004: 2. Lamon gave similar details in the report that he submitted on the 1934 spring season to the Department of Antiquities on 10 October 1934, in the Israel Antiquities Authority Archives (British Mandate Record File SRF_143 [233/233]). On the palace, see Ussishkin 2018: 336–53.
33. Yadin 1960, 1966, 1967, 1970, 1973, 1976, 1980; Yadin, Shiloh, and Eitan 1972; also Dunayevski and Kempinski 1966, 1973; Ussishkin 1966, 1973, 1980, 1990; Eitan 1974; Shiloh 1980; Kempinksi 1989: 162–64; Wightman 1990; Finkelstein 1996a, 1999; Franklin 2001, 2006, 2017; see also Cline 2006; Lehmann and Killebrew 2010; Cline and Samet 2013; see now Ussishkin 2018: 354–62.
34. Letter from Guy to Breasted dated 15 April 1934; see also the letter from Lamon to Breasted dated 1 May 1934, with a similar statement.
35. Handwritten note in the IAA archives dated 25 April 1934.

36. Letter from Guy to the director of antiquities dated 2 May 1934; confirmation of receipt of the objects from Richmond dated 4 May 1934. Both letters are in the Israel Antiquities Authority Archives (British Mandate Administrative Files ATQ_7/6 [3rd Jacket: 277/271]).
37. Letter from May to Fiske dated 9 May 1934.
38. Ussishkin (2018: 109–311) continues to argue for enemy attack, as have previously Harrison (2003 and 2004) and Finkelstein (2002, 2009), but I am convinced that it is an earthquake; for my arguments, with references to all earlier publications, see Cline 2011 (published, ironically, in the festschrift honoring Ussishkin). See now Ussishkin 2018: 283–87, 309–11.
39. Handwritten letter from Irwin to Breasted dated 28 May 1934.
40. Handwritten letter from Irwin to Breasted dated 28 May 1934. See Breasted's polite response to Irwin's "interesting suggestion" in his letter dated 16 June 1934.
41. Letter from Guy to Breasted dated 13 July 1934. See discussion in Harrison 2004: 3. Lamon gave similar details in the report that he submitted on the 1934 spring season to the Department of Antiquities on 10 October 1934.
42. Letter from Guy to Breasted dated 13 July 1934. See also discussions and descriptions in Esse 1992: 88 and n59, figs. 1 and 4; Harrison 2004: 3.
43. Letter from Guy to Breasted dated 13 July 1934. See also discussions and descriptions in Esse 1992: 88 and n59, figs. 1 and 4; Harrison 2004: 3.
44. See Gadot et al. 2006; Gadot and Yasur-Landau 2006; Marco et al. 2006; Cline 2011.
45. See, e.g., Finkelstein 2002, 2011; Harrison 2003; Finkelstein and Piasetski 2008.
46. Letter from Guy to Breasted dated 13 July 1934.
47. Toffolo et al. 2014: 223, 226, 236, 238, 241, tables 2–3, figs. 6–8. See now also Finkelstein et al. 2017a: 265, 269, 275. Ussishkin also cites Toffolo's article, and other related radiocarbon publications, but ultimately suggests the larger range of dates.
48. Ussishkin 2018: 314–15, 326–31, with references to previous discussions and arguments by other scholars.
49. Arie 2006: 248; Arie also provides further references for previous discussions, e.g., Aharoni 1972, as do Esse 1992 and now Ussishkin 2018: 312–13.
50. Ussishkin 2018: 317.
51. Ussishkin 2018: 332.
52. See Finkelstein 1996a: 178–80, 182–83.
53. Letter from Guy to Breasted dated 13 July 1934.
54. Letter from Guy to Breasted dated 13 July 1934; see also the report filed with the Department of Antiquities written by Lamon dated 10 October 1934—with copies in both the Oriental Institute and the Israel Antiquities Authority Archives (British Mandate Administrative Files ATQ_7/6 [3rd Jacket: 277/271]). See also Loud 1948: plate 162:7; for recent discussions, see Ussishkin 2018: 239 and fig. 12:3, citing Singer 1995 and Suter 1999–2000. Megiddo is also mentioned in a letter found at the Hittite capital Hattusa; see Singer 1988.
55. Letter from Lamon to Breasted dated 1 May 1934.
56. Letter from Lamon to Breasted dated 1 May 1934.
57. Letter from Lamon to Breasted dated 1 May 1934.
58. Letter from Breasted to Lamon dated 31 May 1934.
59. Letter from Lamon to Breasted dated 3 July 1934; also letter from Engberg to May dated 11 September 1934 (in the Oberlin College Archives: Series IX, ASOR 1934–1940; with thanks to Julian Hirsch for locating the letter).
60. Letter from Lamon to Breasted dated 3 July 1934; letter from Guy to Breasted dated 13 July 1934; see also subsequent mentions during the fall season, in letters

from Breasted to Lamon dated 25 and 26 September 1934 and Lamon's response to Breasted dated 13 October 1934.

61. Handwritten letter from Irwin to Breasted dated 28 May 1934; reply from Breasted dated 16 June 1934.

CHAPTER XI

1. Memo from Charles Breasted to Breasted dated 11 August 1934; memo from Breasted to Charles Breasted dated 16 August 1934.

2. Drower 1985: 395.

3. Letters from Breasted to Wheeler dated 16 March and 3 May 1935; letter from Wheeler to Breasted dated 5 April 1935.

4. Much of the biographical information in this paragraph and the next regarding Gordon Loud comes from a Loud family history published by C. Everett Loud, *300 Years of Louds in America* (1980: 724), and an article by Judith Cass on p. 19 of the *Chicago Tribune* on 6 September 1938 reporting on Loud's upcoming wedding to Honor Merrell, in which they are also described as "two unusually interesting young persons." Additional information was derived from Ancestry.com (searching for Gordon Loud and Kenneth Gordon Loud), especially from a family tree maintained by Susan Gordon Kern. He appears as "Kenneth Gordon Loud" in the 1910 US Federal Census. See also Ussishkin 2018: 63–71 for his view on Loud and his work at Megiddo, which he castigates as "disastrous"—a verdict that is too harsh since, in my opinion, Loud was better than both Fisher and Guy.

5. Letter from Loud to Charles Breasted dated 24 March 1935.

6. Letter from Charles Breasted to Loud dated 20 February 1935, with response from Loud dated 24 March 1935; letter from Loud to Breasted dated 25 February 1935; letter from Breasted to Loud dated 15 March 1935. See also Harrison 2004: 4.

7. Letter from Charles Breasted to Parker dated 28 August 1934; cables from Charles Breasted to Parker dated 1 and 5 September 1934, with cables sent in reply by Parker dated 5, 7, and 8 September 1934; letters from Parker to Charles Breasted dated 7 and 11 September 1934; letter from Charles Breasted to Parker dated 21 September 1934; cable from Parker to Charles Breasted dated 1 October 1934; letters from Parker to Charles Breasted dated 2 and 15 October 1934; letter from Breasted to Parker dated 2 November 1934; letter from Charles Breasted to Parker dated 7 December 1934; letter from Parker to Charles Breasted dated 9 December 1934.

8. Memo from Breasted to Charles Breasted dated 16 August 1934; letter from Charles Breasted to Lamon dated 1 September 1934; Harrison 2004: 3.

9. Memo from Breasted to Charles Breasted dated 16 August 1934.

10. Letter from Charles Breasted to Lamon dated 1 September 1934; Charles Breasted also sent a much shorter, and more polite and uplifting, letter to Shipton dated 6 September 1934.

11. Letters from Breasted to Lamon, Shipton, and Lind, all dated 25 September 1934; the letter to Lind is in the Olof E. Lind papers in the Library of Congress (lccn.loc .gov/mm2014085935).

12. Letter from Loud to Lind dated 27 September 1934 (retrieved from the Olof E. Lind papers in the Library of Congress <lccn.loc.gov/mm2014085935>). Information about the Altmans was derived from Ancestry.com (searching for Charles B. Altman and Alice Stringham Altman). See also Loud and Altman 1938.

13. Letters from Breasted to Lamon and Shipton, both dated 25 September 1934.

14. Letter from Lamon to Breasted dated 1 October 1934.

15. Letter from Lamon to Charles Breasted dated 6 October 1934.
16. Letter from Charles Breasted to Lamon dated 9 November 1934.
17. Memo regarding Lamon's visit to the Department of Antiquities dated 12 October 1934; see also letter from Richmond to Lamon dated 9 October 1934. Both letters are in the Israel Antiquities Authority Archives (British Mandate Administrative Files ATQ_7/6 [3rd Jacket: 277/271]).
18. Letters from Breasted to Richmond dated 3 November and 15 December 1934; letter from Richmond to Breasted dated 28 November 1934; license no. 244 issued in Lamon's name—all currently in the Israel Antiquities Authority Archives (British Mandate Administrative Files ATQ_7/6 [3rd Jacket: 277/271]); letter from Richmond to Breasted dated 5 February 1935, with response from Breasted dated 25 February 1935, in both the archive of the Oriental Institute and the Israel Antiquities Authority Archives (British Mandate Administrative Files ATQ_7/6 [3rd Jacket: 277/271]).
19. Memo from Breasted to Charles Breasted dated 16 August 1934.
20. Letter from Lamon to Breasted dated 1 October 1934.
21. Letters from Lamon to Breasted dated 13 October and 8 November 1934; cable and letter from Breasted to Lamon, both dated 31 October 1934.
22. Letter from Breasted to Lamon dated 25 September 1934; letters from Lamon to Breasted dated 1 and 13 October as well as 1 November 1934.
23. Letters from Lamon to Breasted dated 1 and 13 October 1934.
24. Letter from Breasted to Lamon dated 25 September 1934; letters from Lamon to Breasted dated 1 October, 8 November, and 28 December 1934; see, subsequently, Lamon and Shipton 1939: xxvii.
25. Letters from Lamon to Breasted dated 8 November and 28 December 1934.
26. Letter from Breasted to Lamon dated 25 September 1934; letter from Allen to Engberg dated 6 October 1934; letter from Allen to Guy dated 12 October 1934; letter from Breasted to Guy dated 13 October 1934; cable and letter from Allen to Guy, both dated 9 November 1934; letter from Guy to Breasted dated 21 November 1934; letter from Breasted to Lamon dated 5 December; letter from Charles Breasted to Guy dated 6 December 1934.
27. Letters from Parker to Charles Breasted dated 2 and 15 October 1934; letter from Lamon to Breasted dated 13 October 1934; handwritten letter from Irwin to Breasted dated 31 October 1934.
28. Letters from Lamon to Breasted dated 13 October and 1 November 1934; letter from Parker to Charles Breasted dated 15 October 1934; handwritten letter from Irwin to Breasted dated 31 October 1934.
29. https://www.mayoclinic.org/diseases-conditions/rheumatic-fever/symptoms-causes/syc-20354588.
30. Letter from Lamon to Breasted dated 8 November 1934.
31. Letter from Irwin to Breasted dated 4 March 1935, with reply from Breasted dated 7 March 1935.
32. https://www.nytimes.com/1967/04/25/archives/william-irwin-a-bible-scholar-exprofessor-at-university-of-chicago.html.
33. Letter from Parker to Charles Breasted dated 2 January 1935.
34. Letter from Lamon to Breasted dated 2 February 1935.
35. Letter from Lamon to Breasted dated 2 February 1935.
36. Letter from Lamon to Breasted dated 2 February 1935.
37. Letter from Lamon to Breasted dated 9 March 1935; cable from Lamon to Breasted dated 10 March 1935.

38. Letter from Lamon to Breasted dated 9 March 1935; cable from Lamon to Breasted dated 10 March 1935.
39. Letter from Lamon to Breasted dated 9 March 1935; Lamon and Shipton 1939: 8.
40. Letter from Lamon to Breasted dated 9 March 1935.
41. Letter from Lamon to Breasted dated 9 March 1935.
42. Letter from Lamon to Breasted dated 9 March 1935; see, subsequently, Lamon and Shipton 1939: 3–7, figs. 5–11, for Stratum V, and 8–61, figs. 12–70 for Stratum IV. On Building 1A, see now Ussishkin 2018: 385–86. Note that, as will be mentioned again below, the debates about the proper assignation of buildings, etc., to various strata continued as soon as both *Megiddo I* and *Megiddo II* appeared, in 1939 and 1948, respectively; see, e.g., Albright 1943: 2–3n1, 29–30n10; Wright 1950a: 42, 1950b: 59–60, 1959: 14–15. See also, in general, Albright 1940, 1949.
43. Letter from Lamon to Breasted dated 9 March 1935.
44. Letter from Lamon to Breasted dated 9 March 1935. See also letter from Lamon to Breasted dated 23 March 1935, with reply from Elizabeth Hauser to Lamon dated 6 April 1935; also letter from Lamon to Breasted dated 4 May 1935.
45. See especially Lamon and Shipton 1939: 58–61, where they point out some of the errors discovered too late to be fixed in May's volume.
46. Letter from Breasted to Lamon dated 16 March 1935, with reply from Lamon dated 15 April 1935.
47. Cable from Breasted to Lamon dated 5 May 1935, with letter sent in response by Lamon dated 19 May 1935; see also cable from Charles Breasted to Parker dated 31 May 1935. See also letter from Loud to Breasted dated 29 April 1935, before his visit to Megiddo, and letter from Loud to Charles Breasted dated 19 May 1935, after his visit to Megiddo.
48. Letter from Breasted to Richmond dated 23 May 1935, with response and license from Richmond dated 25 June 1935—copies in the archives of both the Oriental Institute and the Israel Antiquities Authority Archives (British Mandate Administrative Files ATQ_7/6 [3rd Jacket: 277/271]); letter from Charles Breasted to Loud dated 3 June 1935.
49. Cable and letter from Charles Breasted to Loud, both dated 12 April 1935.
50. Letter from Lamon to Breasted dated 19 May 1935, with a handwritten note in red at the bottom clarifying the misunderstanding; letter from Lamon to Charles Breasted dated 21 November 1935.
51. Letter from Parker to Charles Breasted dated 16 May 1935.
52. Letter from Parker to Charles Breasted dated 16 May 1935.
53. Cable from Charles Breasted dated 31 May 1935 and letter dated 25 June 1935, both sent in response to Parker's letter of 16 May 1935; letter from Charles Breasted to Parker dated 24 May 1935; letter from Lind to his wife, Astrid, dated 9 June 1935 (retrieved from the Olof E. Lind papers in the Library of Congress <lccn.loc.gov/mm2014085935>); letter from Loud to Charles Breasted dated 12 June 1935.
54. Letter from Parker to Charles Breasted dated 16 May 1935, as well as other letters sent over the course of the previous months.
55. Letter from Charles Breasted to Parker dated 24 May 1935.

CHAPTER XII

1. Letter from Loud to Lind dated 2 August 1935 (retrieved from the Olof E. Lind papers in the Library of Congress <lccn.loc.gov/mm2014085935>).
2. Letter from Loud to Breasted dated 1 August 1935.

3. Loud 1948: 1.
4. Letter from Loud to Breasted dated 1 August 1935.
5. Loud field diary, entry dated 6 October 1935; the change to the south dig is recorded in the entry for 19 October 1935, after Breasted had returned from Syria; see also Loud 1948: 1. For some reason, in the *Megiddo II* publication, Loud described these trenches as six meters wide, rather than five—"Three trenches, each about 6 meters wide and 50–70 meters long, were dug" (Loud 1948: 1).
6. Letter from Lamon to Charles Breasted dated 21 November 1935.
7. Memo to Matthews dated 15 August 1935.
8. Letter from Loud to Matthews dated 16 October 1935.
9. Letter from Matthews to the shipping company dated 1 November 1935.
10. Loud field diary, entry dated 12 October 1935.
11. Loud field diary, entries dated 12–14 October 1935.
12. Cable from Breasted to Loud dated 13 October 1935; letter from Breasted to Loud dated 13 November 1935; letters from Loud to Matthews dated 16 and 29 October 1935; letter from Loud to Miss Carlson dated 4 November 1935; letter from Loud to Charles Breasted dated 20 November 1935; letter from Lamon to Charles Breasted dated 21 November 1935. Note that the latter two letters arrived in Chicago after Breasted's death, as noted in subsequent letter from Charles Breasted to Lamon dated 16 December 1935.
13. See the meeting diaries of David H. Stevens, with entries for Hutchins meetings on 15 May and 12 September 1934, in the Rockefeller Archive Center (filed under Rockefeller Foundation records, officers' diaries, RG 12, S-Z; Box 444, Reel M Ste 1, Frames 1 and 18).
14. Rockefeller Archive Center; biography of David H. Stevens (http://dimes.rockarch .org/xtf/view?docId=ead/FA394/FA394.xml;chunk.id=be6a13de5e7a4378b54703cc 1929a44f;brand=default;query=FA394&doc.view=contents).
15. See the meeting diaries of David H. Stevens, with entries for Breasted meeting on 17 February 1934; Hutchins on 15 May and 12 September 1934; and Breasted again on 12 September 1934 and 30 July 1935; all in the Rockefeller Archive Center (filed under Rockefeller Foundation records, officers' diaries, RG 12, S-Z; Box 444, Reel M Ste 1, Frames 1, 18, and 174).
16. Loud field diary, entries dated 17, 19, 20, and 28 October and 2–5 November 1935; letters from Loud to Breasted and to Wilson, both dated 9 November 1935.
17. Loud field diary, entries dated 12–17, 19–24, and 26–28 October 1935.
18. Letters from Loud to Breasted and to Wilson, both dated 9 November 1935.
19. Loud field diary, entries dated throughout November 1935, with one day a week off and a break for Thanksgiving; letters from Loud to Charles Breasted dated 20 November and 7 December 1935; letter from Loud to Matthews dated 10 December 1935.
20. Loud field diary, entry dated 9 December 1935; letter from Loud to Wilson dated 21 December 1935. See eventually Loud 1948: 159, plates 237–38.
21. On Temple 2048, as he called it, see originally Loud 1948: 57, 102, 104–5, figs. 126, 247–63. Kempinski 1989: 181–86; Novacek 2011: 40–41; Adams 2017; Ussishkin 2018: 217–20. Ussishkin calls it the "Tower Temple," which is a translation from the Hebrew (*migdal* = tower); on Tower Temples I–III, see also Ussishkin 2018: 16, 69, 203–17, and elsewhere (see his index at the back of the book).
22. Abt 2011: 390.
23. *New York Times*, 3 December 1935, p. 25.

24. Loud field diary, entry dated 3 December 1935. Wilson was alerted by cable on 30 November 1935 that Breasted was seriously ill, and made plans to return home immediately, but he was not able to arrive before Breasted died; see cable from Charles Breasted to Wilson dated 30 November 1935, with two cables in reply from Wilson dated 1 December 1935, followed by a cable sent to Wilson on 2 December 1935, which read simply, "DIRECTOR DIED THIS MORNING."

25. Letter from Charles Breasted to Lamon dated 16 December 1935; see also letter from Charles Breasted to the high commissioner, also dated 16 December 1935; letter from Charles Breasted to Loud dated 17 December 1935. See also letter from Charles Breasted to Rockefeller dated 11 December 1935, in the Rockefeller Archive Center (filed under Educational Interests; RG III 2G; Box 111, Folder 811).

26. Letter from Breasted to Rockefeller dated 25 October 1935, with reply from Rockefeller to Breasted dated 26 November 1935.

27. For confirmation that Breasted never saw this letter before his death, and the sentence quoted here, see the letter from Charles Breasted to Rockefeller dated 11 December 1935, with the subsequent reply from Rockefeller dated 19 December 1935. See also cable and letter from Rockefeller to Charles Breasted dated 2 and 5 December 1935, respectively, as well as reply from Charles Breasted dated 10 December 1935. Copies of all these letters are in the Rockefeller Archive Center (filed under Educational Interests; RG III 2G; Box 111, Folder 811) as well as in the archives at the Oriental Institute.

28. See the meeting diaries of David H. Stevens, with entries for meetings at the University of Chicago on 16 and 20 December 1935, in the Rockefeller Archive Center (filed under Rockefeller Foundation records, officers' diaries, RG 12, S-Z; Box 444, Reel M Ste 1, Frame 174). See also Abt 2011: 392.

29. Loud field diary, entries dated throughout December 1935.

30. For translations of the Amarna Letters, see Moran 1992. On Biridiya and Megiddo, see Kempinski 1989: 12 and now also brief discussion in Ussishkin 2018: 238–39.

31. Letter from Loud to Wilson dated 21 December 1935.

32. Letter from Loud to Wilson dated 21 December 1935.

33. Letter from Loud to Wilson dated 21 December 1935. Adams 2017: 51 argues that the temple was found in Stratum XII and lasted until Stratum VII.

34. Letter from Loud to Wilson dated 21 December 1935. For the publication of Stratum VIB, see Loud 1948: 33, figs. 80–81.

35. Letter from Loud to Wilson dated 21 December 1935.

36. Loud field diary, entries dated 24 and 27 December 1935.

37. Loud field diary, entry dated 29 December 1935. See also similar statements in letter from Loud to Wilson dated 29 December 1935.

38. Letter from Loud to Wilson dated 21 December 1935; letter from Loud to Matthews dated 7 January 1936; letter from Loud to Charles Breasted dated 14 January 1936.

39. Cable from Wilson to Loud dated 15 January 1936.

40. Letter from Wilson to Loud dated 18 January 1936.

41. Letter from Wilson to Loud dated 18 January 1936.

42. Letter from Wilson to Loud dated 18 January 1936.

43. Letter from Loud to Wilson dated 15 February 1936, with brief response from Wilson dated 2 March 1936.

44. Loud field diary entry from 2 February 1936.

45. Letter from Loud to Wilson dated 8 February 1936. See also earlier letters from Loud to Matthews dated 7 January and 8 February 1936 and from Loud to Charles Breasted dated 14 January and 6 February 1936.

46. Loud field diary entry from 2 February 1936.

47. Letter from Loud to Wilson dated 8 February 1936. On the three statuettes and the dating of the statuette of Thuthotep, see Adams 2017; Ussishkin 2018: 172–74.

48. Letter from Loud to Wilson dated 8 February 1936. On the liver omen, see Ussishkin 2018: 216–17.

49. Loud field diary entries dated 19, 22, and 24–25 February 1936.

50. Letter from Loud to Wilson dated 8 February 1936.

51. Letters from Loud to Wilson dated 15 and 25 March 1936; response from Wilson dated 2 April 1936.

52. Letter from Loud to Wilson dated 25 March 1936; field diary entries from 6, 13, and 15 December 1935, as well as 4, 16, 22, and 25 January, 22 and 24–27 February, 23 March, and 7 April 1936. See previously Guy 1931: 24–29, 45–48, and fig. 14; subsequent discussion and explanation in Loud and Shipton 1939: 74–83 and figs. 86–94. See also Kempinski 1989: 99, 115–16.

53. Letter from Loud to Wilson dated 25 March 1936.

54. Letter from Loud to Wilson dated 25 March 1936. Loud field diary entries for 9 and 18–19 February, 26 and 29 March, and 5 April 1936.

55. Letter from Loud to Wilson dated 25 March 1936. See Loud field diary entries for 23 March 1936 and 21, 23, and 25 March 1937. On the original publication of the Stratum IV gate, which was written up by Lamon, see Loud 1948: 46–57, figs. 104–16; see also letters from Loud to Wilson dated 22 February and 6 and 29 March 1937 for some of the discussion that went on behind the scenes before Lamon's final version was published. See now Ussishkin 2018: 319–36, 387–99; also previously Ussishkin 1980; Yadin 1980; Shiloh 1980; Wightman 1985; Kempinski 1989: 112–15.

56. See, e.g., Yadin's articles in the 1960s and 1970s, already cited in previous footnotes.

57. See again Finkelstein 1996a, 1999, 2013; also Balter 2000; Ussishkin 2018: 323–26; Richelle 2018: 82, 85–88.

58. Letter from Loud to Wilson dated 15 April 1936; Loud field diary entry dated 6 April 1936.

59. Draft of report by Loud on 1936 season for Department of Antiquities dated 14 May 1936, in the Israel Antiquities Authority Archives (British Mandate Record File SRF_143 [233/233]).

60. Draft of report by Loud on 1936 season for Department of Antiquities dated 14 May 1936, in the Israel Antiquities Authority Archives (British Mandate Record File SRF_143 [233/233]). See also Loud field diary entries for many of the days in April 1936. On the various gates, see Loud 1948: 16, 22, 25, 31, 33, 37, 45–46 (also 46–57 by Lamon), figs. 39–45, 63–64, 89–96, 104 (and 105–23 to accompany Lamon's contribution). See also Kempinski 1989: 111, fig. 36, for a single plan with all of the gates shown on it and now Ussishkin 2018: 242–45.

61. Cable from Loud to Wilson dated 17 April 1936; letter from Loud to Wilson dated 24 April 1936.

62. Loud field diary entries dated 28 February and 1 May 1936; letters from Loud to Wilson dated 15 and 25 March, 24 April, and 2 May 1936; letters from Wilson to Loud dated 2 and 31 March; letters from Loud to Matthews dated 9 and 15

May 1936; letter from Loud to the National Carloading Co. dated 15 May 1936. Relevant letters in the Israel Antiquities Authority Archives (British Mandate Administrative Files ATQ_7/6 [4th Jacket: 231/230]) include letters from Richmond to Loud dated 21 January, 7 and 19 February, 8 April, 8 and 18 May 1936; letters from Loud to Richmond dated 15 January, 4 and 17 February, March (day not specified), 7 April, and 15 May 1936.

63. Coded cable from Wilson to Loud dated 22 April 1936.

64. Letter from Wilson to Loud dated 23 April 1936; also letter from Loud to Wilson dated 24 April 1936, sent in response to the coded cable, as well as Abt 2011: 392. See also the meeting diaries of Thomas B. Appleget, with entry for Wilson meeting on 9 March 1936, in the Rockefeller Archive Center (filed under Rockefeller Foundation records, officers' diaries, RG 12 Appleget, Thomas B. 1936, Box 15, Folder 10 of 23).

65. The *Rockefeller Foundation Annual Report* for 1936: 304–5. See also the minutes for the 15 April 1936 meeting of the Rockefeller Foundation (Resolved: FR 36059 and 36060), in the Rockefeller Archive Center (filed under Rockefeller Foundation records, RG 1.1, Series 216R, Box 17, Folder 235), and letter from W. W. Brierley (secretary of the General Education Board) to President Hutchins dated 5 May 1936, in the Rockefeller Archive Center (filed under General Education Board, RG 2324.2, Series 1, Box 659, Folder 6854). See also letter from Charles Breasted to John D. Rockefeller, Jr., dated 23 April 1936, with reply dated 4 June 1936.

66. Letter from Wilson to Loud dated 23 April 1936.

67. Cable from Wilson to Loud dated 7 May 1936.

68. Cable from Wilson to Loud dated 7 May 1936; a longer letter with more details was also sent the same day from Wilson to Loud.

69. Cables from Loud to Wilson on 9, 10, and 11 May 1936; cable in reply from Wilson to Loud dated 12 May 1936.

70. Loud field diary entries for 19, 20, and 22 April 1936.

71. On the events of 1936–39, see, among many others, Bethell 1979: 30, 41; Sachar 1979: 199–208; Armstrong 1996: 383–85; Gilbert 1996: 134, 136, 140–43, 147–48; Smith 1996: 97–101; Hudson 2000: 256; Laqueur and Rubin 2001: 41–43; also brief overview in Cline 2004: 254–56, with further references.

72. Handwritten note from Hamilton to Richmond dated 13 May 1936, in the Israel Antiquities Authority Archives (British Mandate Administrative Files ATQ_7/6 [4th Jacket: 231/230]). A fuller, and much more formal, letter from Loud to Richmond dated 14 May 1936 is in the archives of both the Oriental Institute and the Israel Antiquities Authority; it deals with all sorts of specific issues ranging from the legal status of the buildings that they had constructed to the liquidation of various pieces of equipment, and so on. Subsequent letters include one from Richmond to Loud dated 19 May 1936, one from the chief secretary to Richmond dated 29 May 1936, and a reply from Richmond to the chief secretary dated 2 June 1936, as well as later exchanges between Richmond and the chief secretary dated 15 and 18 September 1936. Those in the Israel Antiquities Authority Archives can be found in the British Mandate Administrative Files ATQ_7/6 (4th Jacket: 231/230).

73. Letter from Shipton to Wilson dated 17 May 1936. There is also a later letter sent by Albright to Herbert May, dated 8 August, in which he remarks how sad it is to hear of the dismantling of the various Oriental Institute expedition houses, but that it was bound to come sooner or later (in the Oberlin College archives: Herbert G. May Papers, IV. Correspondence, W. F. Albright, Box 2).

74. Loud field diary entry dated 16 May 1936.

75. Handwritten letter from Lind to Wilson dated 16 May 1936.
76. Memo to terminate Lind dated 12 June 1936; letter from Wilson to Lind dated 25 June 1936; letter from Matthews to Lind dated 6 July 1936; letter from Lind to Wilson dated 23 July 1936; letter from Wilson to Lind dated 18 August 1936; memo from Matthews to W. J. Mather (bursar) dated 22 October 1936.

CHAPTER XIII

1. See the meeting diaries of David H. Stevens, with entry for Wilson meeting on 14 July 1936, in the Rockefeller Archive Center (filed under Rockefeller Foundation records, officers' diaries, RG 12, S-Z; Box 444, Reel M Ste 1, Frame 293).
2. Letters from Loud to Richmond and to the chief secretary, both dated 12 September 1936, with response from Richmond dated 29 September 1936; the letter sent to the chief secretary is in the archives of the Oriental Institute, while the letters between Loud and Richmond are in the Israel Antiquities Authority Archives (British Mandate Administrative Files ATQ_7/6 [4th Jacket: 231/230]).
3. Cables from Loud to Richmond dated 19 October and 27 October 1936; cable from Richmond to Loud 29 October 1936—all three are in the archives of the Oriental Institute as well as in the Israel Antiquities Authority Archives (British Mandate Administrative Files ATQ_7/6 [4th Jacket: 231/230]). See also letters exchanged between Richmond and the chief secretary regarding what answer to send, dated 21 and 28 October 1936, in the Israel Antiquities Authority Archives (British Mandate Administrative Files ATQ_7/6 [4th Jacket: 231/230]).
4. Cable from Loud to Shipton dated 29 October 1936; letter from Loud to Richmond dated 4 November 1936 and reply from Richmond dated 20 November 1936, both in the Israel Antiquities Authority Archives (British Mandate Administrative Files ATQ_7/6 [4th Jacket: 231/230]).
5. Letters from Allen to Shipton dated 31 October and 27 November 1936, with response from Shipton dated 11 November 1936; letter from Allen to Guy dated 27 November 1936; letter from Loud to Allen dated 27 December 1936. See Albright 1932: xxi and historical discussion by Sharon 2014: 44–45.
6. Loud field diary entry for 14 December 1936.
7. Loud field diary entry for 19 December 1936.
8. Letter from Loud to Wilson dated 27 December 1936.
9. Loud field diary entries for 19 and 20 December 1936.
10. Letter from Loud to Wilson dated 27 December 1936; also letter from Loud to Wilson dated 28 February 1937 and letter from Wilson to Loud dated 10 March 1937.
11. Letter from Loud to Wilson dated 27 December 1936. See also report by Loud on the 1936–37 season, in the Israel Antiquities Authority Archives (British Mandate Record File SRF_143 [233/233]).
12. Loud field diary entry for 24 December 1936.
13. Letter from Loud to Wilson dated 27 December 1936; field diary entry for 20 December 1936.
14. Loud field diary entries for 24 and 31 December.
15. Letters from Loud to Wilson dated 27 December 1936 and 22 February, 6 March, and 17 April 1937; see Loud field diary entry for 9 January 1937 re the number of men and both 21 and 25 March 1937 for the first mention of the massive walls of Strata XIV and XV. See also report filed by Loud at the end of the 1936–37 season, in the Israel Antiquities Authority Archives (British Mandate Record File SRF_143 [233/233]).

16. Letter from Wilson to Loud dated 26 January 1937.
17. Letter from Loud to Wilson dated 22 January 1937.
18. Letters from Loud to Wilson dated 22 January and 1 February 1937.
19. Letters from Wilson to Loud dated 22 February and 14 April 1937; on the final publication of the palace, see Loud 1948: 22–33, figs. 50–79. Loud's field diary entries for 15 and 17 February 1937 mark the first finds of ivories in what will become the Treasury (3073); the shell pavement was recorded in the entry for 18 February 1937, while painted wall plaster, in blue, red, yellow, plum, and green is first noted in the entry for 25 February 1937. See also Ussishkin 2018: 245–49.
20. Letter from Loud to Matthews dated 10 March 1937. See also letter from Loud to Wilson dated 22 February 1937.
21. Loud field diary entry dated 2 March 1937.
22. Cable from Loud to Wilson dated 6 March 1937.
23. Cable from Wilson to Loud dated 8 March 1937. See also subsequent letter from Wilson to Loud dated 10 March 1937.
24. Letter from Loud to Wilson dated 6 March 1937. On the final description of the location, see Loud 1948: 25. Re Iliffe's visit, see Loud field diary entry dated 6 March 1937.
25. Letter from Loud to Wilson dated 6 March 1937; Loud field diary entries dated 2, 6, and 21 March 1937; Loud 1948: 25, 173, figs. 55–58, plates 160, 202, 213, 230–32. See now Ussishkin 2018: 250–52, figs. 12:11–14; previously Negbi 1970: 35–36, Samet 2009: 77, 110, 116, and Hall 2016: 51–56. Hall thinks the objects may actually have been three separate deposits, buried close together in a line against (and/or under) the western wall of the room, at slightly different depths, while Negbi suggested that the hoard may date to Stratum IX rather than to VIII.
26. Loud field diary entry dated 2 March 1937; Loud 1948: 25, 173, with figs. 55–58. See now Hall 2016: 48–49; Ussishkin 2018: 250–52.
27. Loud 1948: 25; Ussishkin 2018: 250–52. On the Stratum VIII palace, see now Yasur-Landau and Samet 2017: 469–73.
28. Hasson 2012; https://english.tau.ac.il/news/tel_megido; Hall 2016: 7–8; Ussishkin 2018: 305–9. See now Arie et al. 2019.
29. Letters from Loud to Wilson dated 6 and 18 March 1937. Re Iliffe's declaration, see Loud field diary entry dated 6 March 1937.
30. Letters from Loud to Wilson dated 6 and 18 March and 3 May 1937.
31. Letters from Wilson to Loud dated 29 March and 14 April 1937.
32. Letter from Wilson to Loud dated 29 March 1937; *St. Louis Post-Dispatch*, 15 March 1937, p. 1.
33. Cable and letter from Loud to Wilson, both dated 3 May 1937; *St. Louis Post-Dispatch*, 1 August 1937, p. 4 and continued on p. 6.
34. Letter from Loud to Wilson dated 6 March 1937; letter from Loud to Matthews dated 10 March 1937.
35. Letter from Loud to Wilson dated 18 March 1937.
36. Letter from Loud to Matthews dated 7 April 1937. Regarding the decoding, see also letter from Wilson to Loud dated 10 March 1937 and letter from Matthews to Loud dated 20 March 1937.
37. Loud field diary entry for 6 March 1937.
38. Loud field diary entries for 7 and 9 March 1937.
39. Loud field diary entries dated from 6 March to 7 April 1937; letter from Loud to Iliffe dated 30 April 1937, in the Israel Antiquities Authority Archives (British Mandate Administrative Files ATQ_7/6 [4th Jacket: 231/230]).

40. See, e.g., letter from Loud to Wilson dated 17 April 1937; Loud 1939: 3, 1948: 29, 31, fig. 75; Feldman 2009: 177.

41. Letter from Loud to Iliffe dated 30 April 1937, in the Israel Antiquities Authority Archives (British Mandate Administrative Files ATQ_7/6 [4th Jacket: 231/230]).

42. Letter from Loud to Iliffe, with included sketch, dated 30 April 1937, in the Israel Antiquities Authority Archives (British Mandate Record File SRF_143 [233/233]; also British Mandate Administrative Files ATQ_7/6 [4th Jacket: 231/230]). See also the handwritten letter from Ben-Dor to Kennedy Shaw dated 1 June 1937, letter from Kennedy Shaw to Loud dated 1 June 1937, and letter from Loud to Kennedy Shaw dated 25 June 1937, all discussing the micro-gridding in terms of proper labeling of the ivories once they had reached the Palestine Museum. All of the above are in the Israel Antiquities Authority Archives (British Mandate Administrative Files ATQ_7/6 [4th Jacket: 231/230]).

43. Letters from Loud to Wilson dated 18 and 29 March as well as 17 April 1937. In addition to Loud's official publication of these items in 1939, later publications include Kantor 1956; Barnett 1982: 25–28; Liebowitz 1986; Singer 1988–89; Kempinski 1989: 137–46; Fischer 2007: 119–27; Feldman 2009; Yasur-Landau and Samet 2017: 474–76; and now Ussishkin 2018: 253–66.

44. Letter from Loud to Wilson dated 17 April 1937. Matson later inherited all of the photographs and negatives belonging to the American Colony Photo Department and subsequently donated them to the Library of Congress; they are now available online—see https://www.loc.gov/collections/g-eric-and-edith-matson-photographs/about-this-collection/.

45. Letters from Loud to Wilson dated 18 and 29 March as well as 17 April 1937; Loud 1939: 13, plates 1–3. See also letters about arranging the loan: letter from Loud to Richmond dated 15 April 1937 and reply from Richmond dated 17 April 1937; and letter from Loud to Richmond dated 3 May 1937, with from Kennedy Shaw to Loud dated 8 May 1937—all in the Israel Antiquities Authority Archives (British Mandate Administrative Files ATQ_7/6 [4th Jacket: 231/230]).

46. Letter from Loud to Wilson dated 17 April 1937; Loud 1939: 9, 11–13, plate 62. See Cline 2014 for more on Ramses III and the events of this period. On this pen case, see also Barnett 1982: 25; Fischer 2007: 157–63; Feldman 2009: 192, with further references; Ussishkin 2018: 270.

47. Loud 1939: 7 and fig. 5.

48. Loud 1939: 7–9, 1948: 31. See also, e.g., Barnett 1982: 25; Singer 1988–89: 102.

49. Barnett 1982: 25; Singer 1988–89; Fischer 2007: 119–27; Feldman 2009: 177–78, 188–89; Martin 2017: 270, 273; now Ussishkin 2018: 253–55.

50. Letter from Loud to Wilson dated 17 April 1937. In his field diary entry for 11 March 1937, Loud had earlier noted that "the ivory rooms look more and more secondary"—i.e., that they had been added in and were not part of the original construction of the palace. Subsequently, in the entry for 18 March 1937, he noted that the original palace appeared "to have its western boundary under the ivory rooms."

51. Loud 1939: 9.

52. Letters from Loud to Wilson dated 6 March and 17 April 1937; field diary entries for 6 and 7 March 1937.

53. Loud 1939: fig. 5; Feldman 2009: fig. 3.

54. See Hachmann 1989: 95–122, 1993: 1–40; Adler 1994: 146–49; Fischer 2007: 119–27; Feldman 2009: 177; Samet 2009: 117–53, esp. 83–85, 120–21, 134; Wagner-Durand 2012.

55. On Kamid el-Loz specifically, see Hachmann 1989: 95–122, 1993: 2–8; Adler 1994: 146–49; Wagner-Durand 2012.

56. I thank Professors Haskel and Tina Greenfield (personal communication, 3 December 2018) for suggesting that the complete animal skeleton looks to be a deliberate burial, which led me to begin reexamining the possibility that the Treasury is, in fact, a tomb and thence to the hypothesis presented here.

57. Loud 1939: 7, 9; Loud 1948: 171 (catalog).

58. Loud field diary entry for 6 March 1937.

59. Feldman 2009: 177, 189–90.

60. I thank Professors Haskel and Tina Greenfield (personal communication, 3 December 2018) for their suggestion, which is based on an examination of the photograph published by Feldman.

61. On equid burials in the ancient Near East, see recently, e.g., Weber 2008; Greenfield, Shai, and Maeir 2012; Way 2013; Silver 2014; Wygnańska 2017. See also previously, e.g., Stiebing 1971.

62. Cline 2014.

63. Finkelstein 1996b: 171–72, 2009; Toffolo et al. 2014; Finkelstein et al. 2017a.

64. Loud 1948: 29, 31; Singer 1988–89: 101; Kempinski 1989: 159–60; Ussishkin 1995: 241; see now also discussion in Martin 2017.

65. Ussishkin 1995, 2018: 276–77.

66. Martin 2017; also Finkelstein et al. 2017a; previously Finkelstein 2009.

67. Letter from Loud to Wilson dated 28 April 1937; field diary entry dated 18 April 1937. Rather surprisingly, the official report on this season is extremely short and succinct; see Loud 1938: 45–46.

68. Loud field diary entries for 7 and 15 April 1937.

69. Ussishkin 2018: 246.

70. See letter from Loud to Richmond dated 15 April 1937 and reply from Richmond dated 17 April 1937; also letter from Richmond to Loud dated 4 May 1937—all currently in the Israel Antiquities Authority Archives (British Mandate Administrative Files ATQ_7/6 [4th Jacket: 231/230]). See also field diary entry for 1 May 1937.

71. Letter from Loud to Wilson dated 3 May 1937.

72. Letter from Loud to Wilson dated 3 May 1937. See also earlier letter from Loud to Wilson dated 28 April 1937.

73. Letter from Loud to Iliffe dated 30 April 1937; see also again the handwritten letter from Ben-Dor to Kennedy Shaw dated 1 June 1937, letter from Kennedy Shaw to Loud dated 1 June 1937, and letter from Loud to Kennedy Shaw dated 25 June 1937, all discussing the proper labeling of the ivories once they had reached the Palestine Archaeological Museum. All of the above are in the Israel Antiquities Authority Archives (British Mandate Administrative Files ATQ_7/6 [4th Jacket: 231/230]).

74. Letters from Wilson to Loud dated 25 February, 10 and 29 March, and 14 April 1937; letters from Loud to Wilson dated 29 March, 17 April, and 3 May 1937. See also handwritten letter of thanks from Shipton to Wilson, on stationery from the Cosmos Club in Washington, DC, dated 7 November 1937, sent as he was on his way back to Megiddo with the others for the beginning of the next season.

75. Letter from Loud to Wilson dated 28 April 1937.

CHAPTER XIV

1. Cable from Wilson to Loud dated 13 November; letter from Loud to Wilson (from aboard the SS *Rex*) dated 19 November 1937; Loud field diary entry dated 13 November 1937.

2. Cable and letter from Wilson to Loud, both dated 25 February 1937, with cabled reply from Loud dated 27 February 1937; also letter from Matthews to Loud dated 9 June 1937; all in contrast to the initial pessimistic letter of 26 January 1937 from Wilson to Loud.

3. Letter to Loud with names of possible applicants, including Frazer, dated 28 May 1937; http://tsla.tnsosfiles.com.s3.amazonaws.com/history/manuscripts/findingaids /FRAZER_GEORGE_PRESTON_PAPERS_1978-1992.pdf.

4. Letter from Loud to the director of antiquities dated 26 November 1937, in the Israel Antiquities Authority Archives (British Mandate Administrative Files ATQ_7/6 [4th Jacket: 231/230]); Loud field diary entry dated 25 November 1937.

5. Letter from Loud to Wilson dated 16 December 1937; Loud field diary entry dated 5 December 1937.

6. Letter from Loud to Wilson dated 16 December 1937; letter from Lind to his wife, Astrid, dated 9 September 1937 (retrieved from the Olof E. Lind papers in the Library of Congress <lccn.loc.gov/mm2014085935>); Loud field diary entries for 11 and 13 December 1937.

7. Letters from Loud to Wilson dated 16 and 26 December 1937; letter from Loud to Matthews dated 18 December 1937; Loud field diary entries dated 11 and 12 December 1937.

8. Report from Loud to the director of antiquities on the results of the 1937–38 season—undated but undoubtedly May 1938—in the Israel Antiquities Authority Archives (British Mandate Record File SRF_143 [233/233]); Loud field diary entries dated 22 January and most of April 1938.

9. Report from Loud to the director of antiquities on the results of the 1937–38 season—undated but undoubtedly May 1938—in the Israel Antiquities Authority Archives (British Mandate Record File SRF_143 [233/233]); Loud field diary entries dated 22 January and most of April 1938.

10. See Lamon and Shipton 1939: 43, fig. 49, now updated by Cline 2006: fig. 8.12. See also Loud 1941: 211; Loud 1948: 116, figs. 279, 414; Franklin 2017: 91.

11. Report from Loud to the director of antiquities on the results of the 1937–38 season—undated but undoubtedly May 1938—in the Israel Antiquities Authority Archives (British Mandate Record File SRF_143 [233/233]); Loud field diary entries dated 22 January and most of April 1938; Loud 1948: 6–8, figs. 6–7. On the Stratum XIII gate, see now Ussishkin 2018: 182–84.

12. Loud field diary entry dated 7 December 1937; Loud 1948: 113; Harrison 2004: 5.

13. Loud field diary entries dated 23, 24, and 29 January 1938, as well as 6 and 9–11 April 1938, among others; Loud 1948: 113–14, 116, figs. 272–79.

14. Coded cable and letter from Wilson to Loud, both dated 20 December 1937; cable sent in reply by Loud dated 22 December 1937, as well as letters from Loud to Wilson and Matthews, both dated 26 December 1937. See also letter from Matthews to Loud dated 4 January 1938.

15. Letter from Wilson to Stevens dated 4 November 1937, mentioning the *Illustrated London News* articles of 16 and 23 October 1937; letter from Brierley to Hutchins dated 10 December 1937, with replies from Hutchins, Matthews, and Wilson dated 13, 15, and 20 December 1937, respectively; letter from Wilson to Stevens

dated 20 December 1937. All are in the Rockefeller Archive Center (filed under International Education Board, RG 1008.1, Series 1, Box 18, Folder 274). See also the brief article on the ivories published by Wilson in the *American Journal of Archaeology* (Wilson 1938).

16. Letter from Wilson to Loud dated 14 January 1938.
17. Letters from Loud to Wilson and Matthews, both dated 26 December 1937; Loud field diary entry dated 22 December 1937. On Haines, see Green 2012: 14; on the Braidwoods, see https://www.nytimes.com/2003/01/17/us/2-archaeologists-robert -braidwood-95-and-his-wife-linda-braidwood-93-die.html.
18. Letter from Matthews to Loud dated 6 December 1937 and Loud's reply dated 26 December 1937.
19. Letter from Loud to Wilson dated 16 December 1937.
20. Letter from Loud to Wilson dated 26 December 1937; letter from Loud to Matthews dated 26 December 1937.
21. Loud field diary entry dated 11 January 1938; see also Nelson Glueck's entry for 11 January (see also 13 January) in Newsletter No. 1 for January 1938, currently in the archives of the American Schools of Oriental Research and available online at http://www.asor-glueck.org/diaries/1938-2/. For a recent examination of the circumstances surrounding Starkey's murder, see Garfinkel 2016 and a response by Ussishkin 2019. For a brief biography of Starkey, see https://www.pef.org.uk /profiles/james-leslie-starkey-1895-1938.
22. Loud field diary entry dated 22 January 1938.
23. Loud field diary entry dated 1 February 1938.
24. Report from Loud to the director of antiquities on the results of the 1937–38 season—undated but undoubtedly May 1938—in the Israel Antiquities Authority Archives (British Mandate Record File SRF_143 [233/233]); published as Loud 1938–39: 162–63. See also brief discussions of these levels in Kempinski 1989: 19–90 as well as now discussions in Ussishkin 2018.
25. Loud field diary entries for 21 and 27 February 1938. See also Kempinski 1989: 19.
26. Loud field diary entry for 27 March 1938. See Loud 1948: 59–60, figs. 128–30, and brief mentions in Kempinski 1989: 19 and Ussishkin 2018: 106.
27. Loud field diary entries from 28–30 December 1937 and then 24 January 1938; see Loud 1948: 61, figs. 135–43, and now Ussishkin 2018: 112–39, with references. See also Ussishkin 2015 on a recent reconsideration of the remains from Strata XX–XIV; previously, among others, Epstein 1965; Dunayevski and Kempinski 1973.
28. Loud field diary entries from 28–30 December 1937 and then 24 January 1938; Loud 1948: 61, figs. 144–46. On the more recent Tel Aviv Expedition findings, see Keinan 2007, 2013; also Ussishkin 2018: 116–19.
29. Loud field diary entries dated 8 January and 1, 3, 6, and 13–22 February 1938. In addition to Loud's 1938 report, see also *Science News Letter*, 6 August 1938, p. 83—"Scientists Find Giant Wall at Famed City of Armageddon," available on JSTOR at https://www.jstor.org/stable/3914922. See Loud 1948: 64, 66, 70, figs. 147–55, and now Ussishkin 2018: 143–46, with references.
30. Loud field diary entry dated 11 January 1938; see also his entries for 12 and 23 January. Final publication is Loud 1948: 59, 73, 76, figs. 164–65. See now Ussishkin 2018: 148–50.
31. See Cline 2014: 228, where I first made this observation. For the publication of the bones, see Wapnish and Hesse 2000; see also Ussishkin 2018: 148–50 on the altar in general.
32. Loud 1948: 70, 73, figs. 156–62.

33. Report from Loud to the director of antiquities on the results of the 1936–37 season, dated May 1937, in the Israel Antiquities Authority Archives (British Mandate Record File SRF_143 [233/233]); this lengthy discussion of the various strata was essentially deleted from the very condensed report on the season that was eventually published as Loud 1938: 45–46.

34. On Strata XVI–XIII, see Loud 1948: 73, 76–87, figs. 168–98. Regarding the wall uncovered in Area K by the recent Tel Aviv Expedition, see now Ussishkin 2018: 180–82 and fig. 9.9.

35. Report from Loud to the director of antiquities on the results of the 1936–37 season, dated May 1937, in the Israel Antiquities Authority Archives (British Mandate Record File SRF_143 [233/233]). See Loud 1948: 87, 92, figs. 197–209, 212. See also now Yasur-Landau and Samet 2017: 464–67, for a possible palace in Stratum XII, reconstructed by Nigro 1994.

36. Loud 1948: 92, 97, 102, figs. 210–28, 230, 236–39.

37. Ussishkin 2018: 207–11.

38. Loud 1948: 102, figs. 242–44. See now Ussishkin 2018: 234–35. Note that, in a lengthy article, Bonfil 2012 argues that Thutmose III actually captured Stratum X, but it remains to be seen whether this is accepted by others.

39. Report from Loud to the director of antiquities on the results of the 1936–37 season, dated May 1937, in the Israel Antiquities Authority Archives (British Mandate Record File SRF_143 [233/233]); see also Loud 1948: 102, 104, figs. 247–49.

40. Report from Loud to the director of antiquities on the results of the 1936–37 season, dated May 1937, in the Israel Antiquities Authority Archives (British Mandate Record File SRF_143 [233/233]).

41. Loud field diary entry dated 1 March 1938.

42. Loud field diary entry dated 1 March 1938.

43. Letter from Loud to Matthews dated 7 March 1938.

44. Letter from Loud to Matthews dated 7 March 1938; Loud field diary entries dated 4–11 March 1938.

45. Loud field diary entry dated 12 March 1938.

46. Loud field diary entry dated 13 March 1938; see also previous entry for 8 February 1938.

47. Loud field diary entries dated 16–24 March 1938.

48. Loud field diary entries dated 24–25 March 1938.

49. Loud field diary entries dated 24–25 March 1938; letter from Matthews to Loud sent from Baghdad and dated 24 April 1938.

50. Loud field diary entry dated 27 March 1938.

51. Loud field diary entry dated 31 March 1938.

52. Loud field diary entry dated 31 March 1938.

53. Loud field diary entries dated 31 March and 2 and 5 April 1938.

54. Letter from Loud to Matthews dated 12 January 1938; letter from Wilson to Loud dated 14 January 1938; letter from Matthews to Loud dated 29 January 1938; cable from Loud to Matthews dated 11 February 1938.

55. Re Pope at Megiddo during the second half of this season, see Loud field diary entries dated 16 February, 14 and 27 April, and 9, 13, and 14 May 1938; see also genealogical details listed at https://www.findagrave.com/memorial/180349047/gustavus-debrille-pope and https://www.geni.com/people/Gustavus-Debrille-Pope-Jr/4908435112840064587.

56. Letters from Loud to the director of antiquities dated 11 April and 10 May 1938; letter from Hamilton (as acting director of antiquities) dated 7 May 1938. All are

in the Israel Antiquities Authority Archives (British Mandate Administrative Files ATQ_7/6 [4th Jacket: 231/230]; see also British Mandate Record File SRF_143 [233/233]). See also Loud field diary entries dated 21 and 27–28 April and 2–5 May 1938.

57. Letter from Loud to Matthews dated 14 May 1938 and cable from Loud to Matthews dated 24 May 1938. See also Loud field diary entry dated 14 May 1938.

CHAPTER XV

1. *Chicago Tribune*, 5 November 1938, p. 15, and 6 November 1938, p. 19. Note that the best man is reported as "Edward Noble," but it seems that the newspaper got the first name wrong, for this is much more likely to have been William H. Noble, to whom Loud refers in his letters as "Hal Noble." The announcement of the engagement had appeared back in September (*Chicago Tribune*, 6 September 1938, p. 19), and so Hamilton sent his congratulations ahead of time in a letter dated 21 October 1938, now in the Israel Antiquities Authority Archives (British Mandate Administrative Files ATQ_7/6 [4th Jacket: 231/230]).

2. *Chicago Tribune*, 5 November 1938, p. 15, and 6 November 1938, p. 19.

3. See details available online at http://www.shippingwondersoftheworld.com/rex .html.

4. *Chicago Tribune*, 5 November 1938, p. 15, and 6 November 1938, p. 19. Regarding the arrivals at Megiddo, see letter from Shipton to Hamilton dated 13 October 1938; letters from Loud to Hamilton dated 4 October and 20 December 1938; letters from Hamilton to Loud dated 21 October and 23 December 1938—all in the Israel Antiquities Authority Archives (British Mandate Administrative Files ATQ_7/6 [4th Jacket: 231/230]). See also letters from Matthews to Loud dated 1 and 22 December 1938; Loud field diary entries, undated, at the front of the pages for the 1938/39 season.

5. Letter from Loud to Matthews dated 29 December 1938; reply from Matthews dated 31 January 1939; Loud field diary entry dated 27 December 1939.

6. Final Report on 1938–39 Season submitted by Loud, dated 6 May 1939, in the Israel Antiquities Authority Archives (British Mandate Record File SRF_143 [233/233]), published as Loud 1941: 210–12.

7. Loud field diary entry dated 27 December 1938. See also Final Report on 1938–39 Season submitted by Loud, dated 6 May 1939, in the Israel Antiquities Authority Archives (British Mandate Record File SRF_143 [233/233]), published as Loud 1941: 210–12.

8. Letter from Loud to Matthews dated 16 January 1939; letter from Loud to Wilson dated 29 January 1939; Loud field diary entries dated 4, 7, 9, and 17 January 1939. See also Final Report on 1938–39 Season submitted by Loud, dated 6 May 1939, in the Israel Antiquities Authority Archives (British Mandate Record File SRF_143 [233/233]), published as Loud 1941: 210–12 (esp. p. 211 on the stables).

9. Letter from Loud to Wilson dated 29 January 1939. On the liver omen, see again Ussishkin 2018: 216–17.

10. Letter from Loud to Wilson dated 29 January 1939.

11. Letter from Wilson to Loud dated 19 January 1939; letter from Loud to Wilson dated 12 February 1938.

12. Letter from Wilson to Loud dated 19 January 1939; reply from Loud dated 12 February 1939.

13. See Sachar 1979: 210–13, 222–26; Armstrong 1996: 385; Gilbert 1996: 150–51, 154–60; Khalidi 1991: 192–95; Smith 1996: 101–8; Hudson 2000: 256; Segev 2000: 436–

43; Wasserstein 2001: 115–16. See also brief overview, with further references, in Cline 2004: 255–56.

14. See again Sachar 1979: 210–13, 222–26; Armstrong 1996: 385; Gilbert 1996: 150–51, 154–60; Khalidi 1991: 192–95; Smith 1996: 101–8; Hudson 2000: 256; Segev 2000: 436–43; Wasserstein 2001: 115–16; Cline 2004: 255–56.

15. Segev 2000: 440.

16. Letter from Lind re divorce dated 24 January 1939 (retrieved from the Olof E. Lind papers in the Library of Congress <lccn.loc.gov/mm2014085935>).

17. Letter from Loud to Wilson dated 29 January 1939.

18. Letter from Loud to Wilson dated 29 January 1939.

19. Glueck, "News-Letter No. 2," dated 1 February 1939; currently in the archives of the American Schools of Oriental Research, available online at http://www.asor-glueck.org/diaries/1939-2/. See also Loud field diary entry dated 28 January 1939.

20. Letter from Loud to Wilson dated 29 January 1939; Loud field diary entry dated 28 January 1939.

21. Letters from Loud to Wilson dated 29 January, 12 February, 12 and 16 March 1939; letter from Loud to Wadsworth dated 28 January 1939; letter from Wadsworth to Loud dated 11 March 1939; letter from Wilson to Loud dated 1 April 1939; Loud field diary entry dated 28 January 1939. Strangely enough, Asfour, the lawyer representing the local man, subsequently contacted the expedition directly with the same demand; see letter from Loud to Wilson dated 9 June 1939, enclosing a letter from Asfour dated 12 May 1939; letters from both Loud and Parker to Wadsworth dated 9 June 1939; also letters from Parker to Loud dated 12 June and 22 July 1939, with replies from Loud dated 30 June and 9 August 1939; letters from Loud to Wilson dated 29 June and 8 July 1939, with response from Wilson to the former dated 5 July 1939; letters from Wilson to Wallace Murray at the Department of State in Washington, DC, dated 12 June and 25 October 1939 and to the chief secretary in Jerusalem dated 12 June 1939 (a copy of this last letter is also in the Israel Antiquities Authority Archives [British Mandate Administrative Files ATQ_7/6 (5th Jacket: 132/126)]); letter from the chief secretary to Loud dated 17 October 1939; letter from the American consul to Loud dated 23 October 1939, with reply from Loud dated 17 November 1939. Also, letters from Kennedy Shaw to the chief secretary dated 12 and 26 July 1939 and a letter from Horton, director of land registration, to the chief secretary dated 20 July 1939—all currently in the Israel Antiquities Authority Archives (British Mandate Administrative Files ATQ_7/6 [5th Jacket: 132/126]).

22. Letter from Loud to Wilson dated 29 January 1939; Loud field diary entries dated 4, 5, and 7 January 1939.

23. Letter from Loud to Wilson dated 29 January 1939; Loud field diary entry dated 19 January 1939.

24. Letter from Loud to Matthews dated 9 February 193; letter from Loud to Wilson dated 12 February 1939, with a photo included (labeled no. 5064); Loud field diary entries dated 15, 16, 19, and 20 February, as well as 1 and 2 March 1939. See Lamon and Shipton 1939: fig. 49 and Cline 2006: fig. 8.12 for the location of the stables in the "K-10" area.

25. Letter from Loud to Wilson dated 12 March 1939; Loud field diary entries dated 26 and 28 February 1939.

26. Letter from Loud to Wilson dated 12 March 1939.

27. Letter from Wilson to Loud dated 1 April 1939.

28. Letters from Loud to Matthews dated 1 and 11 March 1939.

29. Letter from Loud to Wilson dated 12 March 1939.

30. Letter from Wilson to Loud dated 1 April 1939.
31. Letter from Loud to Hamilton dated 8 April 1939, in the Israel Antiquities Authority Archives (British Mandate Administrative Files ATQ_7/6 [4th Jacket: 231/230]); letter from Loud to Wilson dated 6 April 1939; Glueck, "News-Letter No. 7," dated 5 April 1939; currently in the archives of the American Schools of Oriental Research, available online at http://www.asor-glueck.org/diaries/1939-2/.
32. Loud field diary entry dated 4 April 1939; Letter from Matthews to Loud dated 7 April 1939.
33. Letters from Loud to Wilson dated 6 and 29 April 1939; Loud field diary entries dated 27 and 29 March as well as 1, 6, and 18 April 1939. See now Ussishkin 2018: 157–66, with references.
34. Letters from Loud to Wilson dated 6 and 29 April 1939; Loud field diary entry dated 18 April 1939. On the correction, see letter from Loud to Kennedy Shaw dated 11 August 1939. See also Final Report on 1938–39 Season submitted by Loud, dated 6 May 1939, in the Israel Antiquities Authority Archives (British Mandate Record File SRF_143 [233/233]), published as Loud 1941: 211; final publication in Loud 1948: 78, fig. 179. See also Kempinski 1989: 175–78; Ussishkin 2018: 160–61 notes that the temples are dated by scholars to either the Early Bronze Age (EB III) or the Intermediate Bronze Age (IB).
35. Letters from Loud to Hamilton dated 8, 17, 20, and 22 April 1939; letters from Hamilton to Loud dated 13, 19, and 22 April 1939, in the Israel Antiquities Authority Archives (British Mandate Administrative Files ATQ_7/6 [4th Jacket: 231/230]). See also letter from Loud to Wilson dated 29 April 1939; Loud field diary entry dated 20 April 1939.
36. Letter from Loud to Hamilton dated 17 April 1939, in the Israel Antiquities Authority Archives (British Mandate Administrative Files ATQ_7/6 [4th Jacket: 231/230]).
37. Letter from Hamilton dated 19 April 1939, in the Israel Antiquities Authority Archives (British Mandate Administrative Files ATQ_7/6 [4th Jacket: 231/230]); Loud field diary entry dated 29 April 1939.
38. Loud field diary entry dated 29 April 1939; letters from Loud to Hamilton dated 8, 20, and 22 April 1939; letters from Hamilton to Loud dated 13 and 19 April 1939; letter from Kennedy Shaw to Loud dated 1 May 1939 and reply from Loud dated 6 May 1939, in the Israel Antiquities Authority Archives (British Mandate Administrative Files ATQ_7/6 [4th Jacket: 231/230]); the 1 May letter from Kennedy Shaw to Loud is also in British Mandate Record File SRF_143 [233/233]). See also letter from Loud to Wilson dated 29 April 1939 and letter from Loud to Matthews dated 6 May 1939.
39. Letters from Loud to Wilson dated 6 and 29 April 1939; letter from Matthews to Loud dated 7 April 1939; letter from Loud to Matthews dated 6 May 1939; Loud field diary entries dated 3 and 6 May 1939.
40. Letter from Loud to Matthews dated 15 April 1939; letter from Loud to Wilson dated 29 April 1939. On the violence, see again the above references (Sachar; Khalidi; Armstrong; Gilbert; Smith; Hudson; and Wasserstein, among others) and brief discussion in Cline 2004: 255–56.
41. Letter from Shipton to Loud dated 4 June 1939.
42. Letter from Shipton to Loud dated 4 June 1939, with reply from Loud dated 28 June 1939; see also letters from Loud to Wilson dated 23 and 29 June 1939, with replies from Wilson to Loud dated 26 and 29 June and 5 July 1939; letter from

Matthews to Shipton also dated 28 June 1939; letter from Shipton to Loud dated 17 July 1939, with reply from Loud dated 3 August 1939.

43. Letter from Shipton to Loud dated 4 June 1939.

44. A letter from Loud to Parker dated 9 August 1939 mentions his hope that Shipton's pottery volume had arrived in Haifa and that they had seen it by that point.

45. Letter from Loud to Shipton dated 3 August 1939, in response to Shipton's original letter of 4 June and a subsequent letter of 17 July 1939.

46. Letter from Shipton to Loud dated 24 August 1939.

47. Letter from Shipton to Loud dated 24 August 1939.

48. Letter from Tchoub to Loud dated 27 July 1939. Parker wrote to Loud a few times during the summer of 1939 and then frequently, often several times a month, from September 1939 right through October 1941; Tchoub wrote less frequently, but at least once and sometimes twice a month from July 1939 through October 1941.

49. Letter from Tchoub to Loud dated 31 August 1939.

50. Cable from Loud to Parker dated 5 September 1939; letter from Loud to both Shipton and Parker dated 8 September 1939; letter from Loud to Tchoub dated 26 September 1939; letters from Loud to Parker dated 9 October and 10 November 1939; letter from Loud to both Parker and Shipton dated 20 October 1939.

51. Letter from Tchoub to Loud dated 14 October 1939; in a subsequent letter, dated 25 October, Tchoub said that Loud's earlier letters had finally arrived. Ironically, both of these letters from Tchoub arrived on the same day, 21 November, according to a reply that Loud sent that same day.

52. Tobler 1950: 1–2. See also Rothman 2002; Peasnall and Rothman 2003.

53. Cable from Loud to Noble dated 13 November 1939; sequential cables from Tobler to Noble, Noble to Loud, and Loud to Tobler, all dated 15 November 1939; final cable from Tobler to Loud dated 16 November 1939.

54. Letter from Loud to both Shipton and Parker dated 8 September 1939; letters from Loud to Parker dated 9 October and 10 November 1939; cable from Loud to Parker dated 25 October 1939; letters from Loud sent separately to Tchoub and to Parker, both dated 21 November 1939.

55. Letter from Loud to Tchoub dated 21 November 1939.

56. Letter from Loud to Parker dated 21 November 1939.

57. Letter from Shipton to Loud dated 10 December 1939.

58. Letter from Loud to Tobler dated 17 November 1939.

CHAPTER XVI

1. Harrison 2004: 5.

2. Letter from Loud to Parker dated 4 January 1940; letter from Loud to Tchoub dated 23 January 1940; letter from Tchoub to Loud dated 31 January 1940.

3. Letters from Loud to Parker dated 4 and 23 January as well as 21 June 1940; letter from Loud to Parker and Shipton dated 15 February 1940; letters from Loud to Tchoub dated 17 August 1940 and 21 March 1941; letter from Tchoub to Loud dated 3 August 1941.

4. Cables from Loud to Parker dated 29 October 1940 and 28 May 1941; letter from Tchoub to Loud dated 5 January 1941; letter from Loud to Parker dated 10 January 1941; letters from Parker to Loud dated 17 January and 30 April 1941; letter from Loud to Tchoub dated 1 February 1941.

5. Shipton 1942. See correspondence about the writing of the guide, beginning in 1941, in the Israel Antiquities Authority Archives (British Mandate Administrative Files ATQ_16/9 [1st Jacket: 120/111]).

6. Letters from Parker to Loud dated 17 April and 12 June 1941; letters from Tchoub to Loud dated 18 May and 3 August 1941; letter from Loud to Tchoub dated 18 June 1941.

7. Beevor 1991: 252. I think Aren Maeir for bringing this to my attention. A letter from Loud to Wilson dated 19 September 1944 refers to a letter sent by Parker dated 28 July 1944 which states that the "authorities" were handing back the dig house as of the end of July 1944. The obituary for Ian Macpherson was published in the *Telegraph* on 12 January 2011; there is apparently also a memoir that Macpherson wrote of his experiences, entitled *Blurred Recollections*, which was privately printed in 1989, according to the obituary (see https://www.telegraph.co.uk/news/obituaries /military-obituaries/special-forces-obituaries/8255880/Ian-Macpherson.html).

8. Letter from Ethel Schenk to Loud dated 8 May 1942.

9. See especially Kletter 2006: 93; Jones 2009: viii–ix; also references to letters either to or from Loud during this time period cited in O'Sullivan 2012: 259n88, 282n166, 338n3, 2015: 228nn43, 54, 62, and 66, 229n77, 230n103; Wilford 2013: 303n11. See also a very small amount of information at the National Archives II Building at College Park, Maryland, filed under: Loud, Gordon; Record Group 226: Records of the Office of Strategic Services; OSS Personnel Files, 1941–1945; Box 0463, ARC ID 1593270, Entry 224, "Lordi, Joseph to Louttit, Chauncey."

10. Letters from Loud to Wilson dated 18 October, 14 November, and 5 December 1945; letters from Wilson to Loud dated 29 October and 17 November 1945; resignation letter sent from Loud to Wilson dated 14 January 1946. The OSS personnel records at the National Archives indicate that he also resigned from that service as of the end of January 1946. An undated memo in the Oriental Institute archives gives a new address for Loud in Washington, DC, as of January 1955; it is unclear whether he was still working for the Atlantic Refining Company at that time or had retired.

11. Letter from Nelson to Hamilton dated 3 November 1942, with reply from Hamilton dated 9 February 1943; both in the Israel Antiquities Authority Archives (British Mandate Administrative Files ATQ_7/6 [5th Jacket: 132/126]).

12. Letter from Hamilton to Makhouly dated 2 March 1946; letter from Makhouly to Hamilton dated 20 March 1946; letter from Parker to district officer, Jenin, dated 26 March 1946; letter from Parker to Hamilton dated 30 March 1946; letter from Hamilton to Parker dated 4 April 1946; memo from Hamilton re visit to Megiddo with Parker dated 17 May 1946; note from Hamilton to Parker after visit dated 18 May 1946. All of the above are currently in the Israel Antiquities Authority Archives (British Mandate Administrative Files ATQ_7/6 [5th Jacket: 132/126]).

13. Letter from Shipton to Hamilton dated 14 February 1944, with reply from Hamilton dated 21 February 1944; both are currently in the Israel Antiquities Authority Archives (British Mandate Administrative Files ATQ_7/6 [5th Jacket: 132/126]). See also letter from Parker to Chicago dated 30 June 1952, with reply from Director Kraeling dated 2 July 1952, confirming their arrival. Back in 1930, Woolman had noted in a letter to his parents (31 March 1930) that both Parker and Guy were Masons, and they had had two Masonic visitors that day, who were "officers of the Grand Lodge of England, one of them was the Grand Secretary."

14. Letter to Lind (possibly from his brother Erik) dated 4 February 1948; letter to Lind (from a carpenter named Muk-har) dated 16 April 1948; undated note

from after the end of May 1948, noting that Lind left Haifa on 24 May 1948; all retrieved from the Olof E. Lind papers in the Library of Congress (lccn.loc.gov /mm2014085935). Lind spent the next ten years in Sweden, trying to get financial remuneration for the loss of his land, ten thousand fruit trees, and the money in his bank accounts. Eventually he made his way to the United States in 1957 and settled in Statesboro, Georgia, where he served as a caretaker to Ed DeLoach's elderly father. He then remarried; tried to sell his life story thinly disguised as a novel; became an American citizen in 1967; and died in 1971, the same year as Gordon Loud. See letters from Lind to the Swedish chargé d'affaires in Tel Aviv dated 21 May 1951 and 3 April 1952; letter from Lind to a lawyer in Stockholm dated 25 March 1952; letter from Lind to Judge Etsioni, District Court of Haifa, dated 15 May 1952; letter from Bank Leumi Le-Israel to Lind dated 24 July 1958; letter from Chas. A. Jackson to Lind re book manuscript dated 18 May 1962; letter from Lind to Ed and Florence DeLoach dated 28 July 1966, following the death of the senior Mr. DeLoach; naturalization certificate dated 4 December 1967, in Savannah, Georgia; all retrieved from the Olof E. Lind papers in the Library of Congress (lccn.loc.gov/mm2014085935). Further information from Carol DeLoach Fletcher (personal communication, 7 May 2018) and an obituary in the *Savannah Evening Press* dated 31 October 1971.

15. A primary account of the battle, which took place from 30 to 31 May 1948, is available in Hebrew in Etzioni 1959: 207–9; relevant portions were translated into English by Nurith Goshen and Assaf Yasur-Landau and quoted in Cline and Sutter 2011: 165–67. See also Cline 2000: 169–71. Re Serge Tchoub and his wife, see letter from Parker to Kraeling dated 13 April 1954. I thank Raz Kletter (personal communication, 2 December 2018) for his thoughts and input on these details.

16. See detailed discussion in Cline and Sutter 2011.

17. This initial visit was on 28 June 1948; details and quoted translation come from Kletter 2006: 6, 8–9.

18. This second visit was on 29 July 1948; details come from Kletter 2006: 12–13, 15, fig. 2a–b.

19. Details and quoted translations come from Kletter 2006: 12–13, 15, 28–29.

20. Letter from Parker to Wilson dated 14 October 1949.

21. Letter from the Oriental Institute to the Provisional Government of Israel dated 10 February 1949; letter from Wilson to Parker dated 18 March 1949; letter from Parker to Jacobsen dated March 1949; also letter and list written by Tchoub dated 30 August 1948.

22. Letter from Parker to the Ministry of Foreign Affairs dated 2 June 1949.

23. Letter from Parker to Wilson dated 8 June 1949.

24. Letter from the Prudential Assurance Company Limited (incorporated in England) to Parker dated 29 August 1949; letter from Ministry for Foreign Affairs to Parker dated 5 October 1949; letter from Parker to Ministry for Foreign Affairs dated 13 October 1949; letter from Wilson to Parker dated 9 November 1949; letter from Parker to Wilson dated 2 December 1949.

25. Details and quoted translation come from Kletter 2006: 28–29.

26. Letters from Kraeling to Parker dated 23 March, 4 August, and 15 October 1954; letters from Parker to Kraeling dated 13 April, 13 August, and 23 October 1954. Details re Parker's final years are available via records accessible through Ancesty .com (searching for "Ralph Bernard Parker").

27. Letter from Parker to Wilson dated 8 June 1949; letter from Tchoub to Parker dated 9 September 1954; letters from Parker to Kraeling dated 13 August and 23 October 1954.

28. Details and quoted translation come from Kletter 2006: 29–30, 93, 105.

EPILOGUE

1. Guy 1938; Shipton 1939; Loud 1939; Lamon and Shipton 1939; Loud 1948; letters from Loud to Parker dated 4 and 23 January 1940. A letter from the director of antiquities dated 28 January 1939 acknowledges receipt of Guy's 1938 *Megiddo Tombs* book; a letter from Hamilton to Shipton dated 7 November 1939 thanks him for sending a copy of his pottery book, so it had obviously appeared sometime prior to the beginning of November 1939; similarly, a letter from Ben-Dor to Loud dated 3 January 1940 requests a copy of Lamon and Shipton's *Megiddo I* volume (though he mistakenly lists "Shipton—Engberg" as the authors), so it had obviously been published before the end of 1939 as well; and another letter from Ben-Dor to Loud thanks him for the receipt of his 1939 *Megiddo Ivories* volume. All four letters are in the Israel Antiquities Authority Archives (British Mandate Administrative Files ATQ_7/6 [5th Jacket: 132/126]).

2. Loud 1948: vii.

3. Loud 1948: vii.

4. Loud 1948: vii. Nearly half a century later, Tim Harrison, who was then a graduate student at the University of Chicago and is now a professor at the University of Toronto, did exactly that, working on the Stratum VI material in particular and publishing it in 2004 (Harrison 2004). Doug Esse, who died of cancer in 1992 at the age of forty-two, had initiated the restudy of Stratum VI (see Esse 1992), which Harrison saw to completion. Other scholars have since also been engaged in additional work on other Megiddo materials, including Eliot Braun, who published a volume in 2013 specifically concerned with the East Slope excavations (Braun 2013).

5. Crowfoot 1940: 132–47.

6. Letter from May to Albright dated 5–6 February 1940.

7. Albright 1940, 1943: 2–3n1, 29–30n10.

8. Loud 1948: 116; Wright 1950a: 42, 1950b: 59–60, 1959: 14–15. See also Crowfoot 1940; Albright 1940, 1943: 2–3n1, 29–30n10, 1949; Kempinski 1989: 91; Davis 2004: 62–63, 102.

9. Against this, see now Franklin 2006, who argues that we should simply be talking about Strata V and IV, and reassigns the various buildings accordingly.

10. See Finkelstein 1996a.

11. See, e.g., Yadin 1960, 1966, 1967, 1970, 1973, 1976, 1980; Yadin, Shiloh, and Eitan. 1972; also Dunayevski and Kempinski 1966, 1973; Eitan 1974; Shiloh 1980; Ussishkin 1980. See now Ussishkin 2018: 73–78.

12. See, e.g., Finkelstein and Ussishkin 1994; Silberman et al. 1999; Finkelstein, Ussishkin, and Halpern 2000, 2006; Finkelstein, Ussishkin, and Cline 2013. For an overall summary, see now Ussishkin 2018: 79–105.

Bibliography

MEGIDDO PUBLICATIONS RESULTING FROM THE
ORIENTAL INSTITUTE'S EXCAVATIONS

Braun, Eliot. 2013. *Early Megiddo on the East Slope (The "Megiddo Stages")*. *A Report on the Early Occupation of the East Slope of Megiddo. Results of the Oriental Institute's Excavations, 1925–1933*. Oriental Institute Publications 139. Chicago: University of Chicago.

Engberg, Robert M. 1940. Megiddo: Guardian of the Carmel Pass I. *Biblical Archaeologist* 3, no. 4: 41, 43–51.

Engberg, Robert M. 1941. Megiddo: Guardian of the Carmel Pass II. *Biblical Archaeologist* 4, no. 1: 11–16.

Engberg, Robert M., and Geoffrey M. Shipton. 1934. *Notes on the Chalcolithic and Early Bronze Age Pottery of Megiddo*. Studies in Ancient Oriental Civilization 10. Chicago: University of Chicago Press.

Fisher, Clarence S. 1929. *The Excavation of Armageddon*. Oriental Institute Communications 4. Chicago: University of Chicago.

Guy, Philip Langstaffe Ord. 1931. *New Light from Armageddon. Second Provisional Report (1927–29) on the Excavations at Megiddo in Palestine*. Oriental Institute Communications 9. Chicago: University of Chicago.

Guy, Philip Langstaffe Ord. 1932a. Balloon Photography and Archaeological Excavation. *Antiquity* 6: 148–55.

Guy, Philip Langstaffe Ord. 1932b. Excavations in Palestine, 1931: Megiddo. *Quarterly of the Department of Antiquities in Palestine* 1: 161–62.

Guy, Philip Langstaffe Ord. 1934. Excavations in Palestine, 1932–33: Megiddo. *Quarterly of the Department of Antiquities in Palestine* 3: 178–79.

Guy, Philip Langstaffe Ord. 1938. *Megiddo Tombs*. Oriental Institute Publications 33. Chicago: University of Chicago.

Harrison, Timothy P. 2004. *Megiddo 3. Final Report on the Stratum VI Excavations*. Oriental Institute Publications 127. Chicago: University of Chicago.

Lamon, Robert S. 1935. *The Megiddo Water System*. Oriental Institute Publications 32. Chicago: University of Chicago.

Lamon, Robert S., and Geoffrey M. Shipton. 1939. *Megiddo I. Seasons of 1925–34. Strata I–V*. Oriental Institute Publications 42. Chicago: University of Chicago.

Loud, Gordon. 1938. Excavations in Palestine and Trans-Jordan, 1936–37: Megiddo. *Quarterly of the Department of Antiquities in Palestine* 7: 45–46.

Loud, Gordon. 1938–39. Excavations in Palestine and Trans-Jordan, 1937–38: Megiddo. *Quarterly of the Department of Antiquities in Palestine* 8: 162–63.

Loud, Gordon. 1939. *The Megiddo Ivories*. Oriental Institute Publications 52. Chicago: University of Chicago.

Loud, Gordon. 1941. Excavations in Palestine and Trans-Jordan, 1938–39: Megiddo. *Quarterly of the Department of Antiquities in Palestine* 9: 200–212.

Loud, Gordon. 1948. *Megiddo II. Seasons of 1935–39. Text and Plates*. Oriental Institute Publications 62. Chicago: University of Chicago.

May, Herbert G. 1935. *Material Remains of the Megiddo Cult*. Oriental Institute Publications 26. Chicago: University of Chicago.

Shipton, Geoffrey M. 1939. *Notes on the Megiddo Pottery of Strata VI–XX*. Studies in Ancient Oriental Civilization 17. Chicago: University of Chicago Press.

Shipton, Geoffrey M. 1942. *Guide to Megiddo*. Jerusalem: Department of Antiquities, Government of Palestine.

Staples, William E. 1931. An Inscribed Scaraboid from Megiddo. In *New Light from Armageddon. Second Provisional Report (1927–29) on the Excavations at Megiddo in Palestine*, 49–68. Oriental Institute Communications 9. Chicago: University of Chicago.

REVIEWS OF MEGIDDO PUBLICATIONS RESULTING FROM THE ORIENTAL INSTITUTE'S EXCAVATIONS

Albright, William F. 1940. Review of *Megiddo I: Seasons of 1925–34, Strata I–V* and of *Notes on the Megiddo Pottery of Strata VI–XX*. *American Journal of Archaeology* 44, no. 4: 546–50.

Albright, William F. 1949. Review of *Megiddo II: Seasons of 1935–39*. *American Journal of Archaeology* 53, no. 2: 213–15.

Crowfoot, John W. 1940. Megiddo—A Review. *Palestine Exploration Quarterly* 72, no. 4: 132–47.

Wright, G. Ernest. 1950a. The Discoveries at Megiddo 1935–39. *Biblical Archaeologist* 13, no. 2: 28–46.

Wright, G. Ernest. 1950b. Review of *Megiddo II: Seasons of 1935–39*. *Journal of the American Oriental Society* 70, no. 1: 56–60.

PUBLICATIONS ABOUT JAMES HENRY BREASTED AND OTHER MEGIDDO EXCAVATORS

Abt, Jeffrey. 2011. *American Egyptologist: The Life of James Henry Breasted and the Creation of His Oriental Institute*. Chicago: University of Chicago Press.

Braidwood, Robert, and Douglas Esse. 1988. In Memoriam: Geoffrey M. Shipton, 1910–1987. *Bulletin of the American Schools of Oriental Research* 272: 1–2.

Breasted, Charles. 1947. *Pioneer to the Past: The Story of James Henry Breasted, Archaeologist*. New York: Charles Scribner's Sons.

Green, John D. M. 2009. Archaeology and Politics in the Holy Land: The Life and Career of P.L.O. Guy. *Palestine Exploration Quarterly* 141, no. 3: 167–87.

Green, John D. M. 2015. From Chicago to Jerusalem (and Back Again): The Untold Story of E. F. Beaumont. *The Oriental Institute Notes and News* 227 (Autumn): 15–19.

Larson, John A., ed. 2010. *Letters from James Henry Breasted to His Family, August 1919–July 1920: Letters Home during the Oriental Institute's First Expedition to the Middle East*. Oriental Institute Digital Archives 1. Chicago: University of Chicago.

Wilson, John A. 1936. *Biographical Memoir of James Henry Breasted 1865–1935*. Presented to the Academy at the Autumn Meeting, 1936. National Academy of Sciences of the United States of America. Biographical Memoirs, volume XVIII—Fifth Memoir, 93–121. Washington, DC: National Academy of Sciences.

ADDITIONAL RELEVANT PUBLICATIONS RESULTING FROM THE VARIOUS EXCAVATIONS AT MEGIDDO

Adams, Matthew J. 2017. Djehutihotep and Megiddo in the Early Bronze Age. *Journal of Ancient Egyptian Interconnections* 13: 48–58.

Adams, Matthew J., Jonathan David, and Yotam Tepper. 2014. Excavations at the Camp of the Roman Sixth Ferrata Legion in Israel. *Bible History Daily*, 1 May 2014 (originally published 17 October 2013). Available online at: http://www.biblicalarchaeology.org/daily/biblical-sites-places/biblical-archaeology-sites/legio/.

Aharoni, Yohanan. 1972. The Stratification of Israelite Megiddo. *Journal of Near Eastern Studies* 31: 302–11.

Arie, Eran. 2006. The Iron Age I Pottery: Levels K-5 and K-4 and an Intra-Site Spatial Analysis of the Pottery from Stratum VIA. In *Megiddo IV: The 1998–2002 Seasons*, edited by Israel Finkelstein, David Ussishkin, and Baruch Halpern, 1:191–298. Tel Aviv: Tel Aviv University.

Arie, Eran, Elisabetta Boaretto, Mario A. Martin, Dvory Namdar, Orit Shamir, and Naama Yahalom-Mack. 2019. A New Jewelry Hoard from Eleventh-Century BCE Megiddo. *Near Eastern Archaeology* 82, no. 2: 90–101.

Ashkenazi, Eli. 2009. Discovery of World's Oldest Church May Turn Prison into Tourist Site. *Haaretz*, 7 December 2009. Available online at: http://www.haaretz.com/discovery-of-world-s-oldest-church-may-turn-prison-into-tourist-site-1.2676.

Balter, Michael. 2000. The Two Tels: Armageddon for Biblical Archaeology? *Science* 287, no. 5450: 31–32.

Belkin, Lawrence A., and Eileen F. Wheeler. 2006. Reconstruction of the Megiddo Stables. In *Megiddo IV: The 1998–2002 Seasons*, edited by Israel Finkelstein, David Ussishkin, and Baruch Halpern, 2:666–87. Tel Aviv: Tel Aviv University.

Ben Zion, Ilan. 2015. In First, Imperial Roman Legionary Camp Uncovered near Megiddo. *Times of Israel*, 7 July 2015. Available online at: http://www.timesofisrael.com/in-first-imperial-roman-legionary-camp-uncovered-near-megiddo/.

Benzinger, Immanuel. 1904. Die Ausgrabungen auf dem Tell el-Mutesellim. VI. Die Ausgrabungen im Herbst 1903. *Mittheilungen und Nachrichten des Deutschen Palästina-Vereins*, 65–74.

Böhme, Sabine. 2014. "Alltägliches aus Megiddo." Die ersten Funde, ihr Ausgräber, und Berlin. *Antike Welt* 45, no. 5: 41–43.

Bonfil, Ruhama. 2012. Did Thutmose III's Troops Encounter Megiddo X? In *All the Wisdom of the East: Studies in Near Eastern Archaeology and History in Honor of Eliezer D. Oren*, edited by Mayer I. Gruber, Shmuel Ahituv, Gunnar Lehmann, and Zipora Talshir, 129–55. Orbis Biblicus et Orientalis 255. Göttingen: Vandenhoeck & Ruprecht.

Breasted, James H. 1920. The First Expedition of the Oriental Institute of the University of Chicago. *Journal of the American Oriental Society* 40: 282–85.

Breasted, James H. 1922. The Oriental Institute of the University of Chicago: A Beginning and a Program. *American Journal of Semitic Languages and Literatures* 38: 233–328.

Breasted, James H. 1926. Luxor and Armageddon: The Expansion of the Oriental Institute of the University of Chicago. *Art and Archaeology: The Arts throughout the Ages* 22: 155–66.

Breasted, James H. 1928. Armageddon Excavations: The Megiddo Expedition. In *Handbook of the Oriental Institute of the University of Chicago*, 18–24. Chicago: University of Chicago Press.

Breasted, James H. 1931. The Megiddo (Palestine) Expedition. In *Handbook of the Oriental Institute of the University of Chicago*, 38–49. 3rd rev. ed. Chicago: University of Chicago Press.

Cantrell, Deborah O. 2006. Stable Issues. In *Megiddo IV: The 1998–2002 Seasons*, edited by Israel Finkelstein, David Ussishkin, and Baruch Halpern, 2:630–42. Tel Aviv: Tel Aviv University.

Cantrell, Deborah O., and Israel Finkelstein. 2006. A Kingdom for a Horse: The Megiddo Stables and Eighth Century Israel. In *Megiddo IV: The 1998–2002 Seasons*, edited by Israel Finkelstein, David Ussishkin, and Baruch Halpern, 2:643–65. Tel Aviv: Tel Aviv University.

Cline, Eric H. 2006. Chapter 8: Area L (The 1998–2000 Seasons) and Chapter 8: Appendix: The 2004 Season (with Margaret E. Cohen). In *Megiddo IV: The 1998–2002 Seasons*, edited by Israel Finkelstein, David Ussishkin, and Baruch Halpern, 1:104–29. Tel Aviv: Tel Aviv University.

Cline, Eric H. 2011. Whole Lotta Shakin' Going On: The Possible Destruction by Earthquake of Megiddo Stratum VIA. In *The Fire Signals of Lachish: Studies in the Archaeology and History of Israel in the Late Bronze Age, Iron Age, and Persian Period in Honor of David Ussishkin*, edited by Israel Finkelstein and Nadav Na'aman, 55–70. Tel Aviv: Tel Aviv University.

Cline, Eric H. 2017b. "English Lady Owns Armageddon": Rosamond Templeton, Laurence Oliphant, and Tell El-Mutesellim. In *Rethinking Israel: Studies in the History and Archaeology of Ancient Israel in Honor of Israel Finkelstein*, edited by Oded Lipschits, Yuval Gadot, and Matthew J. Adams, 47–56. Winona Lake, IN: Eisenbrauns.

Cline, Eric H., and Inbal Samet. 2013. Chapter 6: Area L. In *Megiddo V: The 2004–2008 Seasons*, edited by Israel Finkelstein, David Ussishkin, and Eric H. Cline, 1:275–85. Tel Aviv: Tel Aviv University.

Cline, Eric H., and Anthony Sutter. 2011. Battlefield Archaeology at Armageddon: Cartridge Cases and the 1948 Battle for Megiddo, Israel. *Journal of Military History* 75, no. 1: 159–90.

Conder, Claude R. 1873. The Survey of Palestine. VII. The Plain of Esdraelon. *Palestine Exploration Quarterly* 5–6: 3–10.

Conder, Claude R. 1877. Megiddo. *Palestine Exploration Quarterly* 9, no. 1: 13–20.

Cradic, Melissa S. 2017. Embodiments of Death: The Funerary Sequence and Commemoration in the Bronze Age Levant. *Bulletin of the American Schools of Oriental Research* 377: 219–48.

Dunayevski, Immanuel, and Aharon Kempinski. 1966. Megiddo. *Israel Exploration Journal* 16, no. 2: 142.

Dunayevski, Immanuel, and Aharon Kempinski. 1973. The Megiddo Temples. *Zeitschrift des Deutschen Palästina-Vereins* 89, no. 2: 161–87.

Eitan, Abraham. 1974. Megiddo. *Israel Exploration Journal* 24: 275–76.

Epstein, Claire. 1965. An Interpretation of the Megiddo Sacred Area during Middle Bronze II. *Israel Exploration Journal* 15, no. 4: 204–21.

Erman, Adolf, and Emil Kautzsch. 1906. Ein Siegelstein mit hebräischer Unterschrift vom Tell el-Mutesellim. *Mittheilungen und Nachrichten des Deutschen Palästina-Vereins*, 33–34.

Esse, Douglas L. 1992. The Collared Pithos at Megiddo: Ceramic Distribution and Ethnicity. *Journal of Near Eastern Studies* 51, no. 2: 81–103.

Feldman, Marian. 2009. Hoarded Treasures: The Megiddo Ivories and the End of the Bronze Age. *Levant* 41, no. 2: 175–94.

Finkelstein, Israel. 1996b. The Stratigraphy and Chronology of Megiddo and Beth-Shan in the 12th–11th Centuries B.C.E. *Tel Aviv* 23, no. 2: 170–84.

Finkelstein, Israel. 2009. Destructions: Megiddo as a Case Study. In *Exploring the Longue Durée, Essays in Honor of Lawrence E. Stager*, edited by David J. Schloen, 113–26. Winona Lake, IN: Eisenbrauns.

Finkelstein, Israel, Eran Arie, Mario A. S. Martin, and Eli Piasetzky. 2017. [= Finkelstein et al. 2017a]. New Evidence on the Late Bronze/Iron I Transition at Megiddo: Implications for the End of the Egyptian Rule and the Appearance of Philistine Pottery. *Egypt and the Levant* 27: 261–80.

Finkelstein, Israel, Dafna Langgut, Meirav Meiri, and Lidar Sapir-Hen. 2017. [= Finkelstein et al. 2017b]. Egyptian Imperial Economy in Canaan: Reaction to the Climate Crisis at the End of the Late Bronze Age. *Egypt and the Levant* 27: 249–59.

Finkelstein, Israel, and David Ussishkin. 1994. Back to Megiddo. *Biblical Archaeology Review* 20, no. 1: 26–43.

Finkelstein, Israel, and David Ussishkin. 2000. Archaeological and Historical Conclusions. In *Megiddo III: The 1992–1996 Seasons*, edited by Israel Finkelstein, David Ussishkin, and Baruch Halpern, 2:576–605. Tel Aviv: Tel Aviv University.

Finkelstein, Israel, David Ussishkin, and Baruch Halpern, eds. 2000. *Megiddo III: The 1992–1996 Seasons*. Vols. 1–2. Tel Aviv: Tel Aviv University.

Finkelstein, Israel, David Ussishkin, and Baruch Halpern, eds. 2006. *Megiddo IV: The 1998–2002 Seasons*. Vols. 1–2 Tel Aviv: Tel Aviv University.

Finkelstein, Israel, David Ussishkin, and Eric H. Cline, eds. 2013. *Megiddo V: The 2004–2008 Seasons*. Vols. 1–3. Tel Aviv: Tel Aviv University.

Franklin, Norma. 2000. Relative and Absolute Chronology of Gallery 629 and the Megiddo Water System: A Reassessment. In *Megiddo III: The 1992–1996 Seasons*, edited by Israel Finkelstein, David Ussishkin, and Baruch Halpern, 2:515–23. Tel Aviv: Tel Aviv University.

Franklin, Norma. 2001. Masons' Marks from the Ninth Century BCE Northern Kingdom of Israel: Evidence of the Nascent Carian Alphabet? *Kadmos* 40, no. 2: 107–16.

Franklin, Norma. 2006. Revealing Stratum V at Megiddo. *Bulletin of the American Schools of Oriental Research* 342: 95–111.

Franklin, Norma. 2013. Who Really Built the Water System at Megiddo? ASOR Blog post, 8 October 2013. Available online at: http://www.asor.org/anetoday/2013/10/who-really-built-the-water-system-at-megiddo/.

Franklin, Norma. 2017. Entering the Arena: The Megiddo Stables Reconsidered. In *Rethinking Israel: Studies in the History and Archaeology of Ancient Israel in Honor of Israel Finkelstein*, edited by Oded Lipschits, Yuval Gadot, and Matthew J. Adams, 87–101. Winona Lake, IN: Eisenbrauns.

Franklin, Norma. 2019a. Megiddo's Stables: Trading Egyptian Horses to the Assyrian Empire. TheTorah.com, 3 September 2019. https://thetorah.com/megiddos-stables-trading-egyptian-horses-to-the-assyrian-empire/.

Franklin, Norma. 2019b. Megiddo and Jezreel Reflected in the Dying Embers of the Northern Kingdom of Israel. In *The Last Days of the Kingdom of Israel*, edited by Shuichi Hasegawa, Christoph Levin, and Karen Radner, 189–208. Beihefte zur Zeitschrift für die alttestamentliche Wissenschaft, Band 511. Berlin: de Gruyter.

Gadot, Yuval, Mario Martin, Noga Blockman, and Eran Arie. 2006. Area K (Levels K-5 and K-4, The 1998–2002 Seasons). In *Megiddo IV: The 1998–2002 Seasons*, edited by Israel Finkelstein, David Ussishkin, and Baruch Halpern, 1:87–103. Tel Aviv: Tel Aviv University.

Gadot, Yuval, and Assaf Yasur-Landau. 2006. Beyond Finds: Reconstructing Life in the Courtyard Building of Level K-4. In *Megiddo IV: The 1998–2002 Seasons*, edited by Israel Finkelstein, David Ussishkin, and Baruch Halpern, 2:583–600. Tel Aviv: Tel Aviv University.

Greenberg, Jonathan D. 2005. "Megiddo Tombs: Bones of Armageddon." Senior honors thesis in archaeology. Washington, DC: George Washington University.

Hall, Erin. 2016. "Hoarding at Tel Megiddo in the Late Bronze Age and Iron Age I." MA thesis. Tel Aviv: Tel Aviv University.

Halpern, Baruch. 2000. Centre and Sentry: Megiddo's Role in Transit, Administration and Trade. In *Megiddo III: The 1992–1996 Seasons*, edited by Israel Finkelstein, David Ussishkin, and Baruch Halpern, 2:535–75. Tel Aviv: Tel Aviv University.

Harrison, Timothy P. 2003. The Battleground: Who Destroyed Megiddo? Was It David or Shishak? *Biblical Archaeology Review* 29, no. 6: 28–35, 60–64.

Hasson, Nir. 2012. Megiddo Dig Unearths Cache of Buried Canaanite Treasure. *Haaretz*, 22 May 2012. Available online at: http://www.haaretz.com/israel-news/megiddo-dig-unearths-cache-of-buried-canaanite-treasure-1.431797.

Joffe, Alexander H., Eric H. Cline, and Oded Lipschitz. 2000. Area H. In *Megiddo III: The 1992–1996 Seasons*, edited by Israel Finkelstein, David Ussishkin, and Baruch Halpern, 1:140–60. Tel Aviv: Tel Aviv University.

Kautzsch, Emil. 1904. Ein althebräisches Siegel vom Tell el-Mutesellim. *Mittheilungen und Nachrichten des Deutschen Palästina-Vereins*, 1–14.

Keinan, Adi. 2007. "The Megiddo Picture Pavement: Evidence for Egyptian Presence in Northern Israel during Early Bronze Age I." MA thesis. Tel Aviv: Tel Aviv University (in Hebrew).

Keinan, Adi. 2013. Chapter 2, Pt. II: Sub-Area Lower J. In *Megiddo V: The 2004–2008 Seasons*, edited by Israel Finkelstein, David Ussishkin, and Eric H. Cline, 1:28–46. Tel Aviv: Tel Aviv University.

Kempinski, Aharon. 1989. *Megiddo. A City State and Royal Centre in North Israel*. Munich: C. H. Beck.

Lehmann, Gunnar, and Ann E. Killebrew. 2010. Palace 6000 at Megiddo in Context: Iron Age Central Hall Tetra-Partite Residencies and the "Bit-Hilani" Building Tradition in the Levant. *Bulletin of the American Schools of Oriental Research* 359: 13–33.

Marco, Shmuel, Amotz Agnon, Israel Finkelstein, and David Ussishkin. 2006. Megiddo Earthquakes. In *Megiddo IV: The 1998–2002 Seasons*, edited by Israel Finkelstein, David Ussishkin, and Baruch Halpern, 2:568–75. Tel Aviv: Tel Aviv University.

Martin, Mario A. S. 2017. The Fate of Megiddo at the End of the Late Bronze IIB. In *Rethinking Israel: Studies in the History and Archaeology of Ancient Israel in Honor of Israel Finkelstein*, edited by Oded Lipschits, Yuval Gadot, and Matthew J. Adams, 267–86. Winona Lake, IN: Eisenbrauns.

McGreal, Chris. 2005. Holy Land's 'Oldest Church' Found at Armageddon. *Guardian*, 7 November 2005. Available online at: http://www.theguardian.com/world/2005/nov/07/israel.artsnews.

Myre, Greg. 2005. Israeli Prisoners Dig Their Way to Early Christianity. *New York Times*, 7 November 2005. Available online at: http://www.nytimes.com/2005/11/07/world/middleeast/israeli-prisoners-dig-their-way-to-early-christianity.html?_r=0.

Niemann, H. Michael, and Gunnar Lehmann. 2006a. One Hundred Years after Gottlieb Schumacher, Carl Watzinger and Excavations at Megiddo with an Extract from Emil Kautzsch's Diary about His Visit to Megiddo in 1904. In *Megiddo IV: The 1998–2002 Seasons*, edited by Israel Finkelstein, David Ussishkin, and Baruch Halpern, 2:688–702. Tel Aviv: Tel Aviv University.

Niemann, H. Michael, and Gunnar Lehmann. 2006b. Gottlieb Schumacher, Carl Watzinger und der Beginn der Ausgrabungen in Megiddo: Rückblick und Konsequenzen nach 100 Jahren. In *Palaestina exploranda: Studien zur Erforschung Palästinas im 19. Und 20. Jahrhundert anläßlich des 125jährigen Bestehens des Deutschen Vereins zur Erforschung Palästinas*, edited by Ulrich Hübner, 174–203. Wiesbaden: Harrassowitz Verlag.

Nigro, Lorenzo. 1994. The "Nordburg" of Megiddo: A New Reconstruction on the Basis of Schumacher's Plan. *Bulletin of the American Schools of Oriental Research* 293: 15–29.

Peersmann, Jennifer. 2000. Assyrian Magiddu: The Town Planning of Stratum III. In *Megiddo III: The 1992–1996 Seasons*, edited by Israel Finkelstein, David Ussishkin, and Baruch Halpern, 2:524–34. Tel Aviv: Tel Aviv University.

Pincus, Jessie, Tim DeSmet, Yotam Tepper, and Matthew J. Adams. 2013. Ground Penetrating Radar and Electromagnetic Archaeogeophysical Investigations at the Roman Legionary Camp at Legio, Israel. *Archaeological Prospection* 20, no. 3: 1–13.

Poolman, Laurel A. 2014. "An Isotopic Perspective on Internationalism in the Late Bronze Age Levant: Stable Strontium and Oxygen Isotopic Analyses from Tel Megiddo, Israel." Senior honors thesis in archaeology. Washington, DC: George Washington University.

Pritchard, James B. 1970. The Megiddo Stables: A Reassessment. In *Near Eastern Archaeology in the Twentieth Century*, edited by James A. Sanders, 268–75. Garden City, NY: Doubleday and Co.

Reich, Ronny. 2003. The Stratigraphic Relationship between Palaces 1369 and 1052 (Stratum III) at Megiddo. *Bulletin of the American Schools of Oriental Research* 331: 39–44.

Samet, Inbal. 2009. "Canaanite Rulership in Late Bronze Age Megiddo." MA thesis. Tel Aviv: Tel Aviv University.

Sapir-Hen, Lidar, Mario A. S. Martin, and Israel Finkelstein. 2017. Food Rituals and Their Social Significance in the Mid-Second Millennium BC in the Southern Levant: A View from Megiddo. *International Journal of Osteoarchaeology*; published online (DOI: 10.1002/oa.2629).

Sapir-Hen, Lidar, Aharon Sasson, Assaf Kleiman, and Israel Finkelstein. 2016. Social Stratification in the Late Bronze and Early Iron Ages: An Intra-Site Investigation at Megiddo. *Oxford Journal of Archaeology* 35, no. 1: 47–73.

Schumacher, Gottlieb B. 1904a. Die Ausgrabungen auf dem Tell el-Mutesellim. I. Die Einrichtung der Arbeit. *Mittheilungen und Nachrichten des Deutschen Palästina-Vereins*, 14–20.

Schumacher, Gottlieb B. 1904b. Die Ausgrabungen auf dem Tell el-Mutesellim. II. Der Tell el-Mutesellim und die Chirbet el-Leddschön. *Mittheilungen und Nachrichten des Deutschen Palästina-Vereins*, 33–56.

Schumacher, Gottlieb B. 1905a. Die Ausgrabungen auf dem Tell el-Mutesellim. VII. Die Ausgrabungen im Frühjahr 1904. *Mittheilungen und Nachrichten des Deutschen Palästina-Vereins*, 1–16.

Schumacher, Gottlieb B. 1905b. Die Ausgrabungen auf dem Tell el-Mutesellim. VII. Die Ausgrabungen im Frühjahr 1904 (Fortsetzung und Schluss). *Mittheilungen und Nachrichten des Deutschen Palästina-Vereins*, 17–26.

Schumacher, Gottlieb B. 1905c. Die Ausgrabungen auf dem Tell el-Mutesellim. VIII. Die Ausgrabungen im Herbst 1904. *Mittheilungen und Nachrichten des Deutschen Palästina-Vereins*, 81–82.

Schumacher, Gottlieb B. 1906a. Die Ausgrabungen auf dem Tell el-Mutesellim. VIII. Die Ausgrabungen im Herbst 1904 (Fortsetzung und Schluss). *Mittheilungen und Nachrichten des Deutschen Palästina-Vereins*, 1–14.

Schumacher, Gottlieb B. 1906b. Die Ausgrabungen auf dem Tell el-Mutesellim. IX. Die Ausgrabungen im Frühjahr 1905. *Mittheilungen und Nachrichten des Deutschen Palästina-Vereins*, 17–30.

Schumacher, Gottlieb B. 1906c. Die Ausgrabungen auf dem Tell el-Mutesellim. X. Die Ausgrabungen im Sommer und Herbst 1905. *Mittheilungen und Nachrichten des Deutschen Palästina-Vereins*, 35–64.

Schumacher, Gottlieb B. 1906d. Die Ausgrabungen auf dem Tell el-Mutesellim. X. Die Ausgrabungen im Sommer und Herbst 1905 (Schluss). *Mittheilungen und Nachrichten des Deutschen Palästina-Vereins*, 65–70.

Schumacher, Gottlieb B. 1908. *Tell el-Mutesellim: Bericht über die 1903 bis 1905 mit Unterstützung Sr. Majestät des Deutschen Kaisers und der Deutschen Orient-gesellschaft vom Deutschen Verein zur Erforschung Palästinas veranstalteten Ausgrabungen. Band I: Fundbericht.* Leipzig: Rudolf Haupt.

Shahack-Gross, Ruth, Ron Shaar, Erez Hassul, Yael Ebert, Mathilde Forget, Norbert Nowaczyk, Shmuel Marco, Israel Finkelstein, and Amotz Agnon. 2018. Fire and Collapse: Untangling the Formation of Destruction Layers Using Archaeomagnetism. *Geoarchaeology*, 1–16.

Shiloh, Yigal. 1980. Solomon's Gate at Megiddo as Recorded by Its Excavator, R. Lamon, Chicago. *Levant* 12: 69–76.

Silberman, Neil A., Israel Finkelstein, David Ussishkin, and Baruch Halpern. 1999. Digging at Armageddon. *Archaeology*, November/December, 32–39.

Singer, Itamar. 1988. Megiddo Mentioned in a Letter from Bogazköy. In *Documentum Asiae Minoris Antiquae (Festschrift Heinrich Otten)*, edited by Erich Neu and Christel Rüster, 327–32. Wiesbaden: Otto Harrassowitz.

Singer, Itamar. 1988–89. The Political Status of Megiddo VIIA. *Tel Aviv* 15–16: 101–12.

Singer, Itamar. 1995. A Hittite Seal from Megiddo. *Biblical Archaeologist* 58, no. 2: 91–93.

Singer-Avitz, Lily. 2014. The Pottery of Megiddo Strata III–II and a Proposed Subdivision of the Iron IIC Period in Northern Israel. *Bulletin of the American Schools of Oriental Research* 372: 123–45.

Suter, Claudia E. 1999–2000. The Hittite Seal from Megiddo. *Aula Orientalis* 17–18: 421–30.

Tepper, Yotam. 2002. Lajjun–Legio in Israel: Results of a Survey in and around the Military Camp Area. In *Limes XVIII: Proceedings of the XVIIIth International Congress of Roman Frontier Studies Held in Amman, Jordan (September 2000)*, edited by Philip Freeman, Julian Bennett, Zbigniew T. Fiema, and Birgitta Hoffmann, 231–42. British Archaeological Reports S1084. Oxford: British Archaeological Reports.

Tepper, Yotam. 2003a. Survey of the Legio Region. *Hadashot Arkheologiyot—Excavations and Surveys in Israel* 115: 29*–31*.

Tepper, Yotam. 2003b. "Survey of the Legio Area near Megiddo: Historical and Geographical Research." MA thesis. Tel Aviv: Tel Aviv University (in Hebrew).

Tepper, Yotam. 2007. The Roman Legionary Camp at Legio, Israel: Results of an Archaeological Survey and Observations on the Roman Military Presence at the Site. In *The Late Roman Army in the Near East from Diocletian to the Arab Conquest: Proceedings of a Colloquium Held at Potenza, Acerenza and Matera, Italy (May 2005)*, edited by Ariel S. Lewin and Pietrina Pellegrini, 57–71. BAR International Series 1717. Oxford: ArchaeoPress.

Tepper, Yotam, and Di Segni, Leah. 2006. *A Christian Prayer Hall of the Third Century CE at Kefar 'Othnay (Legio). Excavations at the Megiddo Prison 2005.* Jerusalem: Israel Antiquities Authority.

Tobler, Arthur J. 1950. *Excavations at Tepe Gawra.* Vol. 2, *Levels IX–XX.* Philadelphia: University of Pennsylvania Press.

Toffolo, Michael B., Eran Arie, Mario A. S. Martin, Elisabetta Boaretto, and Israel Finkelstein. 2014. Absolute Chronology of Megiddo, Israel, in the Late Bronze and Iron Ages: High-Resolution Radiocarbon Dating. *Radiocarbon* 56, no. 1: 221–44.

Tzaferis, Vassilios. 2007. Inscribed "To God Jesus Christ": Early Christian Prayer Hall Found in Megiddo Prison. *Biblical Archaeology Review* 33, no. 2: 42–43, 46.

Ussishkin, David. 1966. King Solomon's Palace and Building 1723 in Megiddo. *Israel Exploration Journal* 16, no. 3: 174–86.

Ussishkin, David. 1973. King Solomon's Palaces. *Biblical Archaeologist* 36: 78–105.

Ussishkin, David. 1980. Was the Solomonic City Gate at Megiddo Built by King Solomon? *Bulletin of the American Schools of Oriental Research* 239: 1–18.

Ussishkin, David. 1990. Notes on Megiddo, Gezer, Ashdod, and Tel Batash in the Tenth to Ninth Centuries B.C. *Bulletin of the American Schools of Oriental Research* 277, no. 278: 71–91.

Ussishkin, David. 1995. The Destruction of Megiddo at the End of the Late Bronze Age and Its Historical Significance. *Tel Aviv* 22, no. 2: 240–67.

Ussishkin, David. 2015. The Sacred Area of Early Bronze Megiddo: History and Interpretation. *Bulletin of the American Schools of Oriental Research* 373: 69–104.

Ussishkin, David. 2018. *Megiddo-Armageddon: The Story of the Canaanite and Israelite City.* Jerusalem: Israel Exploration Society/Biblical Archaeological Society.

Wapnish, Paula, and Brian Hesse. 2000. Mammal Remains from the Early Bronze Sacred Compound. In *Megiddo III: The 1992–1996 Seasons,* edited by Israel Finkelstein, David Ussishkin, and Baruch Halpern, 2:429–62. Tel Aviv: Tel Aviv University.

Watzinger, Carl. 1929. *Tell el-Mutesellim: Bericht über die 1903 bis 1905 mit Unterstützung Sr. Majestät des Deutschen Kaisers und der Deutschen Orient-gesellschaft vom Deutschen Verein zur Erforschung Palästinas veranstalteten Ausgrabungen. Band II: Die Funde.* Leipzig: J. C. Hinrichs.

Weintraub, Pamela. 2015. Rewriting Tel Megiddo's Violent History. *Discover,* 1 October, 1–20. Available online at: http://discovermagazine.com/2015/nov/14-witness-to-armageddon.

Wightman, Greg J. 1985. Megiddo VIA–III: Associated Structures and Chronology. *Levant* 17: 117–29.

Wightman, Greg J. 1990. The Myth of Solomon. *Bulletin of the American Schools of Oriental Research* 277, no. 278: 5–22.

Wilson, John A. 1938. The Megiddo Ivories. *American Journal of Archaeology* 42, no. 3: 333–36.

Wilson, John A. 1968–69. "A Jubilee Shall That Fiftieth Year Be unto You" (Lev. 25:11). In *The Oriental Institute Report for 1968/69 (Fiftieth Anniversary, 1919–1969),* 6–12. Chicago: The Oriental Institute.

Wilson, Scott. 2005. Site May Be 3rd-Century Place of Christian Worship. *Washington Post,* 7 November. Available online at: http://www.washingtonpost.com/wp-dyn/content/article/2005/11/06/AR2005110600478.html.

Woolman, David C. n.d. "In the Shadow of Armageddon: The Megiddo Memoir of an American Architect in Palestine, 1929–1930." Unpublished manuscript.

Wright, G. Ernest. 1959. Israelite Samaria and Iron Age Chronology. *Bulletin of the American Schools of Oriental Research* 155: 13–29.

Yadin, Yigael. 1960. New Light on Solomon's Megiddo. *Biblical Archaeologist* 23, no. 2: 62–68.

Yadin, Yigael. 1966. Megiddo. *Israel Exploration Journal* 16, no. 4: 178–80.

Yadin, Yigael. 1967. Megiddo. *Israel Exploration Journal* 17, no. 2) 119–21.

Yadin, Yigael. 1970. Megiddo of the Kings of Israel. *Biblical Archaeologist* 33: 66–96.

Yadin, Yigael. 1973. A Note on the Stratigraphy of Israelite Megiddo. *Journal of Near Eastern Studies* 32, no. 3: 330.

Yadin, Yigael. 1976. In Defense of the Stables at Megiddo. *Biblical Archaeology Review* 2: 18–22.

Yadin, Yigael. 1980. A Rejoinder to Ussishkin's Solomonic City Gate. *Bulletin of the American Schools of Oriental Research* 239: 19–23.

Yadin, Yigael, Yigael Shiloh, and Abraham Eitan. 1972. Megiddo. *Israel Exploration Journal* 22, nos. 2/3: 161–64.

Yasur-Landau, Assaf, and Inbal Samet. 2017. Resilience and the Canaanite Palatial System: The Case of Megiddo. In *Rethinking Israel: Studies in the History and Archaeology of Ancient Israel in Honor of Israel Finkelstein*, edited by Oded Lipschits, Yuval Gadot, and Matthew J. Adams, 463–81. Winona Lake, IN: Eisenbrauns.

Zarzecki-Peleg, Anabel. 2005. "Tel Megiddo during the Iron Age I and IIA IIB: The Excavations of the Yadin Expedition at Megiddo and Their Contribution for Comprehending the History of This Site and Other Contemporary Sites in Northern Israel." PhD diss., Hebrew University of Jerusalem (in Hebrew).

Zarzecki-Peleg, Anabel. 2016. *Yadin's Expedition to Megiddo. Final Report of the Archaeological Excavations (1960, 1966, 1967, and 1971/2 Season). Text and Plans.* Qedem 56. Jerusalem: Hebrew University of Jerusalem, Institute of Archaeology.

OTHER RELEVANT PUBLICATIONS CITED IN THE TEXT AND ENDNOTES

Adler, Wolfgang. 1994. *Kāmid el-Lōz: Das "Schatzhaus" im Palastbereich: die Befunde de Königsgrabes. SBA* 47. Bonn: Habelt.

Albright, William F. 1932. *The Excavation of Tell Beit Mirsim in Palestine.* Vol. 1, *The Pottery of the First Three Campaigns.* New Haven, CT: Yale University Press.

Albright, William F. 1943. *The Excavation of Tell Beit Mirsim.* Vol. 3, *The Iron Age.* Annual of the American Schools of Oriental Research 21/22. New Haven, CT: American Schools of Oriental Research.

Aleksandrowicz, Or. 2015. "Architecture's Unwanted Child: Building Climatology in Israel, 1940–1977." PhD diss., Vienna: Institut für Architekturwissenschaften.

Armstrong, Karen. 1996. *Jerusalem: One City, Three Faiths.* New York: Alfred A. Knopf.

Barag, Dan. 1966. The Effects of the Tennes Rebellion on Palestine. *Bulletin of the American Schools of Oriental Research* 183: 6–12.

Barnett, Richard D. 1982. *Ancient Ivories in the Middle East.* Qedem 14. Jerusalem: Hebrew University of Jerusalem, Institute of Archaeology.

Beevor, Antony. 1991. *Crete: The Battle and the Resistance.* London, J. Murray.

Bethell, Nicholas. 1979. *The Palestine Triangle: The Struggle between the British, the Jews and the Arabs, 1935–48.* New York: G. P. Putnam's Sons.

Black, Ian, and Benny Morris. 1991. *Israel's Secret Wars: A History of Israel's Intelligence Services.* New York: Grove Weidenfeld.

Blenkinsopp, Joseph. 2002. The Babylonian Gap Revisited: There Was No Gap. *Biblical Archaeology Review* 28, no. 3.

Braund, H.E.W. 1975. *Calling to Mind: Being Some Account of the First Hundred Years (1870–1970) of Steel Brothers and Company Limited.* Oxford: Pergamon Press.

Brocker, Jacqueline. 2006. "Popular History and the Desire for Knowledge: An Examination of James A. Michener's *The Source* as a Popular History of Israel." BA honours thesis. Sydney: University of Sydney.

Cantrell, Deborah O. 2011. *The Horsemen of Israel. Horses and Chariotry in Monarchic Israel (Ninth–Eighth Centuries B.C.E.).* Winona Lake, IN: Eisenbrauns.

Casey, Bart. 2015. *The Double Life of Laurence Oliphant: Victorian Pilgrim and Prophet.* New York: Post Hill Press.

Chapman, Rupert L., III. 2009. Putting Sheshonq I in His Place. *Palestine Exploration Quarterly* 141, no. 1: 4–17.

Chapman, Rupert L., III. 2015. Samaria and Megiddo: Shishak and Solomon. In *Solomon and Shishak: Current Perspectives from Archaeology, Epigraphy, History and Chronology. Proceedings of the Third BICANE Colloquium Held at Sidney Sussex College, Cambridge 26–27 March, 2011*, edited by Peter James and Peter G. van der Veen, 137–47. BAR International Series 2732. Oxford: Archaeopress.

Cline, Eric H. 2000. *The Battles of Armageddon: Megiddo and the Jezreel Valley from the Bronze Age to the Nuclear Age*. Ann Arbor: University of Michigan Press.

Cline, Eric H. 2004. *Jerusalem Besieged: From Ancient Canaan to Modern Israel*. Ann Arbor: University of Michigan Press.

Cline, Eric H. 2007. *From Eden to Exile: Unraveling Mysteries of the Bible*. Washington, DC: National Geographic Books.

Cline, Eric H. 2009. *Biblical Archaeology: A Very Short Introduction*. New York: Oxford University Press.

Cline, Eric H. 2013. *The Trojan War: A Very Short Introduction*. New York: Oxford University Press.

Cline, Eric H. 2014. *1177 BC: The Year Civilization Collapsed*. Princeton, NJ: Princeton University Press.

Cline, Eric H. 2017a. *Three Stones Make a Wall: The Story of Archaeology*. Princeton, NJ: Princeton University Press.

Cohen, Getzel M., and Martha Sharp Joukowsky, eds. 2004. *Breaking Ground: Pioneering Women Archaeologists*. Ann Arbor: University of Michigan Press.

Cohen, Michael J. 2014. *Britain's Moment in Palestine: Retrospect and Perspectives, 1917–1948*. Routledge: Boston.

Conder, Claude R. 1879. *Tent Work in Palestine. A Record of Discovery and Adventure*. Vols. 1–3. London: Richard Bentley & Son.

Conder, Claude R., and Horatio H. Kitchener. 1882. *The Survey of Western Palestine. Memoirs of the Topography, Orography, Hydrography, and Archaeology*. Vol. 2, *(Sheets VII.–XVI. Samaria*. London: Palestine Exploration Fund.

Davis, Miriam C. 2008. *Dame Kathleen Kenyon: Digging Up the Holy Land*. Walnut Creek, CA: Left Coast Press.

Davis, Thomas W. 2004. *Shifting Sands: The Rise and Fall of Biblical Archaeology*. Oxford: Oxford University Press.

Donaldson, James. 2015. The J. H. Iliffe Collection and the Archaeology of Mandate-Era Palestine. *Nova*, July, 7–11.

Drower, Margaret S. 1985. *Flinders Petrie: A Life in Archaeology*. London: Victor Gollancz.

Dunston, Lara. 2016. Revealed: Cambodia's Vast Medieval Cities Hidden beneath the Jungle. *Guardian*, 10 June. Available online at: https://www.theguardian.com/world/2016/jun/11/lost-city-medieval-discovered-hidden-beneath-cambodian-jungle.

Etzioni, Binyamin, ed. 1959. *Tree and Sword: The Route of Battle of the Golani Brigade*. Tel Aviv: Ma'arakhot Publishing (in Hebrew).

Eyal, Gil. 2002. Dangerous Liaisons between Military Intelligence and Middle Eastern Studies in Israel. *Theory and Society* 31, no. 5: 653–93.

Finch, David. 2002. *Field Notes: The Story of the Canadian Society of Petroleum Geologists*. Calgary: Canadian Society of Petroleum Geologists.

Finkelstein, Israel. 1996a. The Archaeology of the United Monarchy: An Alternative View. *Levant* 28: 177–87.

Finkelstein, Israel. 1999. Hazor and the North in the Iron Age: A Low Chronology Perspective. *Bulletin of the American Schools of Oriental Research* 314: 55–70.

Finkelstein, Israel. 2002. The Campaign of Shoshenq I to Palestine: A Guide to the 10th Century BCE Polity. *Zeitschrift des Deutschen Palästina-Vereins* 118, no. 2: 109–35.

Finkelstein, Israel. 2011. Stages in the Territorial Expansion of the Northern Kingdom. *Vetus Testamentum* 61: 227–42.

Finkelstein, Israel. 2013. *The Forgotten Kingdom: The Archaeology and History of Northern Israel*. Atlanta, GA: Society of Biblical Literature.

Finkelstein, Israel, and Eli Piasetzky. 2008. Radiocarbon Dating and the Late-Iron I in Northern Canaan: A New Proposal. *Ugarit-Forschung* 39 (2007; appeared 2008): 247–60.

Fischer, Erika. 2007. *Ägyptische und ägyptisierende Elfenbeine aus Megiddo und Lachish: Inschriftenfunde, Flaschen, Löffel.* AOAT 47. Münster: Ugarit-Verlag.

Fisher, Steven R. 2016. *The Carswell Covenant.* Philadelphia: CreateSpace Independent Publishing Platform.

Forget, Mathilde C. L., and Ruth Shahack-Gross. 2016. How Long Does It Take to Burn Down an Ancient Near Eastern City? The Study of Experimentally Heated Mud-Bricks. *Antiquity* 90, no. 353: 1213–25.

Fosdick, Raymond B. 1956. *John D. Rockefeller, Jr.: A Portrait.* New York: Harper & Brothers, Publishers.

Fosdick, Raymond B. 1962. *Adventure in Giving: The Story of the General Education Board. A Foundation Established by John D. Rockefeller.* New York: Harper & Row.

Fox, Sir Cyril W. 1955. *Offa's Dyke: A Field Survey of the Western Frontier-Works of Mercia in the Seventh and Eighth Centuries A.D.* London: Oxford University Press.

Garfinkel, Yosef. 2016. The Murder of James Leslie Starkey Near Lachish. *Palestine Exploration Quarterly* 148, no. 2: 84–109.

Geere, H. Valentine. 1904. *By Nile and Euphrates: A Record of Discovery and Adventure.* Edinburgh: T. & T. Clark.

Gilbert, Martin. 1996. *Jerusalem in the Twentieth Century.* New York: John Wiley & Sons.

Glatt, Benjamin. 2016. Today in History: James Michener's Visit to the Holy Land. *Jerusalem Post*, 4 February. Available online at: http://www.jpost.com/Christian-News/Today-in-History-James-Micheners-visit-to-the-Holy-Land-443880.

Goldman, Shalom. 2009. *Zeal for Zion: Christians, Jews, and the Idea of the Promised Land.* Chapel Hill: University of North Carolina Press.

Green, John D. M. 2012. Introduction to *Picturing the Past: Imaging and Imagining the Ancient Middle East,* edited by Jack Green, Emily Teeter, and John A. Larson, 13–23. Oriental Institute Museum Publications 34. Chicago: University of Chicago.

Greenfield, Haskel J., Itzhaq Shai, and Aren Maeir. 2012. Being an "Ass": An Early Bronze Age Burial of a Donkey from Tell es-Safi/Gath, Israel. *Bioarchaeology of the Near East* 6: 21–52.

Hachmann, Rolf. 1989. *Kamid-el-Loz 1963–1981: German Excavations in Lebanon. Part I. Berytus* 37.

Hachmann, Rolf. 1993. Kumidi und Byblos. Spatbronzezeitliche Königsgräber im Küstengebiet östlich des Mittelmeers. In *Biblische Welten: Festschrift für Martin Metzger zu seinem 65. Geburtstag,* edited by Wolfgang Zwickel, 1–40. OBO 123. Freiburg and Gottingen: Vandenhoeck & Ruprecht.

Hallote, Rachel. 2006. *Bible, Map, and Spade: The American Palestine Exploration Society, Frederick Jones Bliss, and the Forgotten Story of Early American Biblical Archaeology.* New York: Gorgias Press.

Hallote, Rachel. 2011. Before Albright: Charles Torrey, James Montgomery, and American Biblical Archaeology, 1907–1922. *Near Eastern Archaeology* 74, no. 3: 156–69.

Henderson, Philip. 1956. *The Life of Laurence Oliphant: Traveller, Diplomat and Mystic.* London: Robert Hale.

Herzog, Ze'ev. 1997. *Archaeology of the City: Urban Planning in Ancient Israel and Its Social Implications.* Tel Aviv: Emery and Claire Yass Archaeology Press.

Holladay, Jack S. 1986. The Stables of Ancient Israel. In *The Archaeology of Jordan and Other Studies Presented to Siegfried H. Horn,* edited by T. Lawrence Geraty and Larry G. Herr, 103–166. Berrien Springs, MI: Andrews University Press.

Hudson, Michael C. 2000. The Transformation of Jerusalem 1917–2000 AD. In *Jerusalem in History*, edited by Kamil J. Asali, 249–85. New York: Olive Branch Press.

James, Peter, and Peter G. van der Veen, eds. 2015. *Solomon and Shishak: Current Perspectives from Archaeology, Epigraphy, History and Chronology. Proceedings of the Third BICANE Colloquium Held at Sidney Sussex College, Cambridge 26–27 March, 2011*, 137–47. BAR International Series 2732. Oxford: Archaeopress.

Jones, Howard Andrew. 2009. Foreword to Harold Lamb, *Swords in the Desert*, edited by Howard Andrew Jones, vii–x. Lincoln: University of Nebraska Press.

Kahana, Ephraim. 2006. *Historical Dictionary of Israeli Intelligence*. Lanham, MD: Scarecrow Press.

Kantor, Helene J. 1956. Syro-Palestinian Ivories. *Journal of Near Eastern Studies* 15: 153–74.

Kenyon, Kathleen M. 1957. *Digging Up Jericho*. London: Ernest Benn.

Kenyon, Kathleen M. 1974. *Digging Up Jerusalem*. London: Ernest Benn.

Khalidi, Walid. 1991. *Before Their Diaspora: A Photographic History of the Palestinians, 1876–1948*. Washington, DC: Institute for Palestine Studies.

Kletter, Raz. 2006. *Just Past? The Making of Israeli Archaeology*. London: Equinox.

Kuklick, Bruce. 1996. *Puritans in Babylon: The Ancient Near East and American Intellectual Life, 1880–1930*. Princeton, NJ: Princeton University Press.

Laqueur, Walter, and Barry Rubin, eds. 2001. *The Israel-Arab Reader: A Documentary History of the Middle East Conflict*. 6th rev. ed. New York: Penguin Books.

Lephen [Lefen], Asa. 1987. The Shai: The Paramilitary Intelligence Service. In *Intelligence and National Security*, edited by Avi Kover and Zvi Ofer, 93–111. Tel Aviv: Marachot (in Hebrew).

Levin, Yigal. 2012. Did Pharaoh Sheshonq Attack Jerusalem? *Biblical Archaeology Review*, July/August 2012, 42–52, 66.

Liebowitz, Harold. 1986. Late Bronze II Ivory Work in Palestine: Evidence of a Cultural Highpoint. *Bulletin of the American Schools of Oriental Research* 265: 3–24.

Loud, C. Everett. 1980. *300 Years of Louds in America*. Corning, NY: private publication.

Loud, Gordon, and Charles B. Altman. 1938. *Khorsabad. Part II: The Citadel and the Town*. Oriental Institute Publications 40. Chicago: University of Chicago.

Macalister, Robert Alexander Stewart. 1906. Gezer and Megiddo. *Palestine Exploration Fund Quarterly Statement* 38, no. 1: 62–66.

Magness, Jodi. 2012. *The Archaeology of the Holy Land: From the Destruction of Solomon's Temple to the Muslim Conquest*. Cambridge: Cambridge University Press.

May, Stephen J. 2005. *Michener: A Writer's Journey*. Norman: University of Oklahoma Press.

McCown, Chester W. 1943. *The Ladder of Progress in Palestine: A Story of Archaeological Adventure*. New York: Harper & Bros.

McNeil, Sam. 2015. At Jordan Site, Drone Offers Glimpse of Antiquities Looting. Archaeologists and Criminologists Use New Technologies to Study Global Trade in Stolen Artifacts. *Times of Israel*, 3 April. Available online at: http://www.timesofisrael.com/at-jordan-site-drone-offers-glimpse-of-antiquities-looting/.

Millar, John F. 2014. *The Buildings of Peter Harrison: Cataloguing the World of the First Global Architect, 1716–1775*. Jefferson, NC: McFarland & Company.

Miller, J. Maxwell, and John H. Hayes. 2006. *A History of Ancient Israel and Judah*. 2nd ed. Louisville, KY: Westminster John Knox Press.

Mitter, Sreemati. 2014. "A History of Money in Palestine: From the 1900s to the Present." PhD diss., Cambridge, MA: Harvard University. Available online at: http://nrs.harvard.edu/urn-3:HUL.InstRepos:12269876.

Moran, William L. 1992. *The Amarna Letters*. Baltimore: Johns Hopkins University Press.

Negbi, O. 1970. *The Hoards of Goldwork from Tell el-'Ajjul*. Studies in Mediterranean Archaeology 25. Göteborg: Paul Åströms Forlag.

Newton, Frances E. 1948. *Fifty Years in Palestine*. London: Cold Harbour Press.

Novacek, Gabrielle V. 2011. *Ancient Israel: Highlights from the Collections of the Oriental Institute, University of Chicago*. Chicago: University of Chicago.

Oliphant, Laurence. 1887. *Haifa; or, Life in Modern Palestine*. 2nd ed. London: William Blackwood and Sons.

Oren, Ram. 2012. Alice, Her Husband, Her Lover and 'Hatikva.' *Ha'aretz*, 9 February.

O'Sullivan, Adrian D. W. 2012. "German Covert Initiatives and British Intelligence in Persia (Iran), 1939–1945." DLitt et Phil thesis. Pretoria: University of South Africa.

O'Sullivan, Adrian D. W. 2015. *Espionage and Counterintelligence in Occupied Persia (Iran): The Success of the Allied Secret Services, 1941–45*. London: Palgrave Macmillan.

Ousterhout, Robert G. 2010. Archaeologists and Travelers in Ottoman Lands: Three Intersecting Lives. *Expedition* 52, no. 2: 9–20.

Parcak, Sarah H. 2009. *Satellite Remote Sensing for Archaeology*. Boston: Routledge.

Parcak, Sarah H. 2019. *Archaeology from Space: How the Future Shapes Our Past*. New York: Henry Holt and Co.

Parcak, Sarah H., David Gathings, Chase Childs, Gregory Mumford, and Eric H. Cline. 2016. Satellite Evidence of Archaeological Site Looting in Egypt: 2002–2013. *Antiquity* 90, no. 349: 185–205.

Peasnall, Brian, and Mitchell S. Rothman. 2003. Excavating Tepe Gawra in the Archives of the University of Pennsylvania Museum. *Expedition* 45, no. 3: 34–39.

Pickett, Jordan. 2013. Contextualizing Penn's Excavations at Beth Shean. *Expedition Magazine* 55, no. 1: 14–15. Available online (and for pdf download) at: http://www.penn .museum/sites/expedition/?p=9770.

Richelle, Matthieu. 2018. *The Bible and Archaeology*. Peabody, MA: Hendrickson Publishers Marketing.

Robinson, Edward, and Eli Smith. 1841. *Biblical Researches in Palestine, Mount Sinai and Arabia Petraea: A Journal of Travels in the Year 1838, Undertaken in Reference to Biblical Geography*. 3 vols. Boston: Crocker and Brewster.

Robinson, Edward, and Eli Smith. 1856. *Later Biblical Researches in Palestine, and in the Adjacent Regions: A Journal of Travels in the Year 1852*. Boston: Crocker and Brewster.

Rothman, Mitchell S. 2002. *Tepe Gawra: The Evolution of a Small, Prehistoric Center in Northern Iraq*. Philadelphia: University of Pennsylvania Museum of Archaeology and Anthropology.

Running, Leona G., and David N. Freedman. 1975. *William Foxwell Albright: A Twentieth-Century Genius*. New York: Two Continents.

Sachar, Howard M. 1979. *A History of Israel: From the Rise of Zionism to Our Time*. New York: Alfred A. Knopf.

Sagrillo, Troy L. 2015. Shoshenq I and Biblical Šîšaq: A Philological Defense of Their Traditional Equation. In *Solomon and Shishak: Current Perspectives from Archaeology, Epigraphy, History and Chronology. Proceedings of the Third BICANE Colloquium Held at Sidney Sussex College, Cambridge 26–27 March, 2011*, edited by Peter James and Peter G. van der Veen, 61–81. BAR International Series 2732. Oxford: Archaeopress.

Segev, Tom. 2000. *One Palestine, Complete*. New York: Metropolitan Books.

Sharon, Ilan. 2014. Levantine Chronology. In *The Oxford Handbook of the Archaeology of the Levant, c. 8000–332 BCE*, edited by Margreet L. Steiner and Ann E. Killebrew, 44–65. New York: Oxford University Press.

Silberman, Neil A. 1982. *Digging for God and Country: Exploration, Archeology, and the Secret Struggle for the Holy Land 1799–1917*. New York: Alfred A. Knopf.

Silberman, Neil A. 1993. *A Prophet from Amongst You. The Life of Yigael Yadin: Soldier, Scholar, and Mythmaker of Modern Israel*. Reading, MA: Addison-Wesley Publishing Company.

Silver, Minna. 2014. Equid Burials in Archaeological Contexts in the Amorite, Hurrian and Hyksos Cultural Intercourse. *ARAM* 26, nos. 1 and 2: 335–55.

Smith, Charles D. 1996. *Palestine and the Arab-Israeli Conflict*. 3rd ed. New York: St. Martin's Press.

Smith, George Adam. 1894. *The Historical Geography of the Holy Land, Especially in Relation to the History of Israel and of the Early Church*. 1st ed. London: Hodder and Stoughton.

Smith, George Adam. 1931. *The Historical Geography of the Holy Land, Especially in Relation to the History of Israel and of the Early Church*. 25th ed. London: Hodder and Stoughton.

Stern, Ephraim. 2000. The Babylonian Gap. *Biblical Archaeology Review* 26, no. 6: 45–51, 76.

Stern, Ephraim. 2002. The Babylonian Gap Revisited: Yes There Was. *Biblical Archaeology Review* 28, no. 3.

Stiebing, William H., Jr. 1971. Hyksos Burials in Palestine: A Review of the Evidence. *Journal of Near Eastern Studies* 30, no. 2: 110–17.

Taylor, Anne. 1982. *Laurence Oliphant: 1829–1888*. Oxford: Oxford University Press.

Templeton, Rosamond Dale Owen Oliphant. 1903 (reprinted 1939). *The Mediators*. London: Office of Light.

Templeton, Rosamond Dale Owen Oliphant. 1929. *My Perilous Life in Palestine*. New York: Duffield & Company.

Tornede, Silke. 1992. "In Search of Arcadia: The Life of Rosamond Dale Owen Oliphant Templeton (1846–1937)." MA thesis. Bloomington: Indiana University.

Trombetta, Lorenzo. 2009. The Private Archive of the Sursuqs, A Beirut Family of Christian Notables: An Early Investigation. *Rivista degli studi orientali* 82, fasc. 1/4: 197–228.

Ussishkin, David. 2019. The Murder of James Leslie Starkey: Addendum to the Paper of Yosef Garfinkel. *Palestine Exploration Quarterly* 151, no. 2: 146–54 (DOI: 10.1080/00310328.2019.1626178).

Vogel, Lester I. 1993. *To See a Promised Land: Americans and the Holy Land in the Nineteenth Century*. State College: The Pennsylvania State University Press.

Wagner-Durand, Elisabeth. 2012. The Treasury of Kamid el-Loz and the Late Bronze Age Settlement History of Kumidi: Creating Collective Memory and Falling Victim to Oblivion. ICAANE Warsaw. Workshop: Continuation and Rupture in the Settlement History of Lebanon. Available online at: https://www.academia.edu/2032243/The_treasury_of_Kamid_el-Loz_and_the_Late_Bronze_Age_settlement_history_of_Kumidi_Creating_collective_memory_and_falling_victim_to_oblivion.

Ward, Alexandra. 2013. "Archaeology, Heritage and Identity: The Creation and Development of a National Museum in Wales." PhD diss., Cardiff University.

Warner, Daniel, and Eli Yannai. 2017. Archaeological Views: One Thing Leads to Another. *Biblical Archaeology Review* 43, no. 3: 26–27, 56–57.

Wasserstein, Bernard. 2001. *Divided Jerusalem: The Struggle for the Holy City*. New Haven, CT: Yale University Press.

Waterhouse, Helen. 1986. *The British School at Athens: The First Hundred Years*. BSA Supplementary Volume 19. Athens: British School at Athens.

Way, Kenneth C. 2013. Assessing Sacred Asses: Bronze Age Donkey Burials in the Near East. *Levant* 42, no. 2: 210–25.

Weber, Jill A. 2008. Elite Equids: Redefining Equid Burials of the Mid- to Late 3rd Millennium BC from Umm el-Marra, Syria. *Archaeology of the Near East* 8: 499–519.

Wilford, Hugh. 2013. *America's Great Game: The CIA's Secret Arabists and the Shaping of the Modern Middle East*. New York: Basic Books.

Willets-Burnham, Anita. 1946. *Round the World on a Penny*. Rev. ed. Private publication.

Wilson, John A. 1972. *Thousands of Years: An Archaeologist's Search for Ancient Egypt*. New York: Charles Scribner's Sons.

Wilson, William E. 1964. *The Angel and the Serpent: The Story of New Harmony*. Bloomington: Indiana University Press.

Worrell, William H. 1920. Report of the Director to the Managing Committee of the American School of Oriental Research in Jerusalem. *Bulletin of the Archaeological Institute of America* 11: 34–37.

Wygnańska, Zuzanna. 2017. Equid and Dog Burials in the Ritual Landscape of Bronze Age Syria and Mesopotamia. *ARAM* 29, nos. 1 and 2: 141–60.

Zertal, Adam. 2003. The Province of Samaria (Assyrian *Samerina*) in the Late Iron Age (Iron Age III). In *Judah and the Judeans in the Neo-Babylonian Period*, edited by Oded Lipschits and Joseph Blenkinsopp, 377–412. Winona Lake, IN: Eisenbrauns.

Index

Note: Page numbers in italic type indicate illustrations.

Abt, Jeffrey, 226

Adams, Matt, 314n8

aerial photography, 128–31, *129*, *130*, 133, 147

Ahab, 91, 187, 195, 235, 293, 298–300

Akhenaten, Pharaoh, 228, 270

Albright, William Foxwell, 12, 13–14, 41, 173, 231, 242, 298–99

Alexander the Great, 53, 55

Allen, George, 242

Allenby, Edmund, 7, 9, 266

Altman, Alice, 208, 216, 218, 220, 240, 241, 243–44, 261, 283

Altman, Charles, 208, 216, 218, 220, 237, 240, 241, 243–44, 261, 274, 283, 285

Amarna period, 86

Amenhotep III, Pharaoh, 228, 270

American Colony, Jerusalem, 44, 162, 253, 290

American Journal of Archaeology, 298

American School of Oriental Research, Jerusalem, 10, 12, 14, 114, 162, 277, 289

Amos, 197, 199

Antiquities Department. *See* Department of Antiquities, British Mandate Palestine

Antiquity (journal), 128, 206

anti-Semitism, 64, 103–5

Arab Revolt (1936–39), 239, 261, 265–66

Arabs: British roundups of, 278; and Israeli War of Independence, 293–94; Jews' relations with, 64–65, 103, 166–67; living conditions of, 110; White Paper on Arab-Jewish relations, 276, 279–80, 283

archaeological practices: architectural knowledge valuable for, 170; horizontal excavation, 91–92, 123–24, 154; intelligence work compared to, 172; present-day staffing, 191; publication considerations in, 160–61; study collections as aid to, 180

archaeology: early years of discipline, 11, 22; isolation of, from world events, 265; in Palestine, 10

Area A, 159, *194*

Area AA (northern trench), 220, 229, *230*, 270

Area BB (eastern trench), 220, 224, *226*, 229, *230*, 261, 266, 268, 270, 275

Area CC (southern trench), *194*, 214, 220, 229, *230*, 293, 299

Area DD, 263, 275, 299

Area H, 199, 248, 259

Area K, 199, 269

Area Q, 293

Armageddon. *See* Megiddo/Armageddon

Ashtarte. *See* Astarte

Assyrians, 253

Astarte, 47, 244

Astarte Temple, 53, 215, 298

Atlantic Monthly (magazine), 109

Atlantic Refining Company, 101, 292

Atlit, 148–49

Badè, William, 42, 66–68, 71, 76

Balfour Declaration, 7, 64

balloon photography. *See* aerial photography

bandits/brigands, 8, 243, 265–66, 272–73, 275–77, 280, 282, 285

Barnett, Richard, 255

Beaumont, Ernest Forrest (E. F.), 162–63, 165, 210

Beevor, Antony, 291

Ben-Dor, Immanuel, 281–82, 286, 294
Ben Gurion, David, 276
Bentley's Complete Phrase Code, 118
Ben-Yehuda, Eliezer, 60
Ben-Yehuda, Yemima. *See* Guy, Yemima
Beth Shean, 13–15, 62, 76, 89
Biridiya (ruler of Megiddo), 228, 270
Bliss, Frederick Jones, 11
bones. *See* skeletal material
Braidwood, Robert and Linda, 264, 272
Braun, Eliot, 370n4
Breasted, Charles, 166; and aerial photogra-
    phy, 128; on excavation results, 217; as
    executive director of Oriental Institute, 71;
    and father's death, 227; and film, 146–48;
    and financial matters, 114–15, 168, 228;
    marriage of, 168; and May affair, 176,
    181–82; and personnel matters, 73, 74,
    100–102, 111–14, 116, 119–22, 145, 156,
    182–83, 205–9, 216–17, 220, 332n32;
    photographs of, 34, *35*; and Solomon's
    Stables, 105; successor of, 265; and
    University of Chicago, 96; visits to
    Megiddo by, 93, 95, 107, 114, 119, 146
Breasted, Frances, 100
Breasted, James Henry, v; Albright's
    relationship with, 14; *Ancient Records of
    Egypt*, 7; color identification instituted by,
    132; death of, 226–27, 232; Egyptian
    material as concern of, 30, 71, 92, 123–24,
    131, 150, 185; on excavation strategy and
    results, 123–24, 150, 154, 158–60, 191, 194;
    and film, 147; and financial matters, 11–12,
    15, 17, 18, 39, 43, 96, 115, 140, 151, 160,
    171–72, 201, 222–23, 227–28, 232; and
    Fisher-Higgins friction, 5, 24–25, 35–37,
    39–43; goals of, xx–xxi; Guy's relationship
    with, 132, 150, 153–54, 156–60, 172, 181–83;
    informant of, 19; launch of Megiddo
    excavations by, 7–12, 15–22; as manager of
    Chicago team, xviii, xxiii; master plan of,
    264–65; and May affair, 176–82, 212; as
    model for Michener's fiction, xviii; news
    of excavation site received by, 26, 28, 36–37,
    66–70, 76–78, 80–81, 85–91, 125–27, 131,
    132–33, 135, 140–43, 148, 153–54, 167,
    168–69, 187, 191–98, 200–202, 210, 212–15;
    and objects for Oriental Institute collection,

128, 162, 174–76; *The Oriental Institute*, 206;
    Oriental Institute founded by, 10; and
    Palestine Archaeological Museum, 115–16;
    and personnel matters, 15–19, 36–37, 39–43,
    59, 61–62, 63, 66–68, 74, 101–2, 113–14, 117,
    121–22, 144, 156, 159–66, 169–74, 182–83,
    205–6, 208; photographs of, *xviii*, 28, 34, *35*,
    94, 95; publications as concern of, 98, 118,
    144, 151–53, 157–58, 160, 173, 208; Rockefel-
    ler monetary gift to, 96; and Sheshonq
    fragment, 28, *28*, 30–33; and Solomon's
    Stables, 1–2, 85, 87–91; visits to Megiddo
    by, 7–10, 17–22, 28, 30–31, 34–35, 61, 63,
    93–96, 153, 156–61, 164, 222–23; and
    Wilensky affair, 161–66, 169–72
Breasted, James Henry, Jr., 152, 341n30
brigands. *See* bandits/brigands
British Mandate Palestine, xxii; Arab Revolt
    (1936–39), 239, 261, 265–66; discontinua-
    tion of, 276; riots in (1920/1921), 7; riots in
    (1929), 103
British School of Archaeology, Jerusalem, 10,
    76, 183
Bronze Age, xv, 133, 140–42, 224–25, 257;
    dating scheme for, 242; Early, 86, 117, 142,
    225, 267, 268–69; Intermediate, 269; Late,
    xvii, 124, 140, 200, 224, 229, 234, 235, 281;
    Middle, 86, 138, 141, 224, 229, 235, 243,
    259, 269
bronze statuette of deity, 224–26, *225*
bronze vessel hoard, *195*, 196–97, 198
Bryn Mawr College, 22
burials, 137–38, *138*, 244–45, 251, 256–57
Burnham, Carol-Lou, 98
Buxton (entomologist), 141

Canaanites, 141, 150–52, 199, 224, 228, 235,
    244, 253, 268, 269
Carmel Caves, 148–49, 190
Carter, Howard, 11
Century (magazine), 109
Chalcolithic period, 117, 266, 267
Chancellor, John, 96
Chicago team: accomplishments of, xxi;
    archives of, xxi; budget of, 114, 236–37, 245,
    261, 264, 273; dig house constructed by, xvii,
    27, 34–35, *35*, *38*, 69, 154, 156; everyday/
    leisure activities of, 107–9; field directors of,

xx; food served to, 25, 104, 220–21; goal of, xix; housing for, 25–26, 25, 65, 99–100, 102, 104–5, 108, 113–14, 118; initial members of, 12–22; locals' relations with, 77–78; personnel of, xxi, 12–22, 20, 43–45, 61, 63–64, 71–75, 74, 83–84, 97–98, 97, 101, 116, 167–68, 220, 243, 301–8; preparations of, 34; service staff for, 109, 159–60, 216–17; spouses' contributions to, 121–22, 168; year-round employment of, 75

Christian Science Monitor (newspaper), 109

Churchill, Winston, 64

chutes, at excavation site, 48, 86, 134, 148

City Wall 325, 53, 86, 88, 92, 126, 189, 194

Clark, Mary "Tod," 94, 95

clay tablets, 228

Cline, Diane Harris, xvii

Cline, Hannah, xix

Cline, Joshua, xix

coded communications, 118–19

Collapse, of ancient Near East, 257

color identification, 132

Concannon, Thomas, 165, 210; reconstruction of structures in Stratum IVA, 194

Conder, Claude R., 6–7

Copper Age, xv

Crowfoot, Grace, 154

Crowfoot, Joan, 154

Crowfoot, John, 154, 298, 299

Cyprus, 64, 270, 296

Cyrus the Great, 55

dating of finds, xv, xix–xx, 51, 53, 55, 86, 90–92, 126–27, 140–42, 185–86, 189–90, 195–200, 229, 233–35, 242, 257, 258, 266–70, 298–300

David, King, 197, 199

Decauville (company), 15, 34

deck tennis, 109

deity. *See* bronze statuette of deity

DeLoach, Edward, xxii, 104, 369n14; and aerial photography, 129; as assistant field director, 68; correspondence of, 24–28, 36, 63, 64, 68–70, 100; criticisms of, 99–101, 111–12; death of, 101; departure of, 101, 112–13, 120, 292; health of, 26, 71, 83; marriage of, 98–101; in Megiddo, 23–27; photographs of, 20, 28, 34, 35, 74, 94, 94, 97; as possible love interest, 67, 75–76;

surveying/drafting undertaken by, 9, 38, 63, 100; as team member, 19, 21; vacations of, 99, 111

DeLoach, Florence (née Burnham), 97, 98–99, 101, 104, 106–8, 111, 111–12

Department of Agriculture, British Mandate Palestine, 89

Department of Antiquities, Ashmolean Museum, Oxford, 98

Department of Antiquities, British Mandate Palestine, 10, 24, 31, 45, 59, 68, 70–71, 78, 87, 98, 115, 128, 174–75, 177–80, 196, 209–11, 216, 235, 239–40, 266, 274, 290

Department of Antiquities, Israel. *See* Israel Department of Antiquities and Museums

District Commissioner's Office, Haifa, 146

division of antiquities from Megiddo, 87, 128, 165, 174–75, 236, 259, 273, 281–83

Dohan, Edith Hall, 22

Donovan, "Wild Bill," 291

draftsmen, 19, 38, 73, 88, 102, 121–22

drones, 130

Dyer, A. Murray, 94, 95

dysentery, 211

earthquake: in ancient Megiddo, 197–200, 212; in vicinity of site, 69

eastern trench. *See* Area BB

École biblique et archéologique française, Jerusalem, 10

Edinburgh Evening News (newspaper), 79

Egyptian Gazette (newspaper), 109

Egyptians, ancient, 7, 9–10, 30–32, 54–55, 71, 86, 92, 123–24, 131, 142, 150, 185–86, 194, 200, 228, 232–33, 235, 245, 247–48, 253, 269–70, 281

Egyptian workmen, 20, 21, 23, 34, 39, 43, 49, 50, 61, 65–66, 84, 87, 92, 106, 110, 143, 148, 165, 222, 262, 273. *See also* local workmen

El (god), 225

el-Hussein, Nasir, 77

Engberg, Irene, 117, 165, 168

Engberg, Robert W., 165; background of, 117; as director of American School of Oriental Research, 289; Egyptian material as concern of, 194; on filming, 146; health of, 143, 145; and May affair, 177–78, 181; Oriental Institute fellowship of, 173–74; on

Engberg, Robert W. (cont.)
  pottery, 117, 158, 174, 176, 190, 277;
  publishing contributions of, 117–18, 158,
    183, 184, 190, 241; and skeletons, *117*, 148,
    190; as team member, 116; and tombs, 211;
    on wife's contributions to expedition, 168;
    and Wilensky affair, 166, 169
Esarhaddon (Neo-Assyrian king), 189
espionage. *See* intelligence work
Esse, Doug, 370n4

Feldman, Marian, 255–57
film, 146–48
fine gridding, 252–53
Finkelstein, Israel, xvi, xix–xx, 200, 234–35,
    299–300, 314n8
Fisher, Clarence, xxii; as advisory director, 61;
    archaeological practices of, 47–49, 51–52;
    death of, 289; *The Excavation of Armageddon*,
    33, 98; as field director, xx, xxiii, 5, 17–22,
    36–37, 46; findings of, 53–55, 293, 298;
    firing of, 61–62, 113; Guy and, 68–69,
    76–77; health of, 26, 45, 61; Higgins's
    relationship with, 5, 17, 24–25, 35–37,
    39–40, 42–43; hiring of personnel by,
    44–46; as interim director of American
    School of Oriental Research, 289; later visit
    by, 277; in Megiddo, 23–27; mental state of,
    14–15, 17–18, 61–62; performance of, 52,
    78, 80; photographs of, *13, 20, 34, 35*; and
    pottery, 39; pre-Megiddo career of, 12–15;
    prompting of Breasted by, 12, 15;
    recording system of, 51–52, 89; rumor-
    mongering by, 67, 69; salary of, 18;
    sexuality of, 62–63, 77; and Shipton's
    wedding, 291; stratigraphic errors of,
    213–15
Fisher, Clarence Stanley, Jr., 21
Fisher, Florie, 21
Fisher, Stanley, xxii, 21, 23–24, 39, 45, 70;
    photographs of, *20, 34, 35*
Fleming, Alexander, 212
Fletcher, Carol DeLoach, 318n55, 320n6,
    331n21, 332n35, 334n90, and 369n14
Fosdick, Raymond, 15–17
Fox, Cyril, 116
Franklin, Norma, 141
Frazer, George Preston, 262, 273

gardens, at Megiddo dig house, 108, 156
Garrod, Dorothy, 148–49, 190
Garstang, John, 10, 14, 18–20, 22, 26, 31, 239
gates, to Megiddo, 126–27, 134, 189, 201,
    233–36, *234*, 263, 292
Geere, Valentine, 62–63
General Education Board (GEB), 15, *94*,
    222–23, 228, 231, 236, 245, 264
German Oriental Society, xix
German Protestant Institute of Archaeology,
    Jerusalem, 10
German Society for the Exploration of
    Palestine, xix
Germany, 284
Gezer, 11, 140, 141
Gilgamesh, 53
Glueck, Nelson, 162–63, 252, 277, 280, 289, 291
Golani Brigade, 293
gold. *See* bronze statuette of deity, 202,
    246–49, *246*, 259, 261, 270
Goldman, Hetty, 12–22
Gold Reserve Act, 172, 223
Gordon, George B., 14–15
Graham, William, 161
Grand Lodge of England, 293
Grand Lodge of Scotland, 293
Great Depression, xxi, 106, 172, 231
Great Royal Visit, 93–95, *94*, 222
Great Trench, 30, 36, 47, 82, 114, 263, 275,
    279, 294
Green, Jack, 162
Greenfield, Haskel and Tina, 257
Guy, P.L.O., 104, 242; and aerial photography,
    133; aerial photography undertaken by,
    128–31; on Arab-Jewish relations, 167;
    archaeological practices of, 123–24, 153–54,
    160–61; background on, 59–60; Breasted's
    relationship with, 132, 150, 153–54, 156–60,
    172, 181–83; cablegram sent by, 2; character/
    personality of, 108; and family, 71; family
    of, 60; as field director, xx, 45–46, 59, 61, 63,
    70–71, 84, 110, 115, 183; findings of, 85,
    125–27, 132–33, 142–43, 148–49, 187, 189–202,
    299; firing of, 40, 77, 113, 159, 182–83, 185,
    205, 207; on Fisher, 52; Fisher and, 68–69,
    76–77; health of, 67, 68; housing for, 114, 144,
    160–61; and May affair, 176–83; *Megiddo
    Tombs*, 175, 184, 211, 277; performance of,

65, 67, 108, 111, 123, 182–83; personnel
matters involving, 63–64, 66–69, 75–77,
83–84, 99–100, 102–3, 111–13, 115, 119–23,
144–46, 161–66, 168–72, 174, 176–84;
photographs of, 60, 74, 94, 94, 97; and prison,
146; purchase of Megiddo site by, 78–83;
reports/publications of, 33, 63, 98, 118, 123,
134, 151–53, 157–58, 160–61, 173, 183, 190–98,
200; salary of, 115, 183; snubbed by colleagues
in publications' acknowledgments, 183;
and Solomon's Stables, 1–2, 85–91, 105–6;
stratigraphic errors of, 213–15; vacations
of, 71, 111; and water tunnel, 133–42; and
Wilensky affair, 161–66, 169–72, 183
Guy, Yemima (née Ben-Yehuda), 60, 68–69, 71,
74, 97, 104, 108, 111, 114, 115, 144, 160, 182

Habash (customs official), 178
Hachmann, Rolf, 256
Haganah, xxiii, 171–72
Haifa, 23, 26, 31, 45, 59, 61, 65, 73, 103, 106–7,
109, 160–61, 167, 170, 212, 231, 239, 244,
265, 282–84, 294, 296
Haines, Carl, 264–65
Halpern, Baruch, 314n8
Hamid, Reis, 64, 97, 140
Hamilton, Robert W., 97, 98, 177–80, 239–40,
274, 282, 291, 292, 297
Harding, Gerald Lankester, 252
Harrison (architect), 165
Harrison, Charles C., 14–15
Harrison, Tim, 33, 370n4
Hathor (goddess), 248
Hawes, Harriet Boyd, 22
Hetshepsut, Queen, 123
Hezekiah's Tunnel, 139
Higgins, Daniel, xxii, 66, 105; death of, 43;
family of, 16, 21–22, 23, 38, 40, 42; firing of,
39–43, 113; Fisher's relationship with, 5, 17,
24–25, 35–37, 39–40, 42–43; health of, 26;
housing for, 26–28; in Megiddo, 23–27, 30;
performance of, 5, 19, 26–27, 37–39, 40–43;
photographs of, 34, 35; salary of, 39, 43; as
team member, 16–22
Higgins, Eleanor, 16, 21
Higgins, Ethel, 16, 21–22, 43
Higgins, Mary, 16, 21
Hilprecht (Nippur dig director), 76, 324n14

Hiram of Tyre, 126
Hitler, Adolf, 249, 285
Hittites, 200, 253
hoards, 195, 196, 245–49, 246, 255, 260, 261, 270
horizontal archaeology, 91–92, 123–24, 154
Hrdlička, Aleš, 175
Hucklesby, C. M., 121
The Human Adventure (film), 147–48, 340n13
Humboldt University, 22
Hutchins, Robert M., 222–23
Hyksos period, 235, 243, 263, 269–70

Iliffe, John Henry "Harry," 175, 178, 247, 249,
252, 253, 259–61, 265, 273, 280–83, 291
Illustrated London News (newspaper), 264
intelligence work, 171–72
International Education Board (IEB), 15, 264
Iron Age, xv, 86, 92, 141, 229, 242, 270
Irwin, William A., 173–74, 177, 180, 182,
197–98, 201–2, 211–12
Ishtar. See Astarte
Israel Antiquities Authority, xxi, 83, 116, 176
Israel Defense Forces, 294
Israel Department of Antiquities and
Museums, 183, 296
Israelites, 187, 199–200
Israeli War of Independence (1948). See War of
Independence, Israeli (1948)
Issi-Adad-Aninu (Neo-Assyrian governor), 189
ivories, 158, 202, 245–48, 250–57, 253, 259–61,
270, 273

Jehu, 187
Jeroboam II, king of Israel, 91, 197, 299
Jerusalem: destruction of (586 BCE), 55; Guy's
part-time employment in, 68; riots in
(1920), 7; riots in (1929), 103; unsafe
conditions around, 243, 265, 280
Jesus Christ, 146, 293
Jewish Agency, 171
Jews: Arabs' relations with, 64–65, 103,
166–67; Chicago team members' attitudes
toward, 64, 103–4; and Israeli War of
Independence, 293–94; White Paper on
Jewish-Arab relations, 276, 279–80, 283
Jezreel Valley, 5, 8, 9–10, 56, 79
Josiah, king of Judah, 55, 142
Judson, Henry, 11

Kamid el-Loz, near Damascus, 256
Kefar 'Othnay (Caporcotani), 146
Keith, Arthur, 190
Kellogg, John Payne, 19, 21, 36, 36–37, 40, 47
Kent, Charles, 97, 98
Kent, Charles Foster, 98
Kenyon, Frederic, 154
Kenyon, Kathleen, 154, 156
Kenyon-Wheeler method, 154
Khorsabad, Iraq, 206, 208, 216, 231
King Hiram Lodge, 293
Kitchener, Horatio H., 6–7
Kraeling, Carl, 285

Lamon, Eugenia "Jean" (née Keefe), 153, 168, 220, 240
Lamon, Robert S., 104, 145, 173; and aerial photography, 128; background of, 73; behavior of, 122, 208–9; death of father of, 152–53; and DeLoach's marriage, 98–99; education of, 73, 96; Egyptian material as concern of, 194; as field director, 73; Guy's relationship with, 122–23; health of, 213, 218; and Loud directorship, 220; *Megiddo I*, xx, 54, 73, 134, 158, 208, 213, 241, 297–98; photographs of, 74, 94, 94, 97; post-Guy duties of, 207–17; published material of, 73, 86, 126–27, 140, 183 (see also *Megiddo I*); and skeletons, 137–38; stature of, 102; on stratigraphy, 211, 213–15, 298–99; subsequent career as petroleum geologist, 73, 260; surveying/drafting undertaken by, 73, 107; tenure of, 73; upon termination of expedition, 237, 240; and tombs, 211; and water system, 140–42, 200–201, 208, 210–11; and Wilensky affair, 166, 169
lapis lazuli, 247–48
Lawrence, T. E., 59
Lejjun, 110, 278
LiDAR, 130
lighting, 140
Lind, Astrid, 152, 165, 168, 208, 220, 240, 276
Lind, Olof, 69, 102, 104; and aerial photography, 129; and American Colony, 162; on Arab-Jewish relations, 166–67; at Atlit, 148–49; background of, 44; character/ personality of, 75, 108; death of, 369n14; departure from Palestine of, 293, 369n14;

divorce of, 276; engagement and marriage of, 152; health of, 45; with Loud at Khorsabad, 208; and Loud directorship, 220; model and detail of Solomon's Stables, 90, 105–6; orchard purchased and managed by, 262, 276, 293, 369n14; as photographer, 44, 75, 210, 218; photographs of, 20, 44, 74, 97; social relations of, 70, 99, 113; and termination of expedition, 237, 240, 262; vacations of, 71
Little, Charles, 72, 73, 75–76
liver omens, 233, 275
Liverpool University, 22
local workmen, 21, 70, 106, 110, 191, 193, 222, 223–24, 232, 243–44, 262, 271–72, 278–79. *See also* Egyptian workmen
London Conference (1939), 275–76, 279–80
London Times (newspaper), 109
Loud, Gordon, xxii; and Arab-Jewish tensions, 261, 265–66, 270–73, 275–81; background of, 206, 221; cablegram sent by, 238; character/personality of, 221; death of, 369n14; death threats received by, 270–73; excavation strategy of, 218–20, 243, 244; on father's death, 227; as field director, xx, 158, 206, 215–18; and final year of expedition, 274–86, 289–90; findings of, 244–59, 261, 281–83; health of, 233; marriage of, 274; *Megiddo II*, 158, 185–86, 218, 248, 252, 255, 258, 292, 297–99; performance of, 236; and personnel matters, 216–18; photographs of, 207; project timeline devised by, 232; reports/publications of, 228–29, 231, 235, 245–56, 259–60, 266, 268, 275–84; resignation of, 292; revival of expedition under, 241–43; termination of expedition under, 236–40; vacation of, 283; war service of, 291; work schedule established by, 221–22
Loud, Honor (née Merrell), 274, 283
Low Chronology hypothesis, xx, 235
Luckenbill, Daniel D., 17–19, 30–31, 34, 36–37, 40–41, 43
Luxor, 63, 71, 75, 102, 115, 116, 143

Macalister, R.A.S., 11, 66, 140, 141
Macpherson, Ian, 291
Magidu, 189

Maisler, Benjamin. *See* Mazar, Benjamin

malaria, 26, 34, 44–45, 61–62, 65, 71, 83, 106, 226, 285

Martin, Mario, 258, 314n8

Masonic Order, 292–93

Matson, G. Eric, 253

Matthews, Dagmar, 271–72

Matthews, Howard, 221, 250, 262, 265, 271–73, 279–81

May, Gola Joyce Kina, 168, 173

May, Helen, 121–22, 144, 168, 169, 173, 182

May, Herbert, 117

May, Herbert Gordon: alleged smuggling of antiquities by, 176–82, 212; and ancient earthquake, 197–98; background of, 121–22; criticism by, of dating and assignations, 298; death of, 183; family of, 168, 177, 178; on filming, 161; Guy's relationship with, 121–22, 144, 174, 176–83; *The Material Remains of the Megiddo Cult*, 158, 168, 173, 183, 211, 213–15; Oberlin position taken by, 173, 183; Wilensky and, 163–64, 166, 169, 170–71

Mazar, Benjamin, 294

McCown, Chester, 340n16, 341n40

McCown, Ted, 149, 340n16, 341n40

megaron temples, 281, *282*

Megiddo/Armageddon: aerial views of, *130*, *219*; approach road to, 134; Arab-Jewish relations' effect on, 261, 265–66, 270–73, 275–81; battles involving, 7, 9–10, 31–32, 54–55, 187, 229, 269–70, 293–94; bedrock of, xv, xx, 218, 229, 261, 266; biblical references to, xiii–xiv; burials at, 137–38, *138*, 244–45, 251, 256–57; car purchased for, 220, 290, *290*; chronological span of, xv, *xvi*, xxi; chronology of major events, 303–8; cities within, xv; city walls of, 53, 86, 88, 92, 126, 189, 194, *267*, 268–69, 292; cult remains at, 117; damage to, 81–82, 292, 293–96; derivation of name, xiv; dig house at, xvii, 27, 34–35, *35*, *38*, 69, 99–100, 102, 105, 107–8, 113–14, 118, 144, 154, 156, 159–60, 165, 290–91, 293–96; discovery of, 7; division of antiquities from, 87, 128, 165, 174–75, 236, 259, 273, 281–83; environmental conditions at, xvii, 23, 65; excavations at, 35–39, 42–43, 47–49, *48*, *50*, 65, 85–91, 87,

107, 113, 118, 123–27, 132–43, 148, 151–52, 158–59, 191–202, 222–24, 228–36, *230*, 243–59, 262–64, 266–70, 272–75, 278–79, 281–82; fame of, 1–2; gates to, 126–27, 134, 189, 201, 233–36, *234*, 263, 292; last habitation of, 56; lease/purchase of land, 24, 78–83, 92; lighting at, 140; map of, *9*; as Neo-Assyrian regional capital, 189; nineteenth-century search for, 5–7; parade ground at, 193; physical appearance of, *xiv*, xiv–xv; publicity on, 1, 12, 24, 32, 79, 82, 89, 249, 264; Schumacher's excavation of, 30; silo at, 191; stables at, 126, 144, 189, 192–93, 213, 263, 279, 292, 298 (*see also* Solomon's Stables); stratigraphy of, xv, 30, 33, 51–53, *52*, 87, 90, 211, 213–15, 261, 263, 266–70, 298–99; terminology concerning, 242; tombs at, 38, 86, 117, 142, 151, 157–58, 174, 190, 211, 256, 277; transportation to, xv–xvi, 23, 65, 93, 96, 103, 106–7, 145, 220; water system of, 133–42, *135*, *137*, 156, 158, 189, 200–201, 208, 210–11

Michener, James, *The Source*, xvii–xviii, xviii, 313n6

micro-gridding, 252–53

Migdal Temple. *See* Temple 2048

Monolith Inscription, 91

Montgomery, James A., 62

mosquitoes, xvii, 23, 25–26, 34

Mount Carmel, 8

Mount Gilboa, 8

Mount Tabor, 8

Muir, John, 66

Munsell Book of Color, 132

Murray, Betty, 154, 156

Musmus Pass, 9

Mussolini, Benito, 8

Mycenaeans, 253

Nakht-Amon (Egyptian official), 254

Napoleon Bonaparte, 8, 10

Neanderthals, 149

Nebuchadnezzar, 55

Necho II, Pharaoh, 54–55

Nelson, Harold, 292

Neo-Assyrians, 55, 126–27, 187, 233, 293

Neo-Babylonians, 55, 187, 189

Neolithic period, xv, 266

New Deal, 172

New Kingdom Egypt, 228

newspaper coverage, 1, 12, 24, 32, 79, 82, 89, 153, 249, 264

Newton, Frances E., 78, 80

New York Times (newspaper), 1, 12, 79, 82, 89, 147, 226

New York Tribune (newspaper), 153

1939 White Paper. *See* White Paper (1939)

Nippur, Mesopotamia, 13

Nobel, Peter, 95, 96

Noble, Hal, 274, 285

Northern Natural Gas, 73

Northern Observation Platform, 268

northern trench. *See* Area AA

Office of Strategic Services, 291

Oliphant, Laurence, 78–79

Omri, 91, 187, 195, 235, 293, 299–300

O'Neill, J. G., 66, 67

Oriental Institute, University of Chicago: academic program of, 36; archival materials at, xxi, 39, 42, 176; building construction for, 94; Charles Breasted as executive director of, 71; color identification practices of, 132; damages paid to, 296; Engberg and, 117; film produced by, 147–48; finances of, 18, 114, 227–28, 231–32, 236–38, 245; founding of, 10; James Henry Breasted as director of, 1; May affair and, 180; Megiddo project of, 17, 18, 41, 61, 81–83, 236–41, 292–97; objects in collection of, 128, 162, 174–76, 236, 249, 259–60; other projects of, 115; Wilensky's lawsuit against, 164–66, 169–72; Wilson as director of, 63. *See also* Chicago team

Owen, Robert, 78

Palace 1723, 299

Palace 6000, 195, 299

palaces: Stratum III (Guy directorship), 189; Stratum VA/IVB (Guy directorship), 194–95, 197, 299; Stratum VIIA (Loud directorship), 201–2, 245–48, 252, 259, 263; Stratum VIIB (Loud directorship), 257–59, 263; Stratum VIII (Loud directorship), 259, 263

Palestine, survey of, 6. *See also* British Mandate Palestine

Palestine Archaeological Museum, Jerusalem, 115–16, 146, 175, 265, 281. *See also* Rockefeller Archaeological Museum

Palestine Exploration Fund, 6

Palestine Exploration Quarterly (journal), 298

Palestine Railway Club, Haifa, 109

Pan Arab Corporation of London, 262

parade ground, 193

Parker, Ralph B. "Harry": anti-Jewish sentiments of, 64, 103–5; background of, 63–64; correspondence of, 284–85, 293, 294; and damage to dig house and contents, 294–96; departure and retirement of, 64, 296; Guy's firing and, 182–83; hiring of, 63–64; and Loud directorship, 220, 262, 274, 283; and May affair, 177; photographs of, 74, 94, *94*, 97; post-Guy duties of, 206, 211, 212, 217; problems involving, 64, 69–70, 77, 103–5; and revival of expedition, 241–43; Shipton as nephew of, 73; social life of, 109, 291; and termination of expedition, 237, 239–40, 286, 290; and water tunnel, 140

Peel Commission, 239

pen case with cartouche of Ramses III, *253*, 254, 257

Persians, 55–56, 142, 187, 189

Petrie, William Matthew Flinders, 11, 20, 22, 162, 201–2, 205, 247, 249, 252

Philip II, king of Spain, 53

Philistines, 196–97

Phillips, Dudley W., 116–17, 119

photography. *See* aerial photography

Picture Pavement, 267

Piepkorn, Arthur, 162–63, 286, 342n63

Plumer, Lord, 26

Pope, Gustavus Debrille "Tony," Jr., 273, 274, 283

pottery: as dating mechanism, 11; division of, 259; formal development of, 174–76; May's alleged smuggling of, 176–82; mending of, *155*; Shipton and Engberg on, 117, 158, 174, 176, 190, 210, 266, 277, 284, 298; sorting of, *38*, 39; storage of, *155*, 156

prison, 146

Quarterly of the Department of Antiquities in Palestine (QDAP; journal), 135, 190, 193 race, 175

railway, 15, 20, 34, 47, 49, 86, 125, 133–34, 140, 148, 191

Ramat David airbase, 8, 291

Ramses, Pharaoh, 86

Ramses II, Pharaoh, 123, 142, 185

Ramses III, Pharaoh, 200, 254; pen case with cartouche of, 253, 254, 257

Ramses VI, Pharaoh, 185–86, 200

recording/registration systems, 51–52, 89

Reisner, George, 13, 76, 205

Resheph (god), 235

rheumatic fever, 212

Richardson, Sidney, 165, 166, 170

Richmond, Ernest, 70–71, 177, 179, 181, 209–10, 239, 241–42

riots, in British Mandate Palestine: 1920/1921, 7; 1929, 103

roads, condition of, xv–xvi, 23, 65, 93, 96, 103, 106–7, 145

Robinson, Edward, 5–6

Rockefeller, Abby, 94, 95, 96

Rockefeller, David, 94, 95

Rockefeller, John D., Jr., xxiii, 1, 10, 11–12, 14–17, 31, 93, 94, 95–96, 115, 146, 151, 227–28, 232, 316n20

Rockefeller, John D., III, 95

Rockefeller, Nelson, 96

Rockefeller Archaeological Museum, East Jerusalem, 31. See also Palestine Archaeological Museum, Jerusalem

Rockefeller Archive Center, xxi

Rockefeller family, 93–96

Rockefeller Foundation (RF), 15, 94, 222–23, 228, 231, 236–37, 245, 264

Romans, 55–56, 107

Ronzevalle, Carlos, 83

Room 3100, 246–47, 246

Roosevelt, Franklin, 172

Rowe, Alan, 14, 62, 72, 185

Russia, 284

Saad, Feiz, 278

Saad, Hassan, 24, 81–82

Said (kitchen staff), 216–17

Samaria, 187, 299

Sargon II (Neo-Assyrian king), 187, 189

satellite imagery, 130

scarabs, 53, 118, 142, 175, 247, 259

Schliemann, Heinrich, 11, 30

Schumacher, Gottlieb, xv, xix, 7, 30–33, 38, 47, 49, 79, 126, 133–34, 187, 193, 197, 263, 275

Scientific American (magazine), 109

Segev, Tom, 276

serpentine, 247

Shalmaneser III (Neo-Assyrian king), 91, 187

Shalmaneser V (Neo-Assyrian king), 187

Shaw Commission, 103

Sheshonq, Pharaoh, 30–31, 199–200. See also Shishak, Pharaoh

Sheshonq fragment, 28, 28, 29, 30–33

Shipton, Geoffrey M., 77, 103, 134; background of, 72–73; departure of, 283–84; Guide to Megiddo, 290–91; and Lamon's marriage, 99; and Loud directorship, 220, 261, 274, 283; marriage of, 291; and Masons' request for stones, 292–93; Megiddo I, xx, 54, 73, 158, 208, 213, 241, 284, 297–98; photographs of, 74, 94, 94, 97; as possible love interest, 75; post-Guy duties of, 208; on pottery, 158, 174, 176, 190, 210, 266, 277, 284, 298; published material of, 86, 126–27, 158, 183, 190, 284 (see also Megiddo I); as recorder, 121–22, 173; and revival of expedition, 242–43; Spinney's position of, 283–84, 291; on stratigraphy, 211, 213–15, 298–99; tenure of, 73; upon termination of expedition, 237, 240

Shipton, Hester (née Wood), 291

Shishak, Pharaoh, 32. See also Sheshonq, Pharaoh

Sierra Club, 66

silo, 191

Siloam Inscription, 139

Singer, Itamar, 258

skeletal material: deposited at Smithsonian, 175, 345n116; Engberg and, 117, 148, 190; found with ivories in Treasury, 250–52, 251, 255–57; Lind's photographs of, 149; near Stone Altar, 268; photographs of, 117, 138, 196, 251; from tombs, 117, 148, 175, 190, 345n116; in water system, 137–38, 138

Smith, Eli, 5–6

Smith, George Adam, 7

Smith, J.M.P., 122

Smith College, 22

Smithsonian Institution, 175, 190, 345n116

Solomon, King, xx–xxi, 1–2, 32, 89–91, 126, 195, 199–200, 293, 298, 299

Solomon's city, xix–xx, xxi, 299–300

Solomon's Stables, xxi, 1–2, *2*, 85–91, *88*, 105–6, *129*, 156, 183, 214, 299; model and detail of, *90*

Sorial, Labib, *20*

Southern Palace, 195, 197

southern trench. *See* Area CC

Spinney's, 73, 283–84

Standard Oil, 73

Standard Oil Company of Indiana, 95

Staples, Elizabeth, 121

Staples, Margaret "Ruth," 74, *74*, 97, 104, 108, 110, 111, 120–21

Staples, William: academic career of, 120–21, 336n120; background of, 74, 122; chapter contributed to report, 118; character/ personality of, 108; at DeLoach's wedding, 99; departure of, 120; family of, 120–21; leisure activities of, 108, 110; photographs of, *74*, *97*; as recorder, 74; salary of, 114; vacations of, 104, 111

Starkey, James, 265

statue-base, 185–86, *186*, 200

Stead, K. W., 177–79

Sterling Rubber Company, 128

Stevens, David, 223, 228, 241

Stewart, Robert, 95

St James' Place Conference. *See* London Conference (1939)

St. Louis Post-Dispatch (newspaper), 1, 24, 32, 249

Stone Altar 4017, 268, *269*, 281, *282*

stratigraphy, 11, 154. *See also* Megiddo: stratigraphy of

Stratum I, *53–55*, *54*, 92, 187, 191

Stratum II, *53–55*, 142, 187, 191

Stratum III (Fisher's/Guy's Sub-II), 53, 86, *90*, 126–27, 134, 189, 211, 224, 233, 293; plan of, 187, *188*, 189

Stratum IV (Fisher's/Guy's III), 53, 86, 89, 91, 134, 211, 214, 224, *234*, 298–99; plan of, *192*

Stratum IVA, 91, 141, 187, 189, 200, 299; reconstruction of structures in, *194*

Stratum IVB, 214, 299

Stratum V (Guy's IV), 86, 214–15, 224, 298, 299

Stratum VA, 299

Stratum VA/IVB, 195, 197, 200, 299

Stratum VB, 199–200, 299, 300

Stratum VI (Guy's V), 86, 224, 243, 258, 270

Stratum VIA, 186, 195–99, 212, 224, 229, 300

Stratum VII, 124, 200, 202, 224, 228, 229, 233–34, 235, 243, 263, 270, 275

Stratum VIIA, 186, 248, 252, 257–58, 270

Stratum VIIB, 185–86, 200, 257–58, 270

Stratum VIII, 124, 224, 229, 233–34, 235, 243–44, *246*, 247–48, 258, 263, 270, 275

Stratum IX, 224, 235, 243, 270, 279

Stratum X, 224, 229, 269, 279

Stratum XI, 269, 279

Stratum XII, 269

Stratum XIII, 263–64, 268, 269

Stratum XIV, 245, 268

Stratum XV, 268, 275, 281

Stratum XVI, 268

Stratum XVII, 244, 245, 268

Stratum XVIII, 267–68, *267*

Stratum XIX, 267

Stratum XX, 266

strike, labor, 223–24

study collections, 180

Sukenik, Eliezer, 252

surveyors/surveying, xxiii, 6, 17, 19, 21, 24, 37–38, 40, 42–43, 63, 70–73, 81, 87, 100, 121, 162–63, 165

Syrians, 228

Tchoub, Serge, 70, 216–17, 220, 284–86, 291, 293, 294, 296

Tel Aviv Megiddo Expedition, xvii–xx, xix–xx, 33, 90, 91, 195, 198–99, 248, 258, 263, 267–69, 293

Tell el-Ajjul, 257

Tell el-Hesi, 11, 89

Tell el-Mutesellim, 5–7, 79, 82

Tell en-Nasbeh, 66

Tell es-Safi, 257

tells, 11

Tell Tayinat, Syria, 264

Temple 2048 (Migdal Temple), 224, *226*, 229, 231–33, 235, 262–63, 270

Temple 4050, 267

temples, 267; 4050, 267; megaron, 281, *282*; 2048, 224, *226*, 229, 231–33, 235, 262–63, 270
Templeton, James, 78–79
Templeton, Rosamond Dale Owen Oliphant, 78–83, 92; memorial plaque for, *82, 83*
Ten Lost Tribes of Israel, 187
tennis court, 96, 107, 109, 114, 156
Tepe Gawra, Iraq, 285–86
Terentieff, Ivan, 72, 73, *74*, 87
Thutmose III, Pharaoh, 7, 9–10, 142, 224, 266, 270
Thutmose III's city, xxi
Tiglath-Pileser III (Neo-Assyrian king), 187
Tobler, Arthur J., 285–86
tombs, at Megiddo, 38, 86, 117, 142, 151, 157–58, 174, 190, 211, 256, 277
Toscanini, Arturo, 244
Transfiguration of Christ, 8
Treasury, 250–57, *250, 251*
Troy and Trojan War, 11, 30
Tufnell, Olga, 252
Tutankhamen, 11, 226–27
Twain, Mark, 164
Tyrian gateway, 126–27

Ugaritic motifs, 253
Umm el-Fahm, 24, 266
United Monarchy, 200, 300
University Museum, University of Pennsylvania, 13–16
University of Chicago: finances of, 15, 222–23; physics department of, 128; students from, 19, 73, 116, 117, 162. *See also* Chicago team; Oriental Institute, University of Chicago
University of London, 22
Ussishkin, David, xix, 199–200, 248, 255, 258, 259, 300, 314n12

vacations, 71, 75, 97, 99, 101, 111, 260
Via Maris, 9–10, 55
Victoria College, University of Toronto, 120–21

Vincent, Pere, 77
volunteers, at Megiddo, xv, xvii, xix, 106

Wadi Ara pass, 110, 266
Wall 4045, *267*, 268
War of Independence, Israeli (1948), 14, *56*, 64, 83, 278, 293–94
water tunnel, 133–42, *135, 137*, 156, 158, 189, 200–201, 208, 210
Watzinger, Carl, 30
Wheeler, Mortimer, 154, 205
Wheeler, Noel F., 205–6
White Paper (1939), 276, 280, 283
Wilensky, Emmanuel, 72, 87, 144–46, 156–57, 161–66, 169–72, 183
Wilensky, Mrs., 149–50, 170
Willets-Burnham, Anita, 98
Wilson, John A., 63, 65, 222–24, 227–29, 231–32, 235–41, 245–47, 249–50, 253, 255, 259–62, 264–65, 271, 275, 278–80, 285, 292, 296
Wilson, Mary, 63, 65, 222
Wood, Hester. *See* Shipton, Hester
Woodley, Ruby, *20*, 43, 45, 67, 69, 70, 75–76, 78
Woolley, Leonard, 59, 106
Woolman, David, 104, 332n36
Woolman, Janet, 101–3, 106–9, 111–13, 116, 131, 133
Woolman, Laurence, xxii, 101–16, 131, 154, 157; model and detail of Solomon's Stables, *90*, 105–6, 113
workmen. *See* Egyptian workmen; local workmen
World's Fair (Chicago, 1933), 106
World War II, 285, 289, 291–92, 298
Wright, G. Ernest, 299

Yadin, Yigael, xix, 141, 195, 234, 299–300
Yeivin, Shemuel, 294, 296

Zarzecki-Peleg, Anabel, 138
Zionism, 60, 170

Also by
ERIC H. CLINE

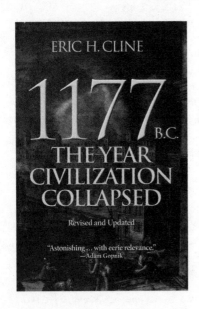 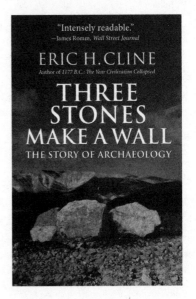

PRINCETON UNIVERSITY PRESS

Available wherever books are sold.
For more information visit us at www.press.princeton.edu